Shojo Beat

Yona of the Dawn

35

Story & Art by
Mizuho Kusanagi

YONA OF THE DAWN

Story Thus Far

Hak

One of the greatest heroes in the nation, known as the "Thunder Beast." He'd obeyed King Il's orders and became bodyguard to his childhood friend, Yona. He walks away from his position as Wind Tribe general in order to protect his people.

Yona

Princess of the Kingdom of Kohka and reincarnation of the Crimson Dragon King. Thanks to her and the Dragon Warriors intervening in national affairs, the public's awareness of her soared, and an alliance proposed by Keishuk brought her back to Hiryuu Palace.

Su-won

A young man descended from the Crimson Dragon King. Now king, he is attempting to make Kohka more powerful by uniting the Five Tribes. He is afflicted with the Crimson Sickness, an illness unique to the Crimson Dragon King's lineage.

Keishuk

As Su-won's advisor, he holds great authority. He adored Su-won's father, Yu-hon, and assisted Su-won in taking the throne. He is torn between the threat Hak presents and the strategic advantage of keeping Yona and the Dragon Warriors around.

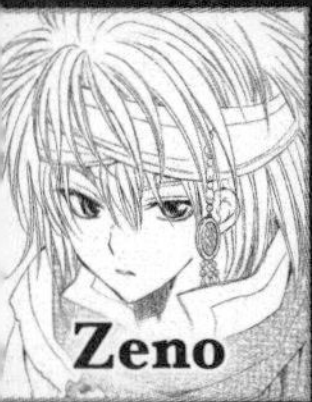
Zeno

'he Yellow Dragon of the 'our Dragon Warriors. Ie has the power of a ragon in his body—the ower of immortality! He s one of the first Dragons vho served the Crimson)ragon King, and he inally met Yona after nany years of waiting.

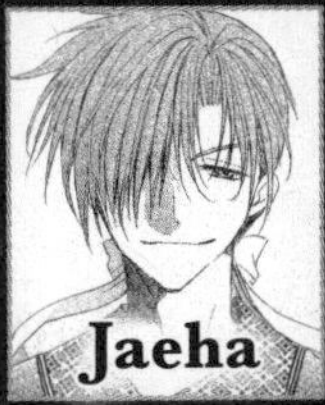
Jaeha

The Green Dragon of the Four Dragon Warriors. With the power of a dragon in his right leg, he can leap to tremendous heights. He loves freedom and hates the idea of being tied down to duty as one of the Four Legendary Dragons.

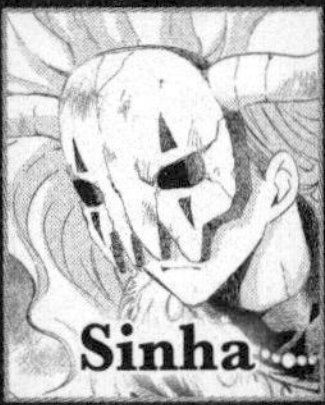
Sinha

The Blue Dragon of the Four Dragon Warriors. With the power of a dragon in his eyes, he can paralyze anyone he looks at. He grew up being hated and feared for his incredible power.

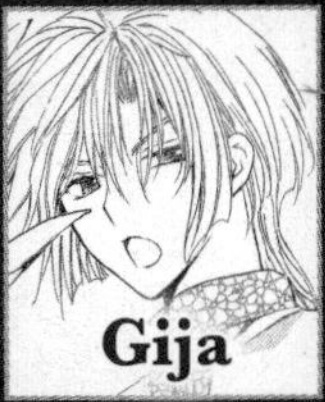
Gija

The White Dragon, one of the Four Dragon Warriors. His right hand contains a dragon's might and is more powerful than ten men. He adores Yona and finds fulfillment in his role as one of the Four Legendary Dragons.

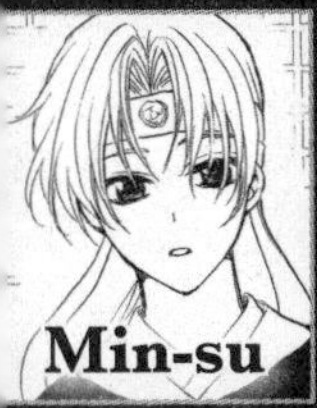
Min-su

'ormerly one of King Il's attendants. Ie is now Su-won's rimary physician and s looking for a cure for he Crimson Sickness.

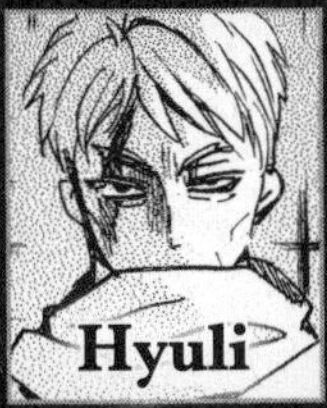
Hyuli

Su-won's sword instructor and bodyguard. He served Su-won's father Yu-hon and was the bodyguard of Yu-hon's wife, Yon-hi.

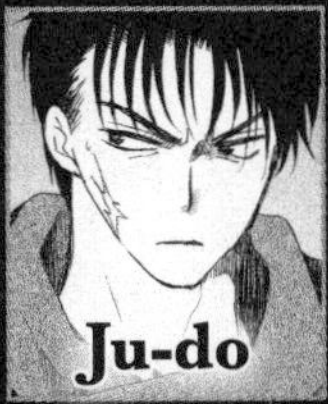
Ju-do

The Sky Tribe's general. He's serious, stuffy, and wary of Hak.

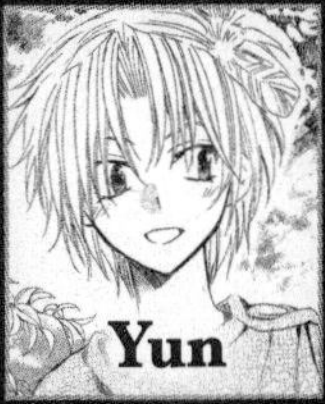
Yun

An intelligent boy who takes care of others and is like a mother to Yona and her friends. Knowledgeable about medicinal herbs, he is learning new medical techniques at the palace.

'our Dragon Warriors… In the Age of Myths, a dragon god took on human form and founded a nation. As the Crimson on King, he was the first ruler of the Kingdom of Kohka. Four other dragons shared their blood with humans so that they l protect him. Those warriors became known as the Four Legendary Dragons, or the Four Dragon Warriors, and their r has been passed down for generations.

STORY

Yona, the princess of the Kingdom of Kohka, has deep feelings for her cousin Su-won, a companion childhood. On her 16th birthday, she sees her father King Il being stabbed to death—by Su-won!

Driven from the palace, Yona and Hak meet a priest named Ik-su who tells Yona a prophecy that leads o gather the Four Dragon Warriors together. Yona then decides to take up arms and defend her nation with 'our Dragon Warriors at her side.

War between Xing and Kohka is narrowly averted thanks to Yona and her friends. After this tension Hak tells Yona the truth about his feelings for her.

After Yona and her friends form an alliance with Kohka and return to Hiryuu Palace, she is immediately rated from Hak and the Dragons. She soon learns that Su-won is displaying symptoms of the Crimson ness, an illness found only among the Crimson Dragon King's descendants. She also finds a journal that nged to Su-won's mother, Yon-hi, and finally learns some truths about how the legend of the Crimson on King affected their respective parents' lives—and deaths.

When Su-won suffers a severe attack from his illness, Yona decides to attend a meeting with a delegation South Kai in his place.

Kingdom of Kohka is a coalition of five tribes: Fire, Water, Wind, Earth, and Sky. The throne is held by the tribe with the est influence, so the current royal family are of the Sky Tribe. The royal capital is Kuuto. Each tribe's chief also holds the of general, and the Meeting of the Five Tribes is the nation's most powerful decision-making body.

Yona of the Dawn

Volume 35

CONTENTS

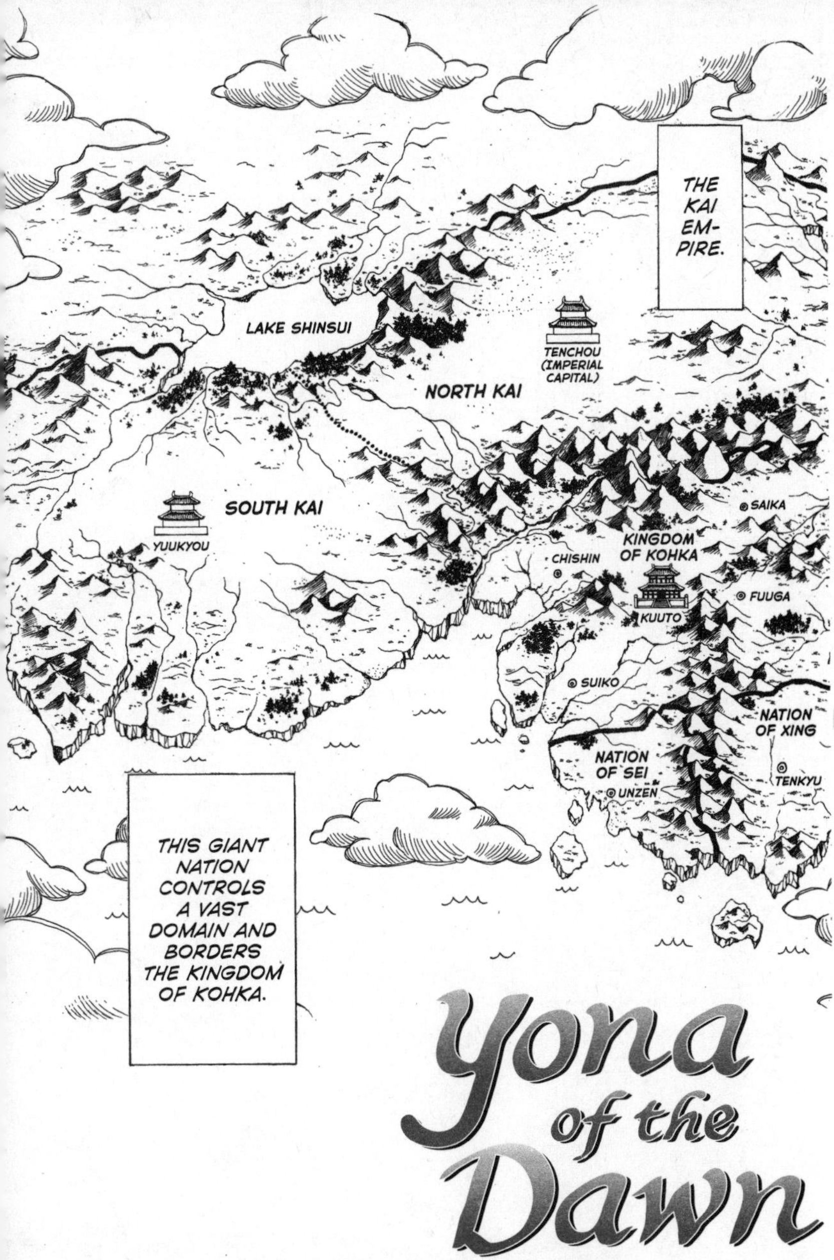
THE KAI EMPIRE.
THIS GIANT NATION CONTROLS A VAST DOMAIN AND BORDERS THE KINGDOM OF KOHKA.
LAKE SHINSUI
TENCHOU (IMPERIAL CAPITAL)
NORTH KAI
SOUTH KAI
YUUKYOU
SAIKA
KINGDOM OF KOHKA
CHISHIN
KUUTO
FUUGA
SUIKO
NATION OF XING
NATION OF SEI
UNZEN
TENKYU

Yona of the Dawn

CHAPTER 199: A VIP FROM SOUTH KAI

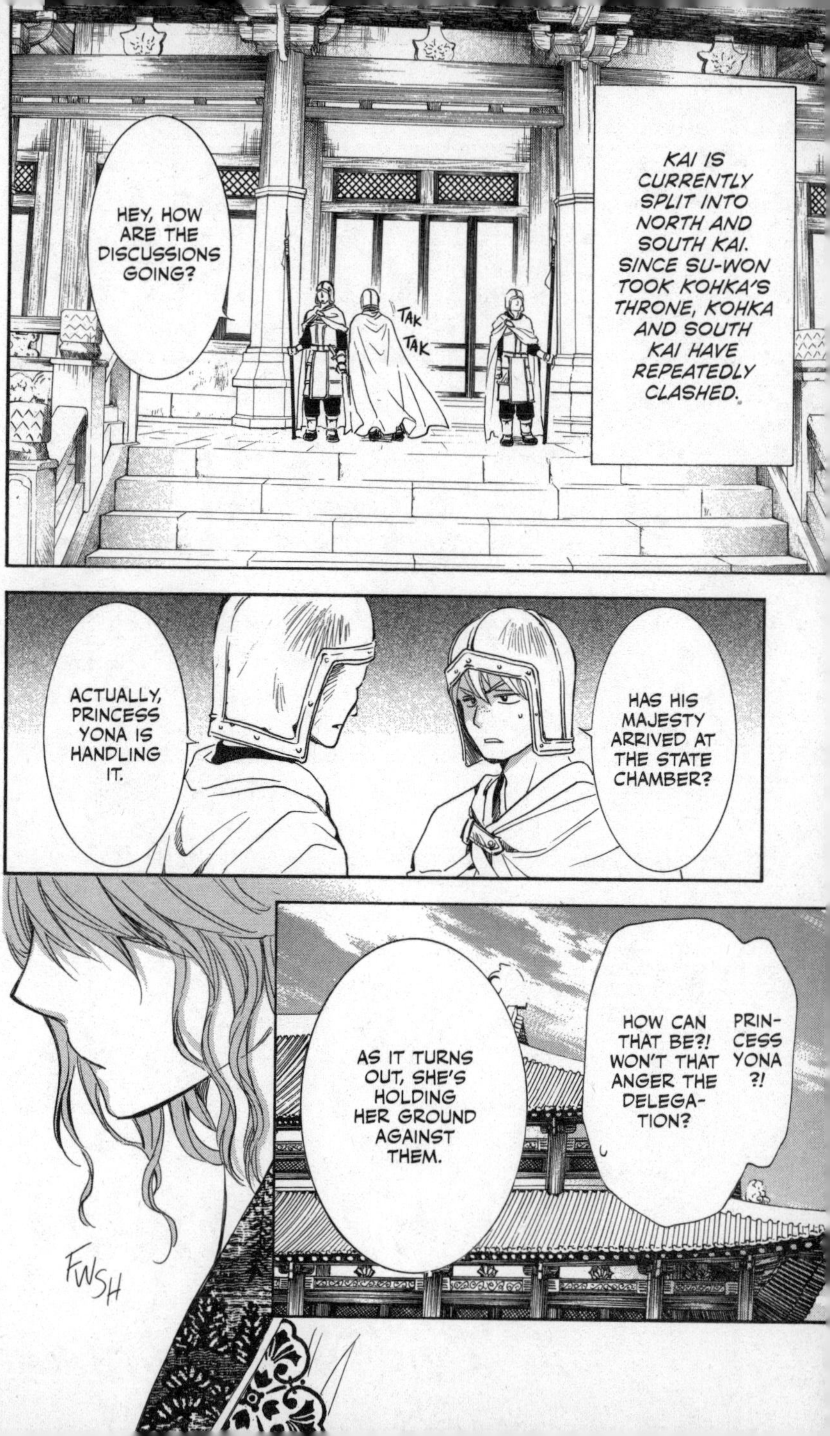
KAI IS CURRENTLY SPLIT INTO NORTH AND SOUTH KAI. SINCE SU-WON TOOK KOHKA'S THRONE, KOHKA AND SOUTH KAI HAVE REPEATEDLY CLASHED.
TAK TAK
HEY, HOW ARE THE DISCUSSIONS GOING?
HAS HIS MAJESTY ARRIVED AT THE STATE CHAMBER?
ACTUALLY, PRINCESS YONA IS HANDLING IT.
PRIN-CESS YONA?!
HOW CAN THAT BE?! WON'T THAT ANGER THE DELEGA-TION?
AS IT TURNS OUT, SHE'S HOLDING HER GROUND AGAINST THEM.
FWSH

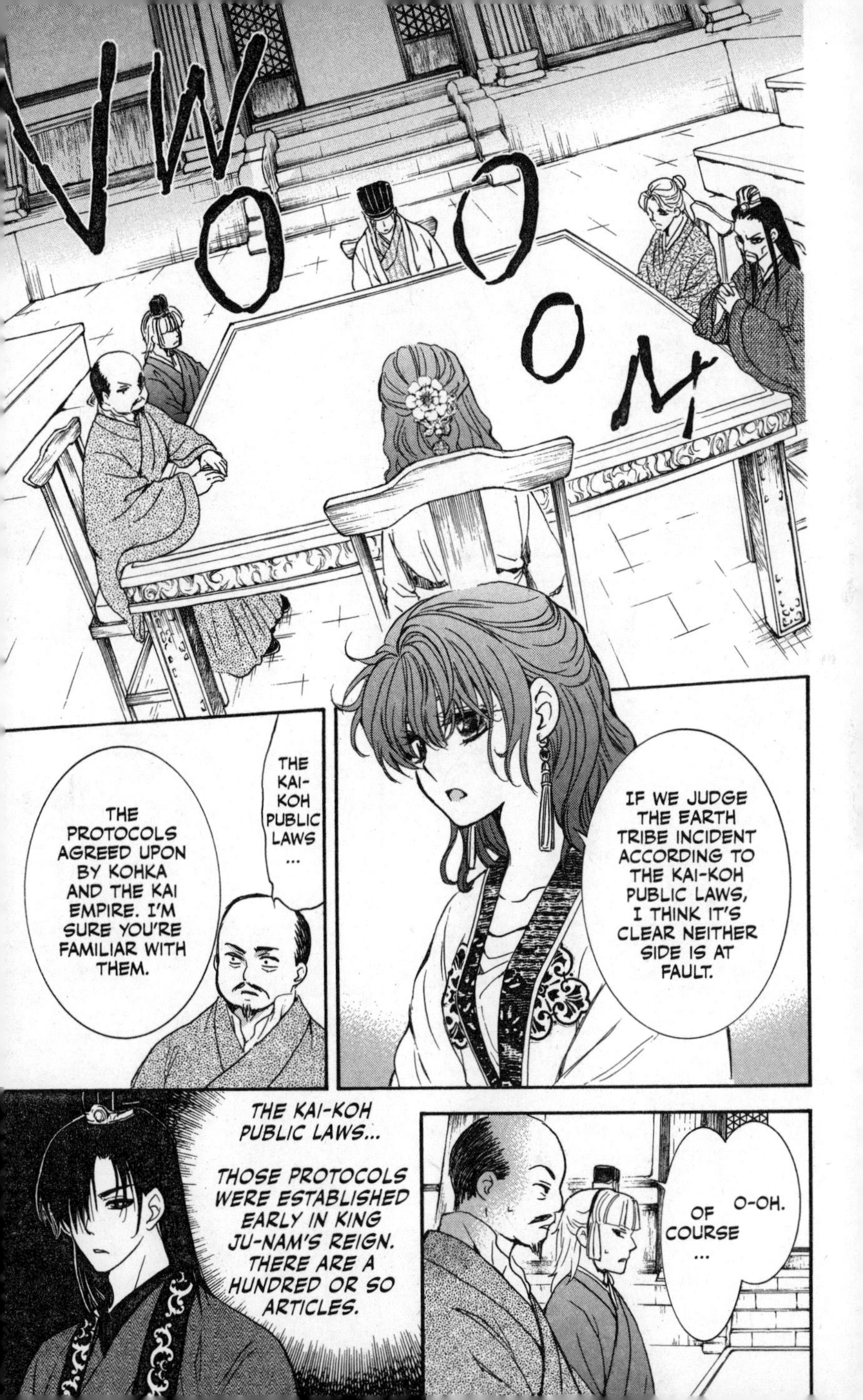
VWOOOM
IF WE JUDGE THE EARTH TRIBE INCIDENT ACCORDING TO THE KAI-KOH PUBLIC LAWS, I THINK IT'S CLEAR NEITHER SIDE IS AT FAULT.
THE KAI-KOH PUBLIC LAWS...
THE PROTOCOLS AGREED UPON BY KOHKA AND THE KAI EMPIRE. I'M SURE YOU'RE FAMILIAR WITH THEM.
O-OH.
OF COURSE...
THE KAI-KOH PUBLIC LAWS...
THOSE PROTOCOLS WERE ESTABLISHED EARLY IN KING JU-NAM'S REIGN. THERE ARE A HUNDRED OR SO ARTICLES.

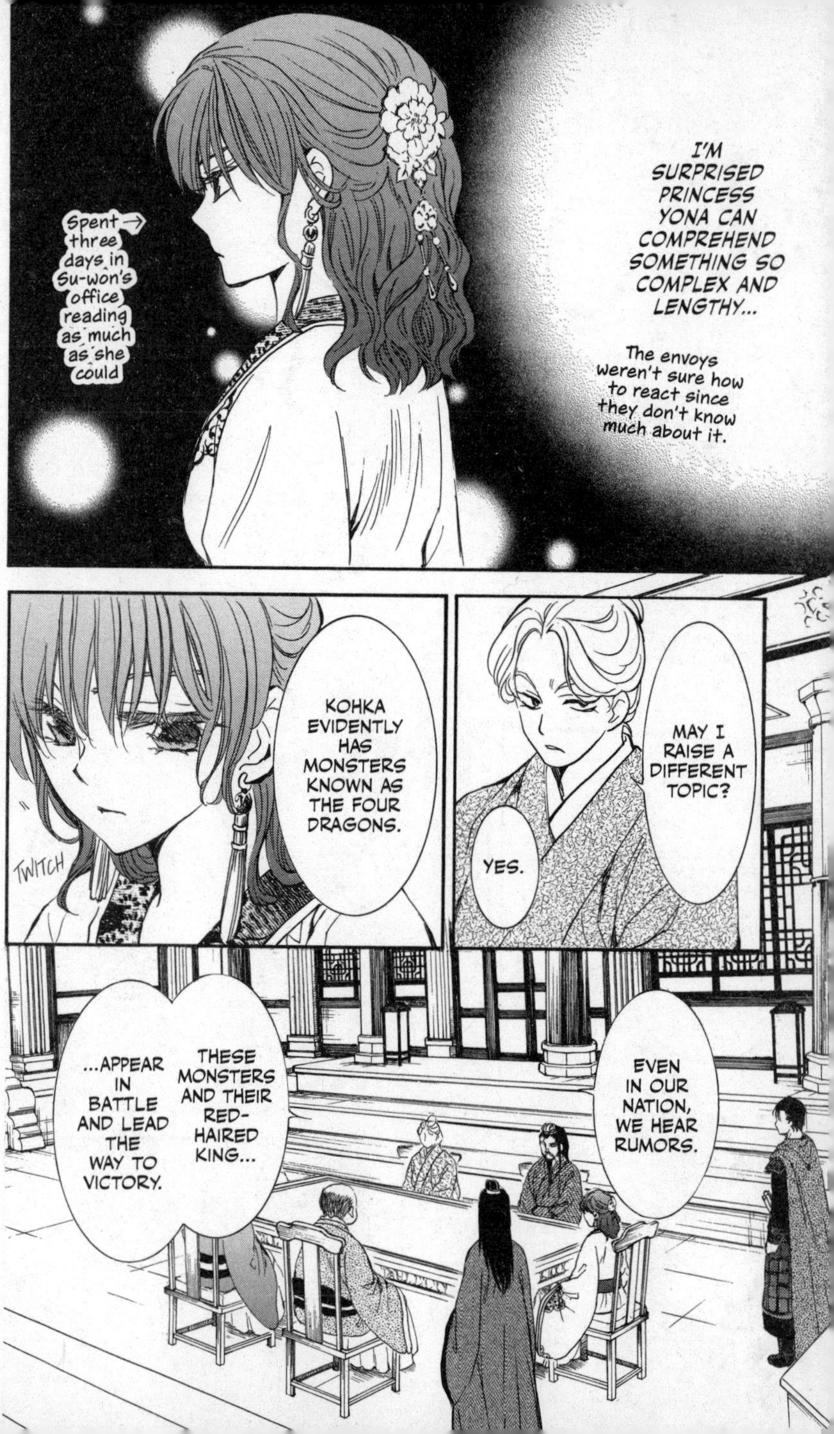
I'M SURPRISED PRINCESS YONA CAN COMPREHEND SOMETHING SO COMPLEX AND LENGTHY...
The envoys weren't sure how to react since they don't know much about it.
Spent three days in Su-won's office reading as much as she could
MAY I RAISE A DIFFERENT TOPIC?
YES.
KOHKA EVIDENTLY HAS MONSTERS KNOWN AS THE FOUR DRAGONS.
TWITCH
EVEN IN OUR NATION, WE HEAR RUMORS.
THESE MONSTERS AND THEIR RED-HAIRED KING...
...APPEAR IN BATTLE AND LEAD THE WAY TO VICTORY.

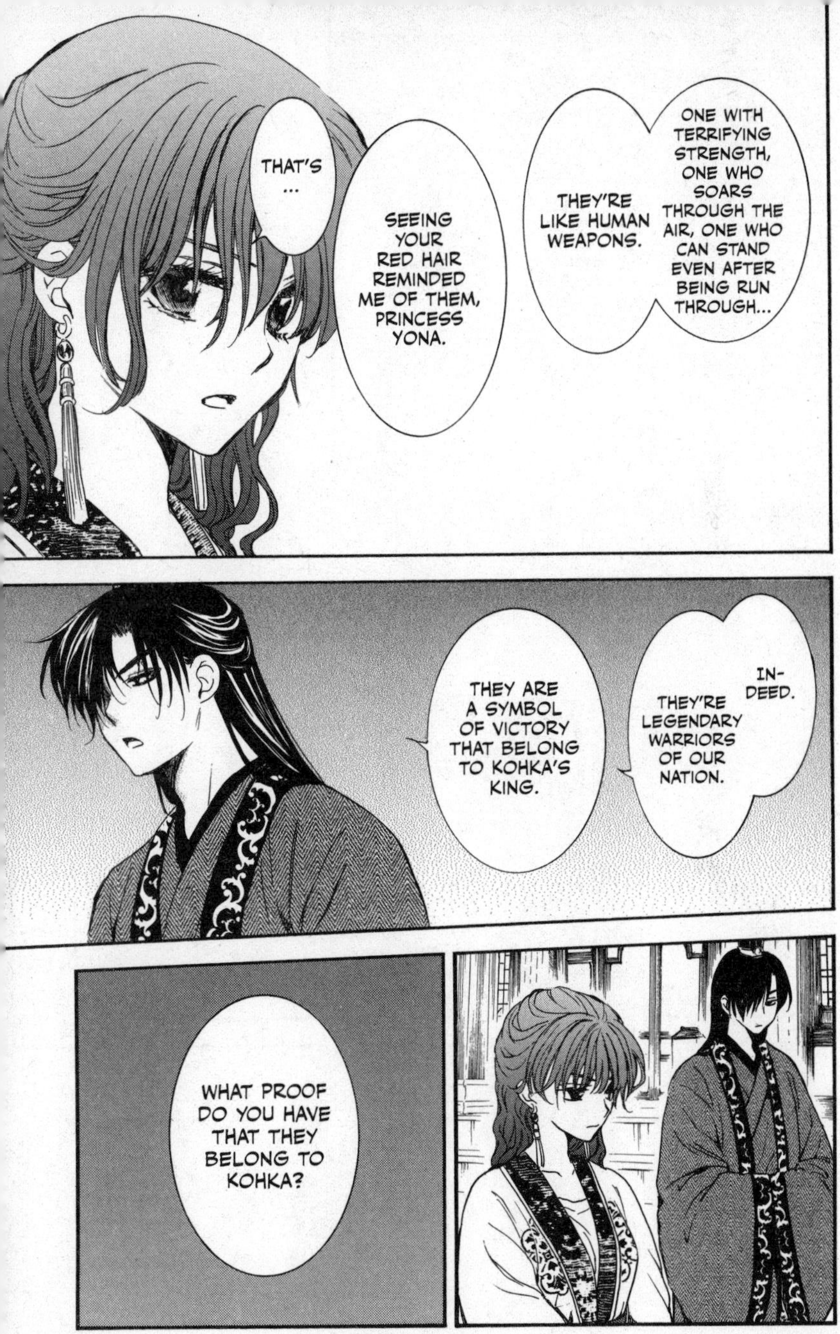
ONE WITH TERRIFYING STRENGTH, ONE WHO SOARS THROUGH THE AIR, ONE WHO CAN STAND EVEN AFTER BEING RUN THROUGH...
THEY'RE LIKE HUMAN WEAPONS.
SEEING YOUR RED HAIR REMINDED ME OF THEM, PRINCESS YONA.
THAT'S ...
IN-DEED.
THEY'RE LEGENDARY WARRIORS OF OUR NATION.
THEY ARE A SYMBOL OF VICTORY THAT BELONG TO KOHKA'S KING.
WHAT PROOF DO YOU HAVE THAT THEY BELONG TO KOHKA?

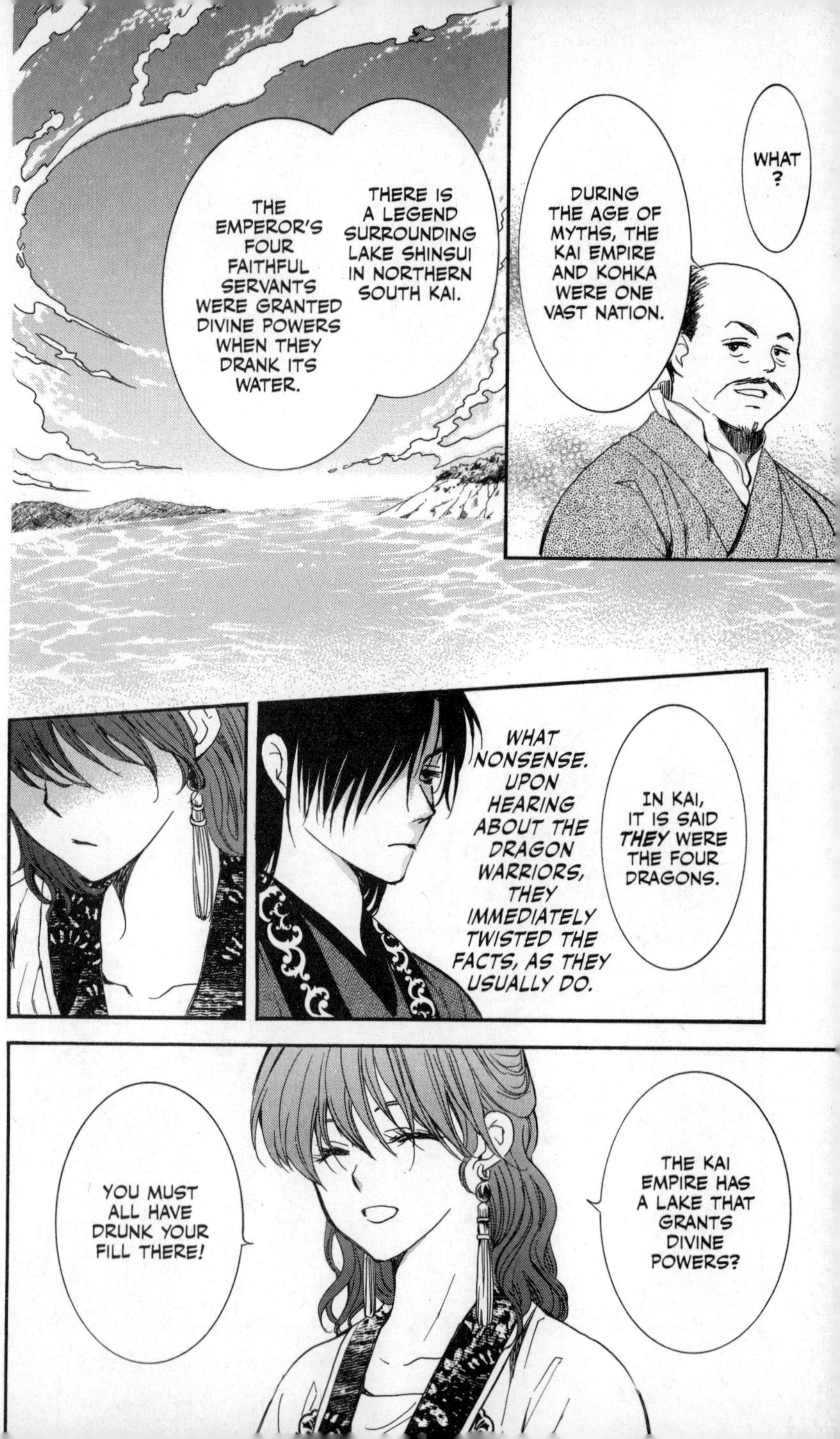
WHAT?
DURING THE AGE OF MYTHS, THE KAI EMPIRE AND KOHKA WERE ONE VAST NATION.
THERE IS A LEGEND SURROUNDING LAKE SHINSUI IN NORTHERN SOUTH KAI.
THE EMPEROR'S FOUR FAITHFUL SERVANTS WERE GRANTED DIVINE POWERS WHEN THEY DRANK ITS WATER.
IN KAI, IT IS SAID *THEY* WERE THE FOUR DRAGONS.
WHAT NONSENSE. UPON HEARING ABOUT THE DRAGON WARRIORS, THEY IMMEDIATELY TWISTED THE FACTS, AS THEY USUALLY DO.
THE KAI EMPIRE HAS A LAKE THAT GRANTS DIVINE POWERS?
YOU MUST ALL HAVE DRUNK YOUR FILL THERE!

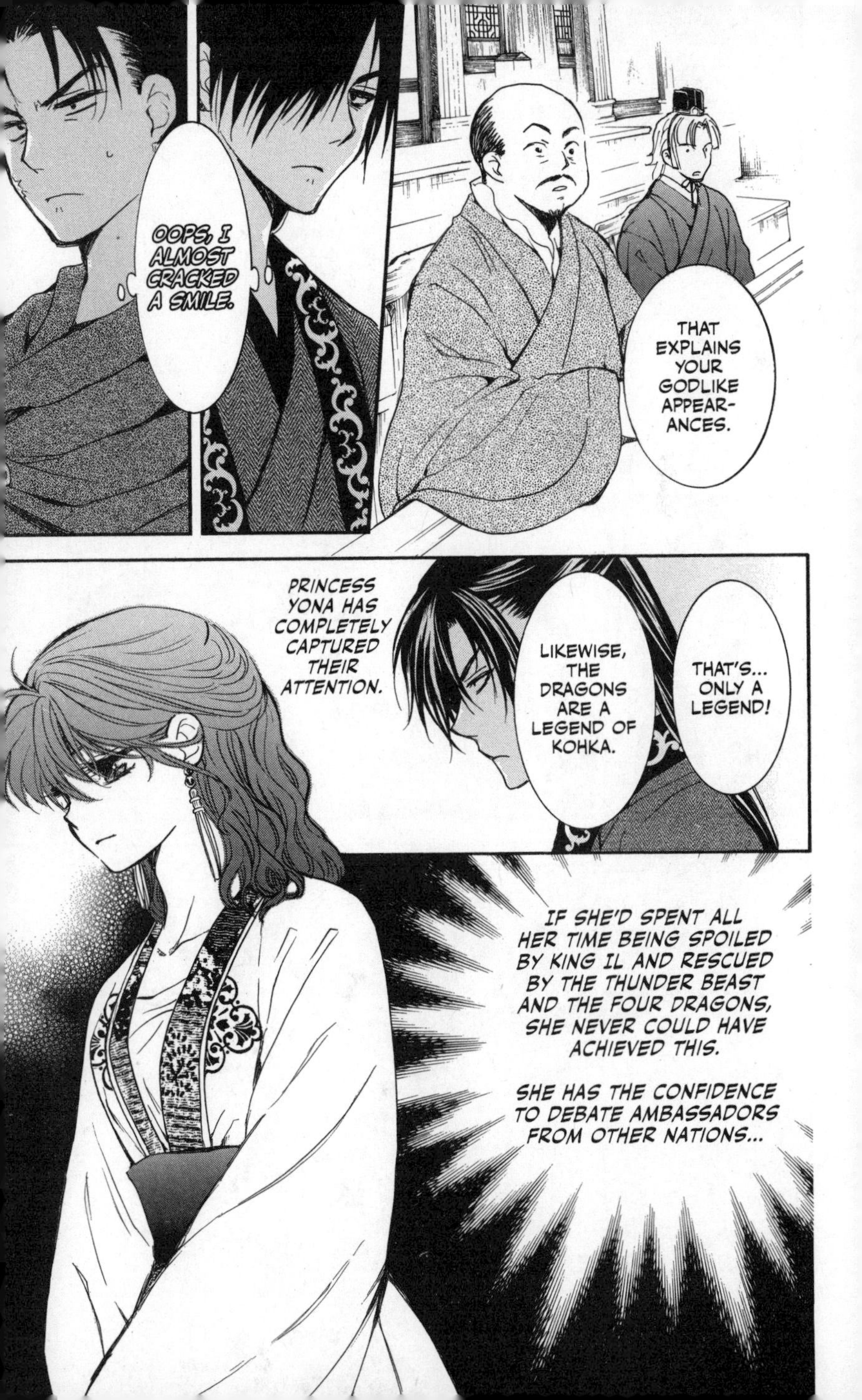
THAT EXPLAINS YOUR GODLIKE APPEAR-ANCES.
OOPS, I ALMOST CRACKED A SMILE.
THAT'S... ONLY A LEGEND!
LIKEWISE, THE DRAGONS ARE A LEGEND OF KOHKA.
PRINCESS YONA HAS COMPLETELY CAPTURED THEIR ATTENTION.
IF SHE'D SPENT ALL HER TIME BEING SPOILED BY KING IL AND RESCUED BY THE THUNDER BEAST AND THE FOUR DRAGONS, SHE NEVER COULD HAVE ACHIEVED THIS.
SHE HAS THE CONFIDENCE TO DEBATE AMBASSADORS FROM OTHER NATIONS...

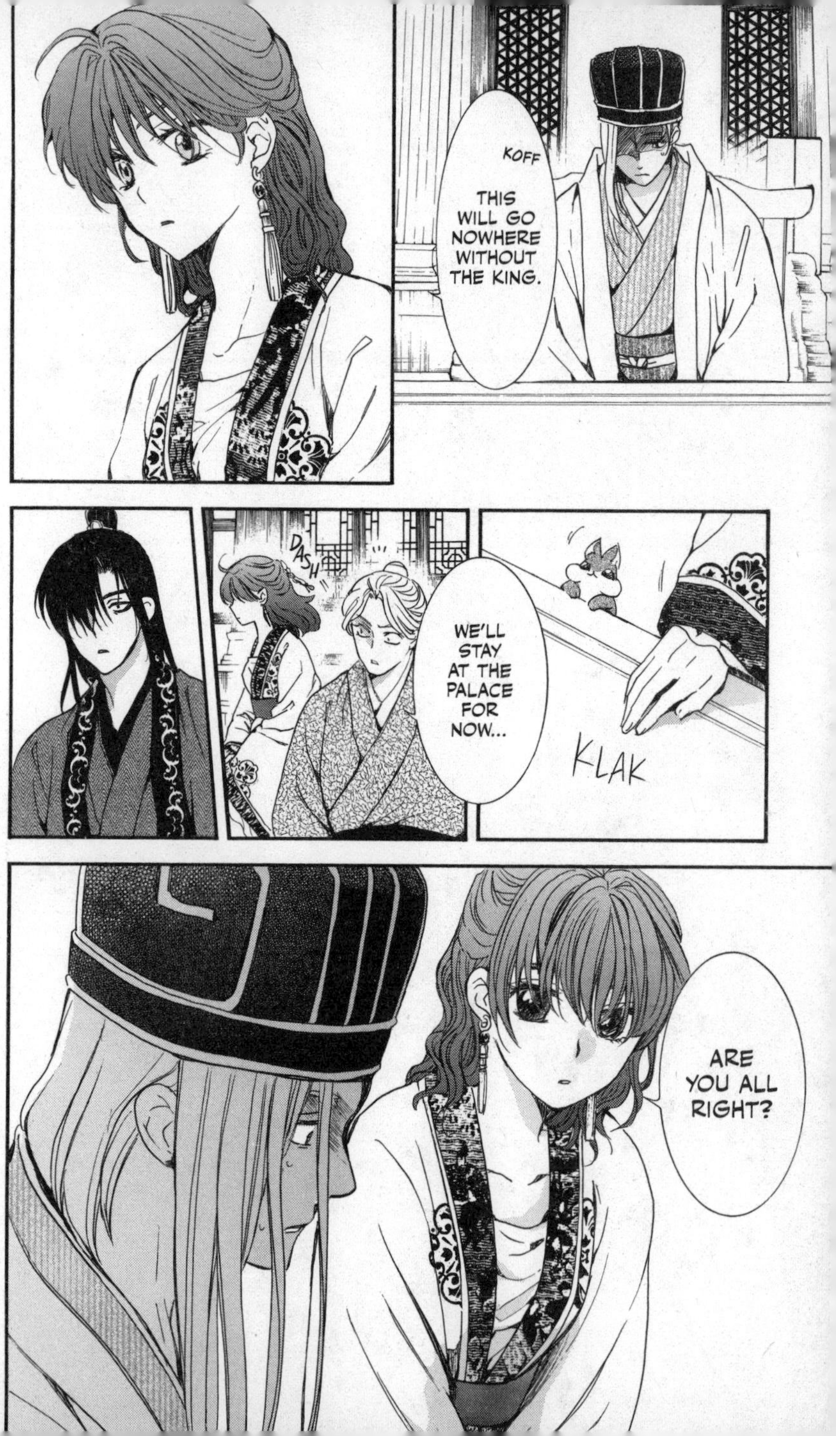
KOFF
THIS WILL GO NOWHERE WITHOUT THE KING.
KLAK
WE'LL STAY AT THE PALACE FOR NOW...
DASH
ARE YOU ALL RIGHT?

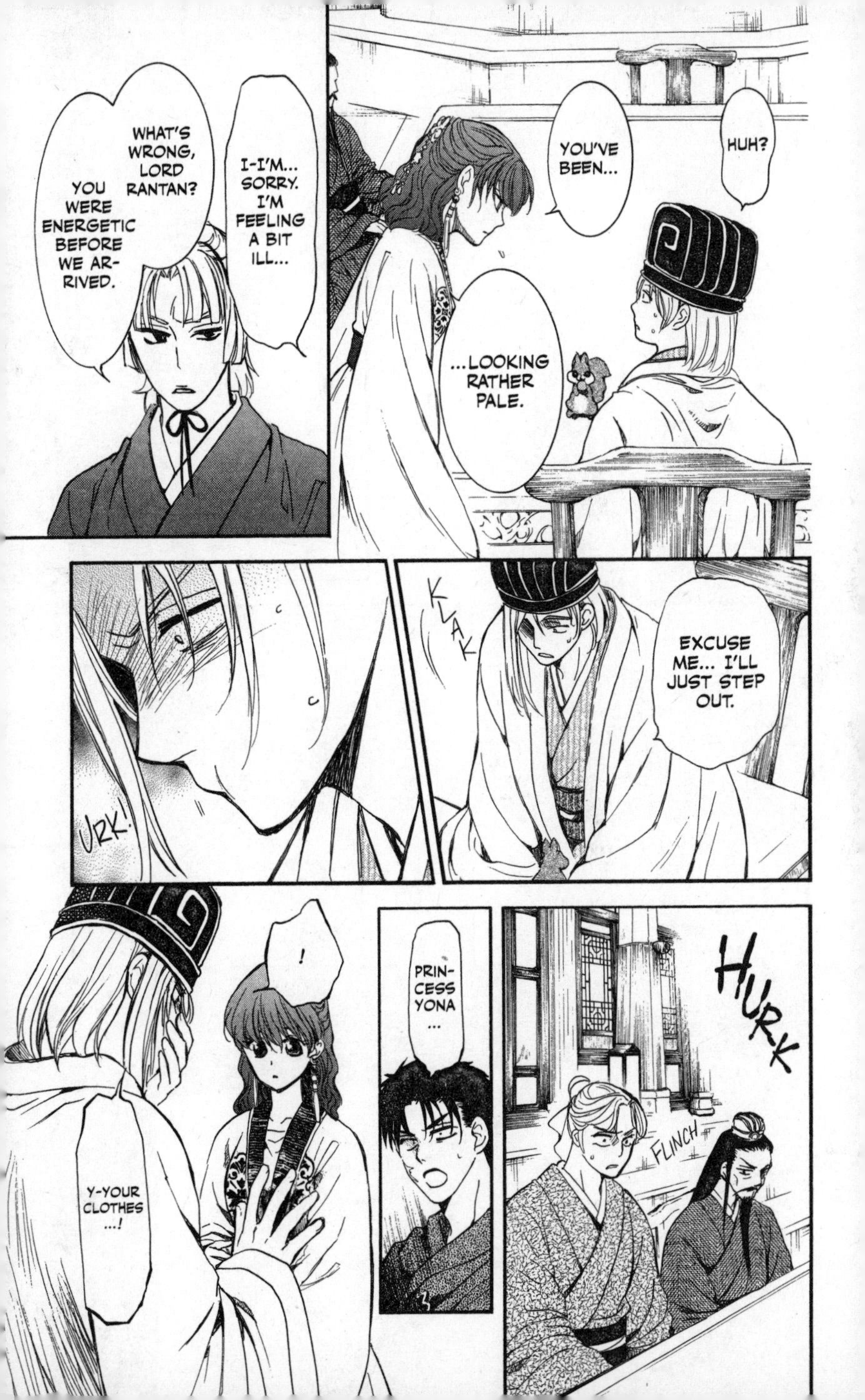
HUH?
YOU'VE BEEN...
...LOOKING RATHER PALE.
WHAT'S WRONG, LORD RANTAN? YOU WERE ENERGETIC BEFORE WE AR-RIVED.
I-I'M... SORRY. I'M FEELING A BIT ILL...
EXCUSE ME... I'LL JUST STEP OUT.
KLAK
URK!
HURK
FLINCH
PRIN-CESS YONA...
!
Y-YOUR CLOTHES...!

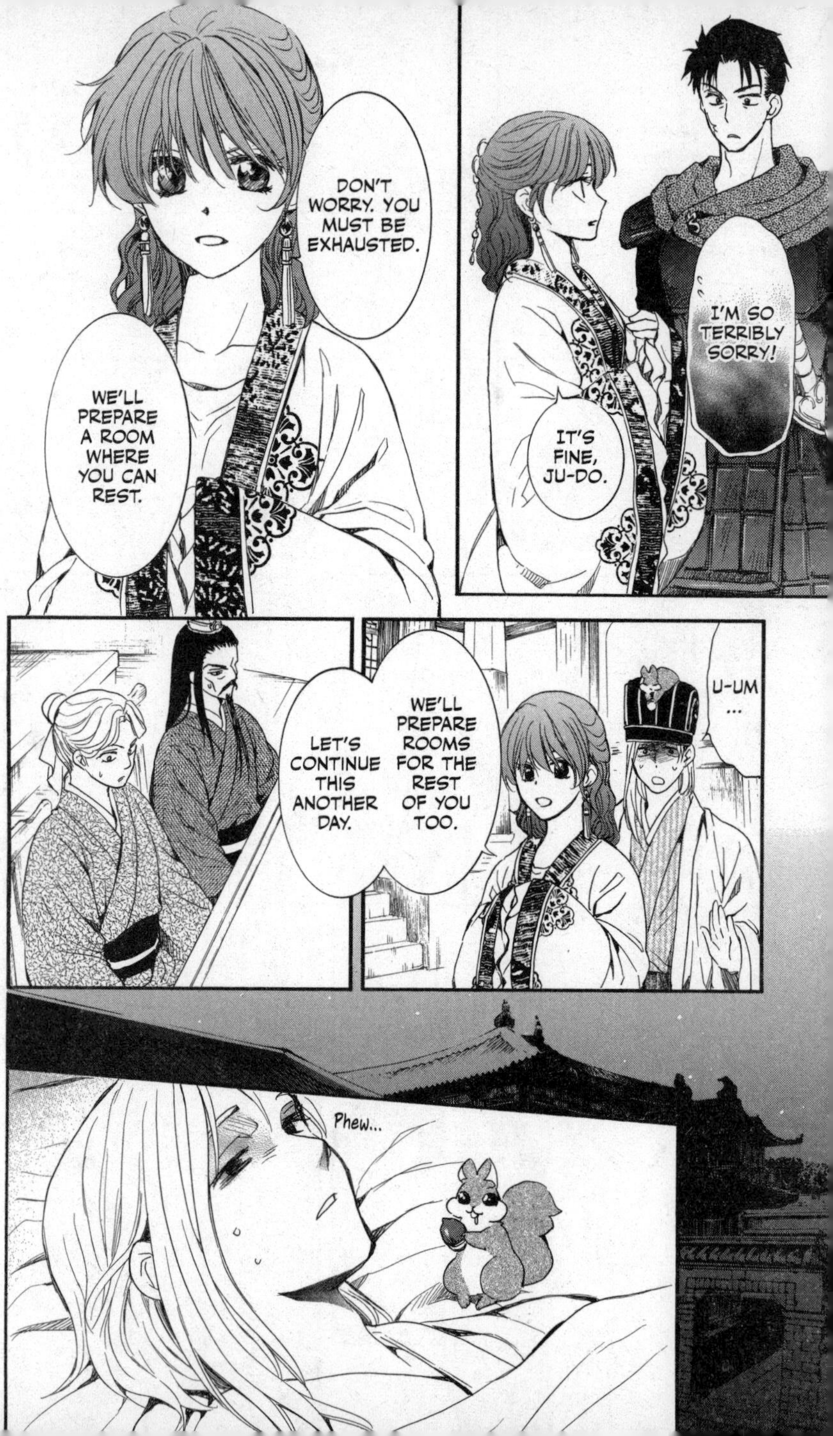
I'M SO TERRIBLY SORRY!
IT'S FINE, JU-DO.
DON'T WORRY. YOU MUST BE EXHAUSTED.
WE'LL PREPARE A ROOM WHERE YOU CAN REST.
U-UM...
WE'LL PREPARE ROOMS FOR THE REST OF YOU TOO.
LET'S CONTINUE THIS ANOTHER DAY.
Phew...

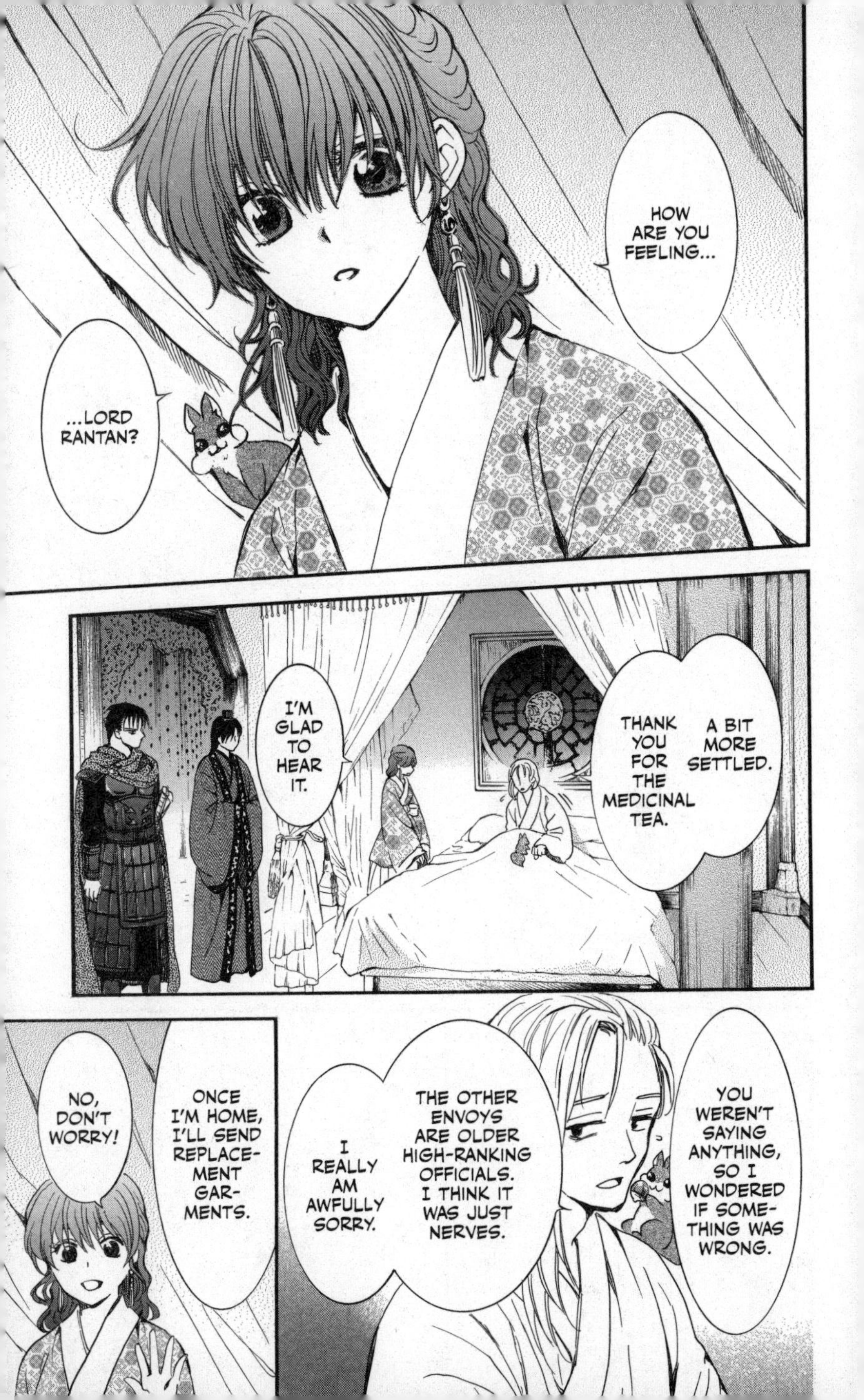
HOW ARE YOU FEELING...
...LORD RANTAN?
A BIT MORE SETTLED.
THANK YOU FOR THE MEDICINAL TEA.
I'M GLAD TO HEAR IT.
YOU WEREN'T SAYING ANYTHING, SO I WONDERED IF SOME-THING WAS WRONG.
THE OTHER ENVOYS ARE OLDER HIGH-RANKING OFFICIALS. I THINK IT WAS JUST NERVES.
I REALLY AM AWFULLY SORRY.
ONCE I'M HOME, I'LL SEND REPLACE-MENT GAR-MENTS.
NO, DON'T WORRY!

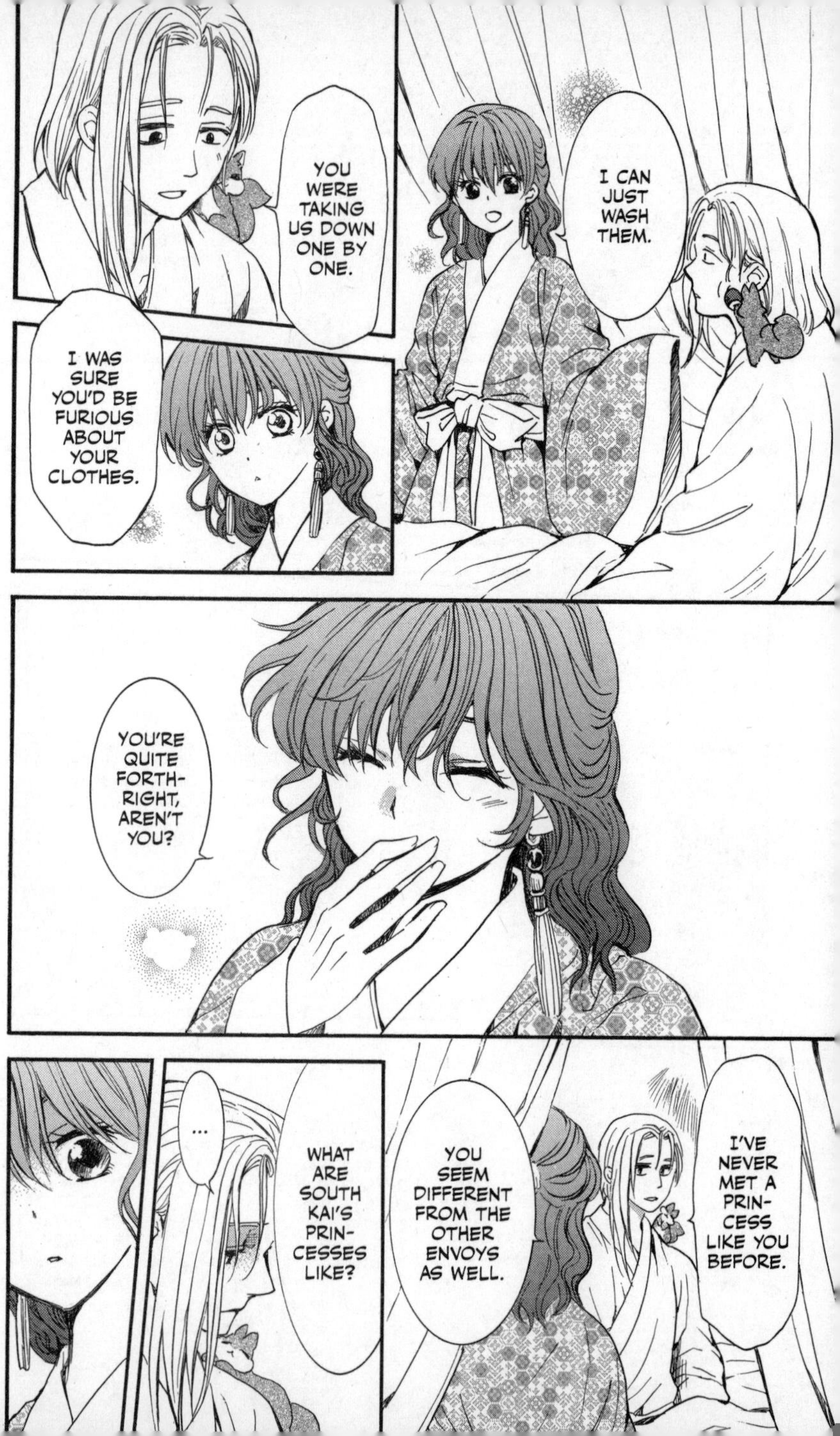

I CAN JUST WASH THEM.
YOU WERE TAKING US DOWN ONE BY ONE.
I WAS SURE YOU'D BE FURIOUS ABOUT YOUR CLOTHES.
YOU'RE QUITE FORTH-RIGHT, AREN'T YOU?
I'VE NEVER MET A PRIN-CESS LIKE YOU BEFORE.
YOU SEEM DIFFERENT FROM THE OTHER ENVOYS AS WELL.
WHAT ARE SOUTH KAI'S PRIN-CESSES LIKE?
...

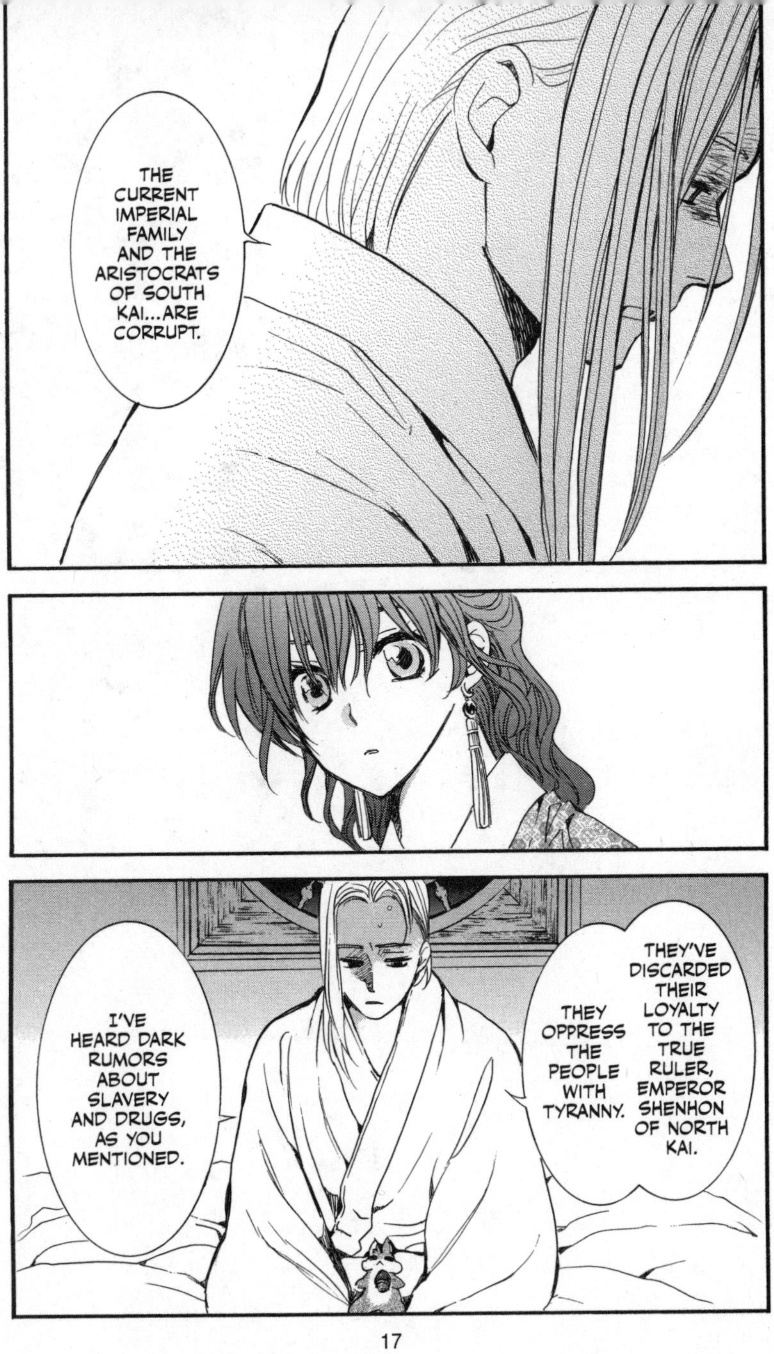
THE CURRENT IMPERIAL FAMILY AND THE ARISTOCRATS OF SOUTH KAI...ARE CORRUPT.
THEY'VE DISCARDED THEIR LOYALTY TO THE TRUE RULER, EMPEROR SHENHON OF NORTH KAI.
THEY OPPRESS THE PEOPLE WITH TYRANNY.
I'VE HEARD DARK RUMORS ABOUT SLAVERY AND DRUGS, AS YOU MENTIONED.

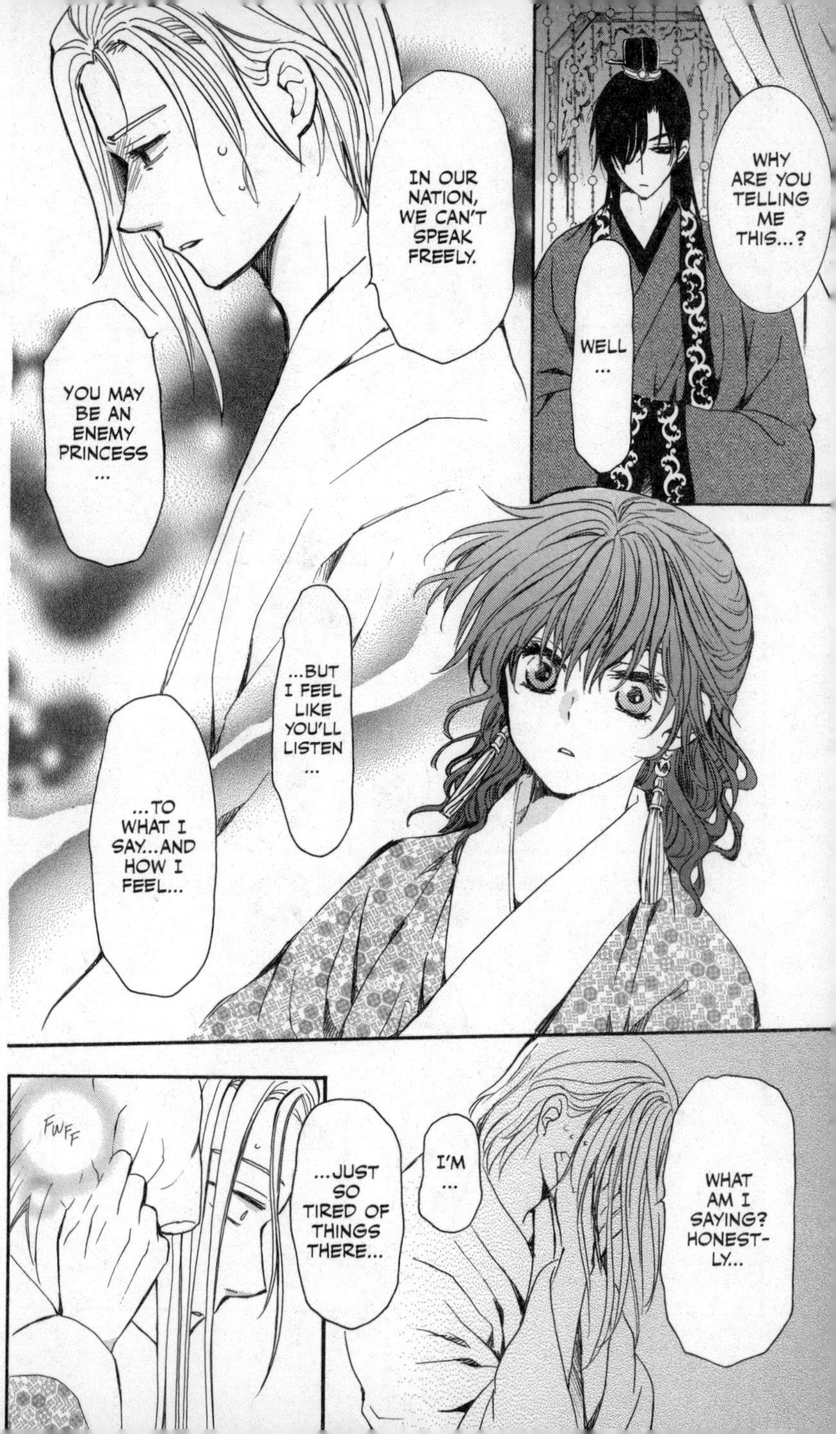
WHY ARE YOU TELLING ME THIS...?
WELL...
IN OUR NATION, WE CAN'T SPEAK FREELY.
YOU MAY BE AN ENEMY PRINCESS...
...BUT I FEEL LIKE YOU'LL LISTEN...
...TO WHAT I SAY...AND HOW I FEEL...
WHAT AM I SAYING? HONEST-LY...
I'M...
...JUST SO TIRED OF THINGS THERE...
FWFF

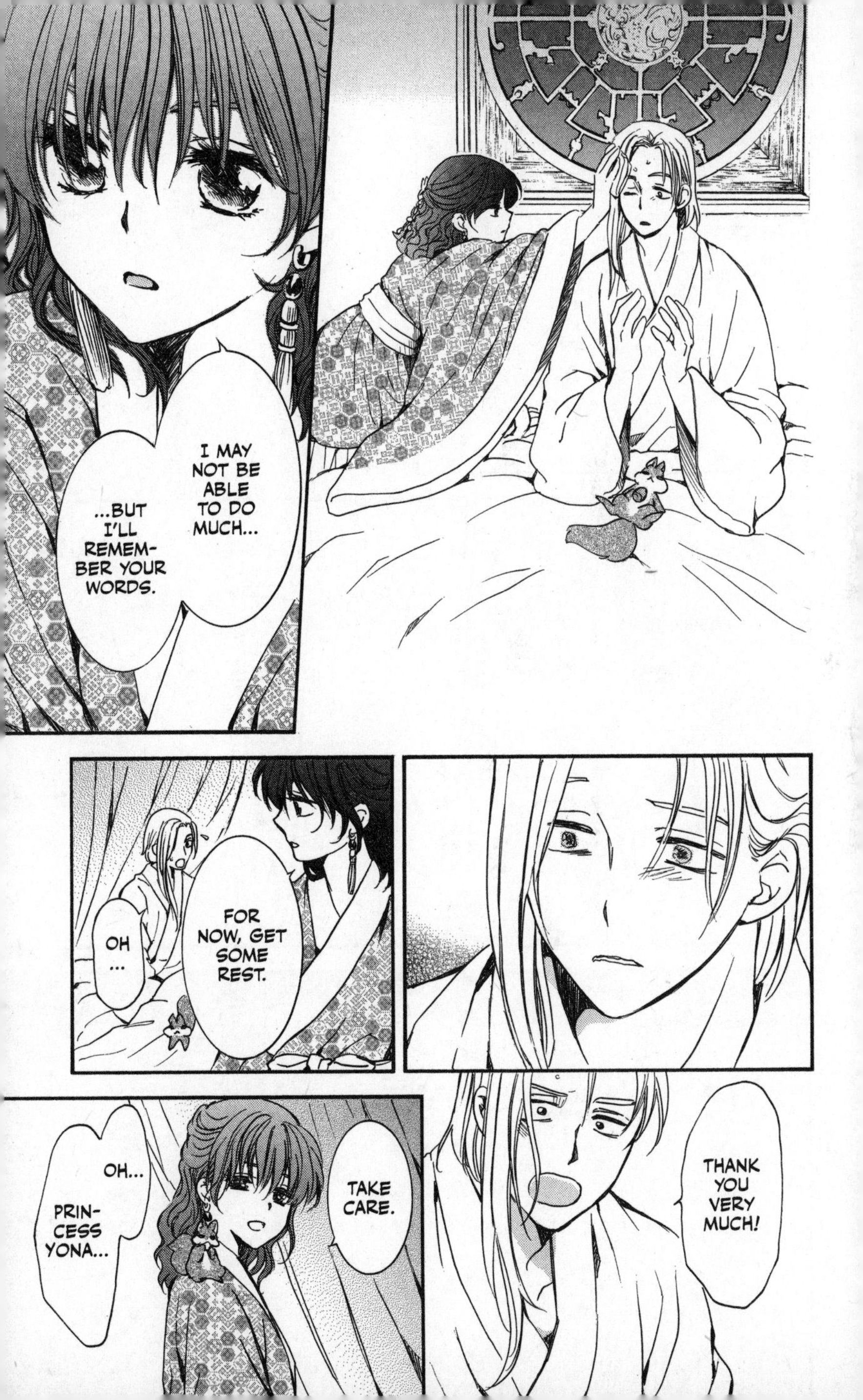
I MAY NOT BE ABLE TO DO MUCH...
...BUT I'LL REMEMBER YOUR WORDS.
FOR NOW, GET SOME REST.
OH ...
THANK YOU VERY MUCH!
TAKE CARE.
OH...
PRINCESS YONA...

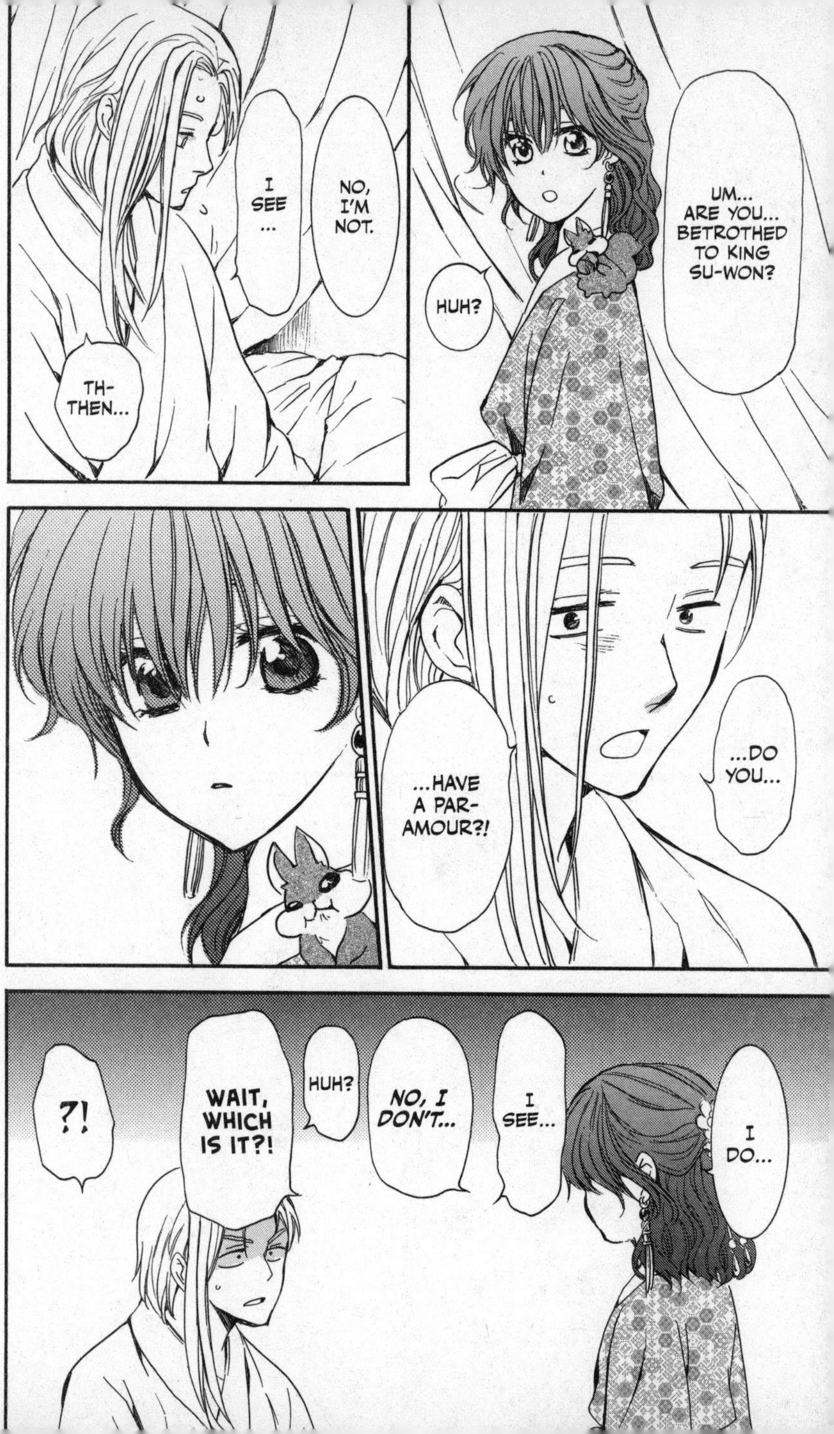
UM... ARE YOU... BETROTHED TO KING SU-WON?
HUH?
NO, I'M NOT.
I SEE...
TH-THEN...
...DO YOU...
...HAVE A PAR-AMOUR?!
I DO...
I SEE...
NO, I DON'T...
HUH?
WAIT, WHICH IS IT?!
?!

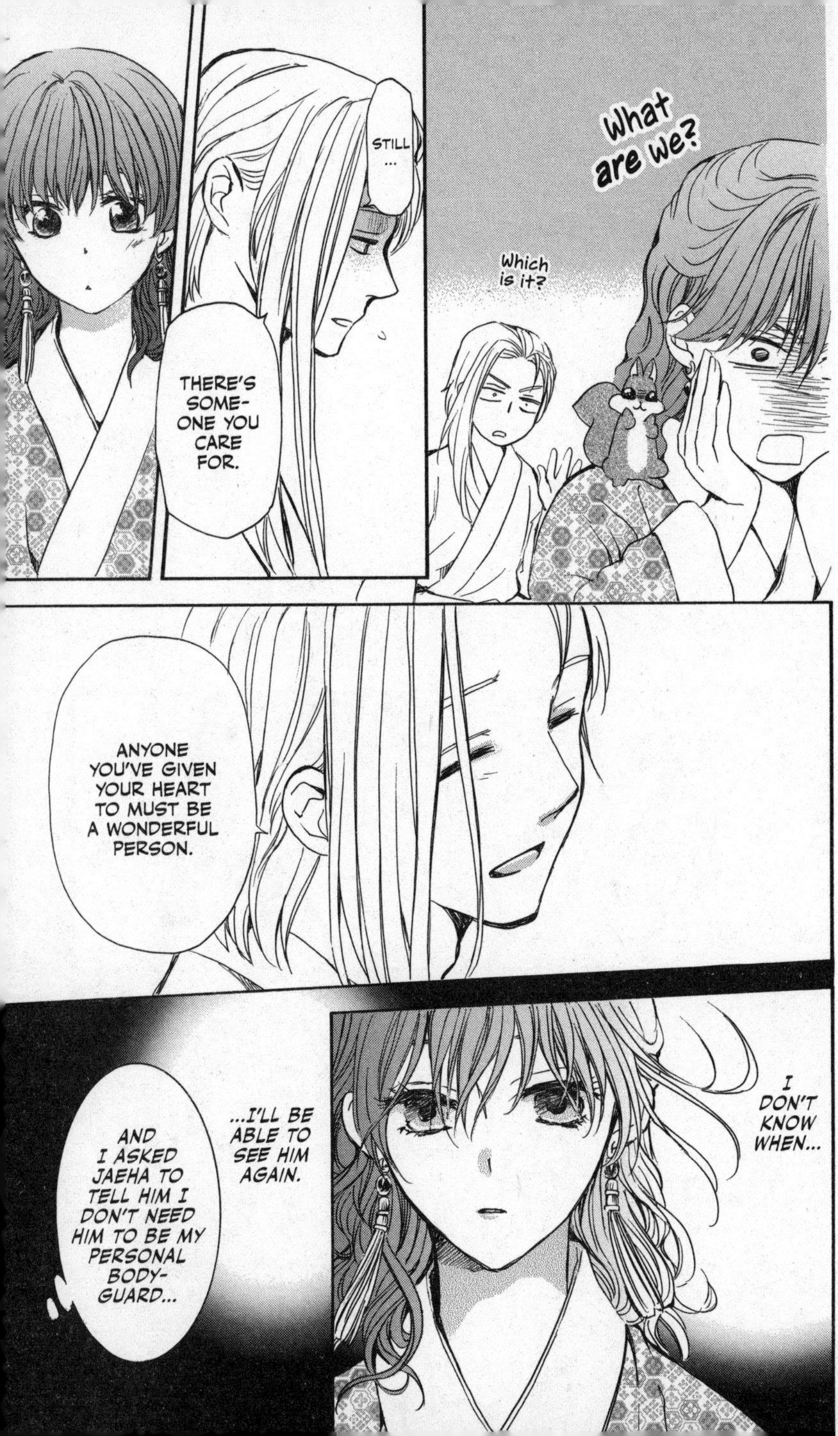
What are we?
Which is it?
STILL ...
THERE'S SOME-ONE YOU CARE FOR.
ANYONE YOU'VE GIVEN YOUR HEART TO MUST BE A WONDERFUL PERSON.
I DON'T KNOW WHEN...
...I'LL BE ABLE TO SEE HIM AGAIN.
AND I ASKED JAEHA TO TELL HIM I DON'T NEED HIM TO BE MY PERSONAL BODY-GUARD...

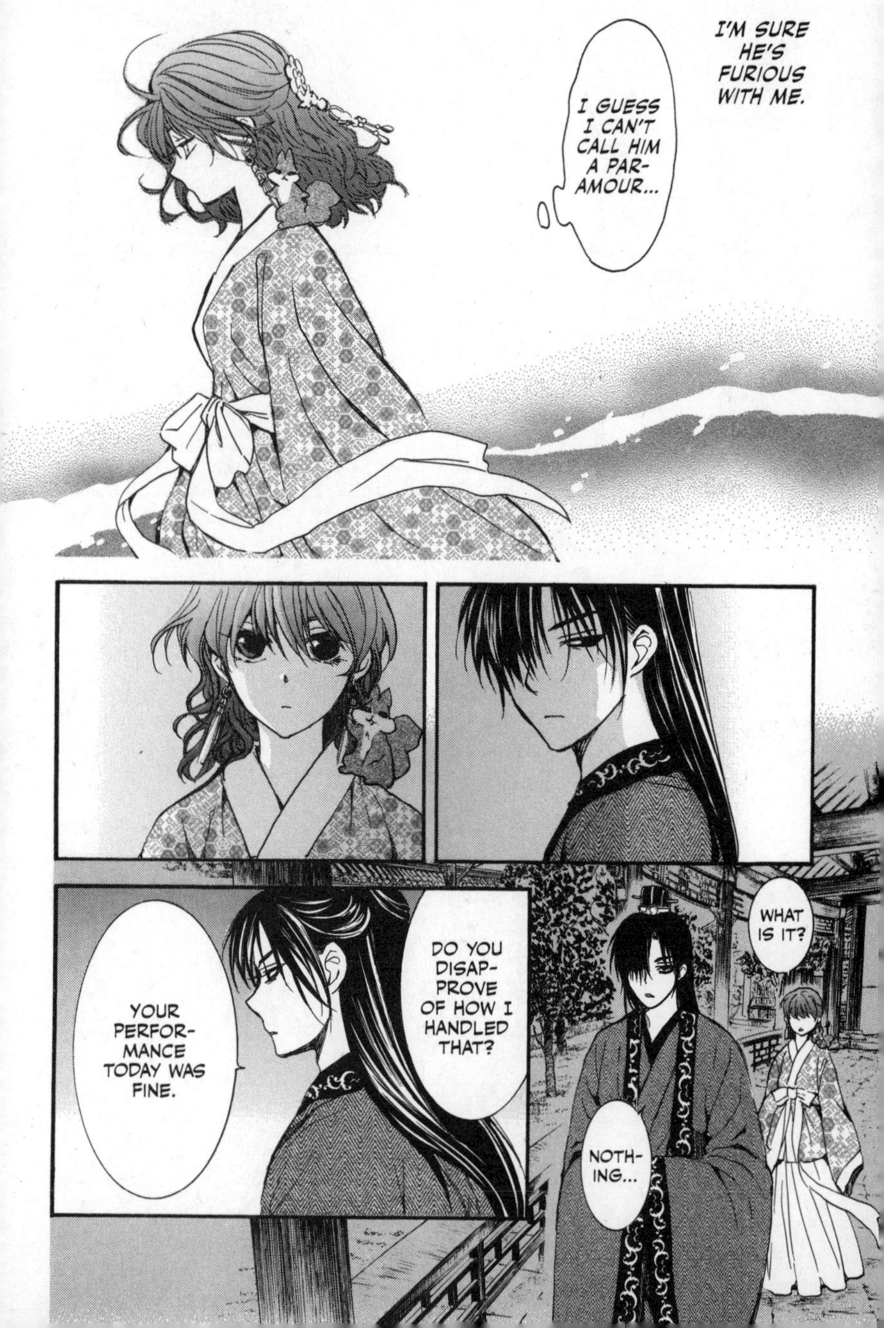
I'M SURE HE'S FURIOUS WITH ME.
I GUESS I CAN'T CALL HIM A PAR-AMOUR...
WHAT IS IT?
NOTH-ING...
DO YOU DISAP-PROVE OF HOW I HANDLED THAT?
YOUR PERFOR-MANCE TODAY WAS FINE.

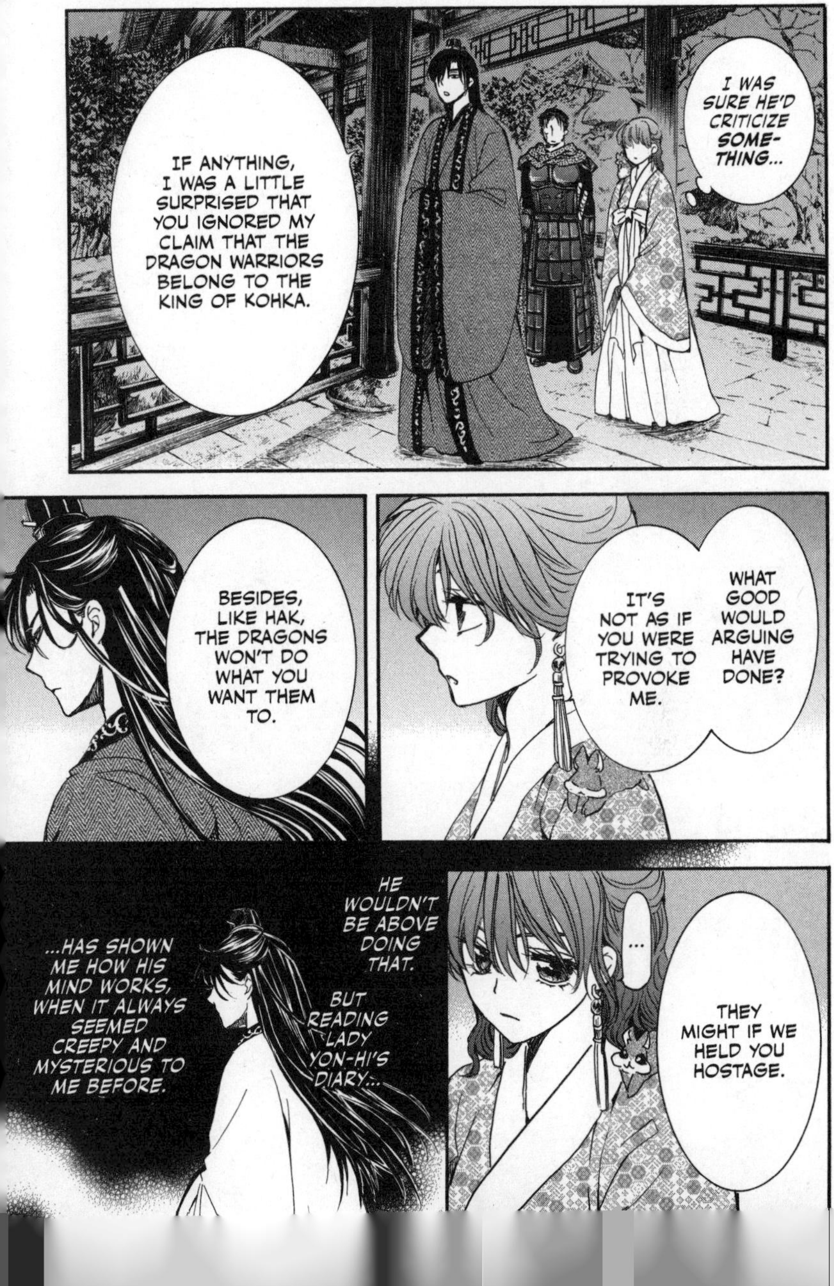
I WAS SURE HE'D CRITICIZE SOMETHING...
IF ANYTHING, I WAS A LITTLE SURPRISED THAT YOU IGNORED MY CLAIM THAT THE DRAGON WARRIORS BELONG TO THE KING OF KOHKA.
WHAT GOOD WOULD ARGUING HAVE DONE?
IT'S NOT AS IF YOU WERE TRYING TO PROVOKE ME.
BESIDES, LIKE HAK, THE DRAGONS WON'T DO WHAT YOU WANT THEM TO.
...
THEY MIGHT IF WE HELD YOU HOSTAGE.
HE WOULDN'T BE ABOVE DOING THAT.
BUT READING LADY YON-HI'S DIARY...
...HAS SHOWN ME HOW HIS MIND WORKS, WHEN IT ALWAYS SEEMED CREEPY AND MYSTERIOUS TO ME BEFORE.

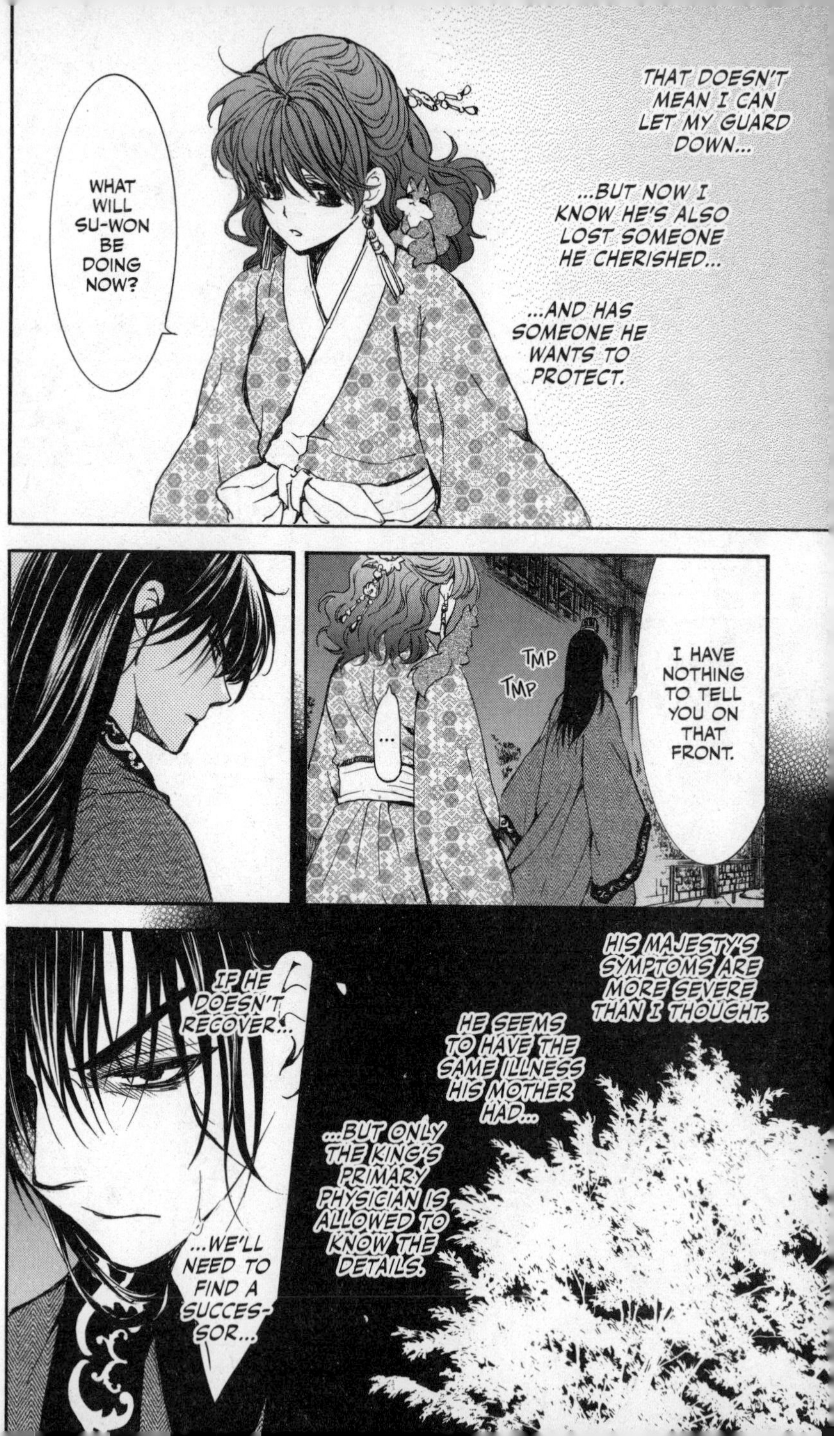
THAT DOESN'T MEAN I CAN LET MY GUARD DOWN...
...BUT NOW I KNOW HE'S ALSO LOST SOMEONE HE CHERISHED...
...AND HAS SOMEONE HE WANTS TO PROTECT.
WHAT WILL SU-WON BE DOING NOW?
I HAVE NOTHING TO TELL YOU ON THAT FRONT.
TMP
TMP
...
HIS MAJESTY'S SYMPTOMS ARE MORE SEVERE THAN I THOUGHT.
HE SEEMS TO HAVE THE SAME ILLNESS HIS MOTHER HAD...
...BUT ONLY THE KING'S PRIMARY PHYSICIAN IS ALLOWED TO KNOW THE DETAILS.
IF HE DOESN'T RECOVER...
...WE'LL NEED TO FIND A SUCCES-SOR...

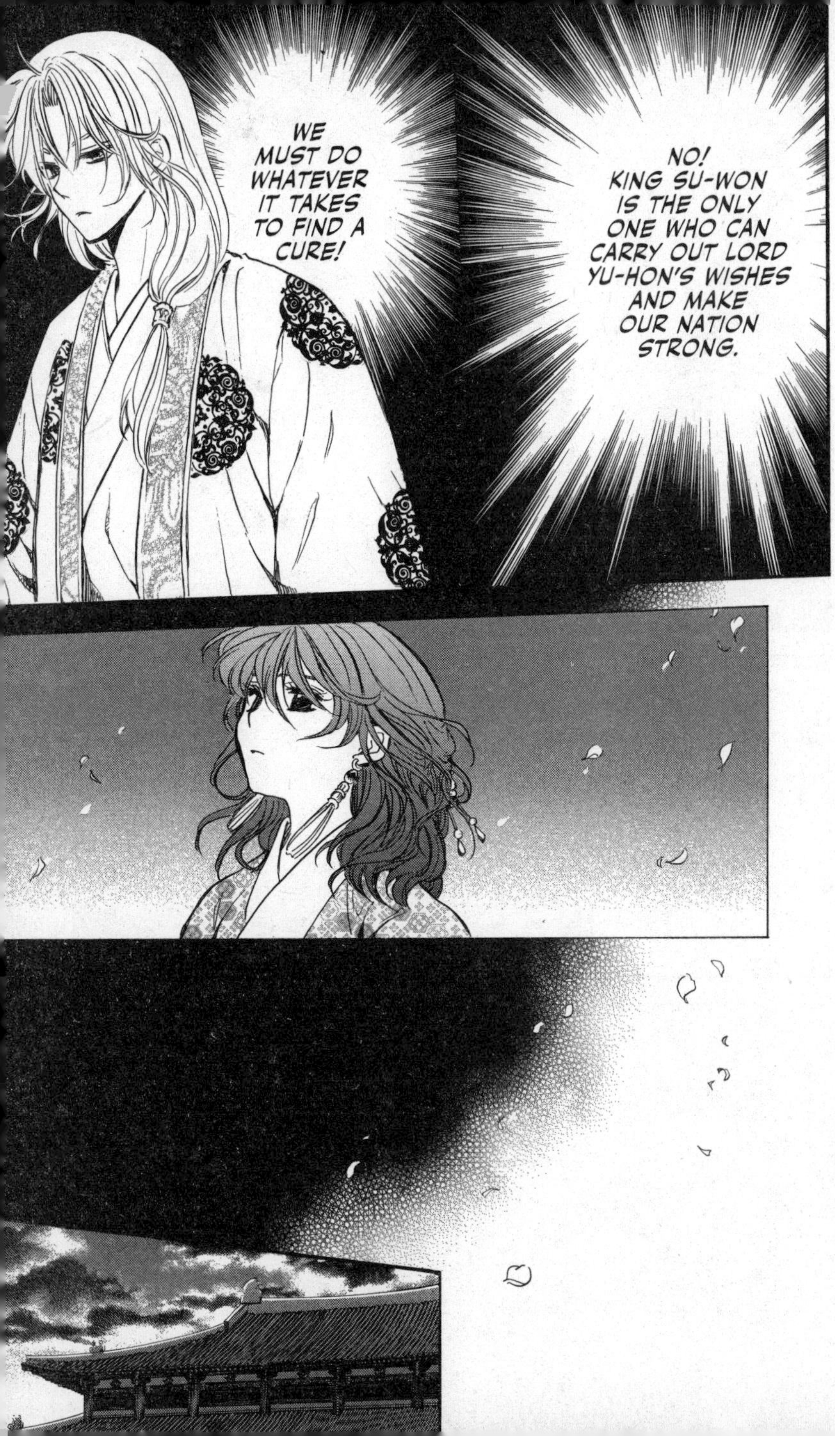
NO! KING SU-WON IS THE ONLY ONE WHO CAN CARRY OUT LORD YU-HON'S WISHES AND MAKE OUR NATION STRONG.
WE MUST DO WHATEVER IT TAKES TO FIND A CURE!

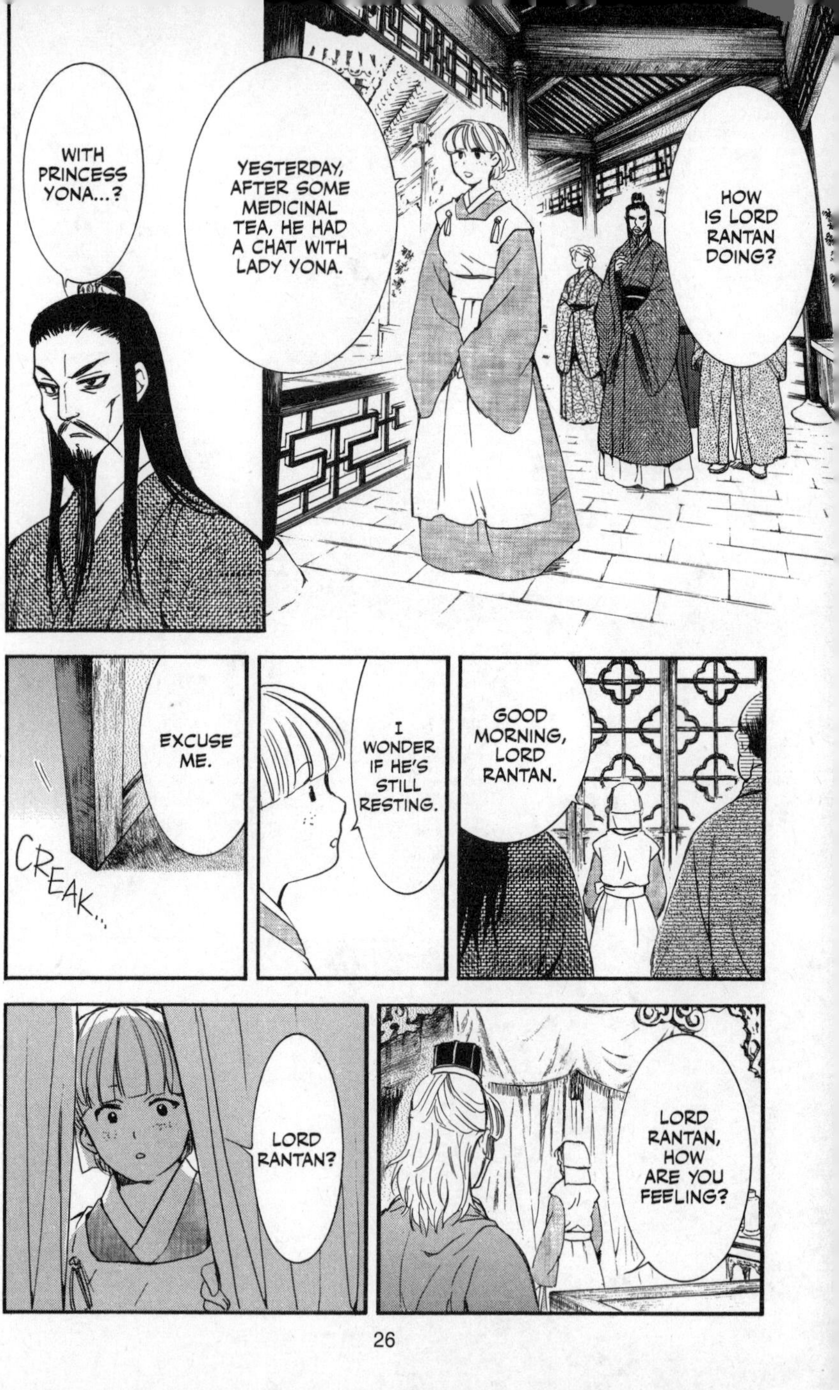
HOW IS LORD RANTAN DOING?
YESTERDAY, AFTER SOME MEDICINAL TEA, HE HAD A CHAT WITH LADY YONA.
WITH PRINCESS YONA...?
GOOD MORNING, LORD RANTAN.
I WONDER IF HE'S STILL RESTING.
EXCUSE ME.
CREAK...
LORD RANTAN, HOW ARE YOU FEELING?
LORD RANTAN?

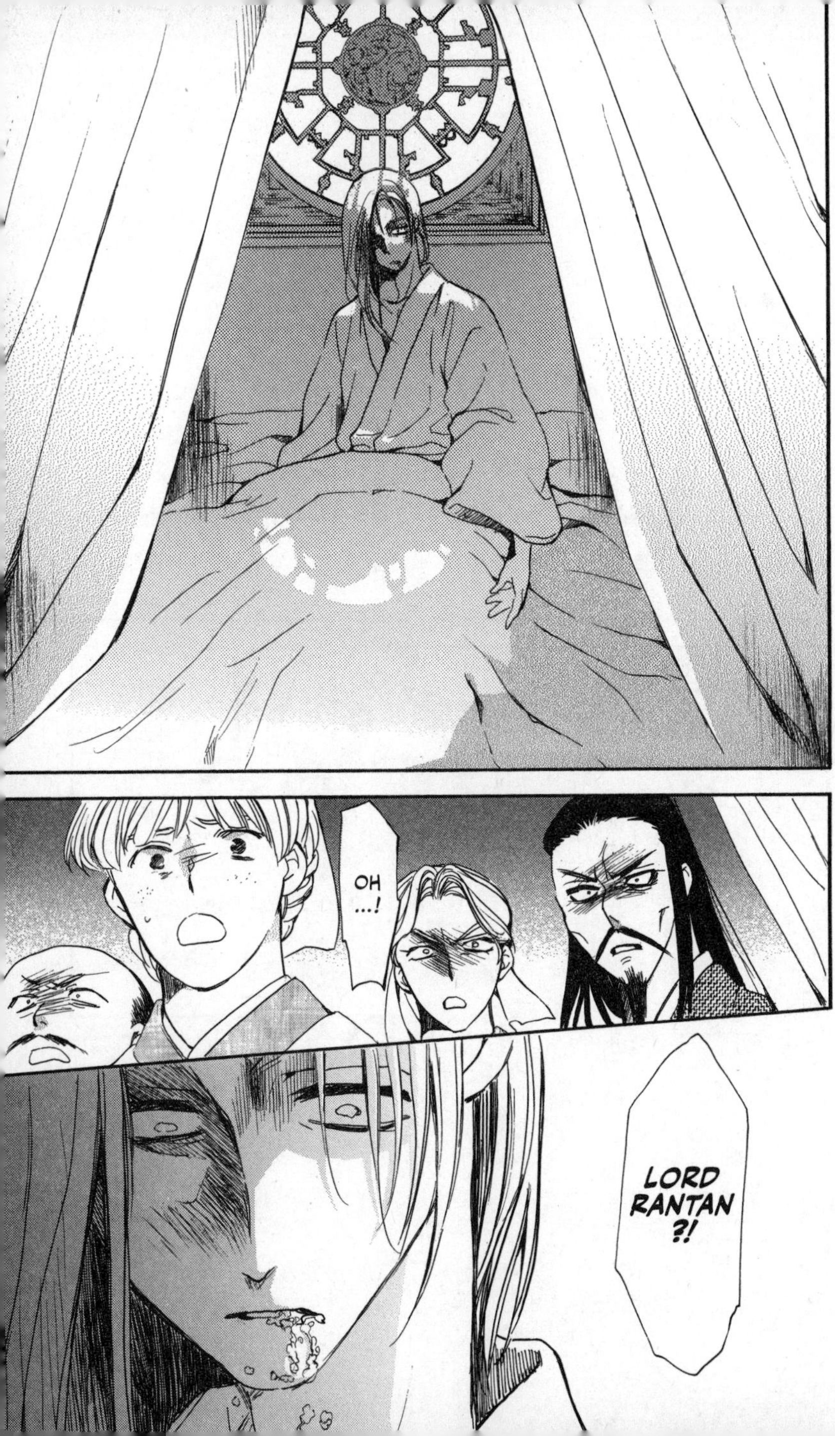
OH ...!
LORD RANTAN ?!

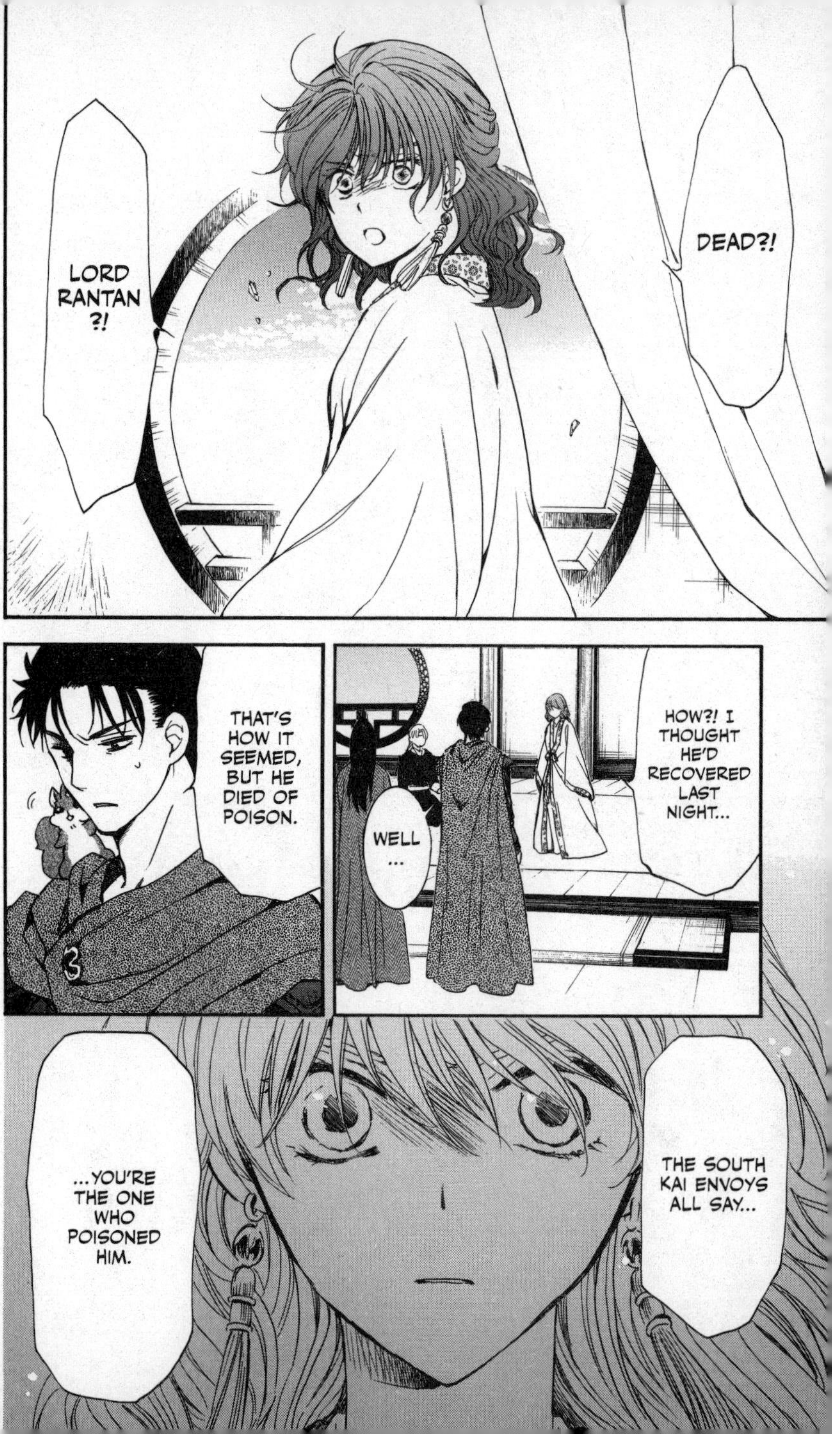
DEAD?!
LORD RANTAN ?!
HOW?! I THOUGHT HE'D RECOVERED LAST NIGHT...
WELL ...
THAT'S HOW IT SEEMED, BUT HE DIED OF POISON.
THE SOUTH KAI ENVOYS ALL SAY...
...YOU'RE THE ONE WHO POISONED HIM.

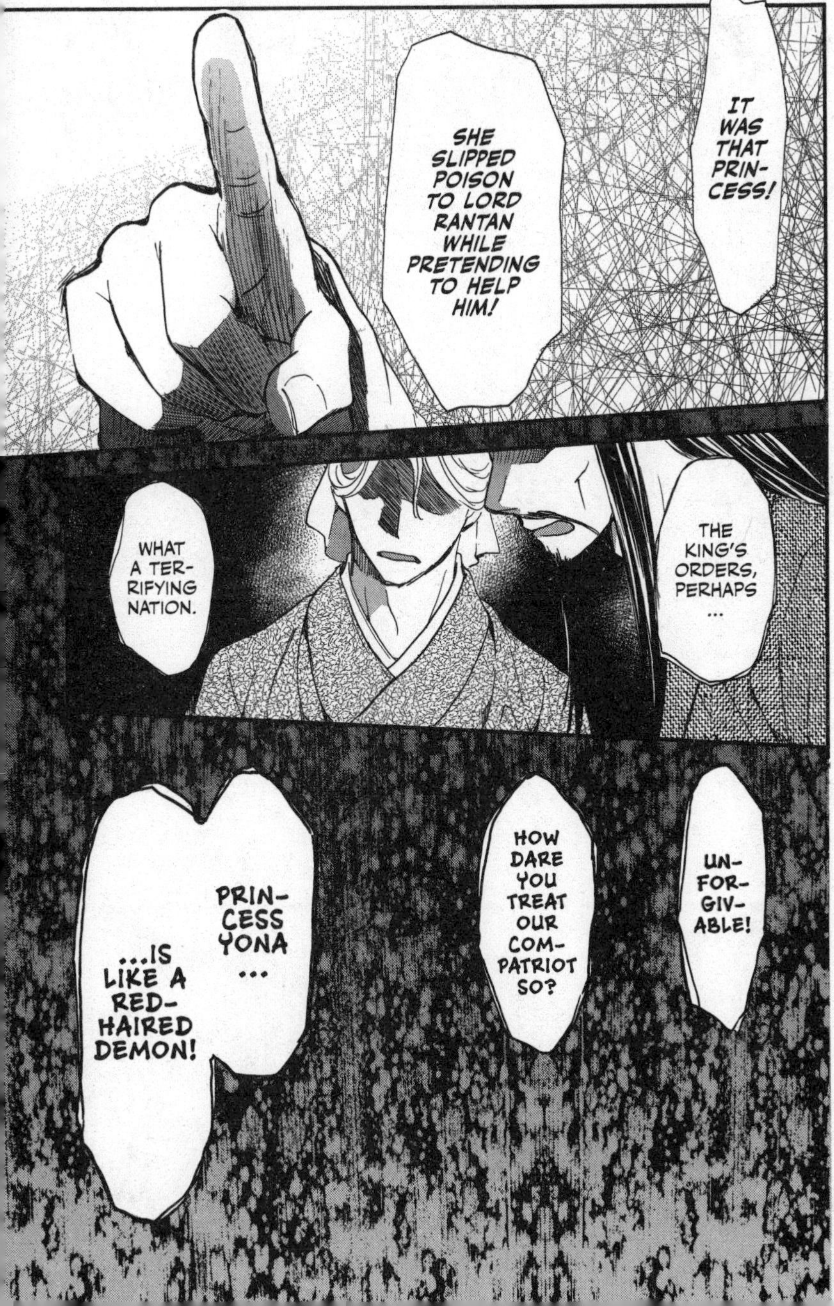
IT WAS THAT PRIN-CESS!
SHE SLIPPED POISON TO LORD RANTAN WHILE PRETENDING TO HELP HIM!
THE KING'S ORDERS, PERHAPS ...
WHAT A TER-RIFYING NATION.
UN-FOR-GIV-ABLE!
HOW DARE YOU TREAT OUR COM-PATRIOT SO?
PRIN-CESS YONA ...
...IS LIKE A RED-HAIRED DEMON!

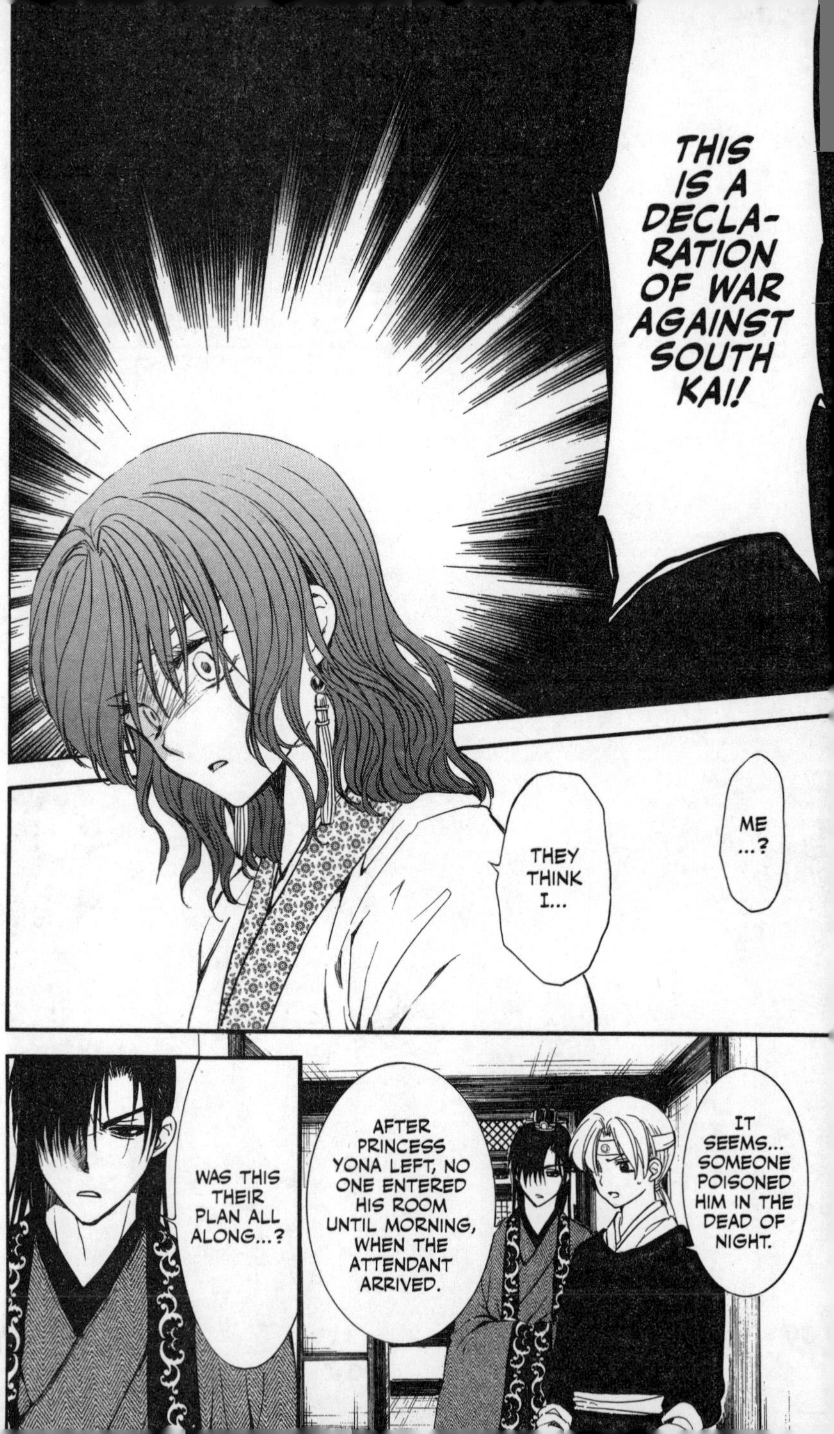
THIS IS A DECLARATION OF WAR AGAINST SOUTH KAI!
ME ...?
THEY THINK I...
IT SEEMS... SOMEONE POISONED HIM IN THE DEAD OF NIGHT.
AFTER PRINCESS YONA LEFT, NO ONE ENTERED HIS ROOM UNTIL MORNING, WHEN THE ATTENDANT ARRIVED.
WAS THIS THEIR PLAN ALL ALONG...?

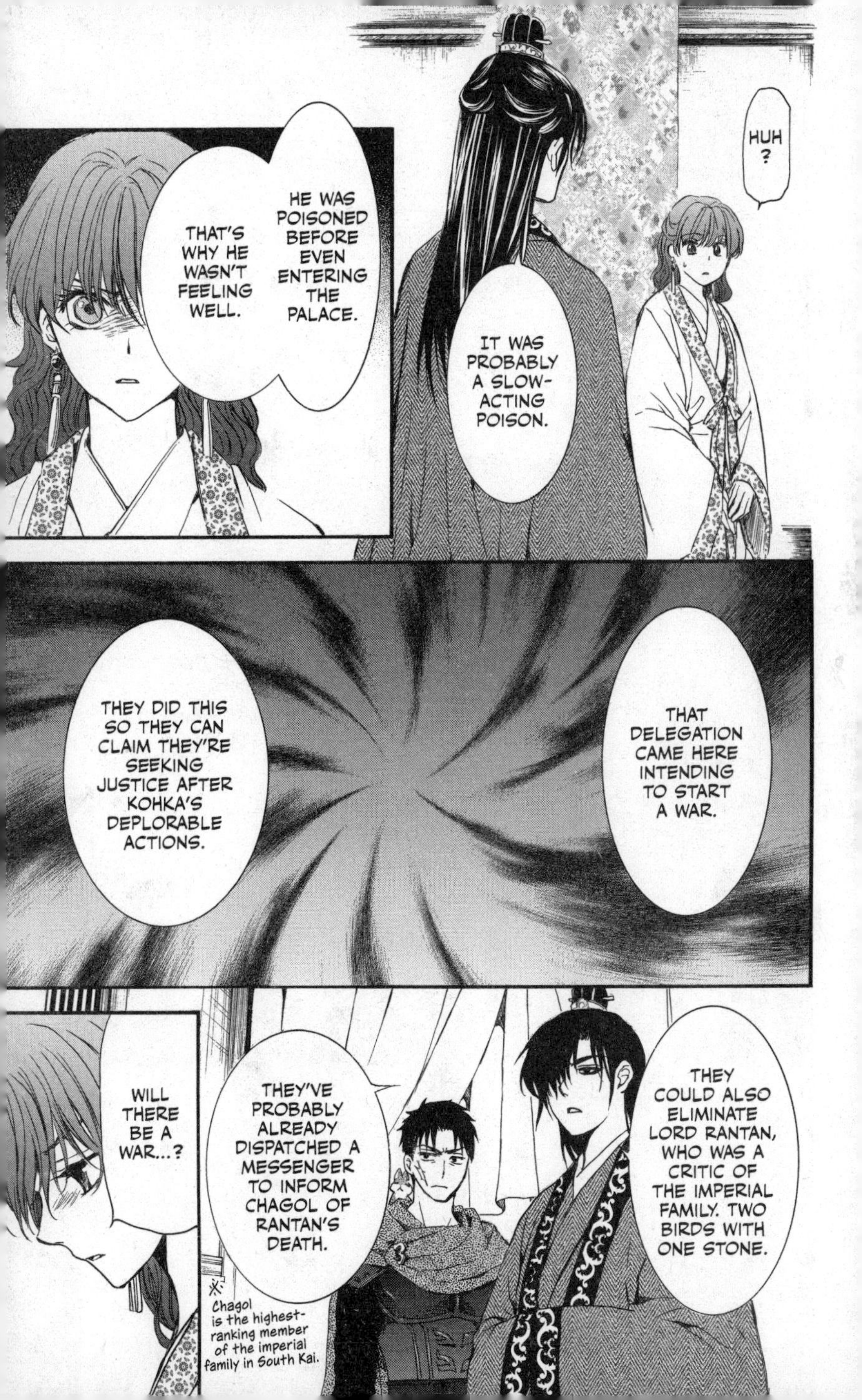
HUH?
IT WAS PROBABLY A SLOW-ACTING POISON.
HE WAS POISONED BEFORE EVEN ENTERING THE PALACE.
THAT'S WHY HE WASN'T FEELING WELL.
THAT DELEGATION CAME HERE INTENDING TO START A WAR.
THEY DID THIS SO THEY CAN CLAIM THEY'RE SEEKING JUSTICE AFTER KOHKA'S DEPLORABLE ACTIONS.
THEY COULD ALSO ELIMINATE LORD RANTAN, WHO WAS A CRITIC OF THE IMPERIAL FAMILY. TWO BIRDS WITH ONE STONE.
THEY'VE PROBABLY ALREADY DISPATCHED A MESSENGER TO INFORM CHAGOL OF RANTAN'S DEATH.
WILL THERE BE A WAR...?
※ Chagol is the highest-ranking member of the imperial family in South Kai.

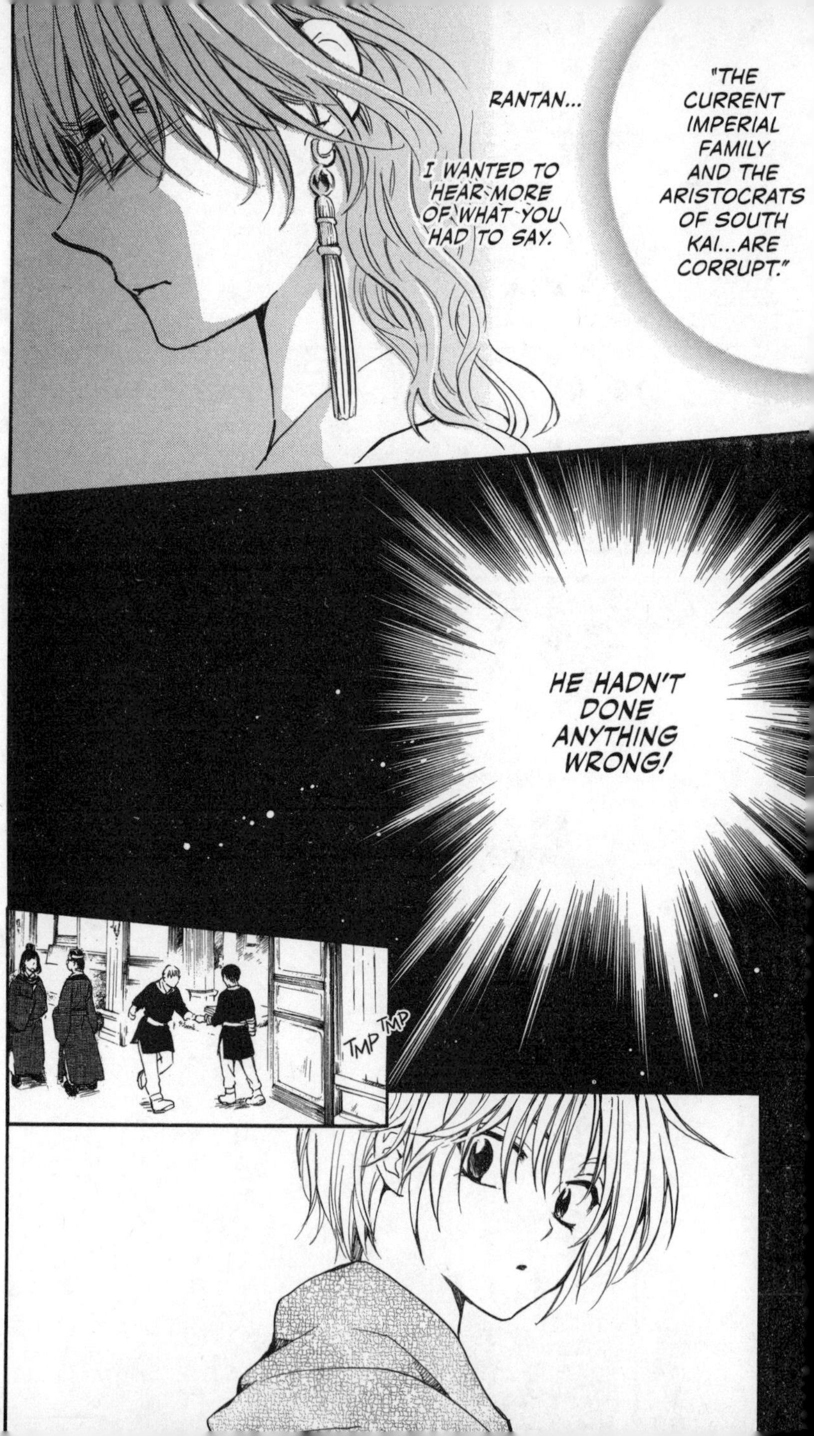
"THE CURRENT IMPERIAL FAMILY AND THE ARISTOCRATS OF SOUTH KAI...ARE CORRUPT."
RANTAN...
I WANTED TO HEAR MORE OF WHAT YOU HAD TO SAY.
HE HADN'T DONE ANYTHING WRONG!
TMP TMP

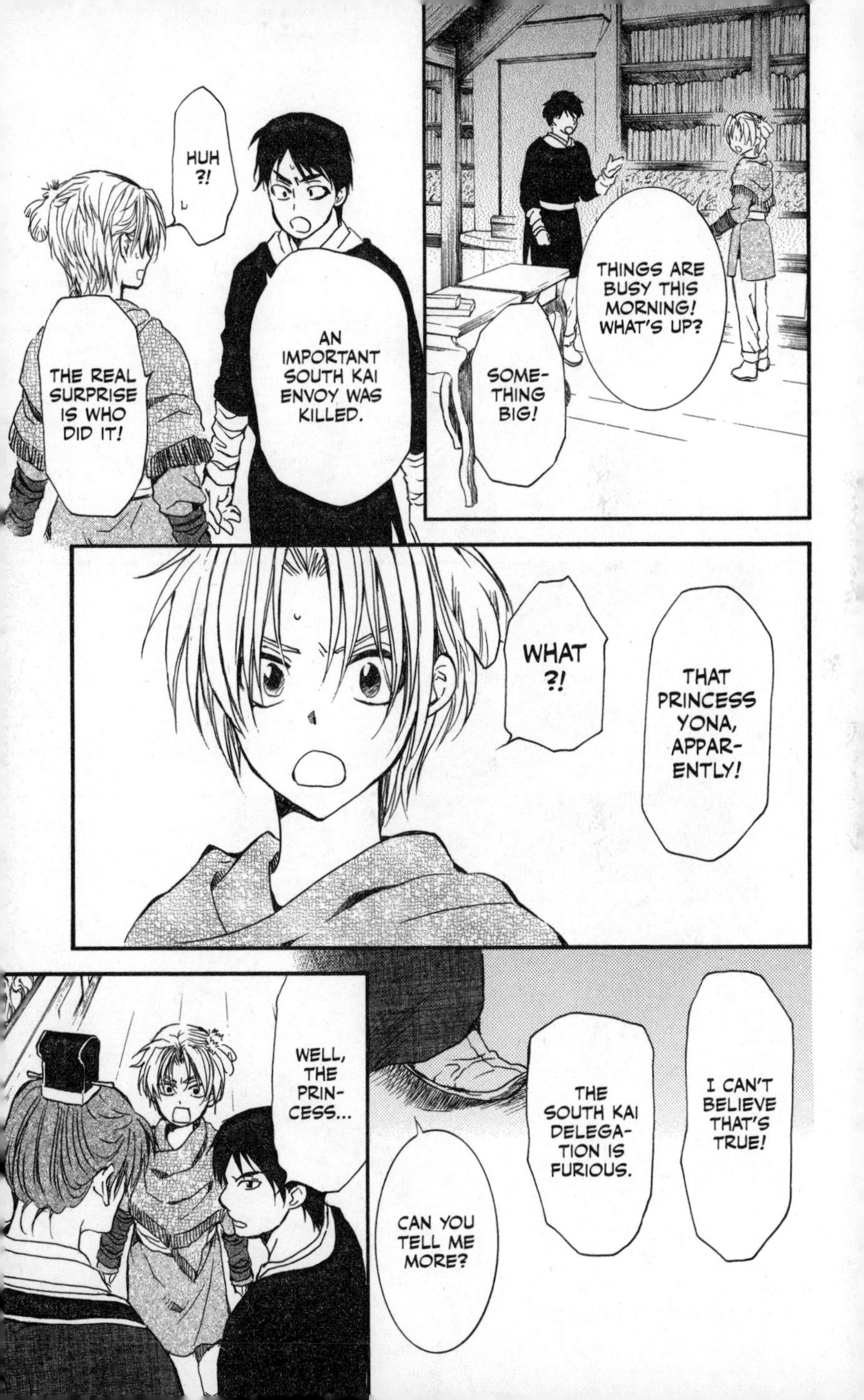
THINGS ARE BUSY THIS MORNING! WHAT'S UP?
SOME-THING BIG!
AN IMPORTANT SOUTH KAI ENVOY WAS KILLED.
HUH?!
THE REAL SURPRISE IS WHO DID IT!
THAT PRINCESS YONA, APPAR-ENTLY!
WHAT?!
I CAN'T BELIEVE THAT'S TRUE!
THE SOUTH KAI DELEGA-TION IS FURIOUS.
CAN YOU TELL ME MORE?
WELL, THE PRIN-CESS...

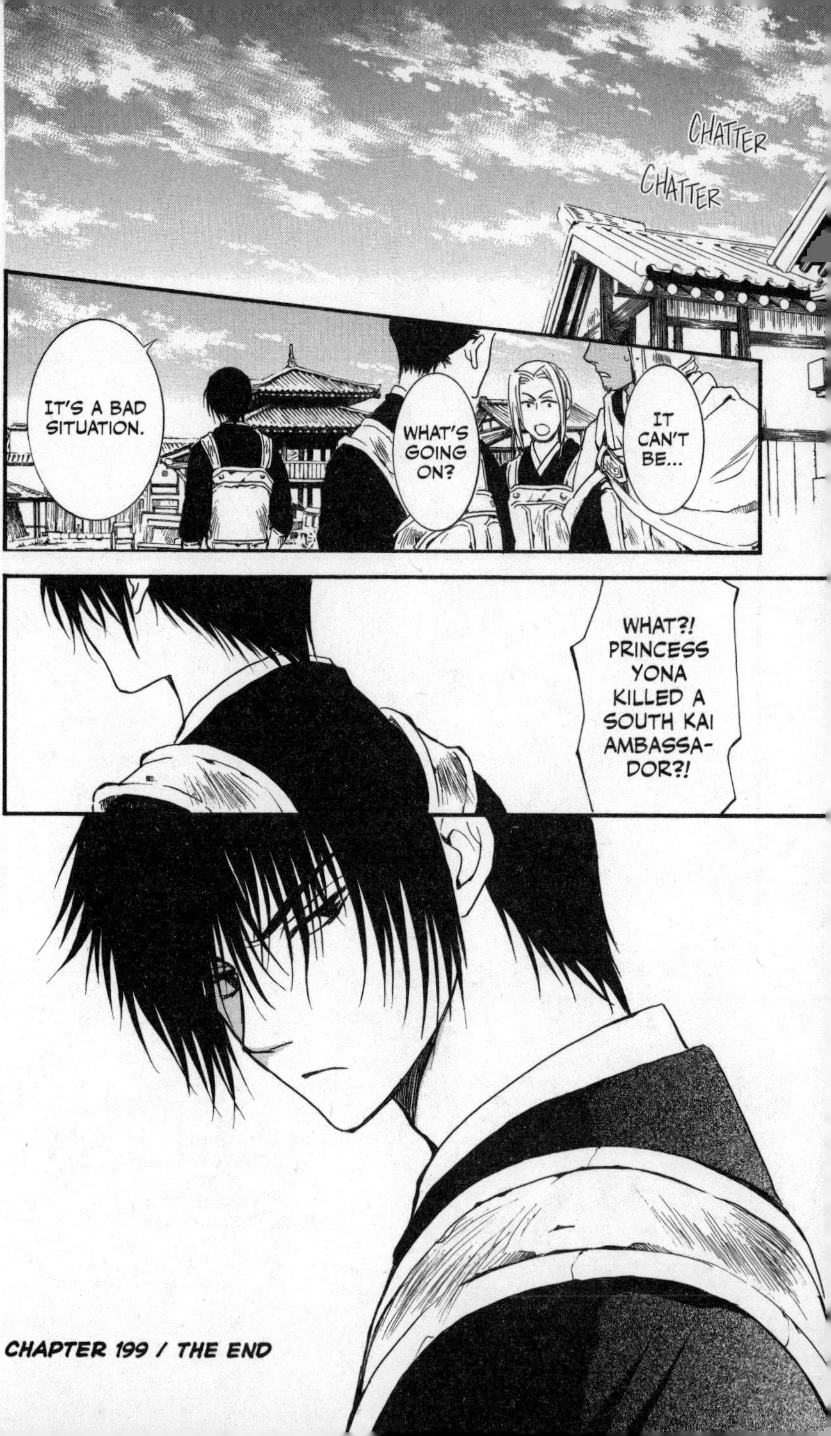
CHATTER
CHATTER
IT CAN'T BE...
WHAT'S GOING ON?
IT'S A BAD SITUATION.
WHAT?! PRINCESS YONA KILLED A SOUTH KAI AMBASSADOR?!
CHAPTER 199 / THE END

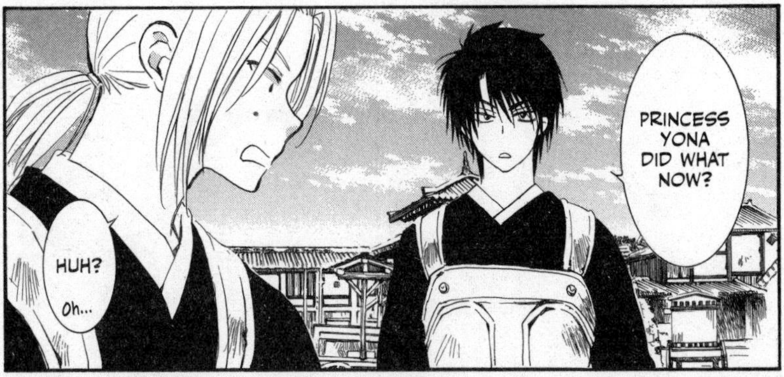
PRINCESS YONA DID WHAT NOW?
HUH?
Oh...

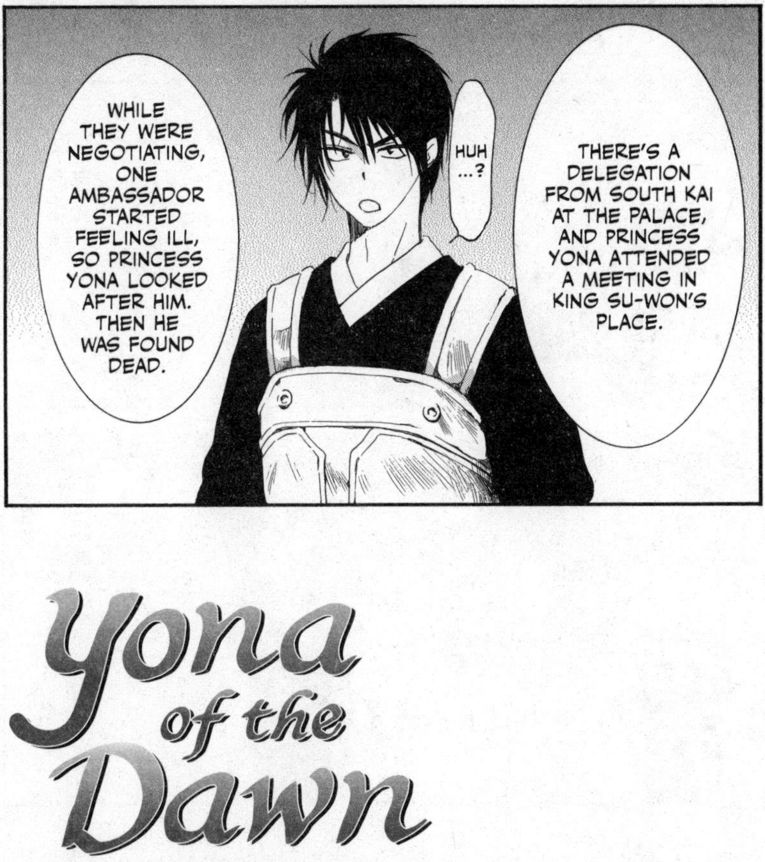
THERE'S A DELEGATION FROM SOUTH KAI AT THE PALACE, AND PRINCESS YONA ATTENDED A MEETING IN KING SU-WON'S PLACE.
HUH ...?
WHILE THEY WERE NEGOTIATING, ONE AMBASSADOR STARTED FEELING ILL, SO PRINCESS YONA LOOKED AFTER HIM. THEN HE WAS FOUND DEAD.

Yona of the Dawn

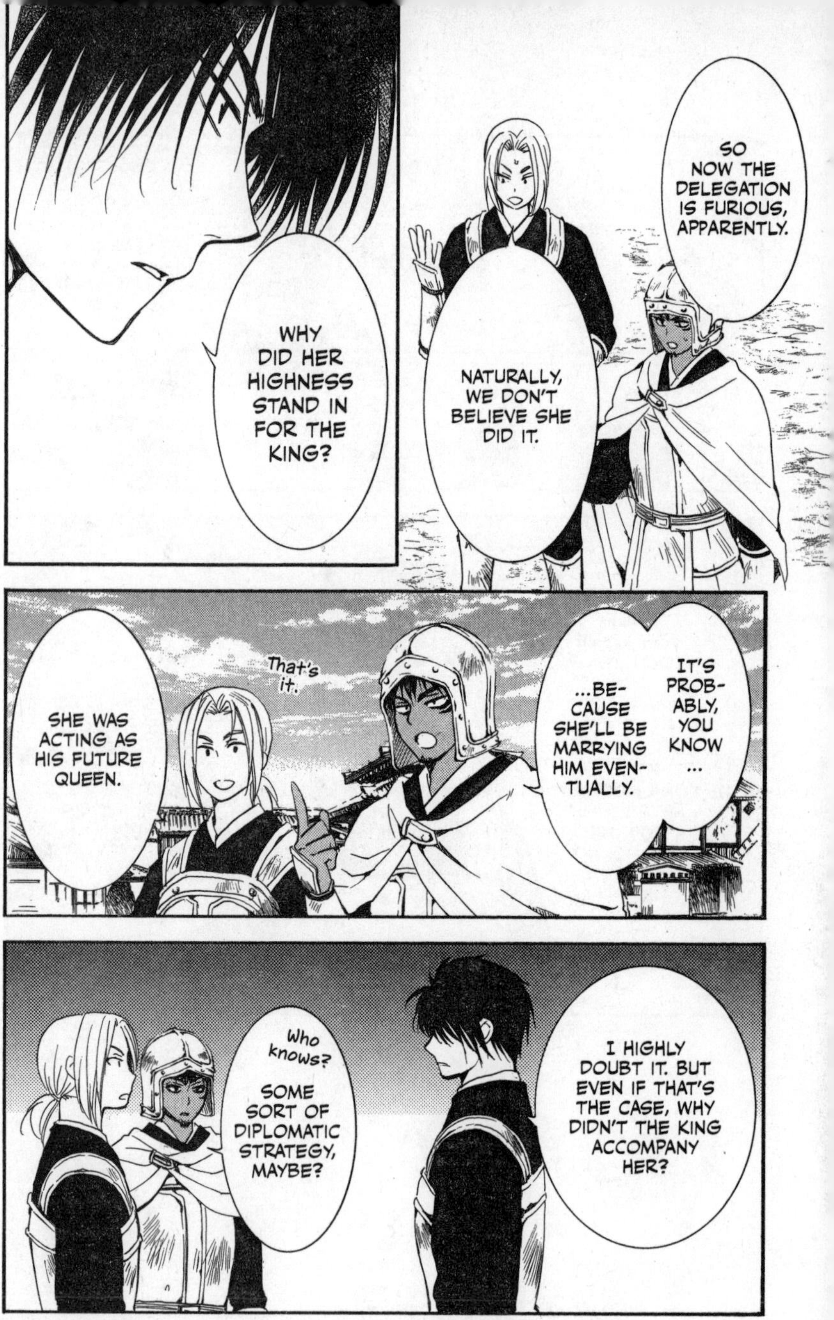
SO NOW THE DELEGATION IS FURIOUS, APPARENTLY.
NATURALLY, WE DON'T BELIEVE SHE DID IT.
WHY DID HER HIGHNESS STAND IN FOR THE KING?
IT'S PROBABLY, YOU KNOW ...
...BECAUSE SHE'LL BE MARRYING HIM EVENTUALLY.
That's it.
SHE WAS ACTING AS HIS FUTURE QUEEN.
I HIGHLY DOUBT IT. BUT EVEN IF THAT'S THE CASE, WHY DIDN'T THE KING ACCOMPANY HER?
Who knows?
SOME SORT OF DIPLOMATIC STRATEGY, MAYBE?

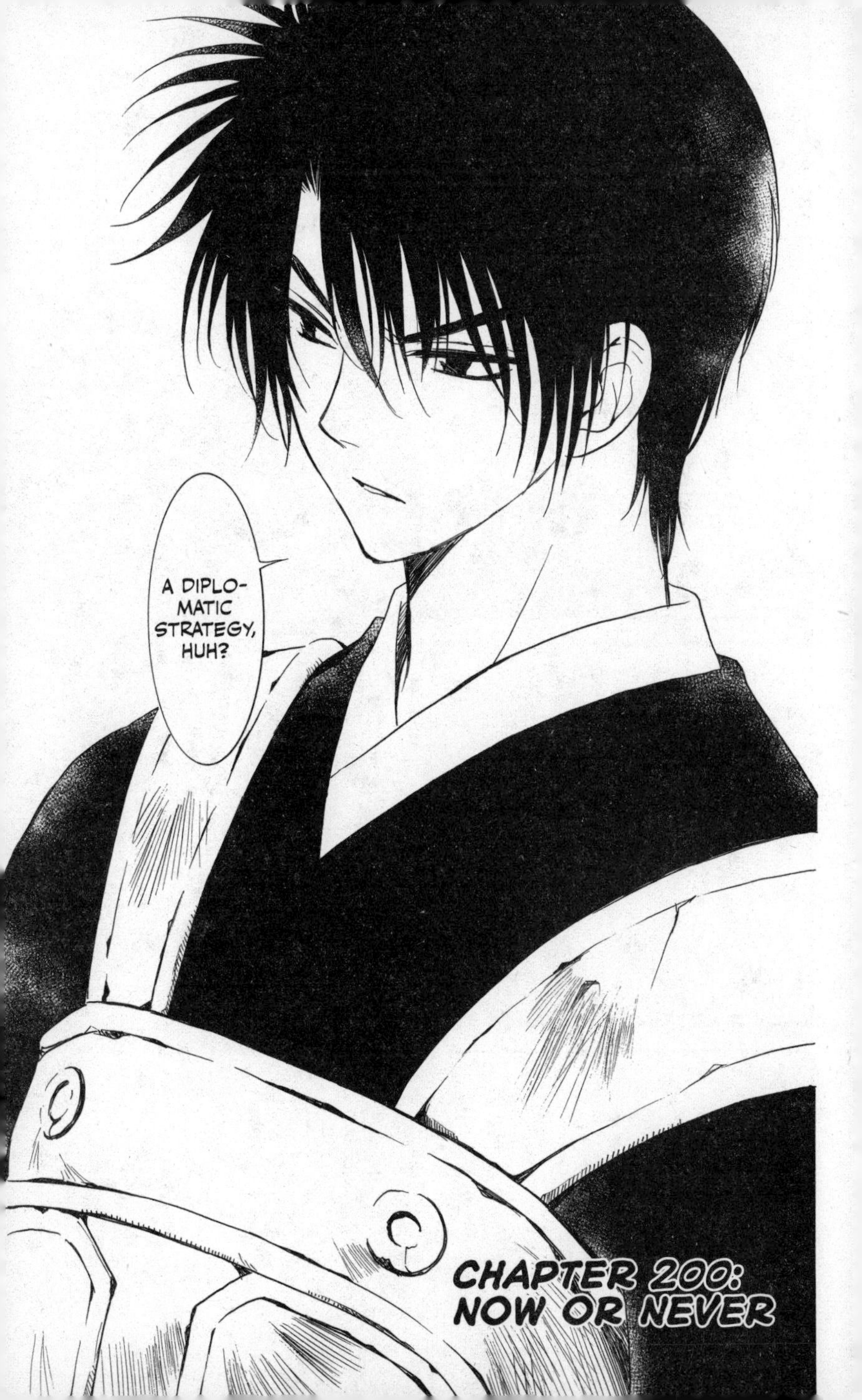
A DIPLOMATIC STRATEGY, HUH?

CHAPTER 200: NOW OR NEVER

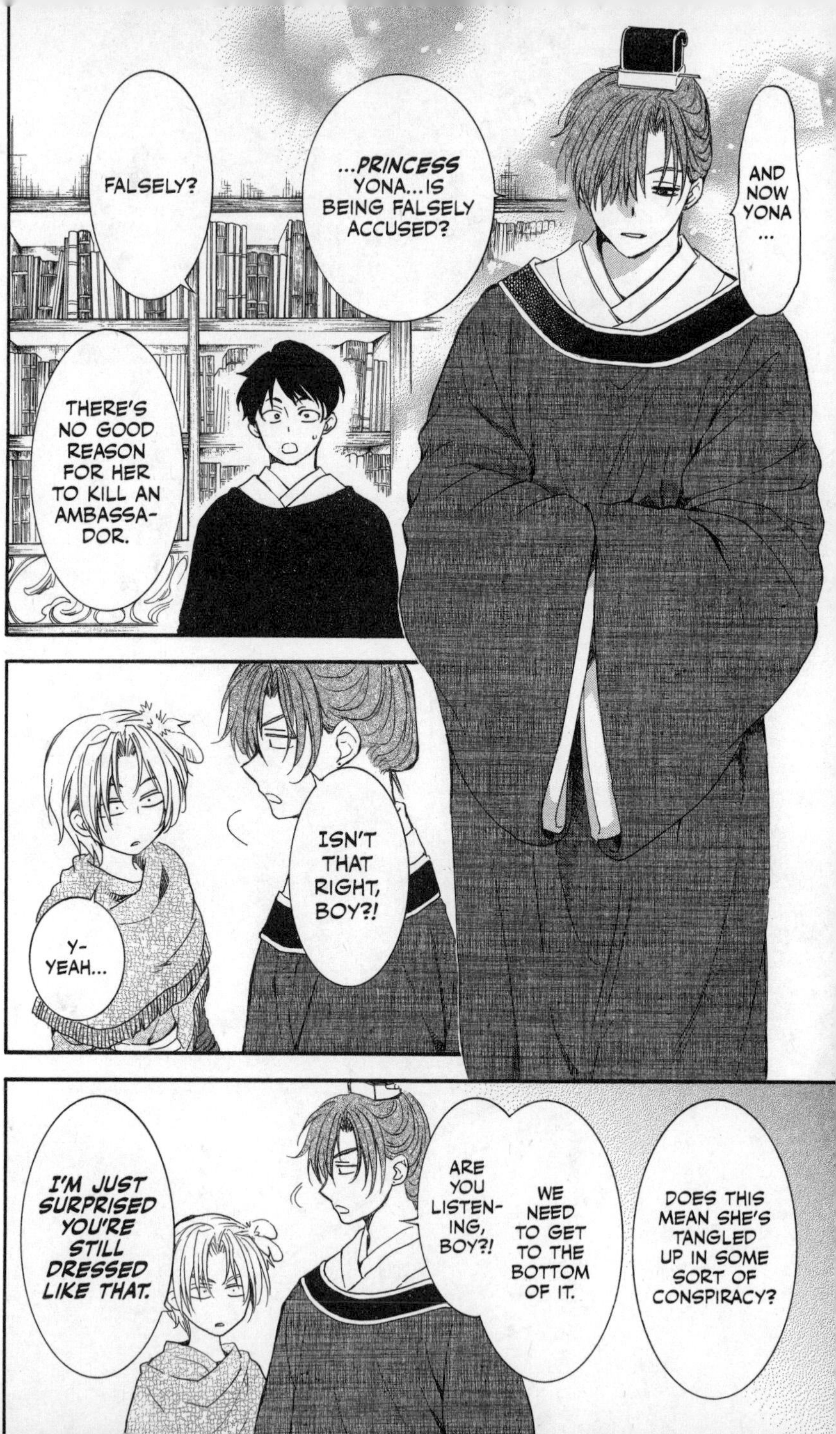
AND NOW YONA ...
...*PRINCESS* YONA...IS BEING FALSELY ACCUSED?
FALSELY?
THERE'S NO GOOD REASON FOR HER TO KILL AN AMBASSADOR.
ISN'T THAT RIGHT, BOY?!
Y-YEAH...
DOES THIS MEAN SHE'S TANGLED UP IN SOME SORT OF CONSPIRACY?
WE NEED TO GET TO THE BOTTOM OF IT.
ARE YOU LISTENING, BOY?!
I'M JUST SURPRISED YOU'RE STILL DRESSED LIKE THAT.

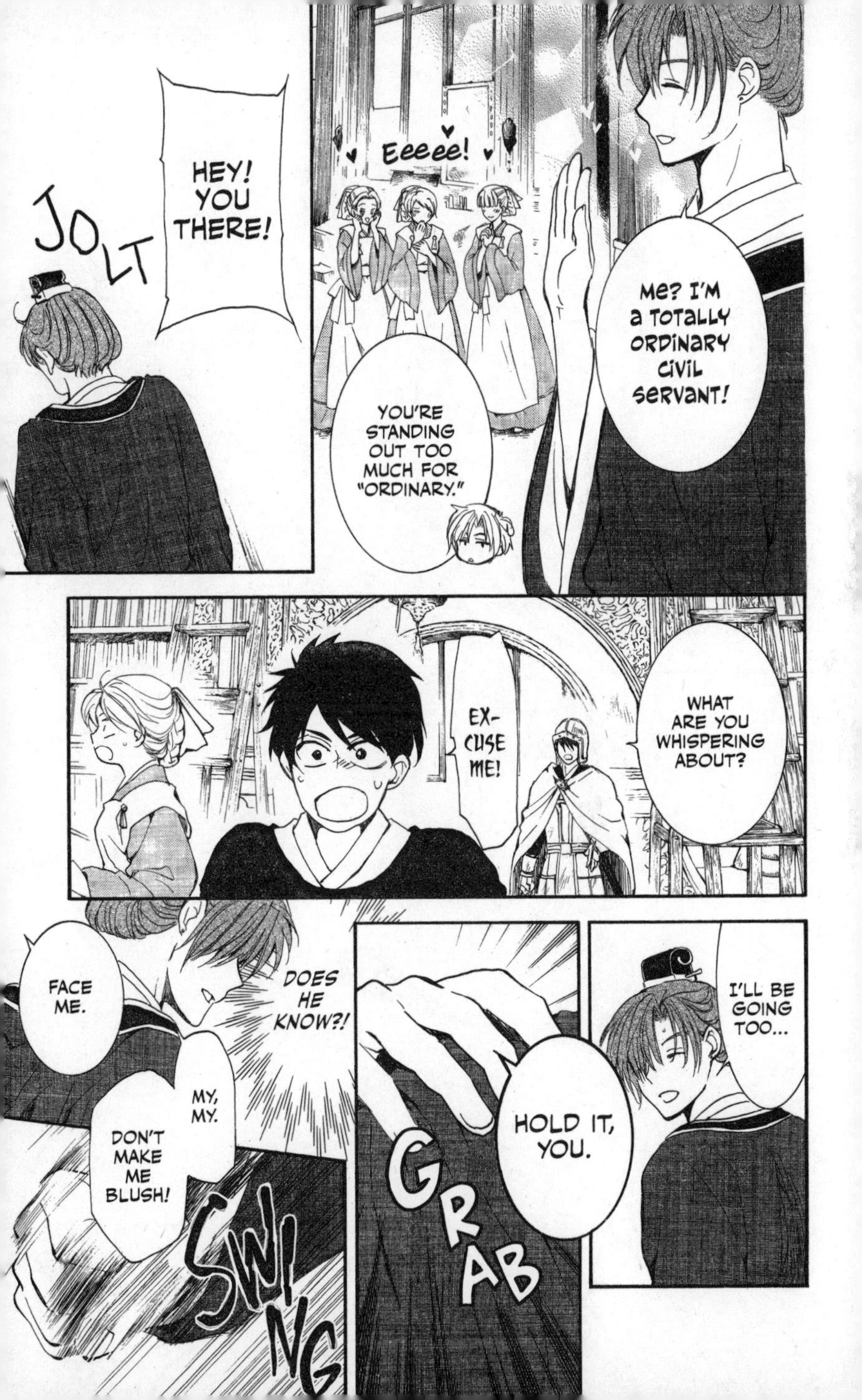
Eeeee!
Me? I'm a totally ordinary civil servant!
You're standing out too much for "ordinary."
Hey! You there!
JOLT
What are you whispering about?
Ex-cuse me!
I'll be going too...
Hold it, you.
GRAB
Face me.
Does he know?!
My, my. Don't make me blush!
SWING

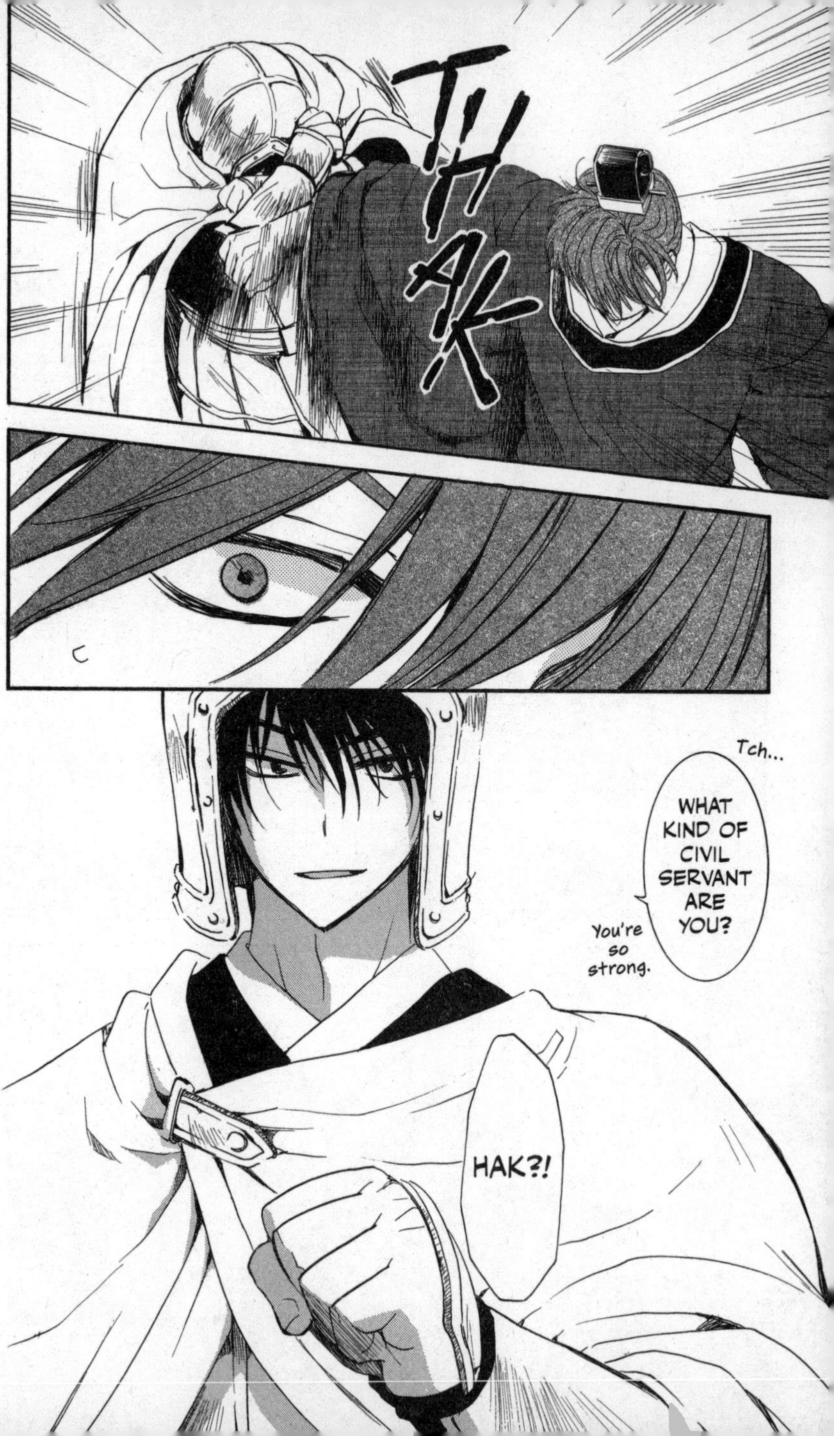
THAK
Tch...
WHAT KIND OF CIVIL SERVANT ARE YOU?
You're so strong.
HAK?!

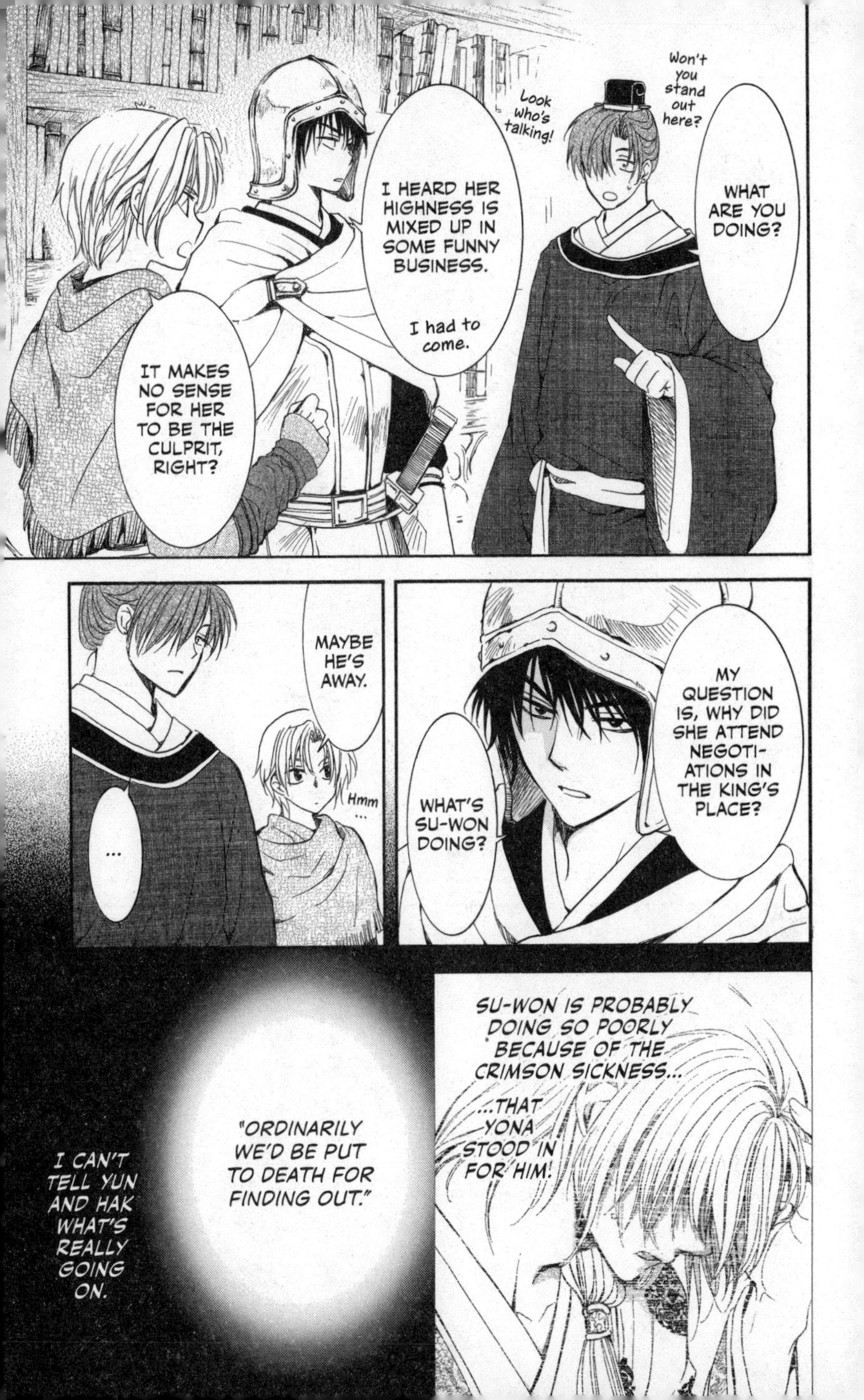
WHAT ARE YOU DOING?
Won't you stand out here?
Look who's talking!
I HEARD HER HIGHNESS IS MIXED UP IN SOME FUNNY BUSINESS.
I had to come.
IT MAKES NO SENSE FOR HER TO BE THE CULPRIT, RIGHT?
MY QUESTION IS, WHY DID SHE ATTEND NEGOTI-ATIONS IN THE KING'S PLACE?
WHAT'S SU-WON DOING?
MAYBE HE'S AWAY.
Hmm ...
...
SU-WON IS PROBABLY DOING SO POORLY BECAUSE OF THE CRIMSON SICKNESS...
...THAT YONA STOOD IN FOR HIM.
"ORDINARILY WE'D BE PUT TO DEATH FOR FINDING OUT."
I CAN'T TELL YUN AND HAK WHAT'S REALLY GOING ON.

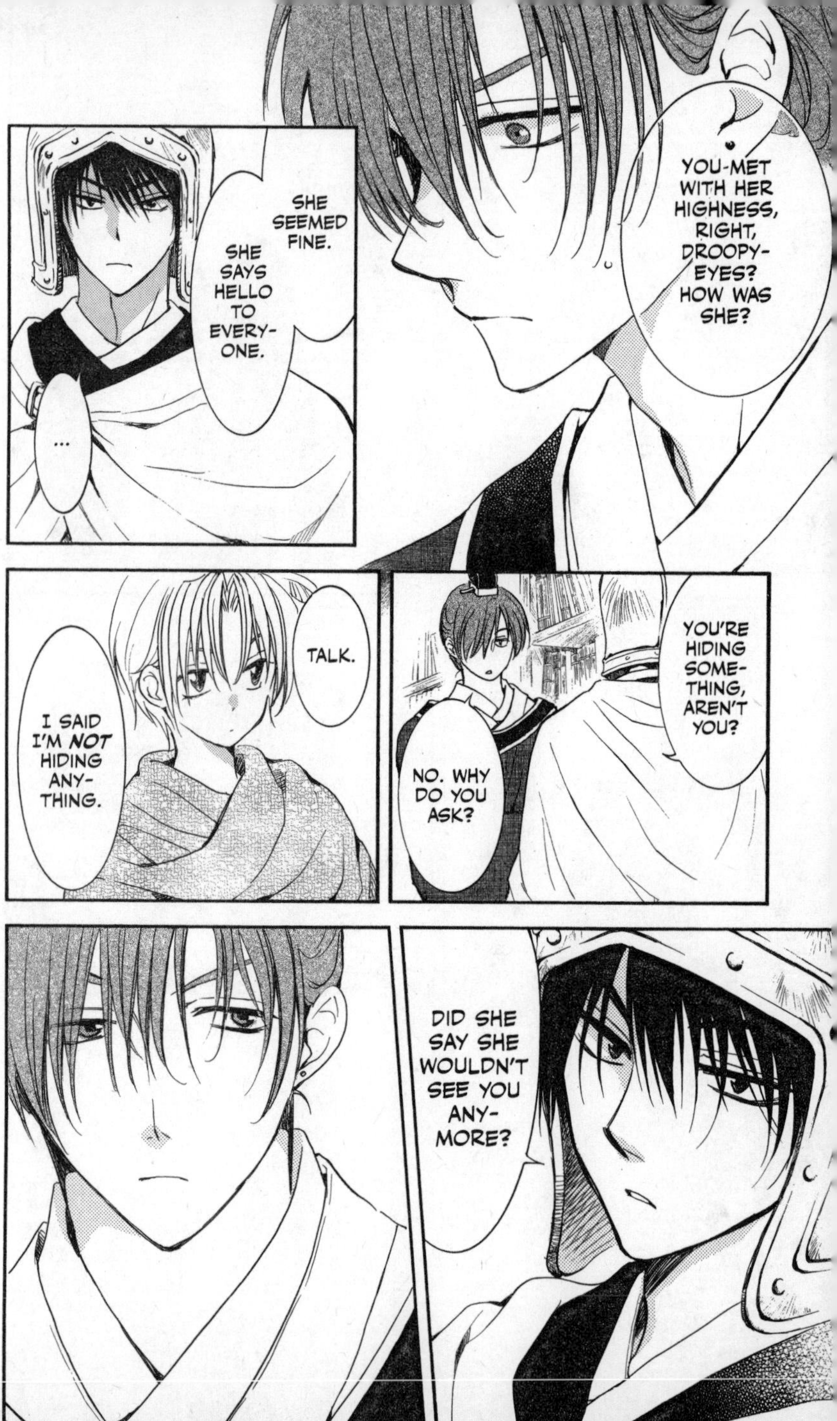
YOU-MET WITH HER HIGHNESS, RIGHT, DROOPY-EYES? HOW WAS SHE?
SHE SEEMED FINE.
SHE SAYS HELLO TO EVERY-ONE.
...
YOU'RE HIDING SOME-THING, AREN'T YOU?
NO. WHY DO YOU ASK?
TALK.
I SAID I'M *NOT* HIDING ANY-THING.
DID SHE SAY SHE WOULDN'T SEE YOU ANY-MORE?

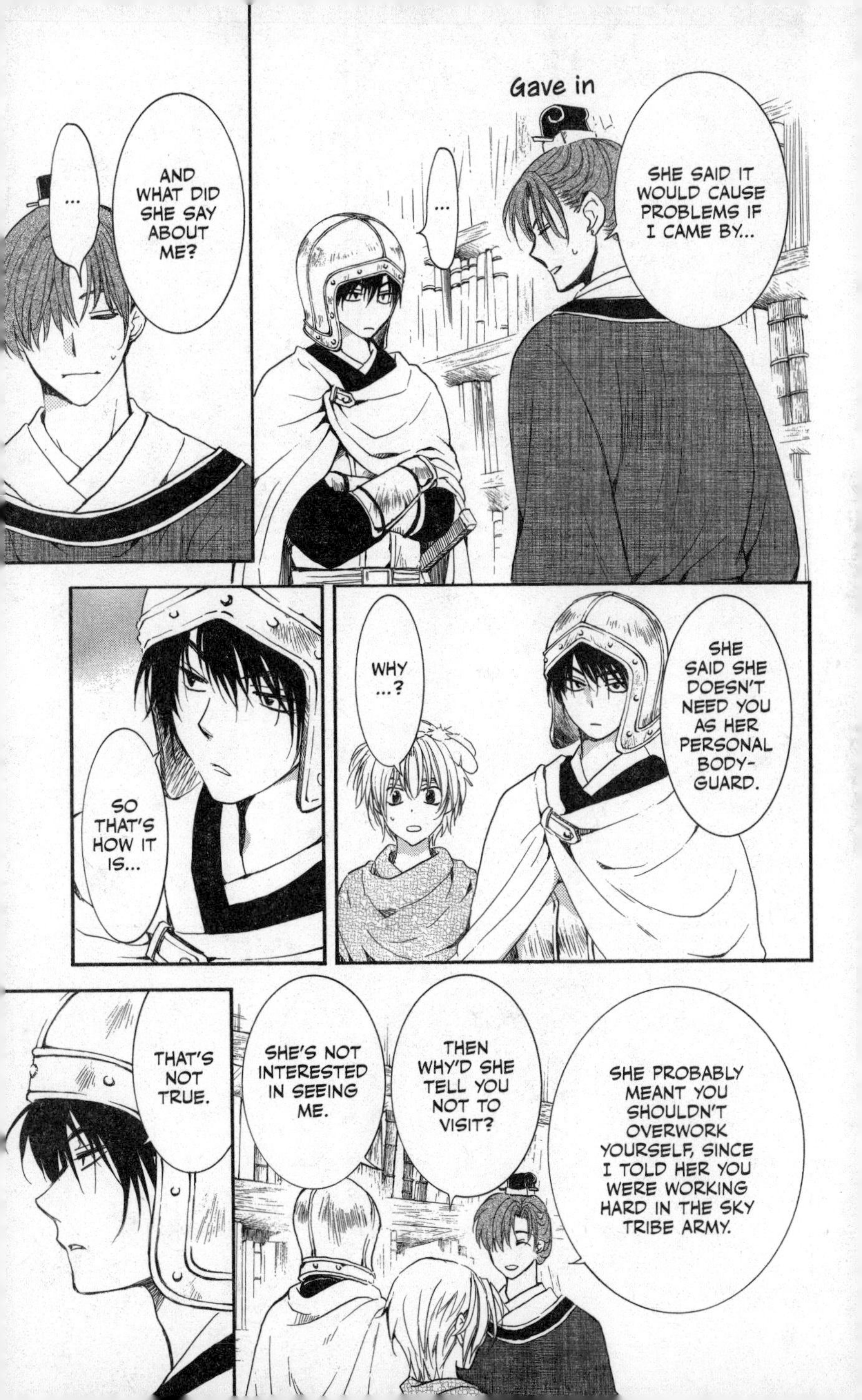
Gave in
SHE SAID IT WOULD CAUSE PROBLEMS IF I CAME BY...
...
AND WHAT DID SHE SAY ABOUT ME?
...
SHE SAID SHE DOESN'T NEED YOU AS HER PERSONAL BODY-GUARD.
WHY ...?
SO THAT'S HOW IT IS...
SHE PROBABLY MEANT YOU SHOULDN'T OVERWORK YOURSELF, SINCE I TOLD HER YOU WERE WORKING HARD IN THE SKY TRIBE ARMY.
THEN WHY'D SHE TELL YOU NOT TO VISIT?
SHE'S NOT INTERESTED IN SEEING ME.
THAT'S NOT TRUE.

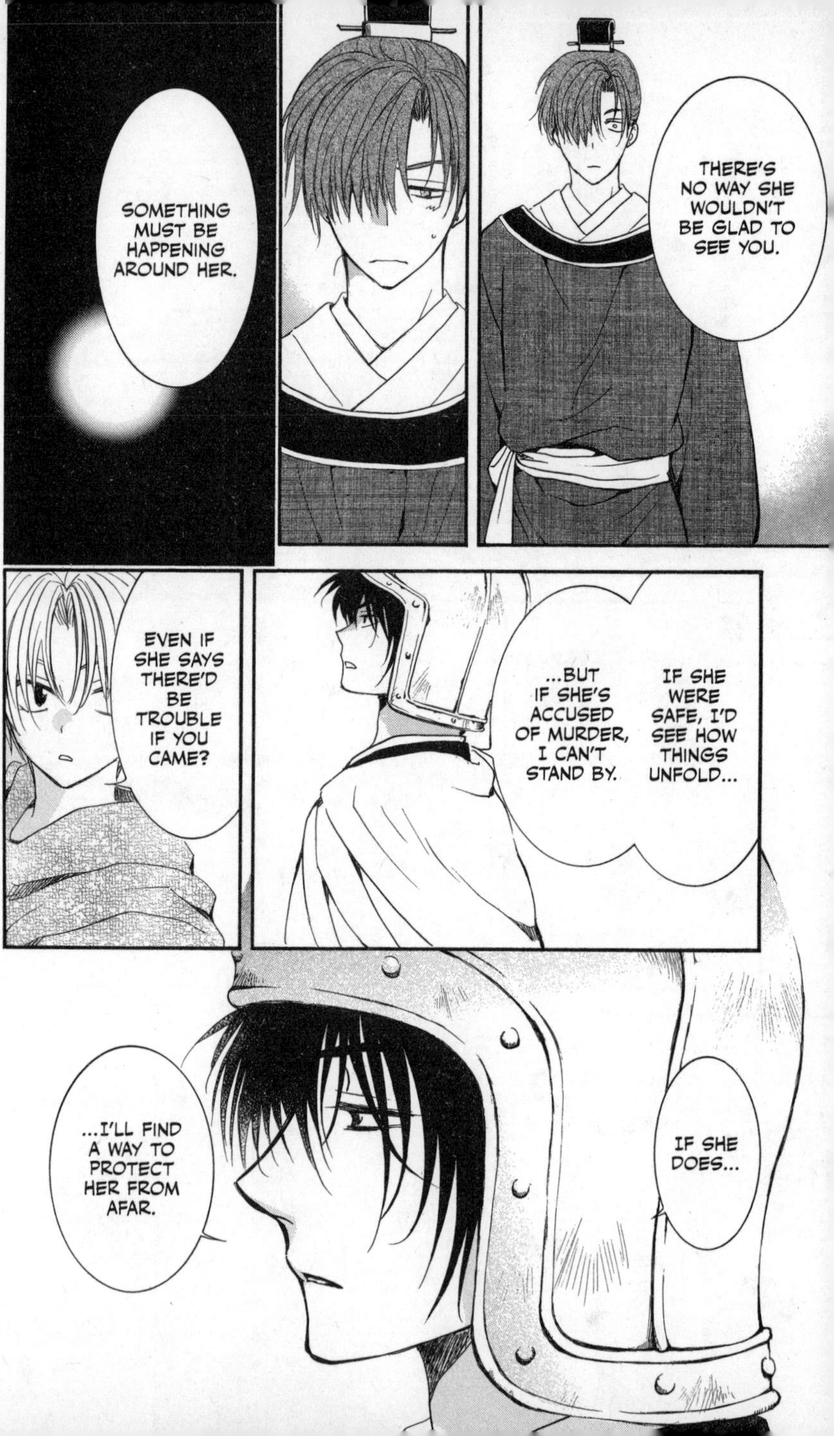
THERE'S NO WAY SHE WOULDN'T BE GLAD TO SEE YOU.
SOMETHING MUST BE HAPPENING AROUND HER.
IF SHE WERE SAFE, I'D SEE HOW THINGS UNFOLD...
...BUT IF SHE'S ACCUSED OF MURDER, I CAN'T STAND BY.
EVEN IF SHE SAYS THERE'D BE TROUBLE IF YOU CAME?
IF SHE DOES...
...I'LL FIND A WAY TO PROTECT HER FROM AFAR.

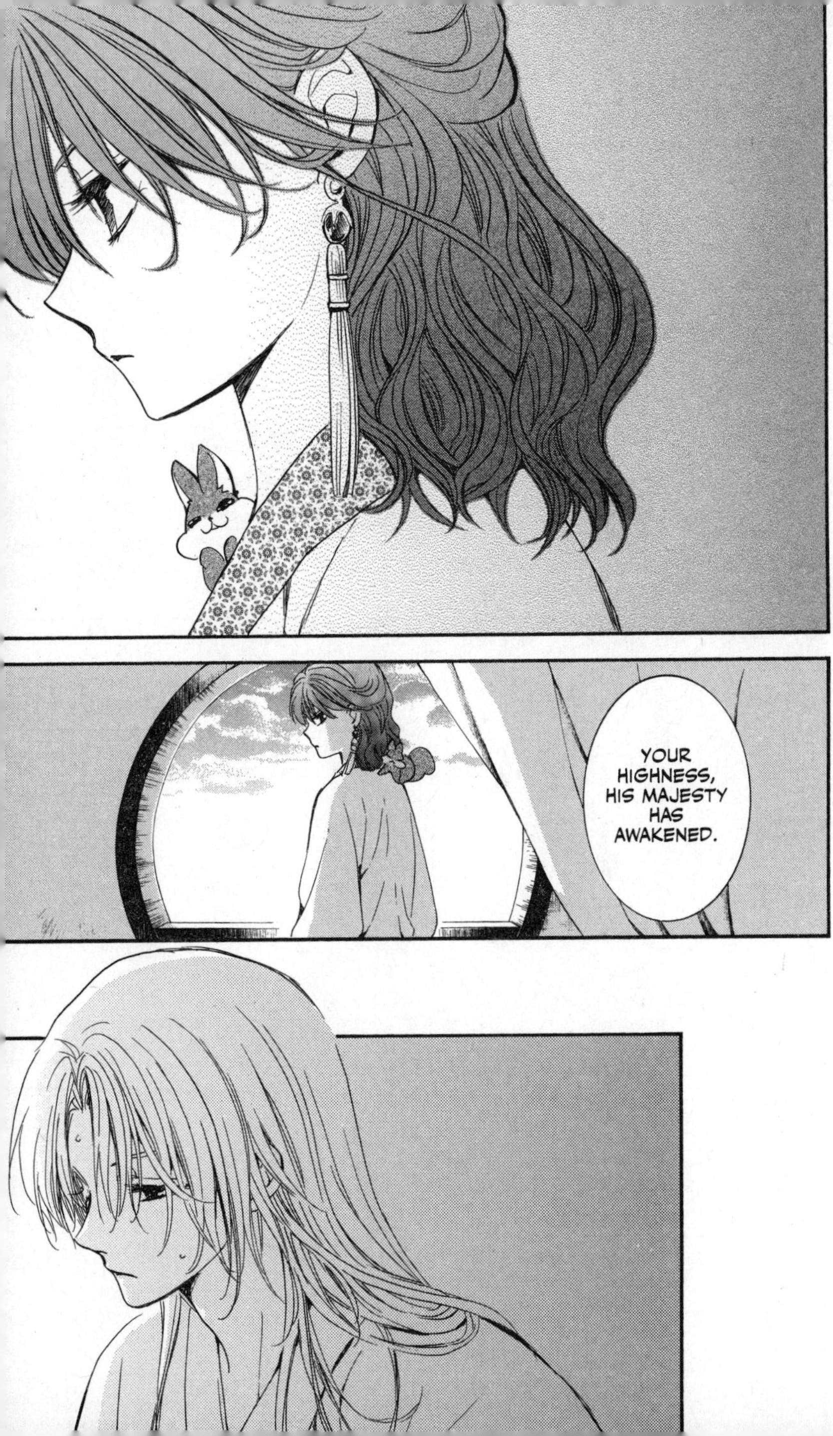
YOUR HIGHNESS, HIS MAJESTY HAS AWAKENED.

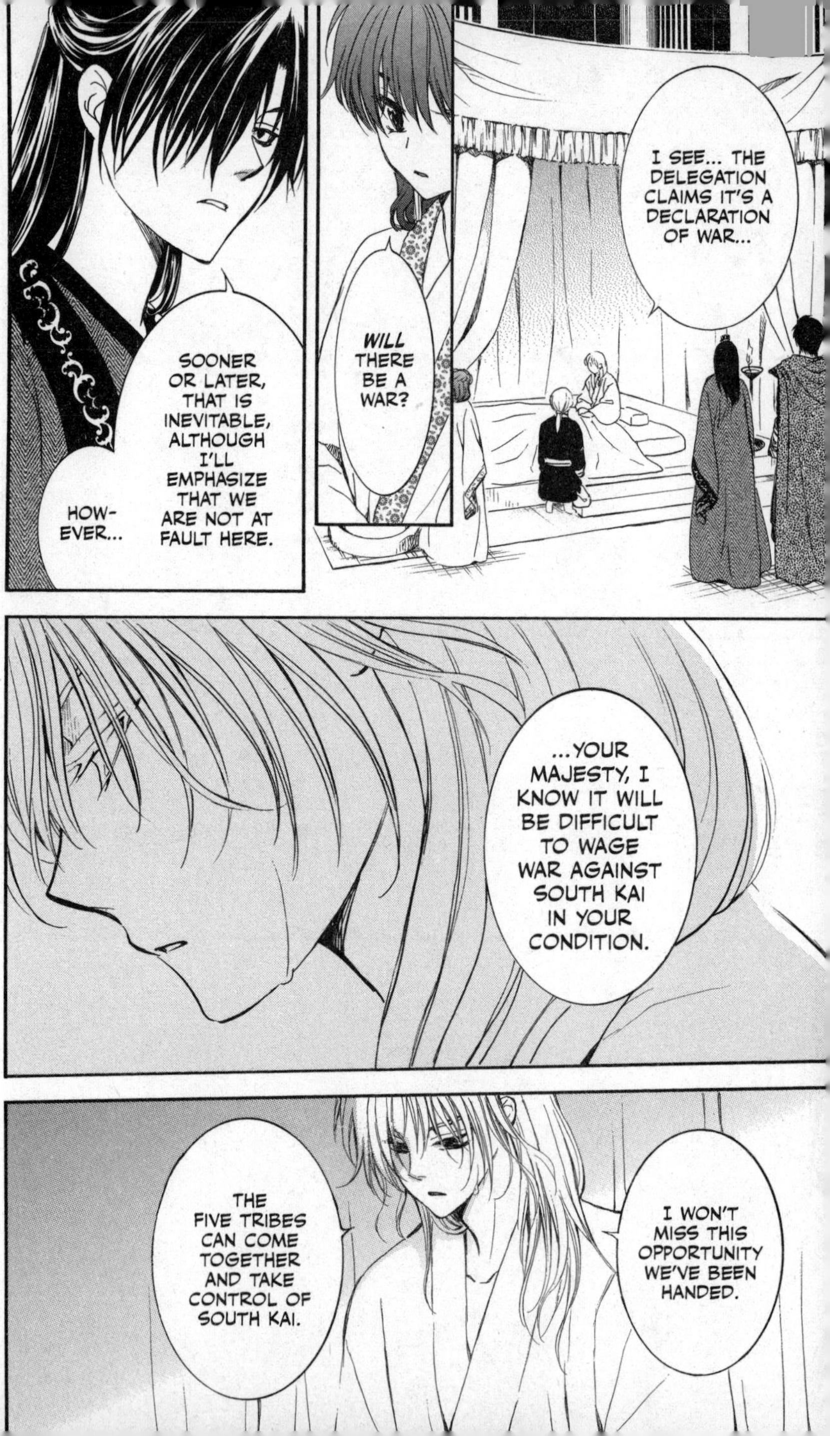
I SEE... THE DELEGATION CLAIMS IT'S A DECLARATION OF WAR...
WILL THERE BE A WAR?
SOONER OR LATER, THAT IS INEVITABLE, ALTHOUGH I'LL EMPHASIZE THAT WE ARE NOT AT FAULT HERE.
HOW-EVER...
...YOUR MAJESTY, I KNOW IT WILL BE DIFFICULT TO WAGE WAR AGAINST SOUTH KAI IN YOUR CONDITION.
I WON'T MISS THIS OPPORTUNITY WE'VE BEEN HANDED.
THE FIVE TRIBES CAN COME TOGETHER AND TAKE CONTROL OF SOUTH KAI.

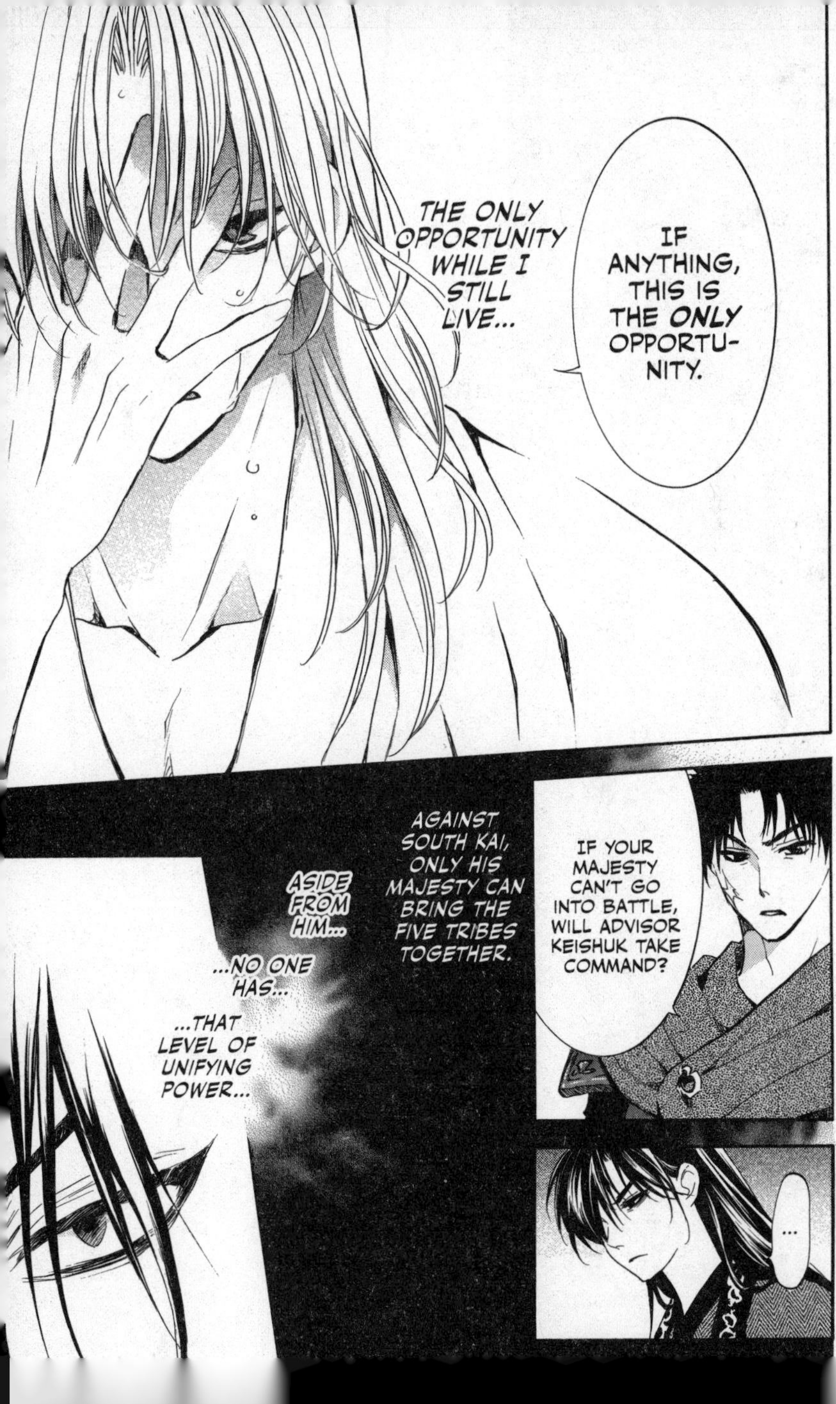
IF ANYTHING, THIS IS THE ONLY OPPORTUNITY.
THE ONLY OPPORTUNITY WHILE I STILL LIVE...
IF YOUR MAJESTY CAN'T GO INTO BATTLE, WILL ADVISOR KEISHUK TAKE COMMAND?
...
AGAINST SOUTH KAI, ONLY HIS MAJESTY CAN BRING THE FIVE TRIBES TOGETHER.
ASIDE FROM HIM...
...NO ONE HAS...
...THAT LEVEL OF UNIFYING POWER...

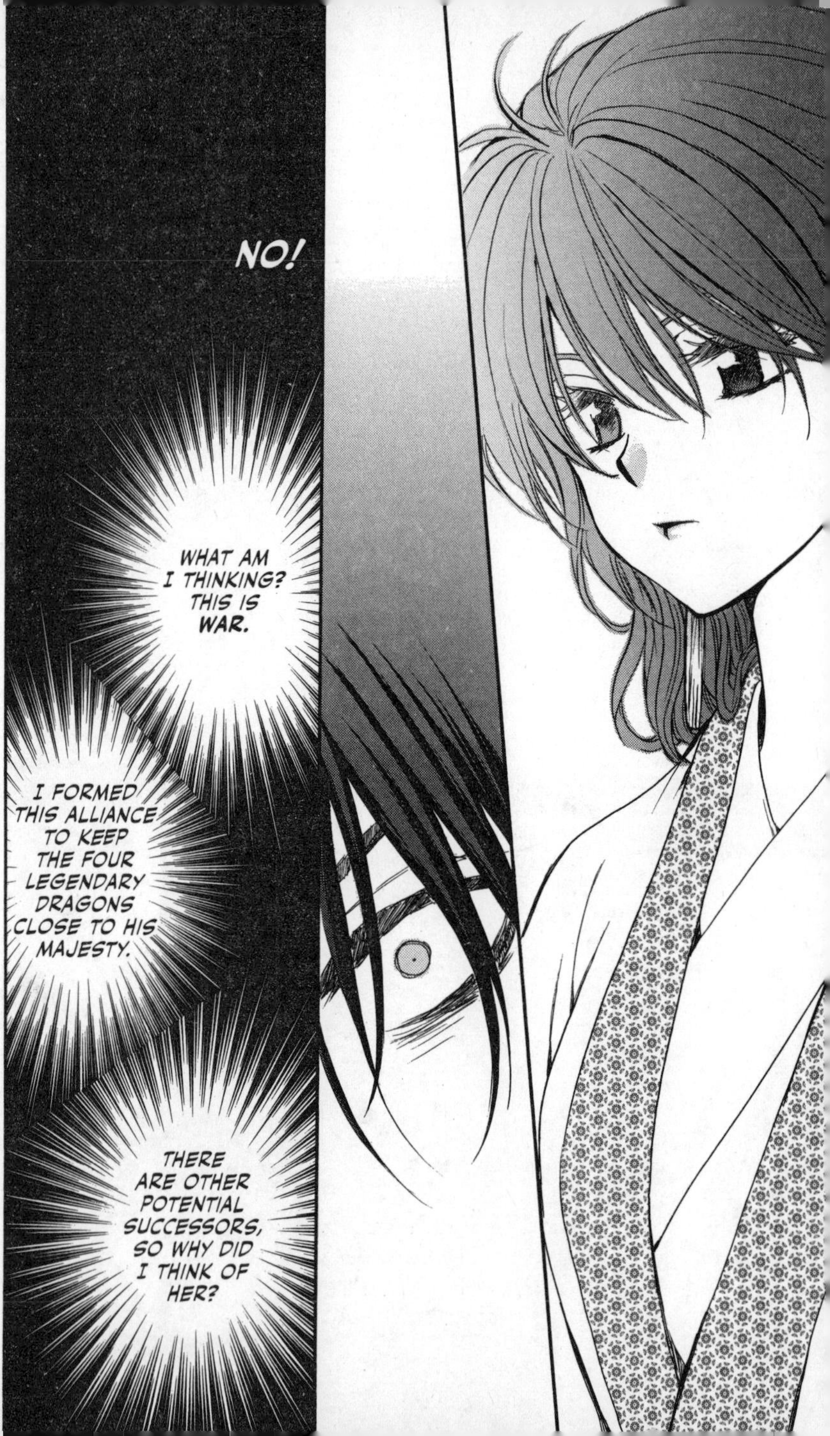
NO!
WHAT AM I THINKING? THIS IS WAR.
I FORMED THIS ALLIANCE TO KEEP THE FOUR LEGENDARY DRAGONS CLOSE TO HIS MAJESTY.
THERE ARE OTHER POTENTIAL SUCCESSORS, SO WHY DID I THINK OF HER?

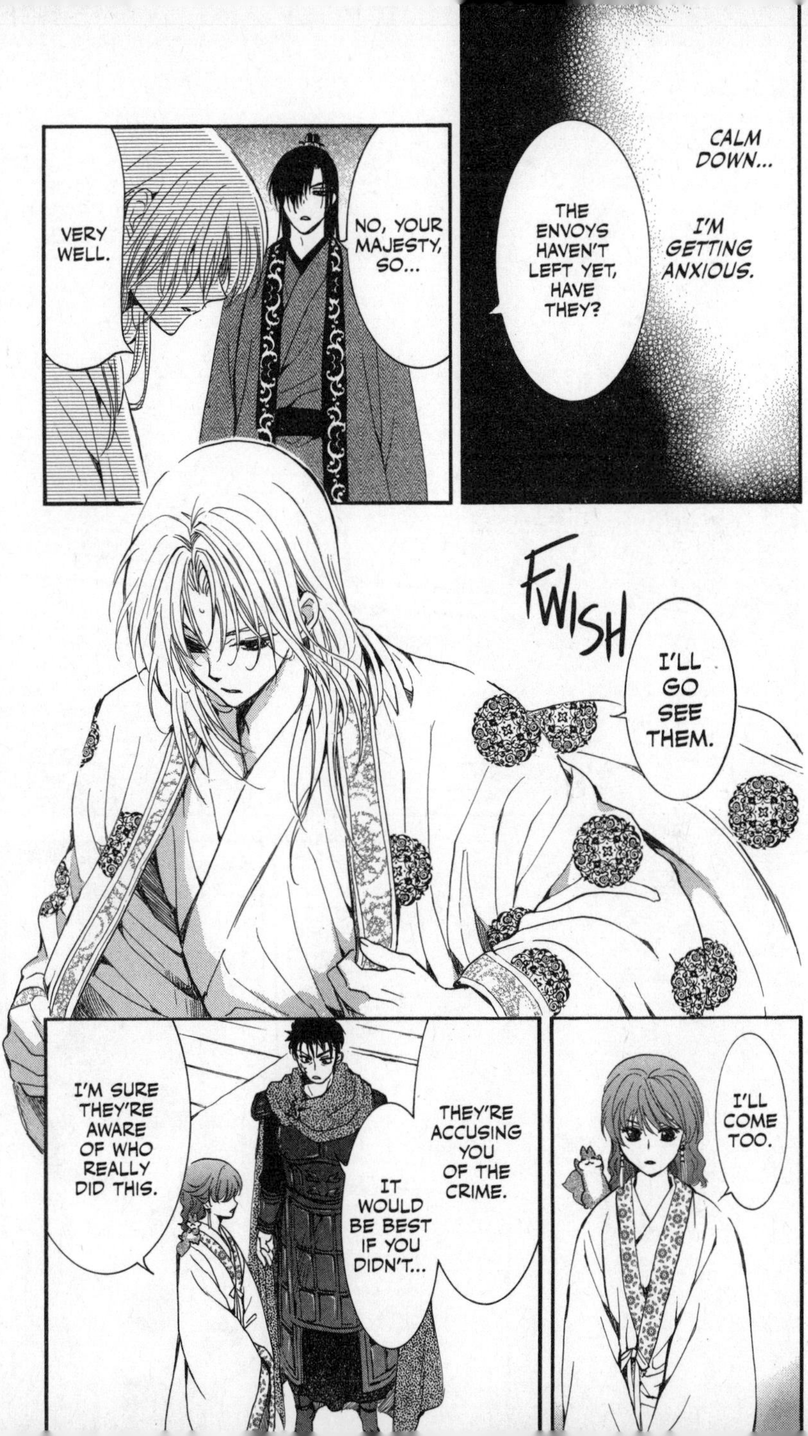
CALM DOWN...
I'M GETTING ANXIOUS.
THE ENVOYS HAVEN'T LEFT YET, HAVE THEY?
NO, YOUR MAJESTY, SO...
VERY WELL.
FWISH
I'LL GO SEE THEM.
I'LL COME TOO.
THEY'RE ACCUSING YOU OF THE CRIME.
IT WOULD BE BEST IF YOU DIDN'T...
I'M SURE THEY'RE AWARE OF WHO REALLY DID THIS.

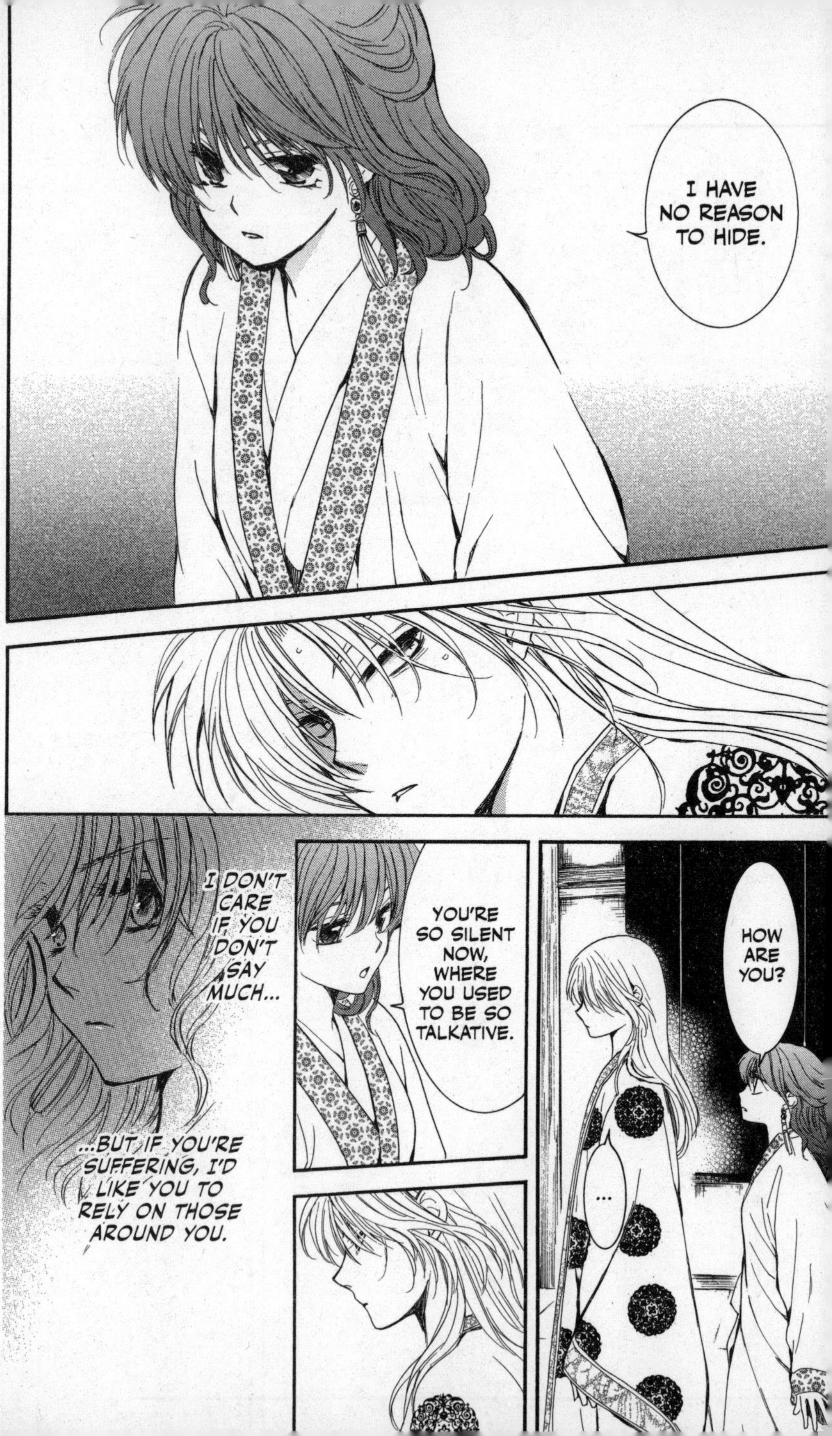
I HAVE NO REASON TO HIDE.
HOW ARE YOU?
...
YOU'RE SO SILENT NOW, WHERE YOU USED TO BE SO TALKATIVE.
I DON'T CARE IF YOU DON'T SAY MUCH...
...BUT IF YOU'RE SUFFERING, I'D LIKE YOU TO RELY ON THOSE AROUND YOU.

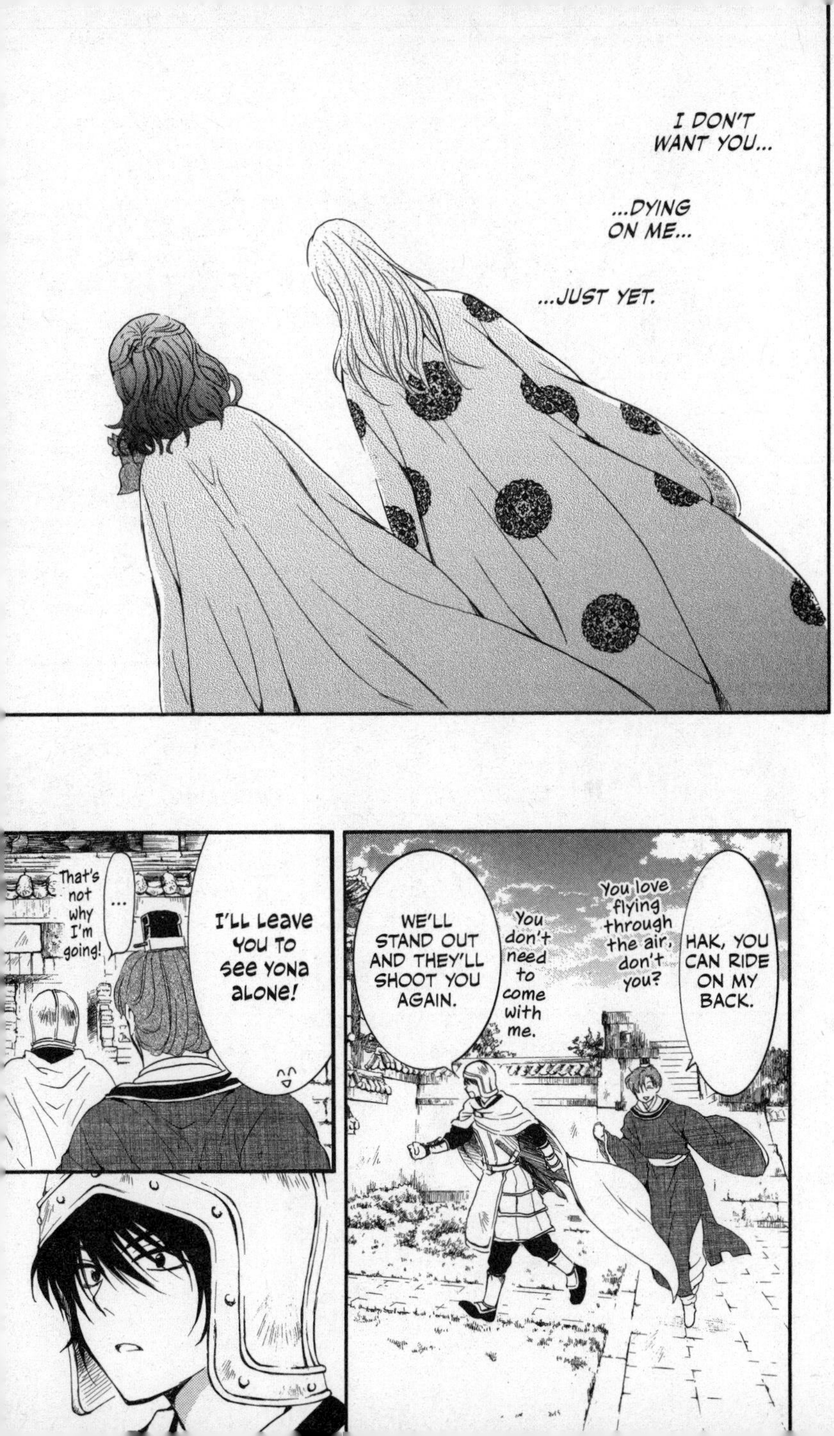
I DON'T WANT YOU...
...DYING ON ME...
...JUST YET.
HAK, YOU CAN RIDE ON MY BACK.
You love flying through the air, don't you?
You don't need to come with me.
WE'LL STAND OUT AND THEY'LL SHOOT YOU AGAIN.
I'LL LEAVE YOU TO SEE YONA ALONE!
...
That's not why I'm going!

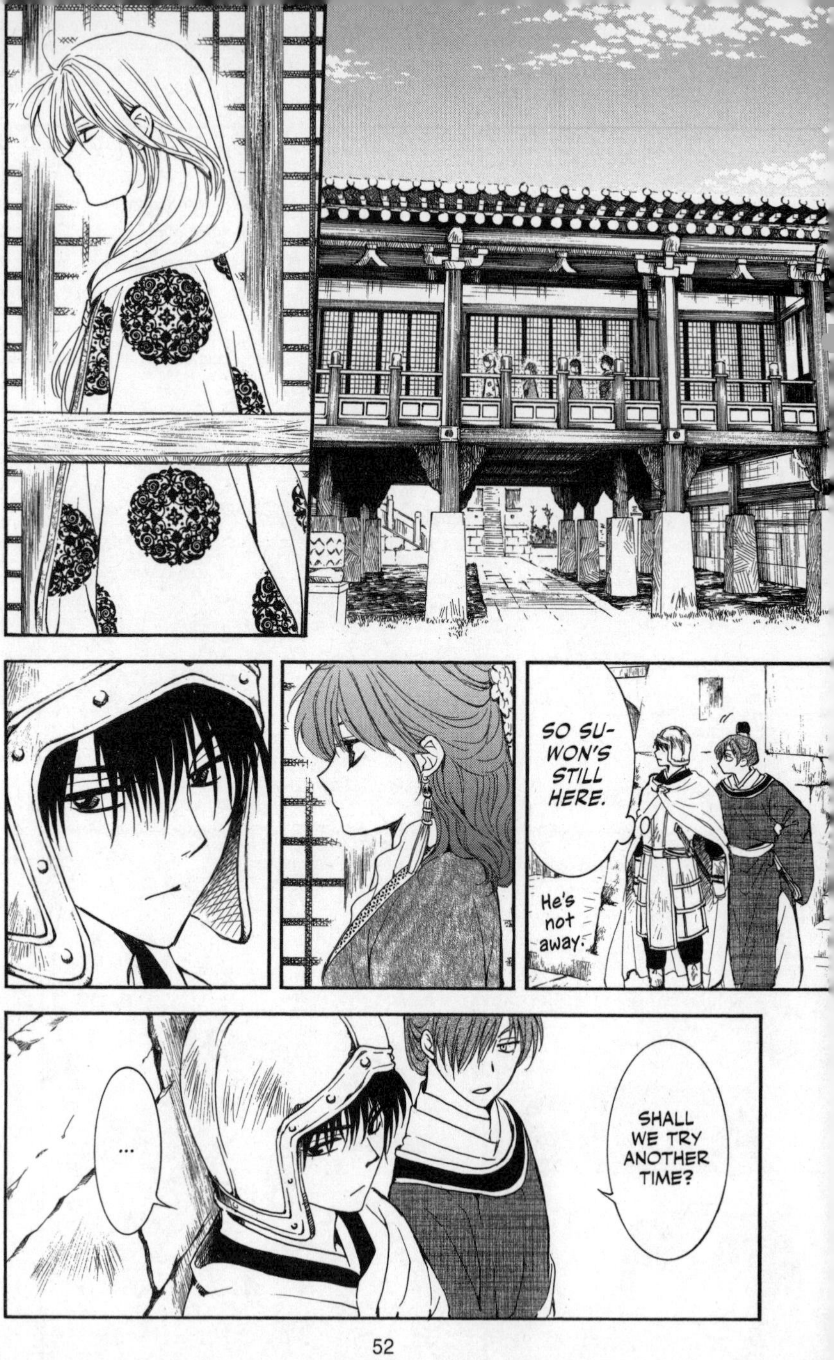
SO SU-WON'S STILL HERE.
He's not away.
SHALL WE TRY ANOTHER TIME?
...

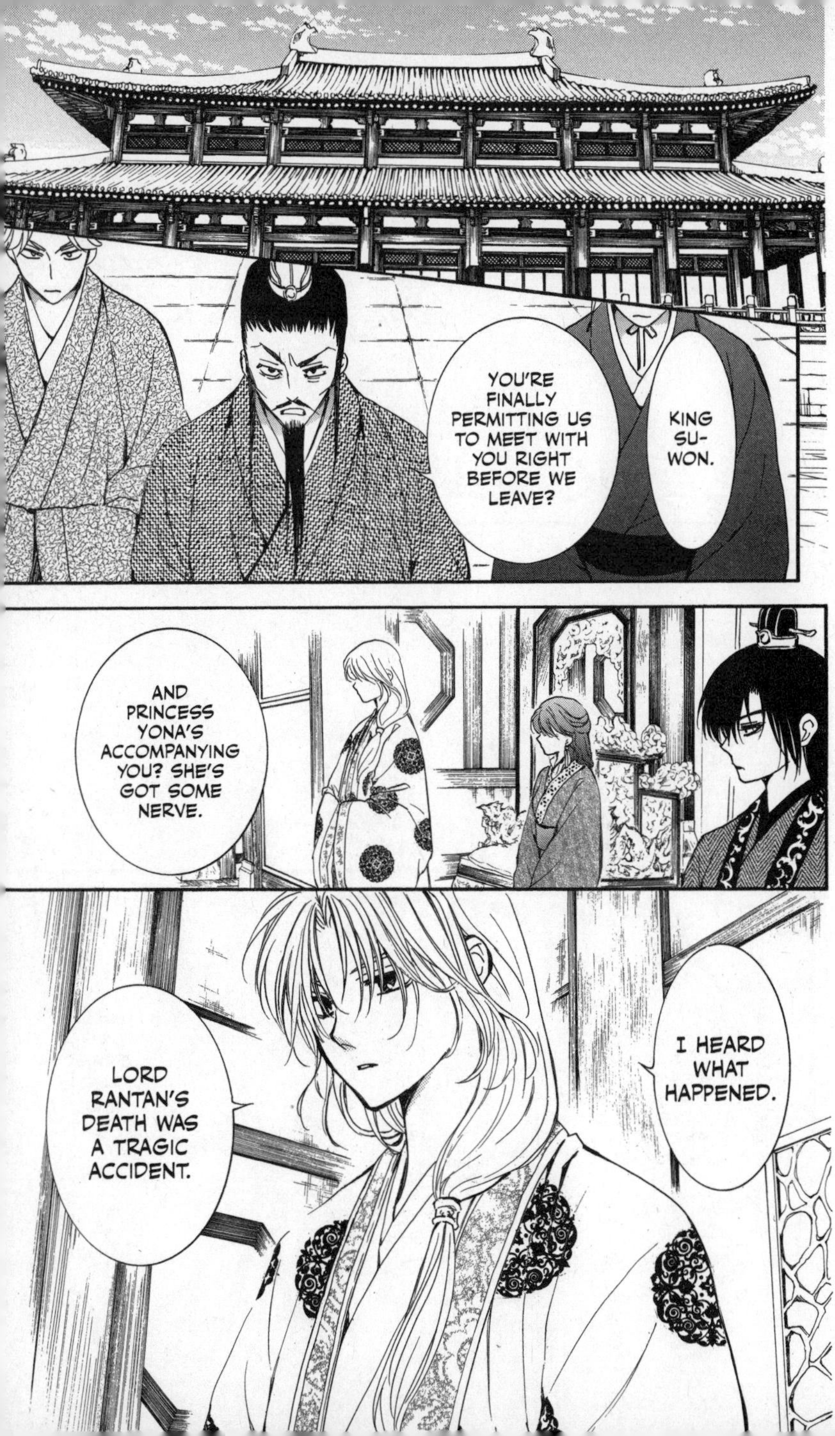
KING SU-WON.
YOU'RE FINALLY PERMITTING US TO MEET WITH YOU RIGHT BEFORE WE LEAVE?
AND PRINCESS YONA'S ACCOMPANYING YOU? SHE'S GOT SOME NERVE.
I HEARD WHAT HAPPENED.
LORD RANTAN'S DEATH WAS A TRAGIC ACCIDENT.

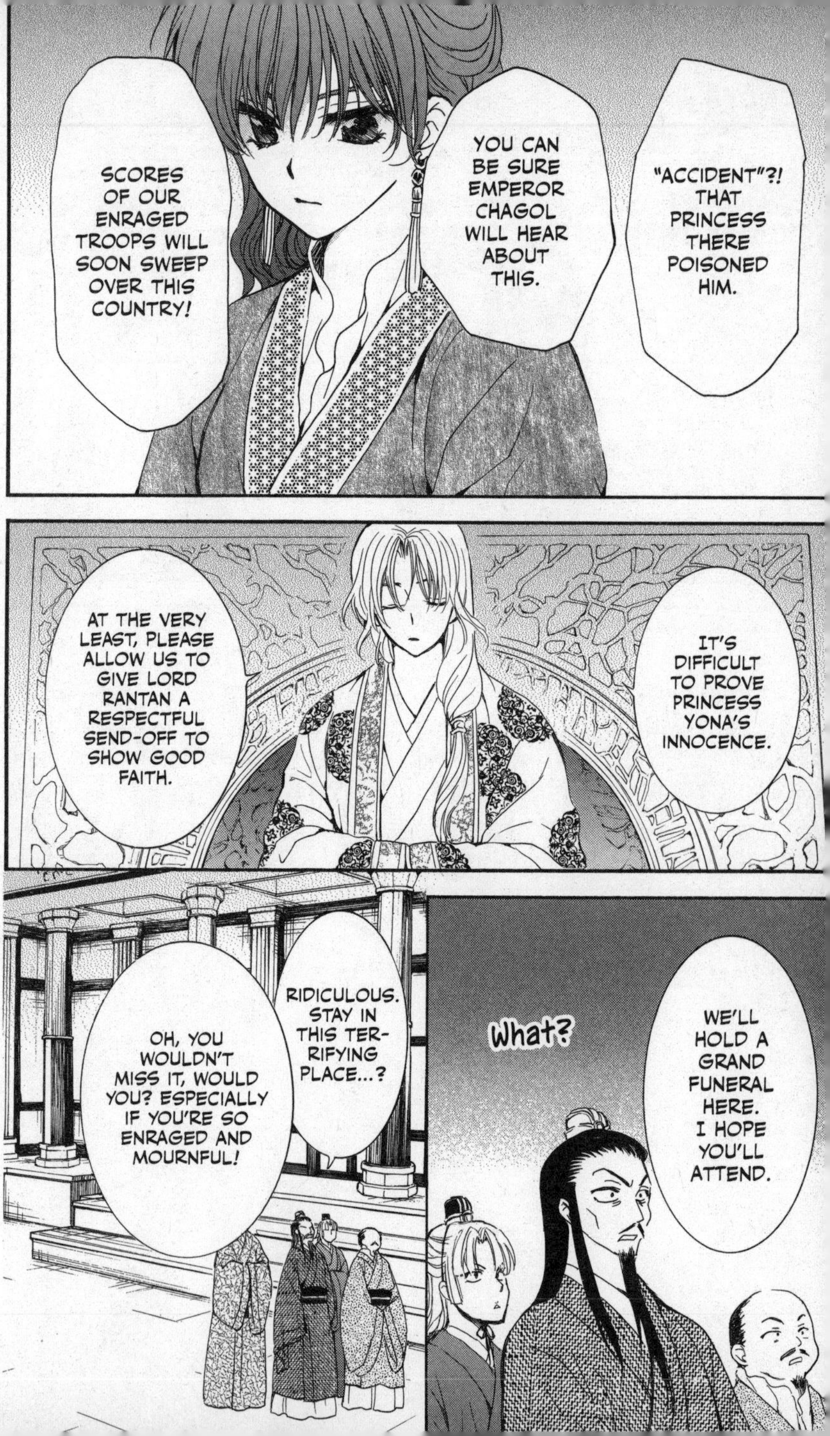
"ACCIDENT"?! THAT PRINCESS THERE POISONED HIM.
YOU CAN BE SURE EMPEROR CHAGOL WILL HEAR ABOUT THIS.
SCORES OF OUR ENRAGED TROOPS WILL SOON SWEEP OVER THIS COUNTRY!
IT'S DIFFICULT TO PROVE PRINCESS YONA'S INNOCENCE.
AT THE VERY LEAST, PLEASE ALLOW US TO GIVE LORD RANTAN A RESPECTFUL SEND-OFF TO SHOW GOOD FAITH.
WE'LL HOLD A GRAND FUNERAL HERE. I HOPE YOU'LL ATTEND.
What?
RIDICULOUS. STAY IN THIS TER-RIFYING PLACE...?
OH, YOU WOULDN'T MISS IT, WOULD YOU? ESPECIALLY IF YOU'RE SO ENRAGED AND MOURNFUL!

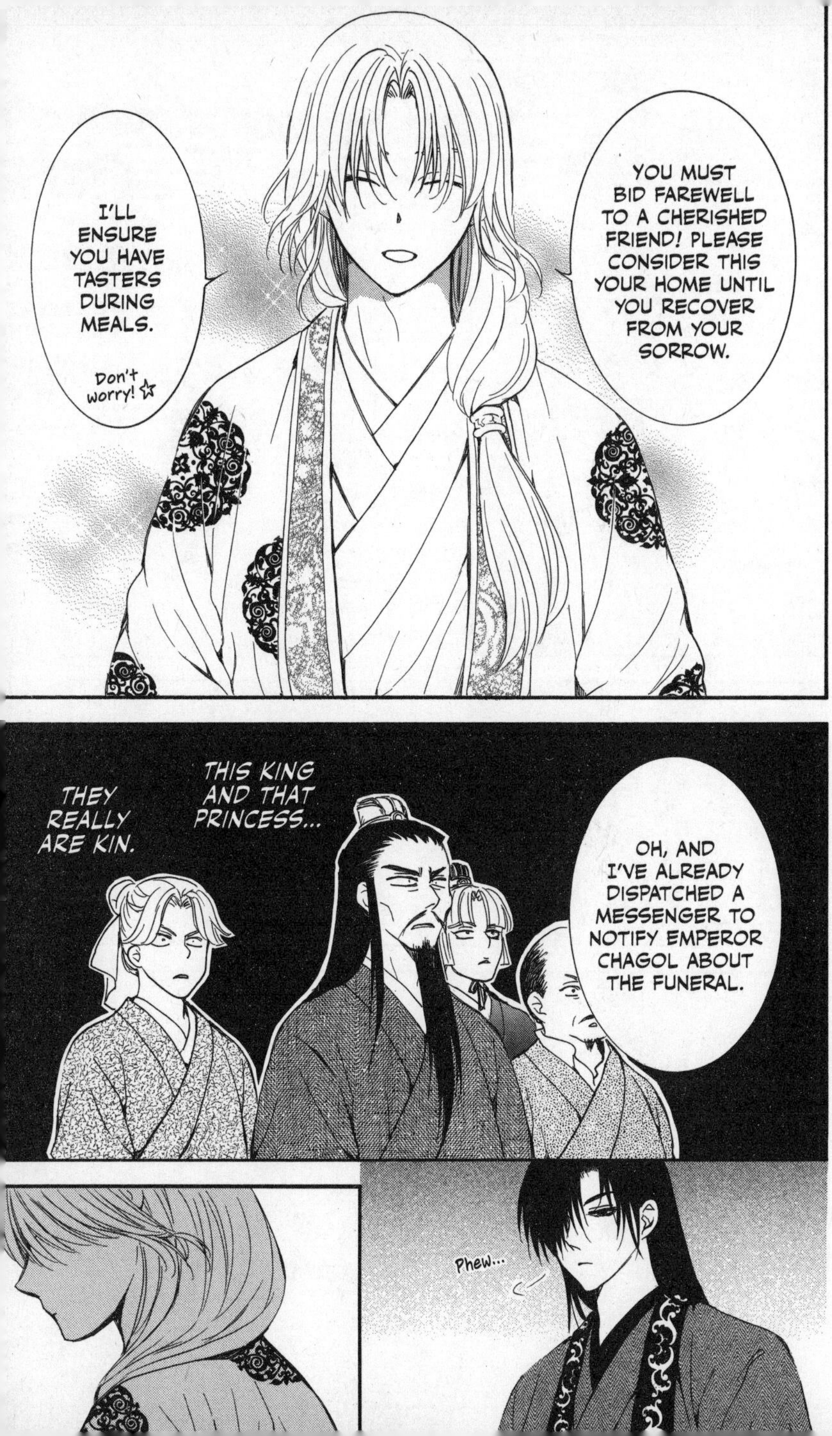
YOU MUST BID FAREWELL TO A CHERISHED FRIEND! PLEASE CONSIDER THIS YOUR HOME UNTIL YOU RECOVER FROM YOUR SORROW.
I'LL ENSURE YOU HAVE TASTERS DURING MEALS.
Don't worry! ☆
OH, AND I'VE ALREADY DISPATCHED A MESSENGER TO NOTIFY EMPEROR CHAGOL ABOUT THE FUNERAL.
THIS KING AND THAT PRINCESS...
THEY REALLY ARE KIN.
Phew...

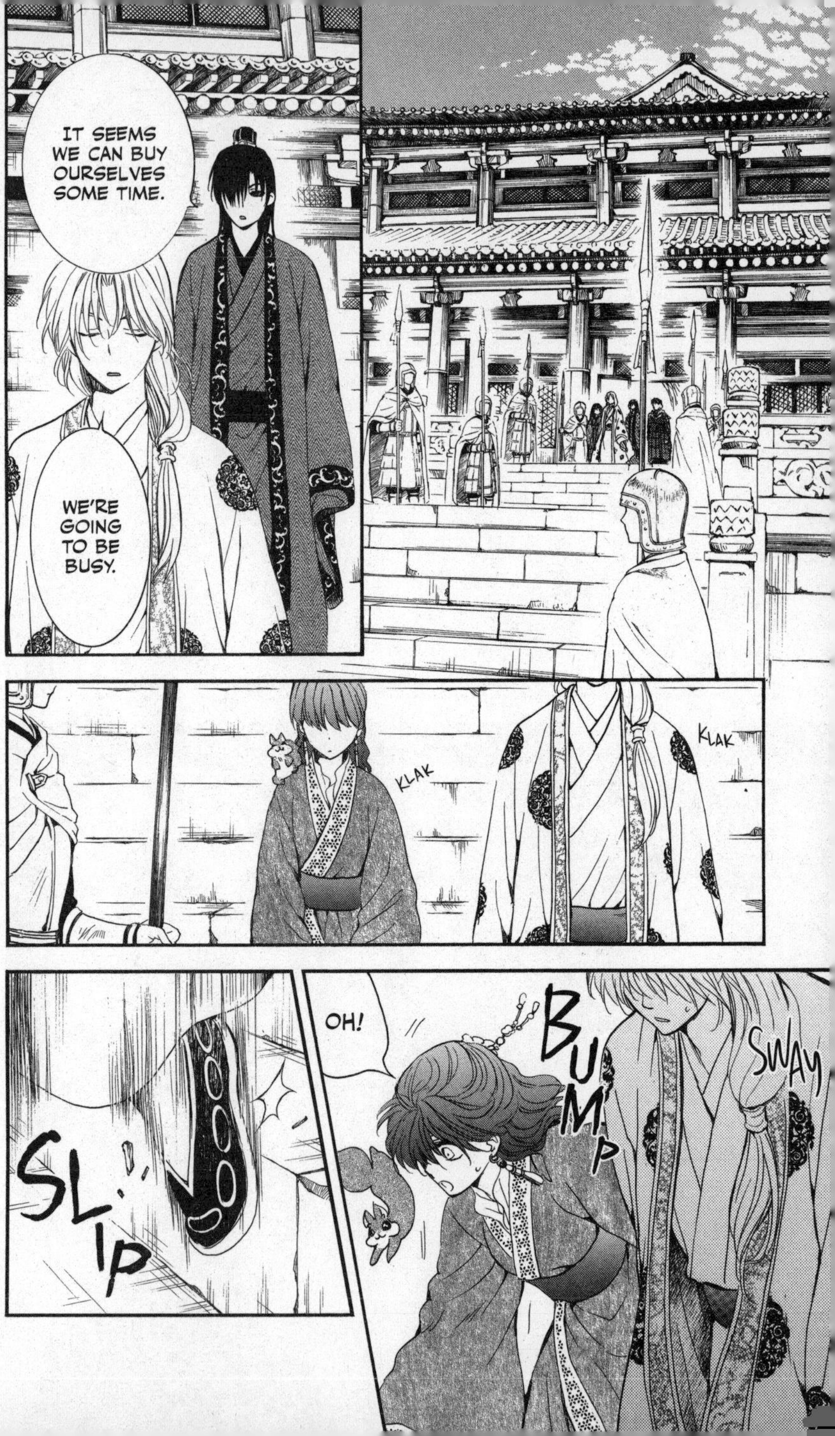
IT SEEMS WE CAN BUY OURSELVES SOME TIME.
WE'RE GOING TO BE BUSY.
KLAK
KLAK
OH!
BUMP
SWAY
SLIP

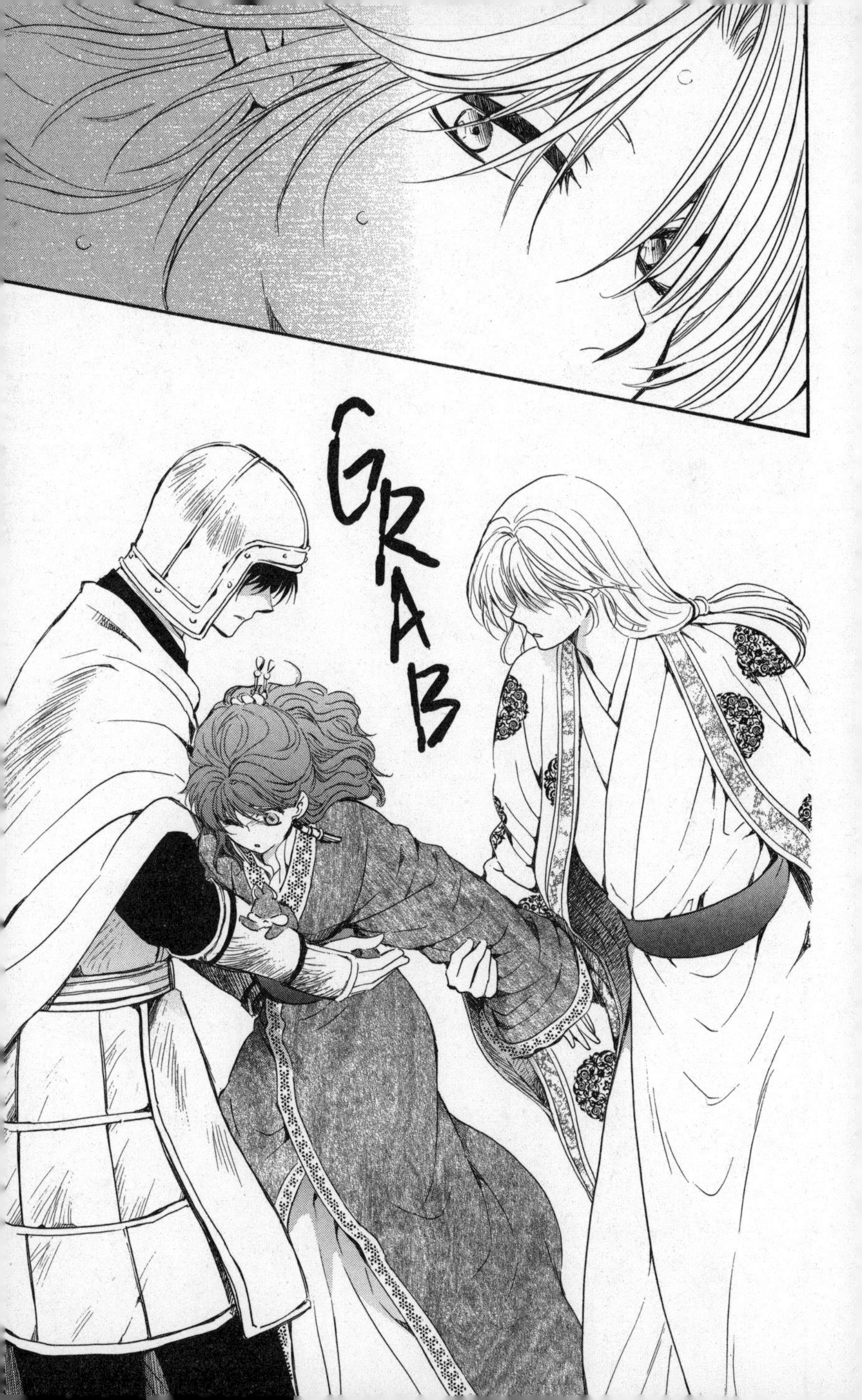
GRAB

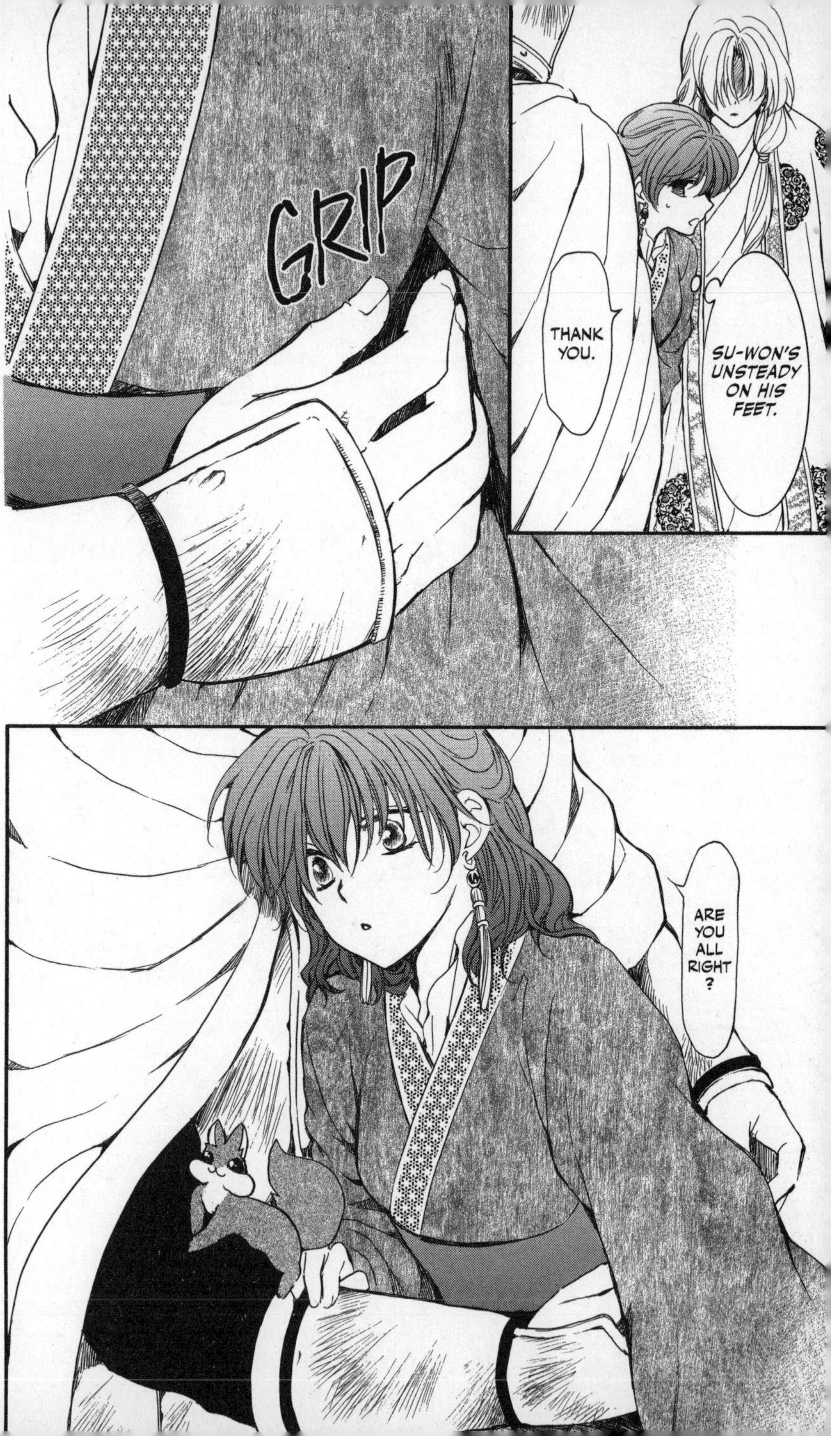
SU-WON'S UNSTEADY ON HIS FEET.
THANK YOU.
GRIP
ARE YOU ALL RIGHT?

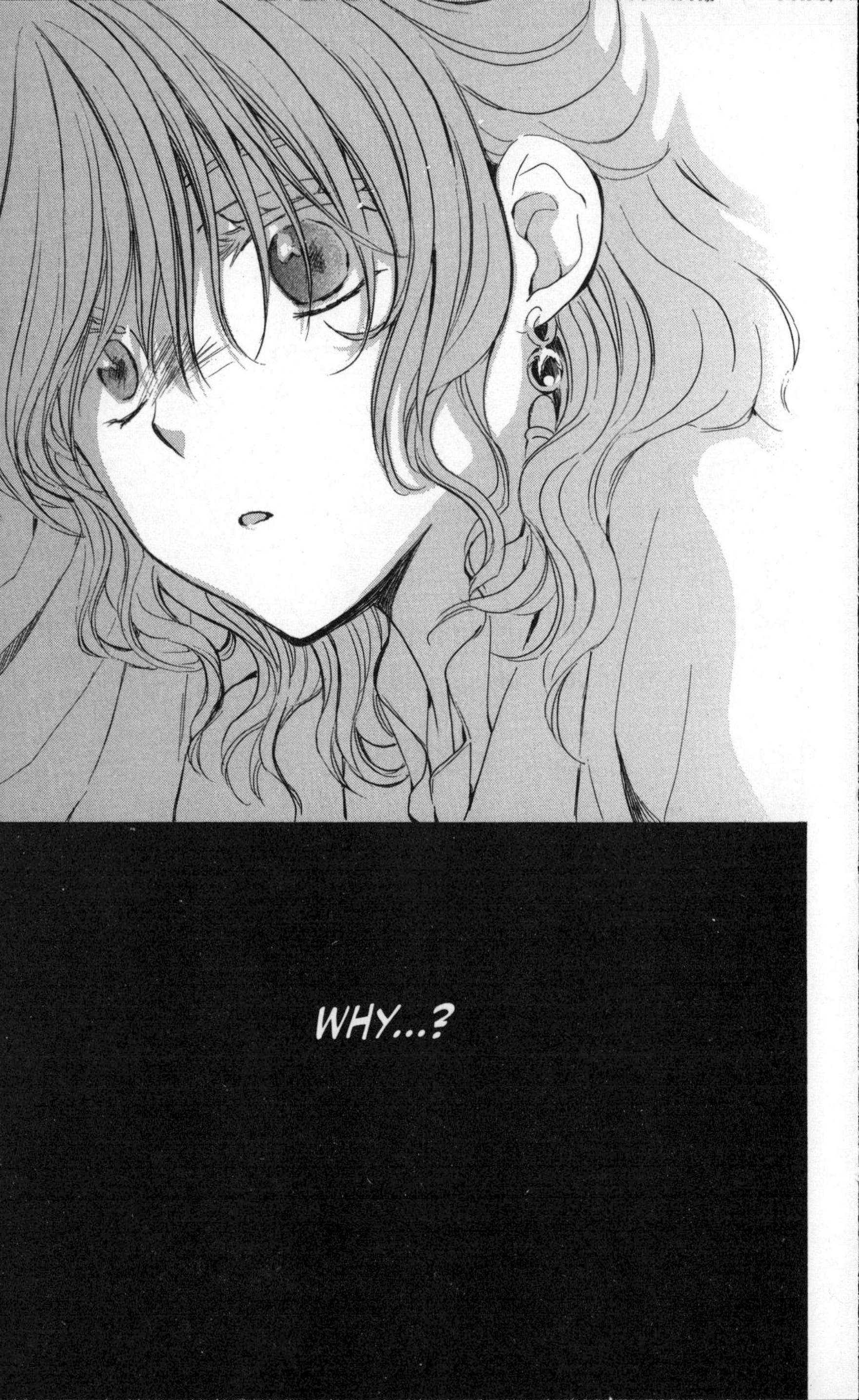
WHY...?

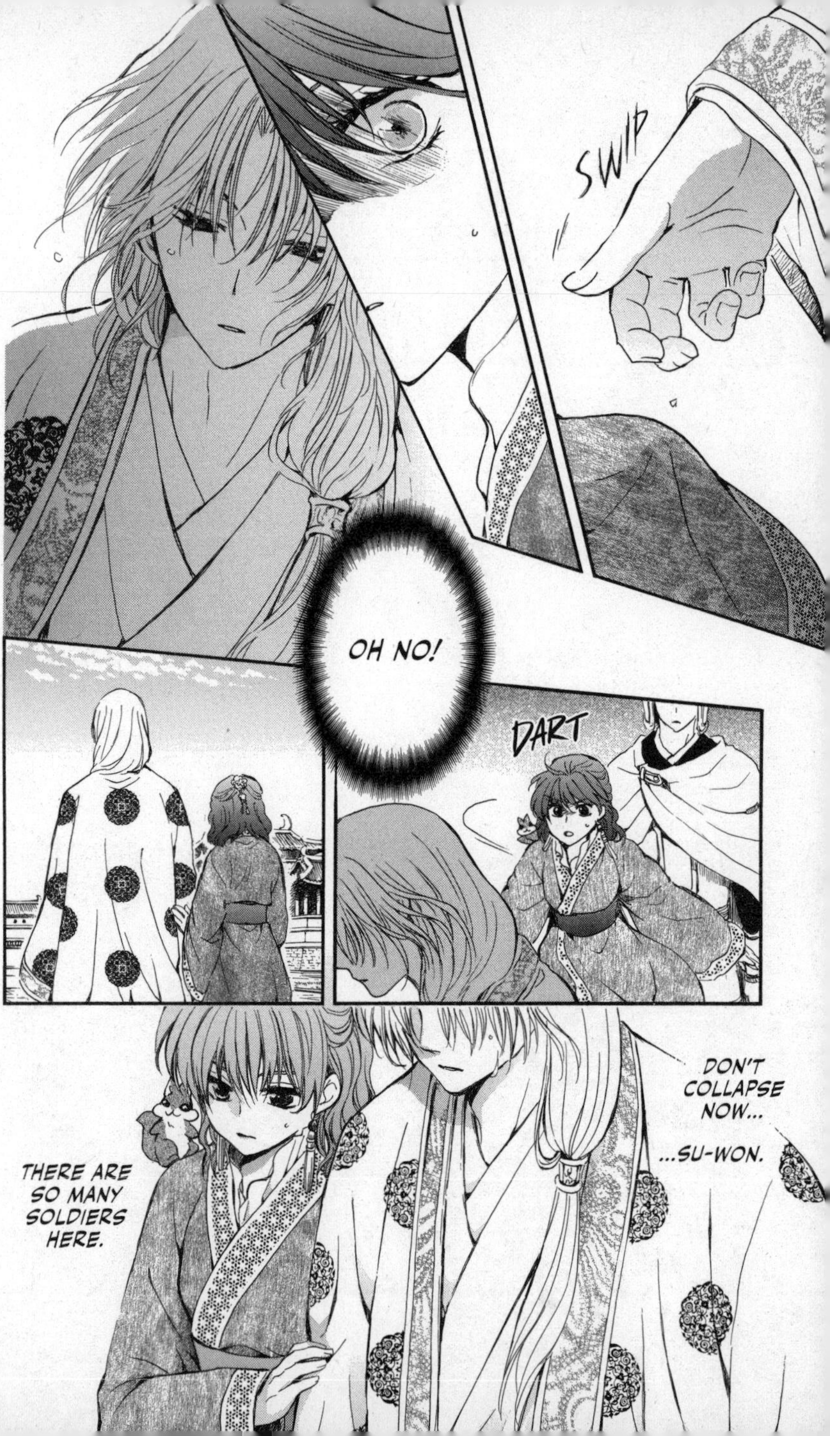
SWIP
OH NO!
DART
DON'T COLLAPSE NOW...
...SU-WON.
THERE ARE SO MANY SOLDIERS HERE.

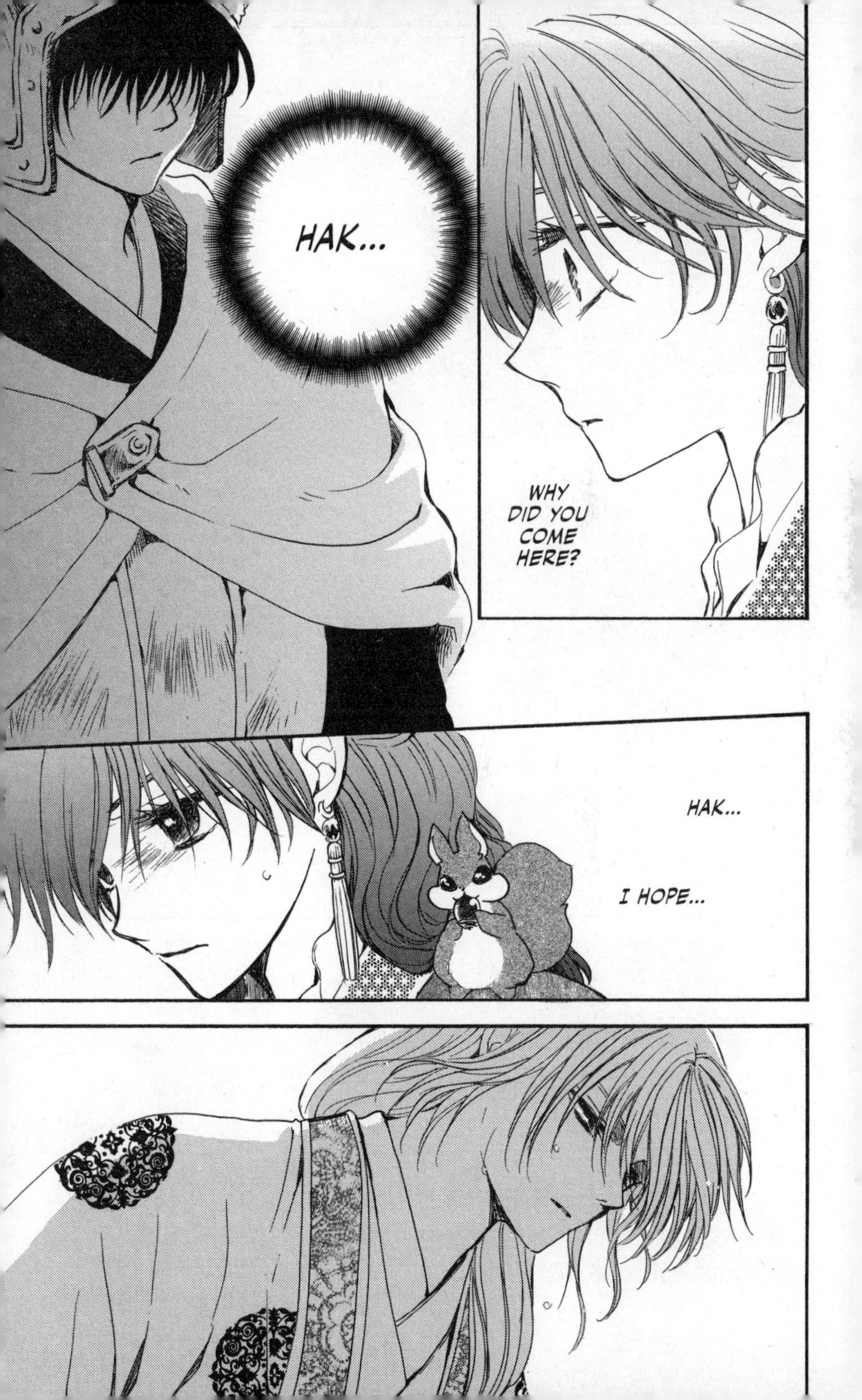
HAK...
WHY DID YOU COME HERE?
HAK...
I HOPE...

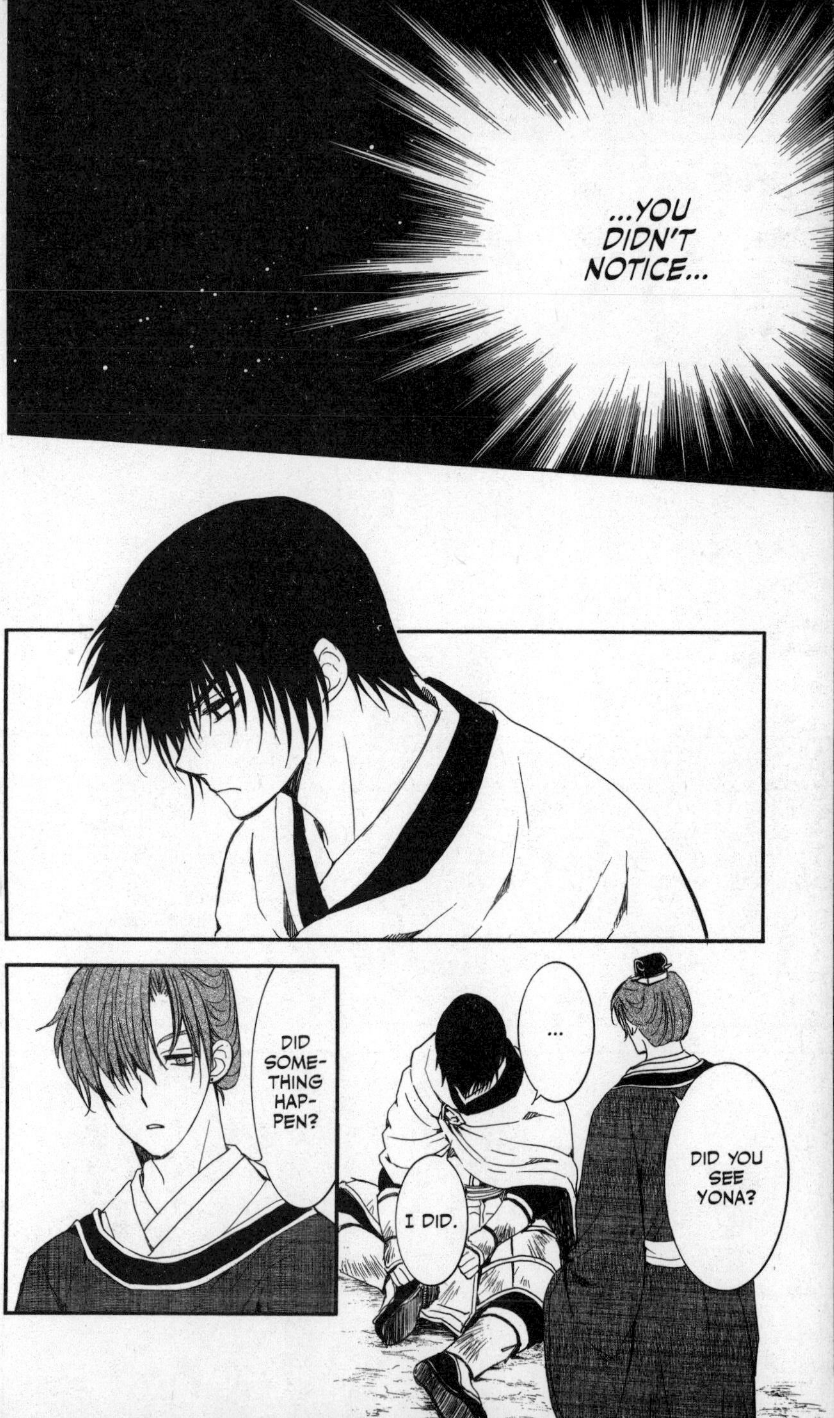
...YOU DIDN'T NOTICE...
DID YOU SEE YONA?
I DID.
...
DID SOME-THING HAP-PEN?

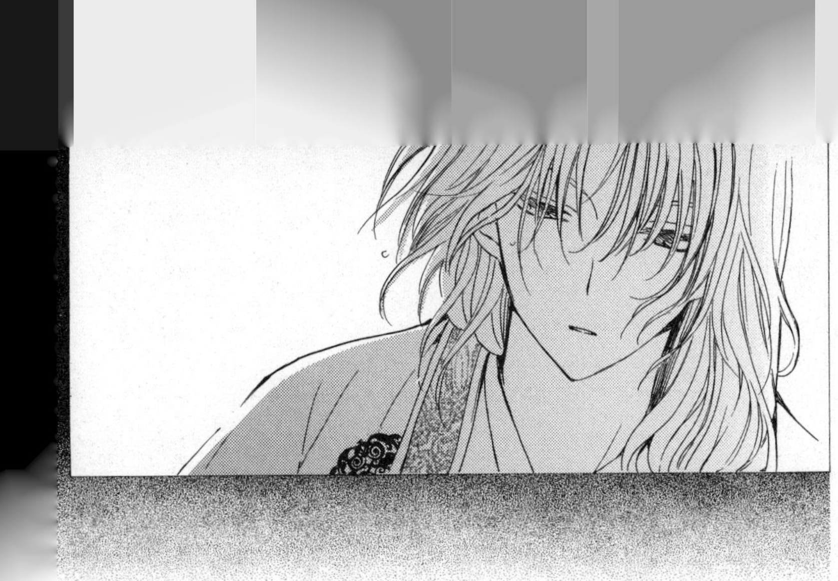

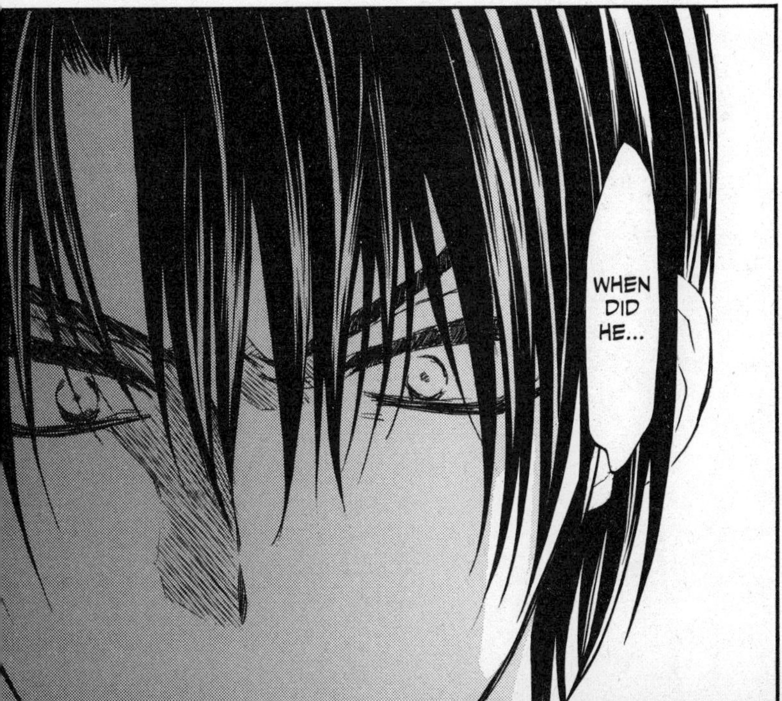
WHEN DID HE...

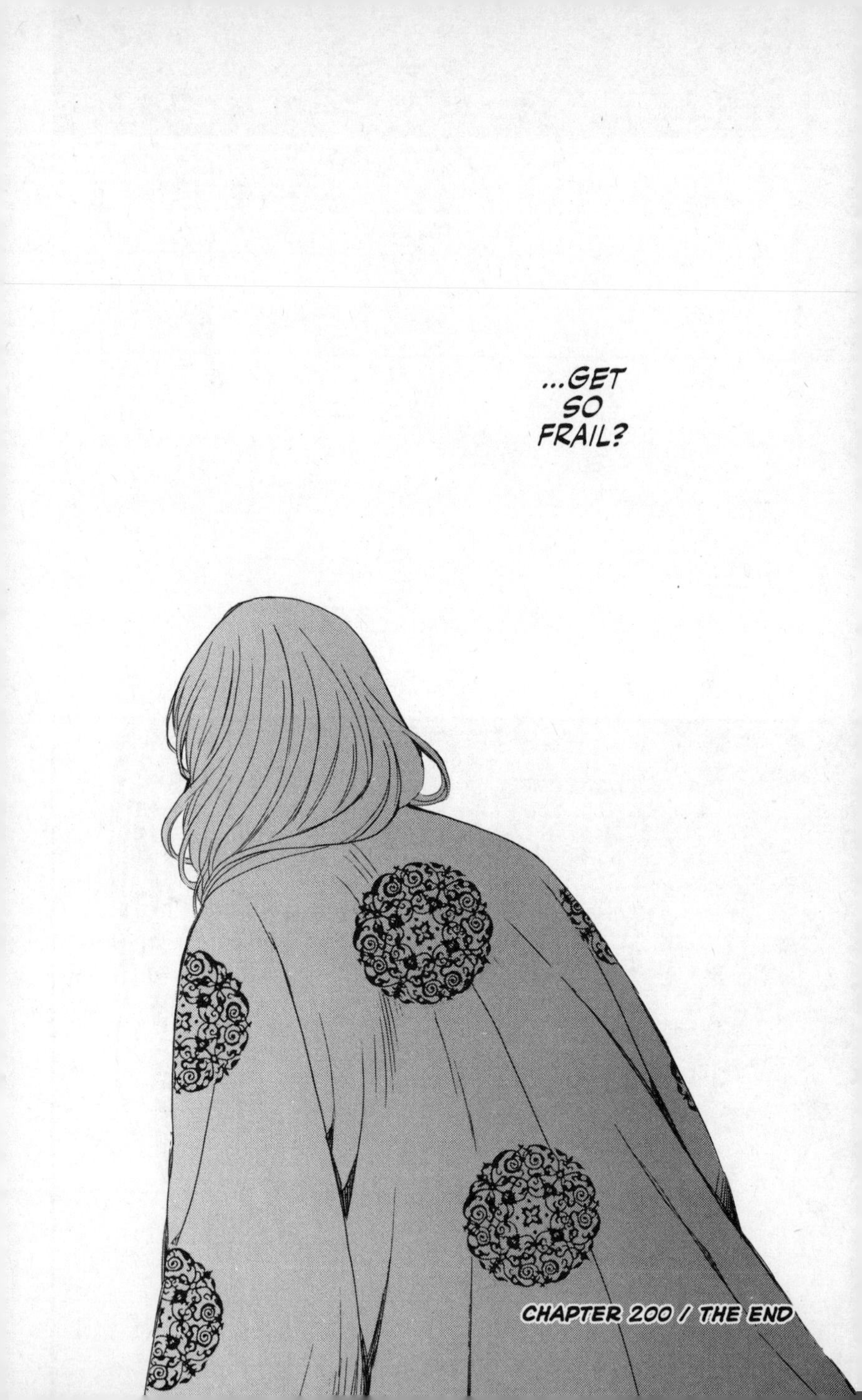
...GET SO FRAIL?
CHAPTER 200 / THE END

Min-su

After Su-won took the throne, Min-su became his primary physician. That was when Min-su's mother, Suimei, told him about the Crimson Sickness. Until then, he knew nothing about it.

As a child, he was quite close to Su-won and Keishuk and studied many things with them.

He still cherishes the memory of his time serving Il.

Age 10

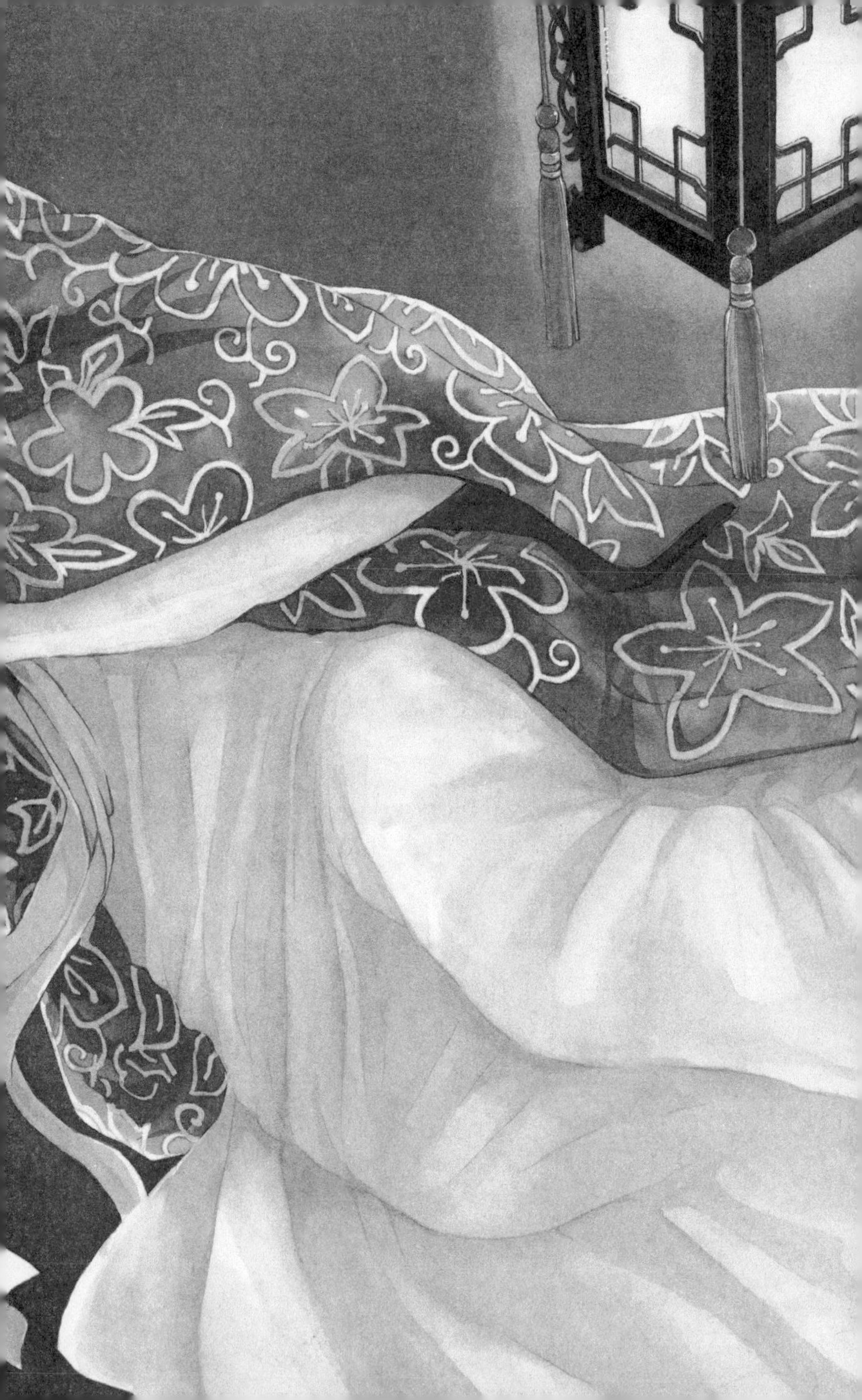

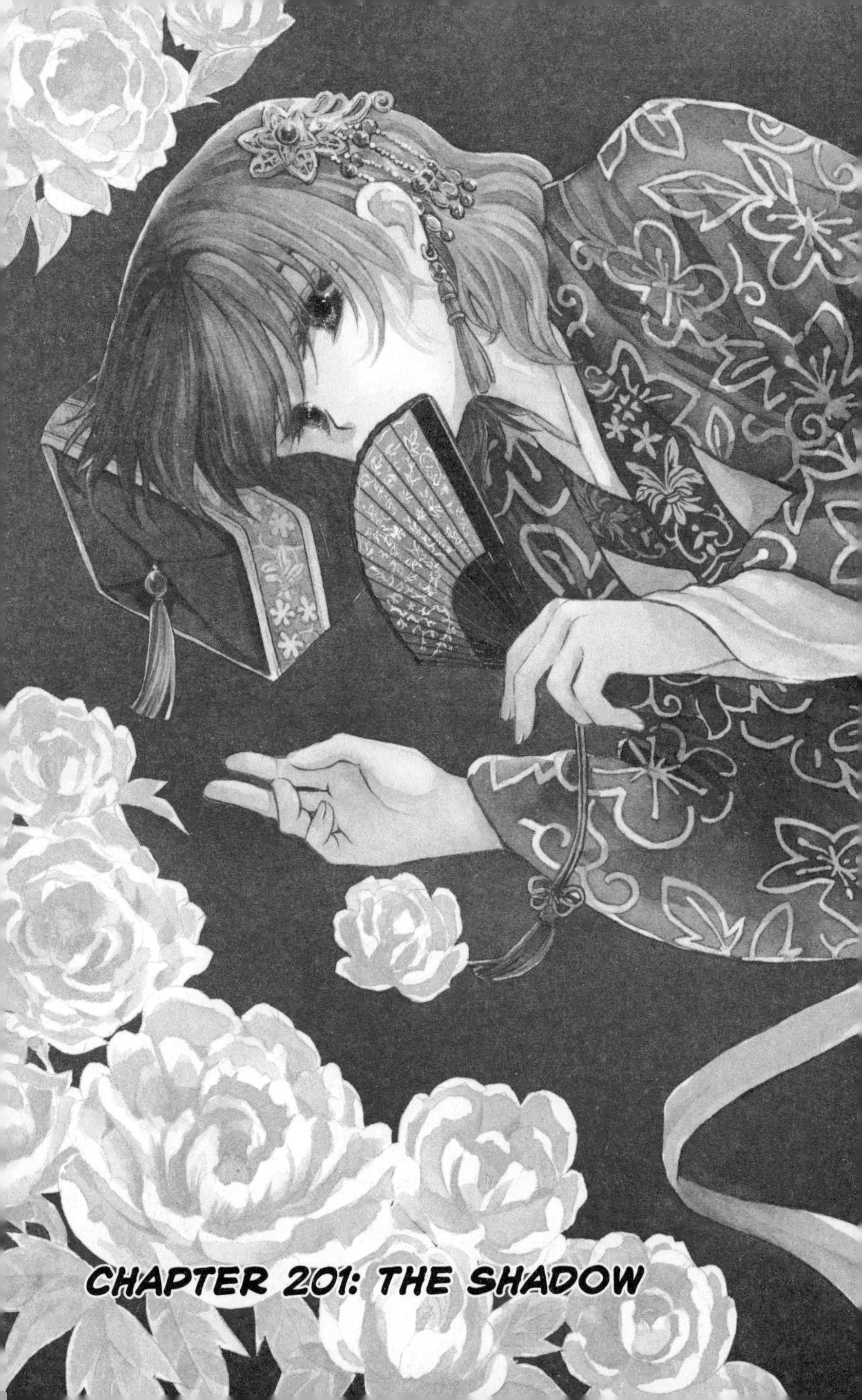
CHAPTER 201: THE SHADOW

yona
of the
Dawn

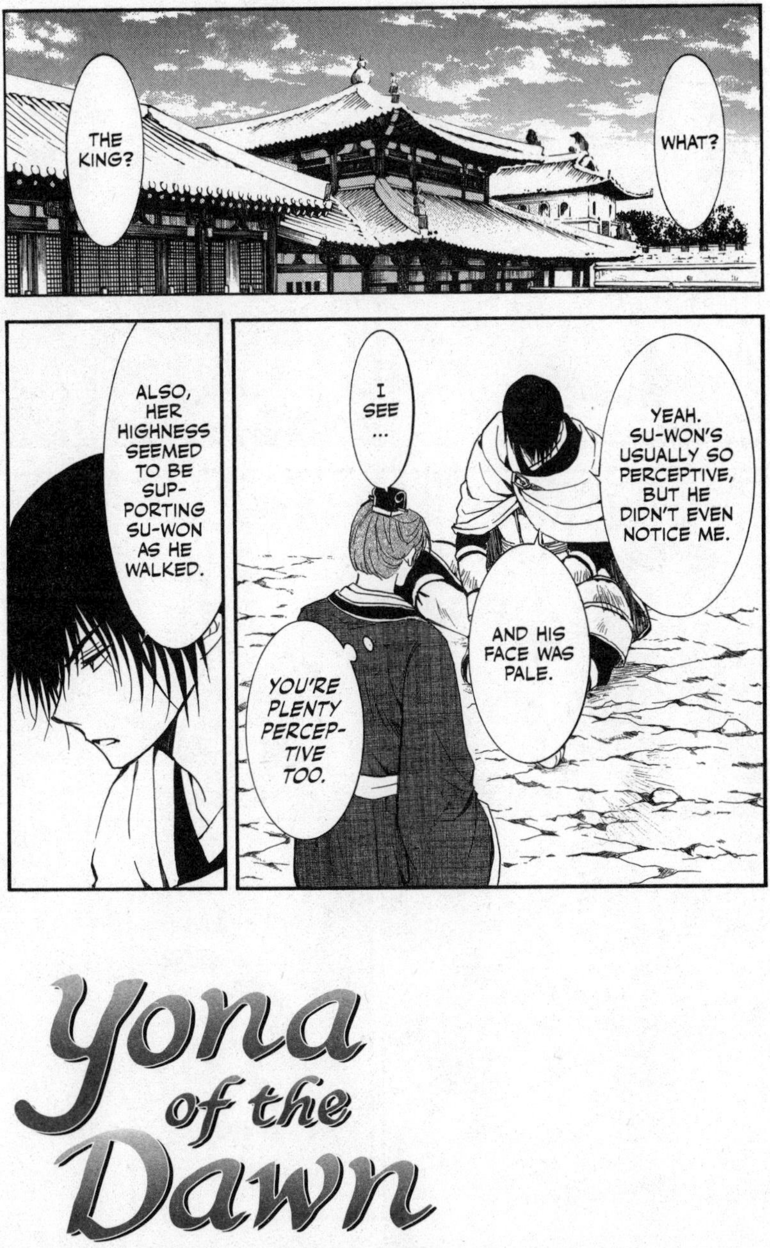
WHAT?
THE KING?
YEAH. SU-WON'S USUALLY SO PERCEPTIVE, BUT HE DIDN'T EVEN NOTICE ME.
I SEE...
AND HIS FACE WAS PALE.
YOU'RE PLENTY PERCEPTIVE TOO.
ALSO, HER HIGHNESS SEEMED TO BE SUPPORTING SU-WON AS HE WALKED.

Yona of the Dawn

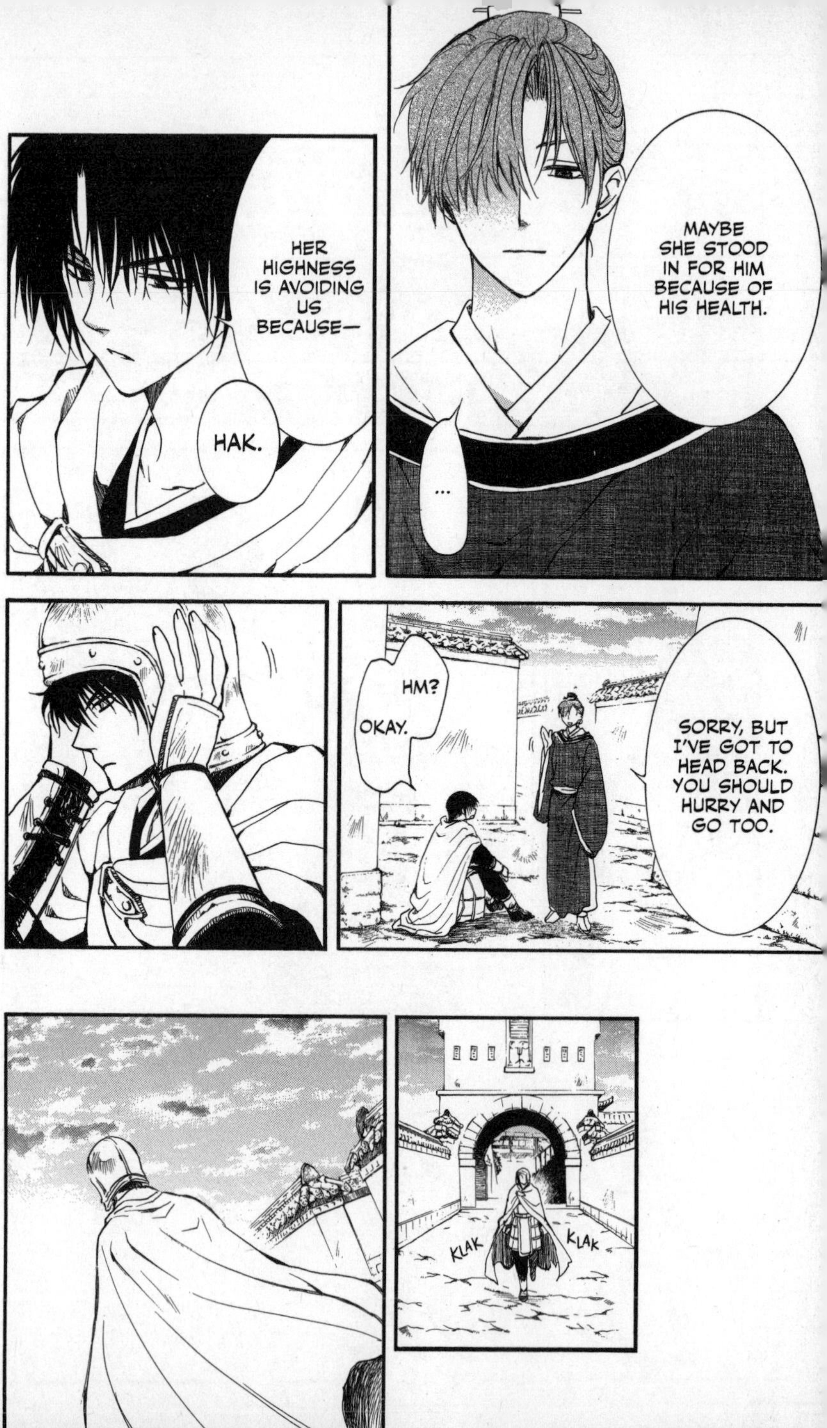
MAYBE SHE STOOD IN FOR HIM BECAUSE OF HIS HEALTH.
...
HER HIGHNESS IS AVOIDING US BECAUSE—
HAK.
SORRY, BUT I'VE GOT TO HEAD BACK. YOU SHOULD HURRY AND GO TOO.
HM?
OKAY.
KLAK
KLAK

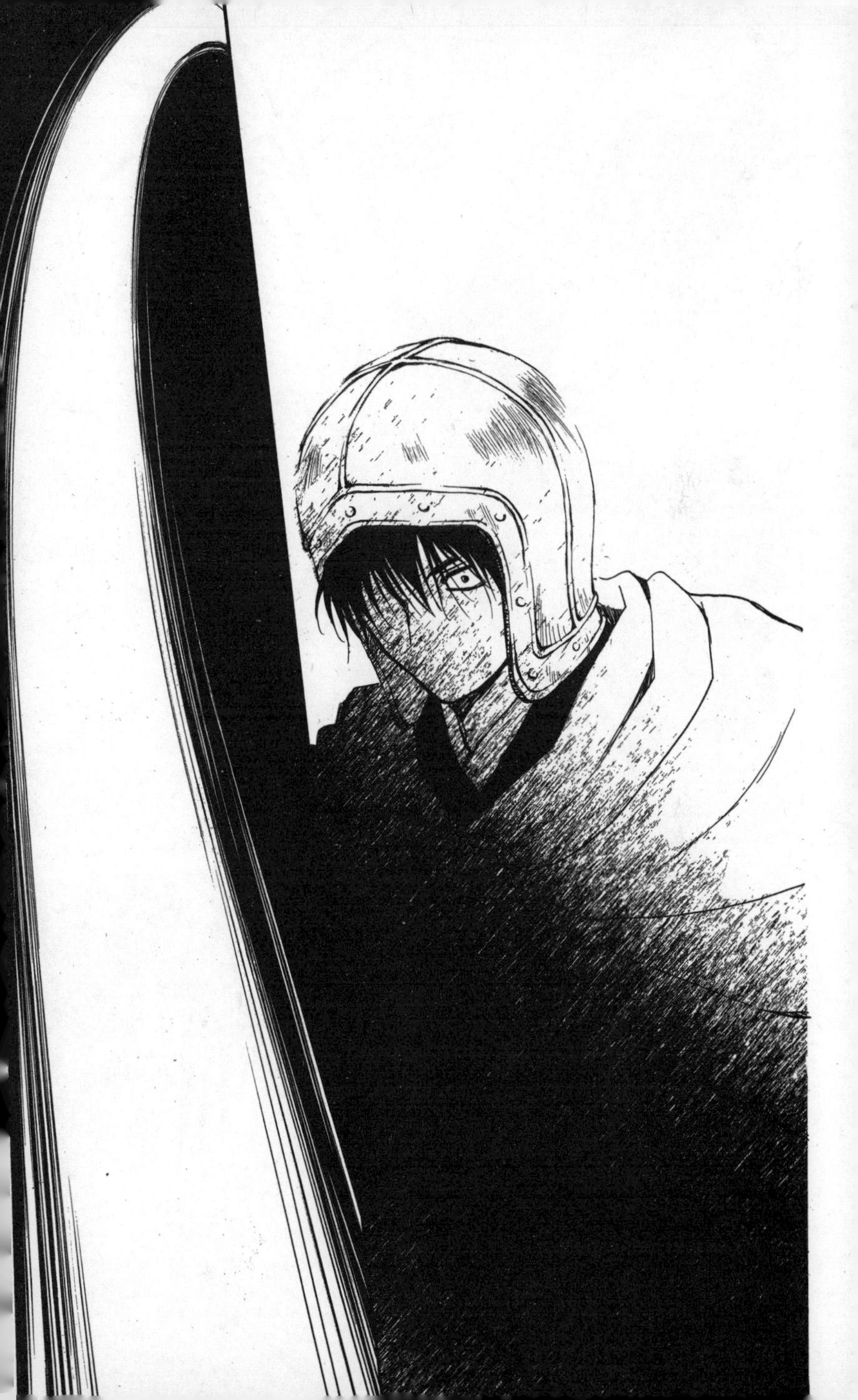

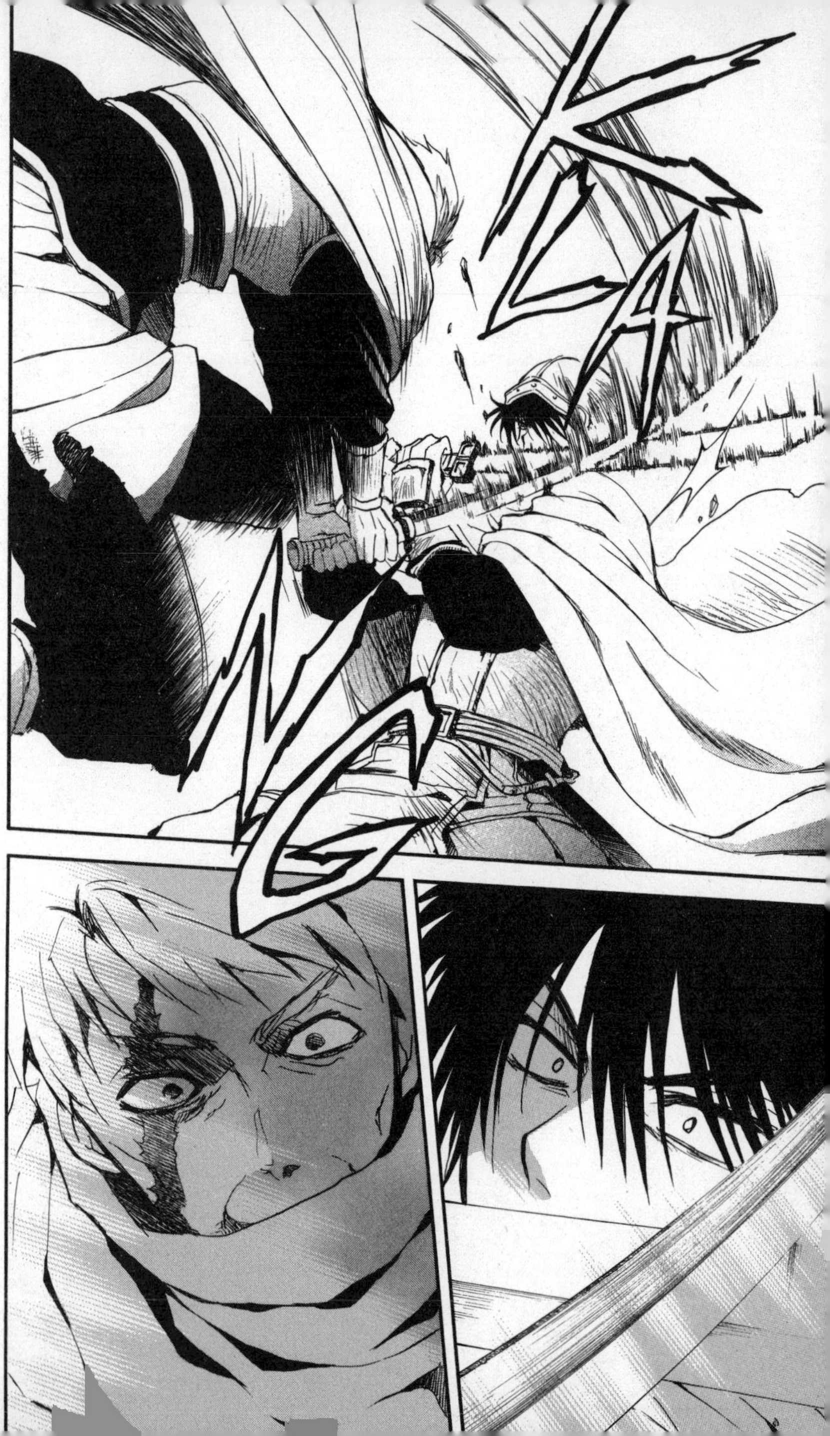
KCANG

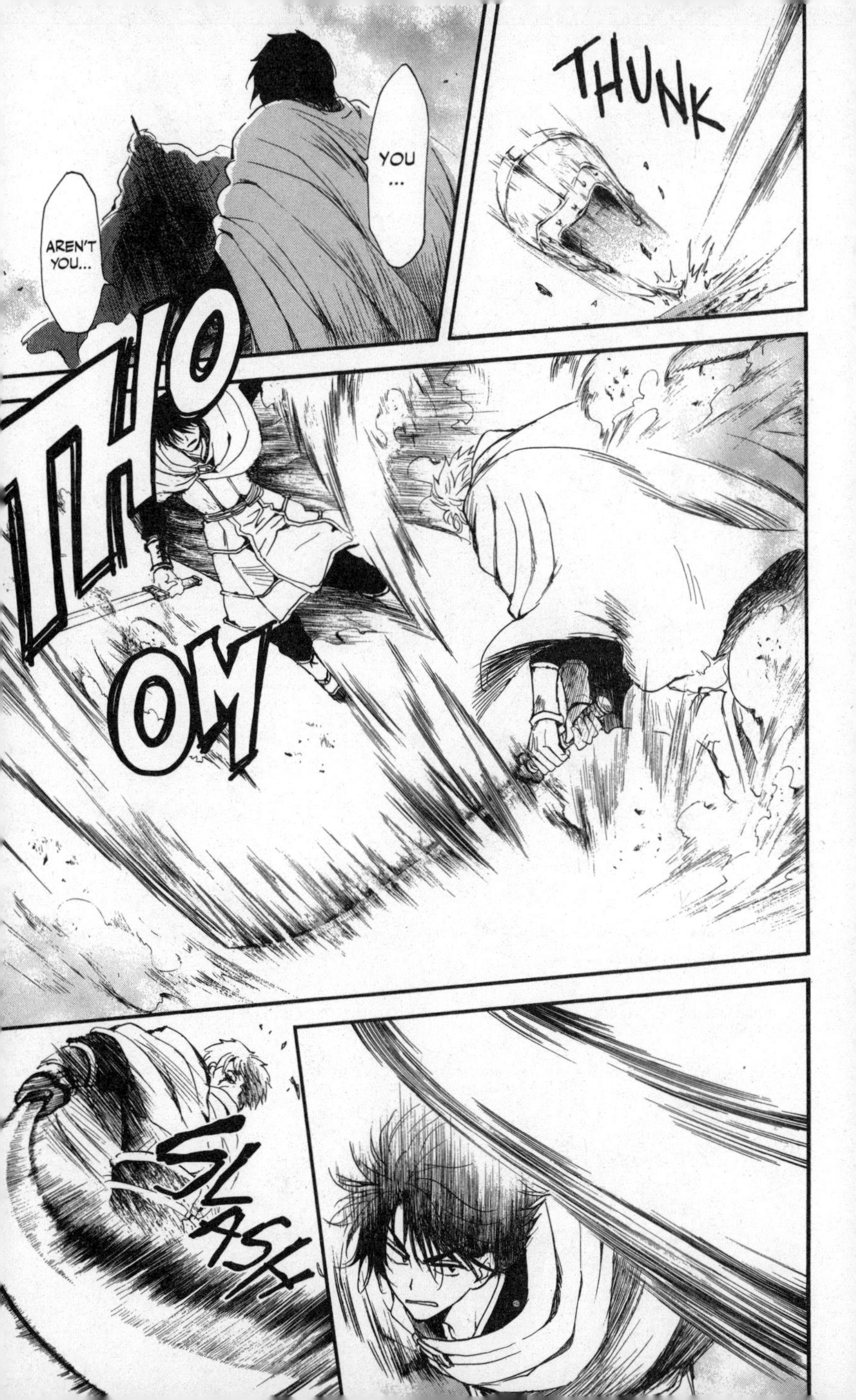
THUNK
YOU ...
AREN'T YOU...
THOOM
SLASH

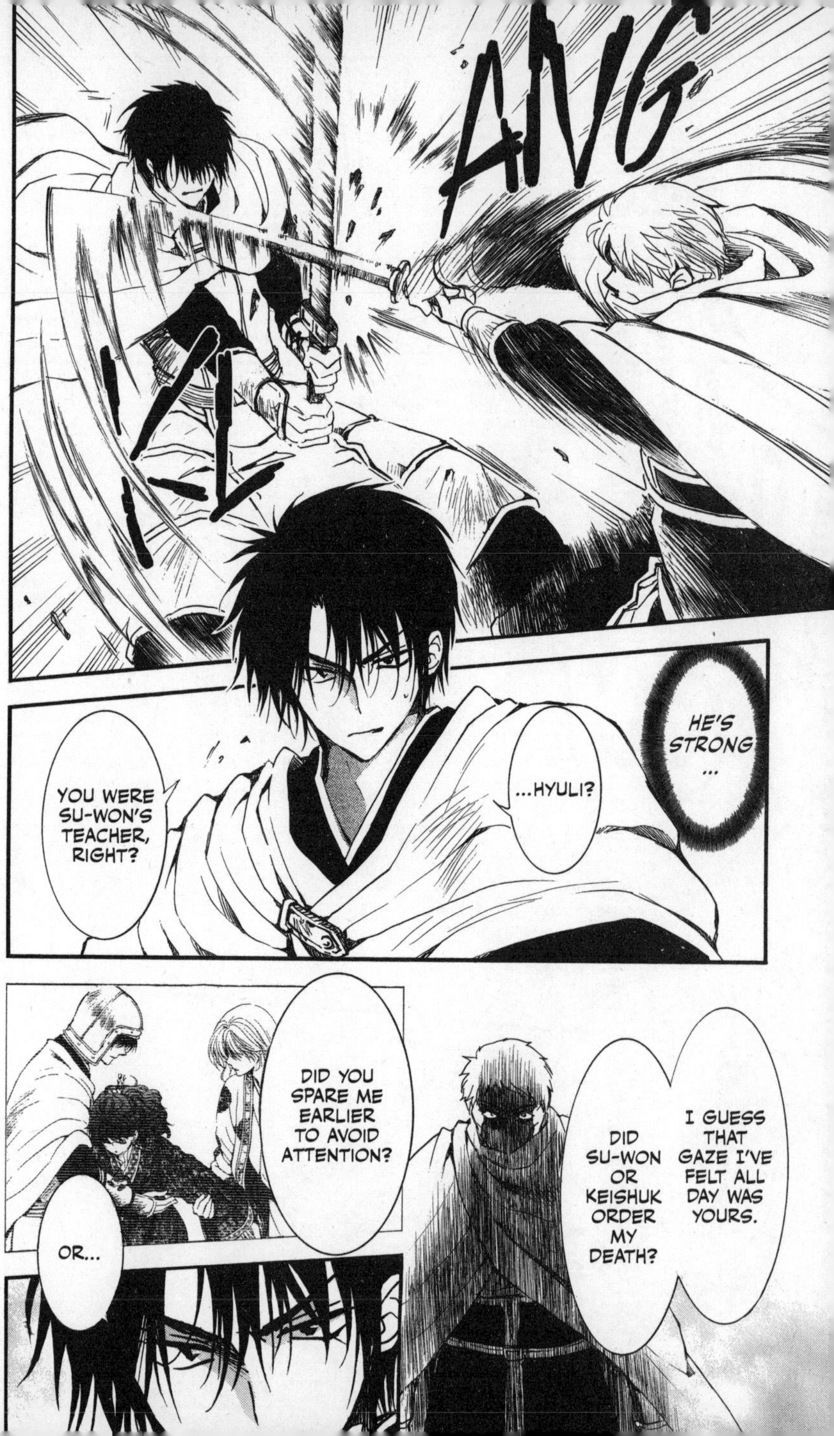
ANG
HE'S STRONG ...
...HYULI?
YOU WERE SU-WON'S TEACHER, RIGHT?
I GUESS THAT GAZE I'VE FELT ALL DAY WAS YOURS.
DID SU-WON OR KEISHUK ORDER MY DEATH?
DID YOU SPARE ME EARLIER TO AVOID ATTENTION?
OR...

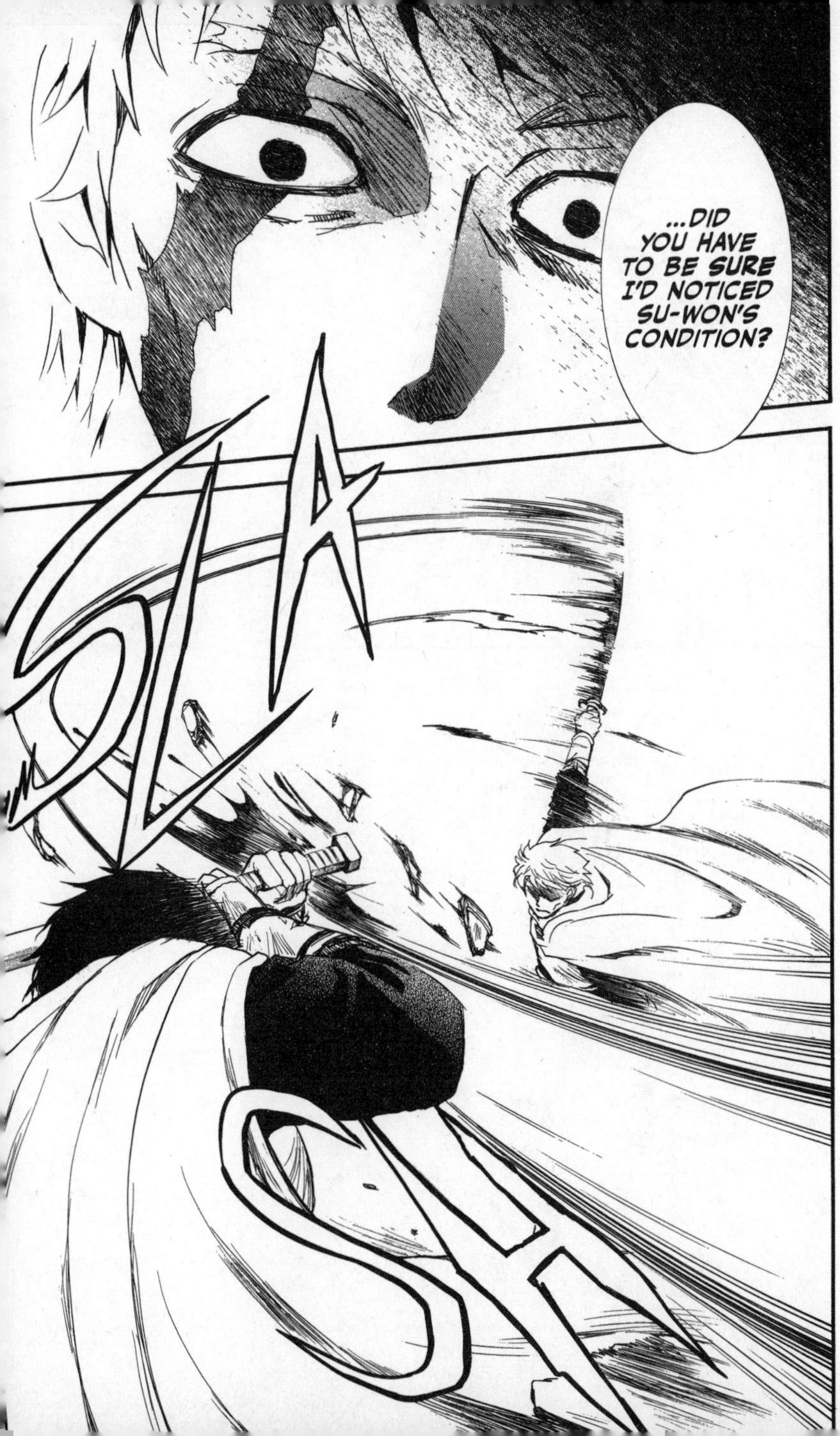
...DID YOU HAVE TO BE SURE I'D NOTICED SU-WON'S CONDITION?
SLA

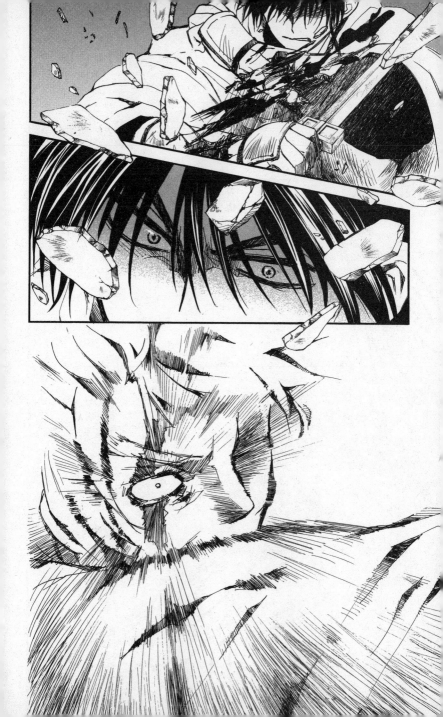

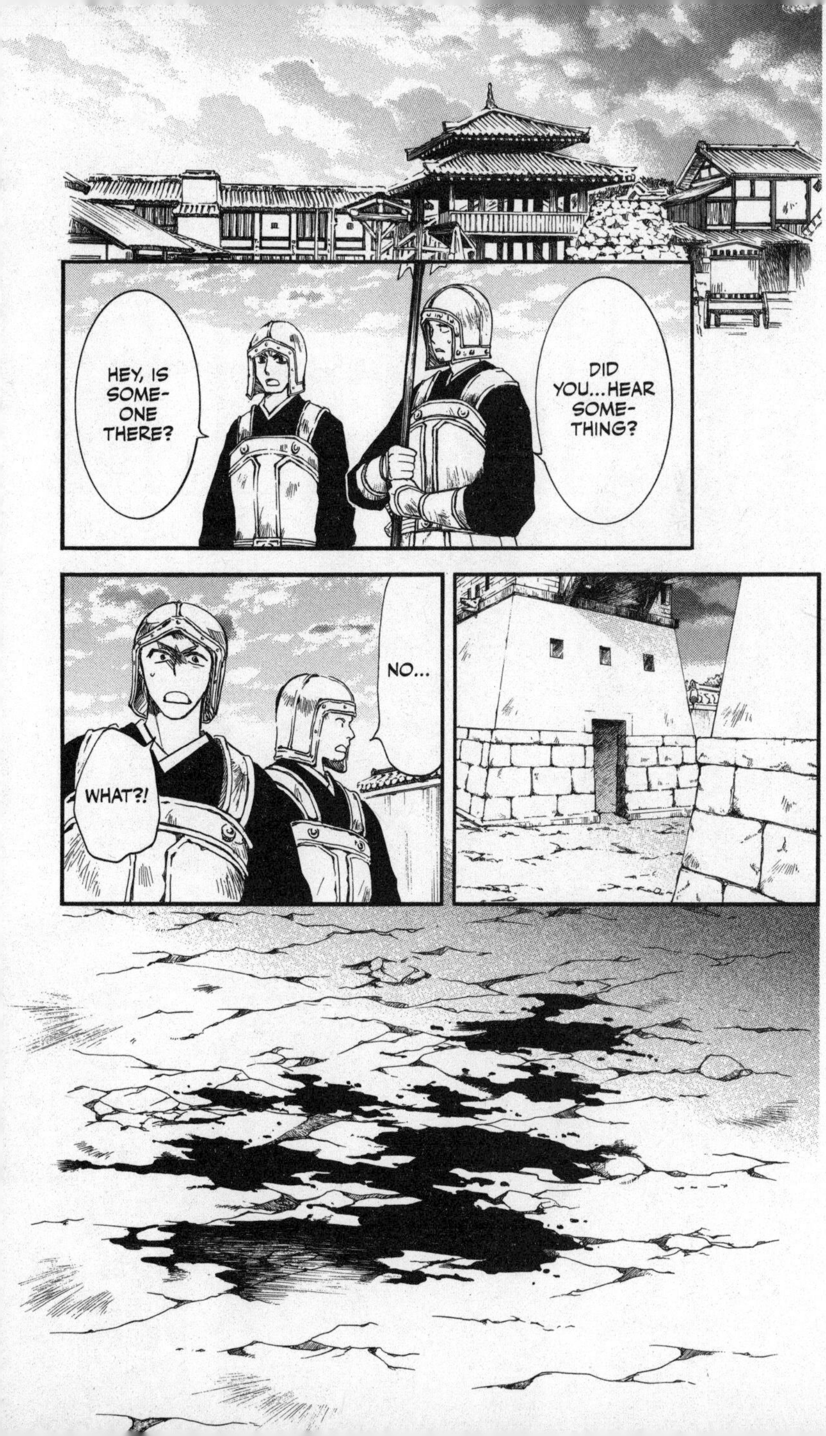
DID YOU...HEAR SOMETHING?
HEY, IS SOMEONE THERE?
NO...
WHAT?!

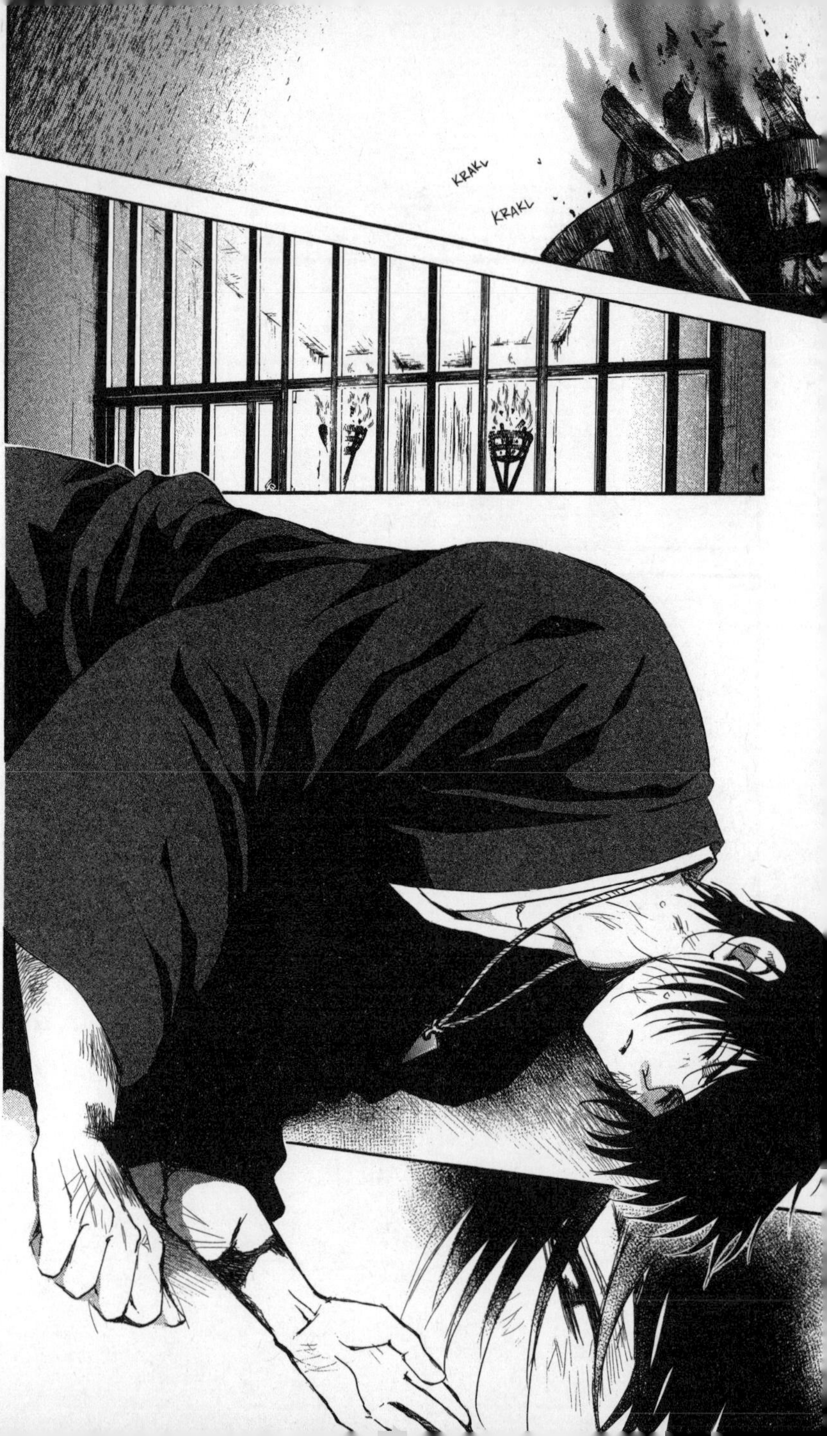
KRAKL
KRAKL

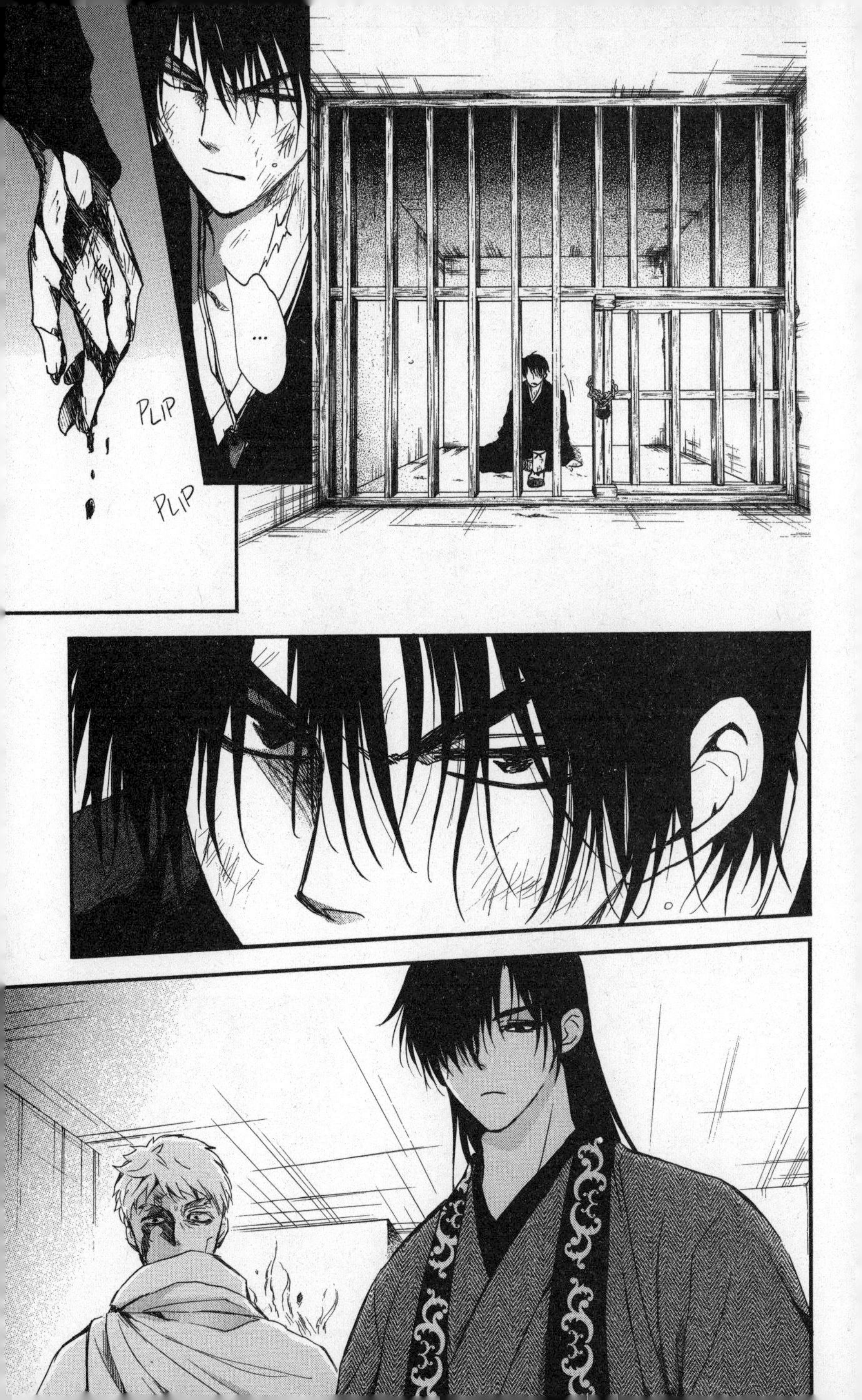
...
PLIP
PLIP

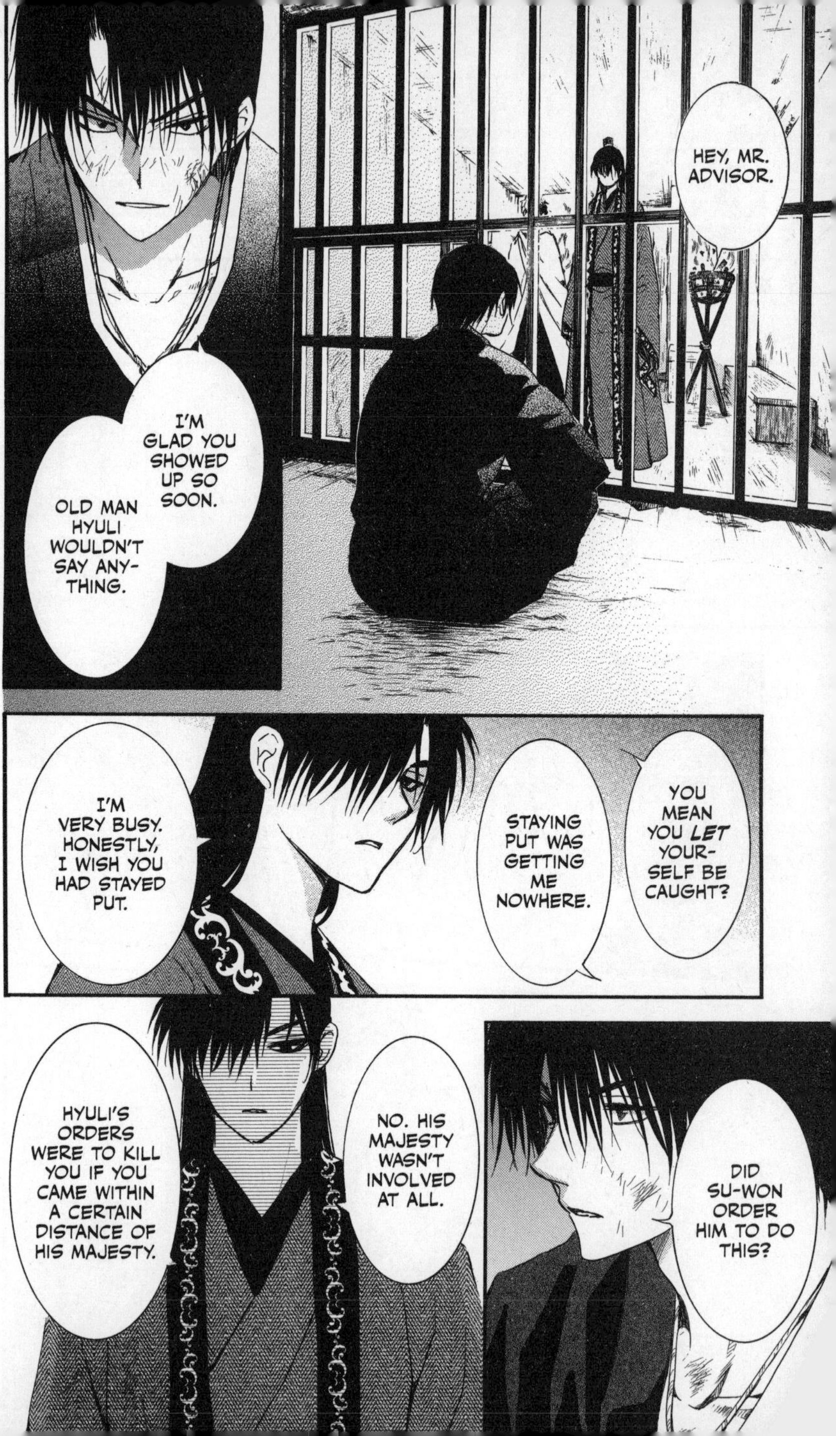
HEY, MR. ADVISOR.
I'M GLAD YOU SHOWED UP SO SOON.
OLD MAN HYULI WOULDN'T SAY ANYTHING.
YOU MEAN YOU *LET* YOURSELF BE CAUGHT?
STAYING PUT WAS GETTING ME NOWHERE.
I'M VERY BUSY. HONESTLY, I WISH YOU HAD STAYED PUT.
DID SU-WON ORDER HIM TO DO THIS?
NO. HIS MAJESTY WASN'T INVOLVED AT ALL.
HYULI'S ORDERS WERE TO KILL YOU IF YOU CAME WITHIN A CERTAIN DISTANCE OF HIS MAJESTY.

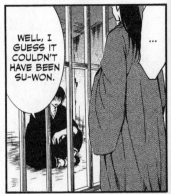

I THOUGHT I WARNED YOU.
THEN WHY AM I STILL ALIVE?
...
WELL, I GUESS IT COULDN'T HAVE BEEN SU-WON.
HE WAS SO FRAIL THAT HE DIDN'T EVEN NOTICE ME.
SAYING THAT MADE YOU AND HYULI BLANCH.
DID HER HIGHNESS STAND IN FOR THE KING BECAUSE OF HIS HEALTH?
...

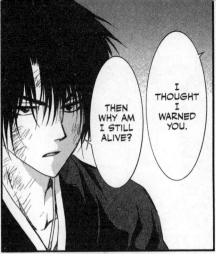

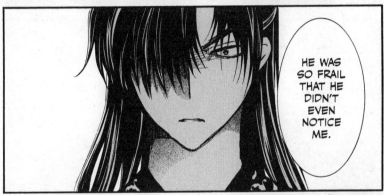

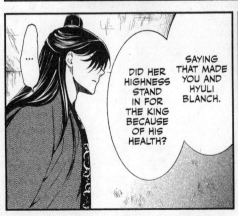

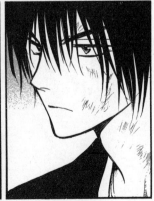

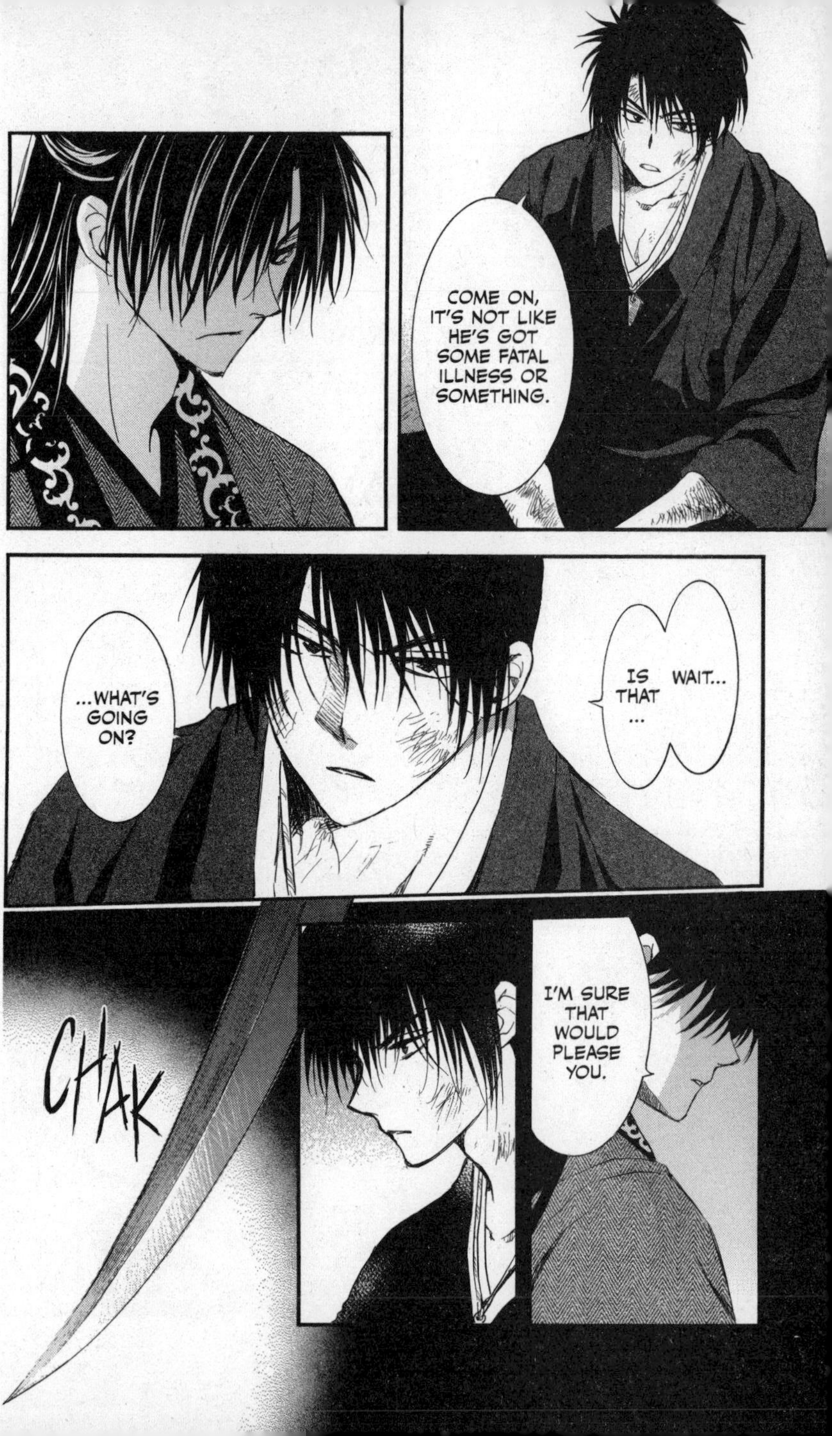
COME ON, IT'S NOT LIKE HE'S GOT SOME FATAL ILLNESS OR SOMETHING.
WAIT...
IS THAT ...
...WHAT'S GOING ON?
I'M SURE THAT WOULD PLEASE YOU.
CHAK

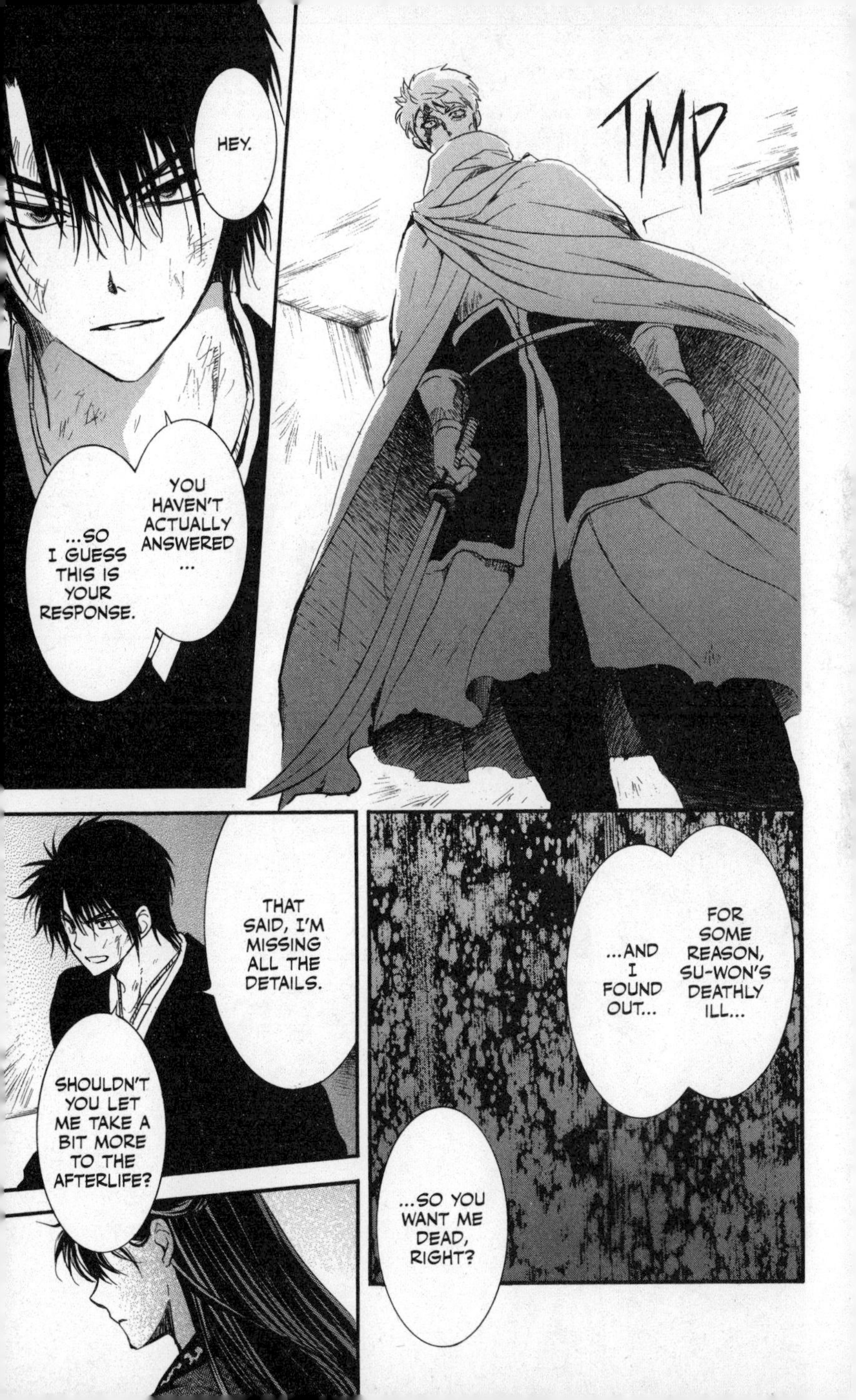
TMP
HEY.
YOU HAVEN'T ACTUALLY ANSWERED ...
...SO I GUESS THIS IS YOUR RESPONSE.
FOR SOME REASON, SU-WON'S DEATHLY ILL...
...AND I FOUND OUT...
...SO YOU WANT ME DEAD, RIGHT?
THAT SAID, I'M MISSING ALL THE DETAILS.
SHOULDN'T YOU LET ME TAKE A BIT MORE TO THE AFTERLIFE?

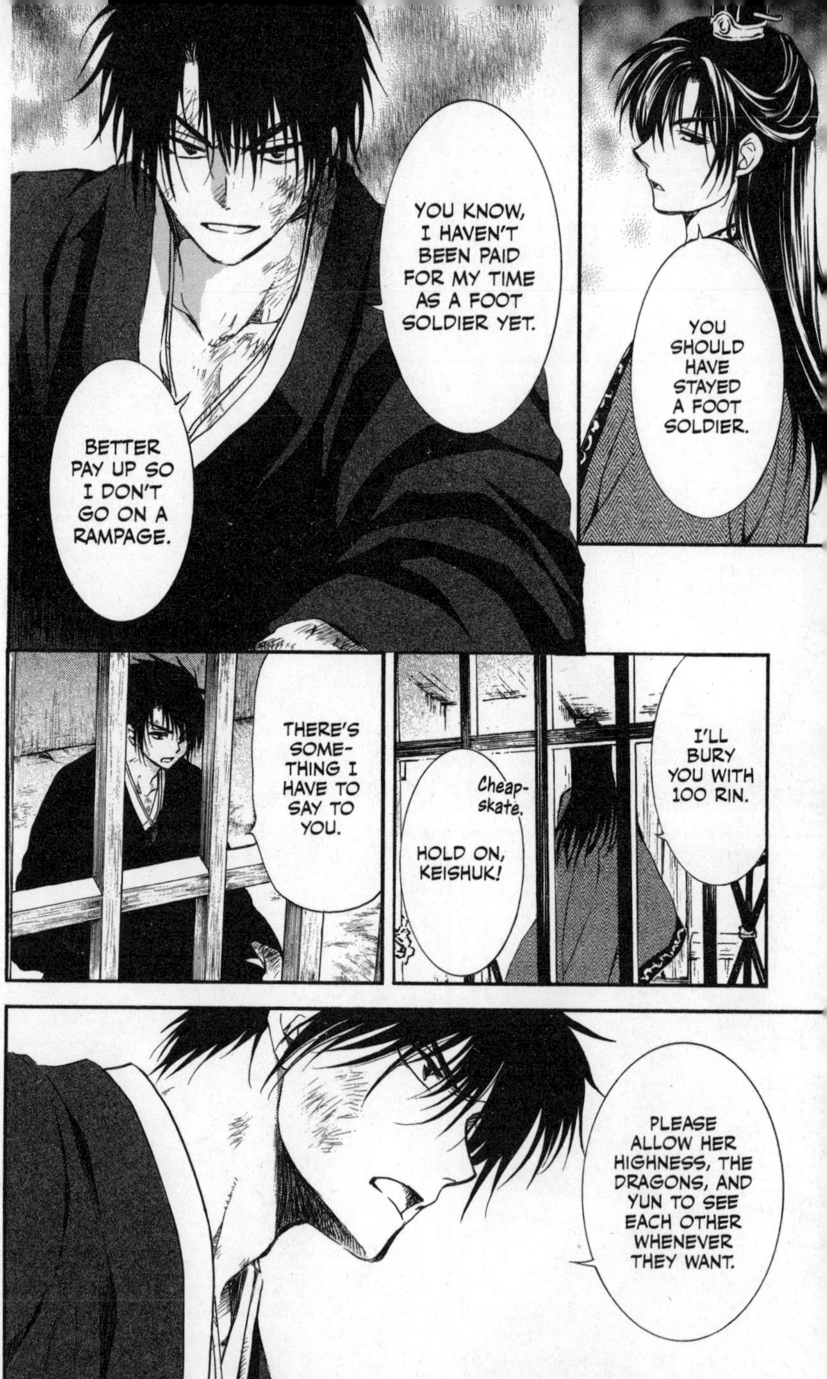
YOU SHOULD HAVE STAYED A FOOT SOLDIER.
YOU KNOW, I HAVEN'T BEEN PAID FOR MY TIME AS A FOOT SOLDIER YET.
BETTER PAY UP SO I DON'T GO ON A RAMPAGE.
I'LL BURY YOU WITH 100 RIN.
Cheap-skate.
HOLD ON, KEISHUK!
THERE'S SOME-THING I HAVE TO SAY TO YOU.
PLEASE ALLOW HER HIGHNESS, THE DRAGONS, AND YUN TO SEE EACH OTHER WHENEVER THEY WANT.

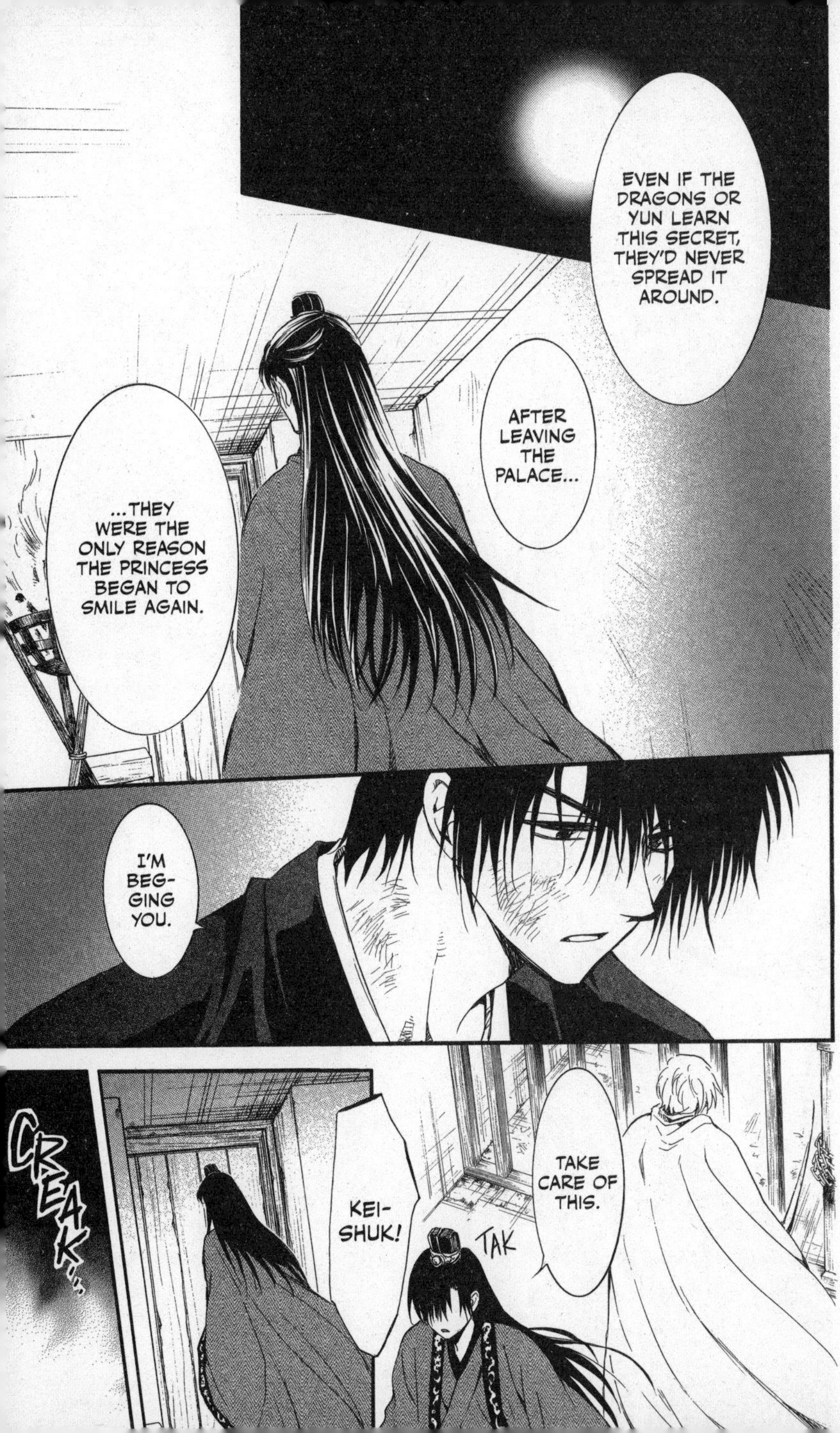
EVEN IF THE DRAGONS OR YUN LEARN THIS SECRET, THEY'D NEVER SPREAD IT AROUND.
AFTER LEAVING THE PALACE...
...THEY WERE THE ONLY REASON THE PRINCESS BEGAN TO SMILE AGAIN.
I'M BEG-GING YOU.
TAKE CARE OF THIS.
TAK
KEI-SHUK!
CREAK...

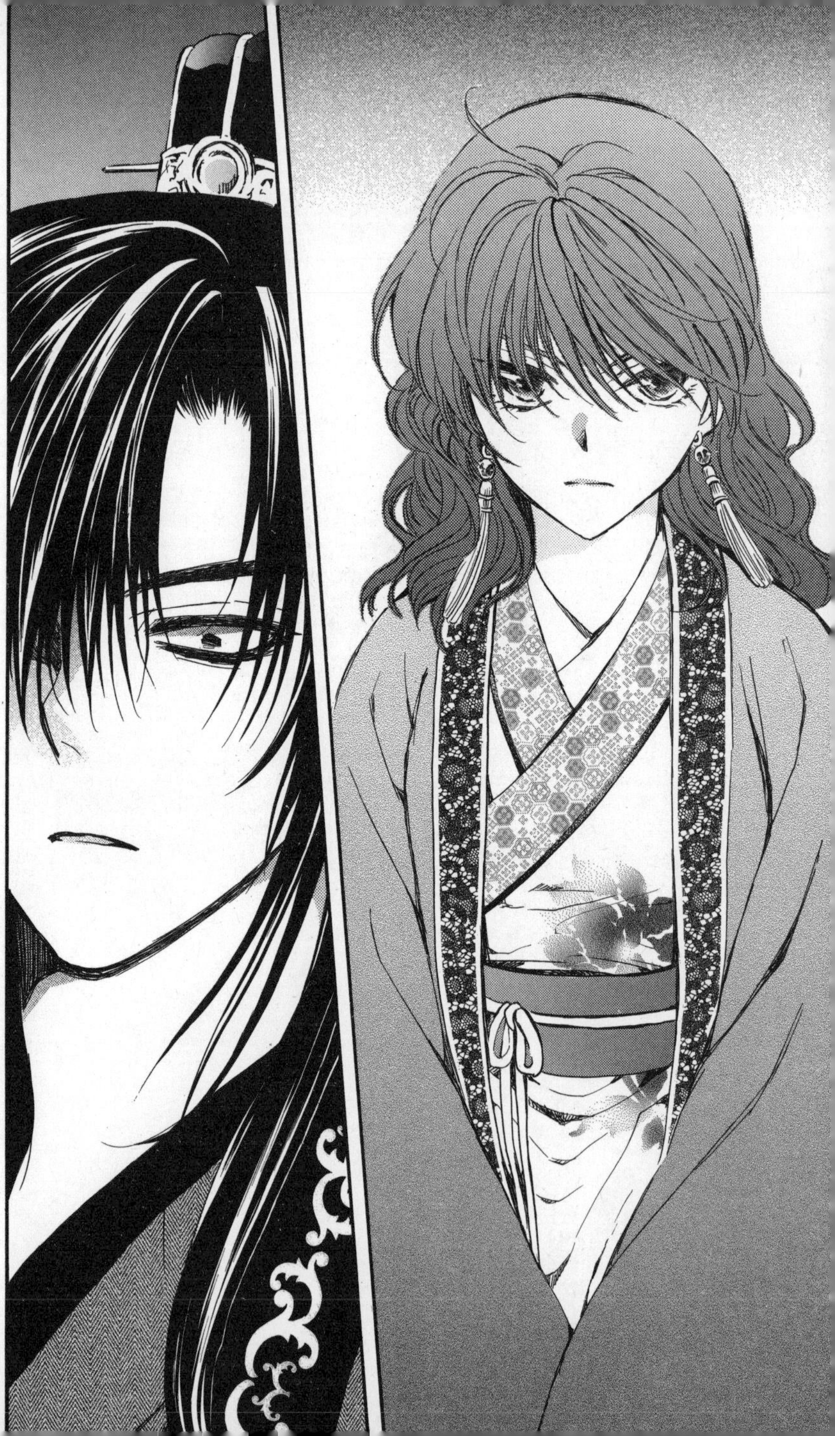

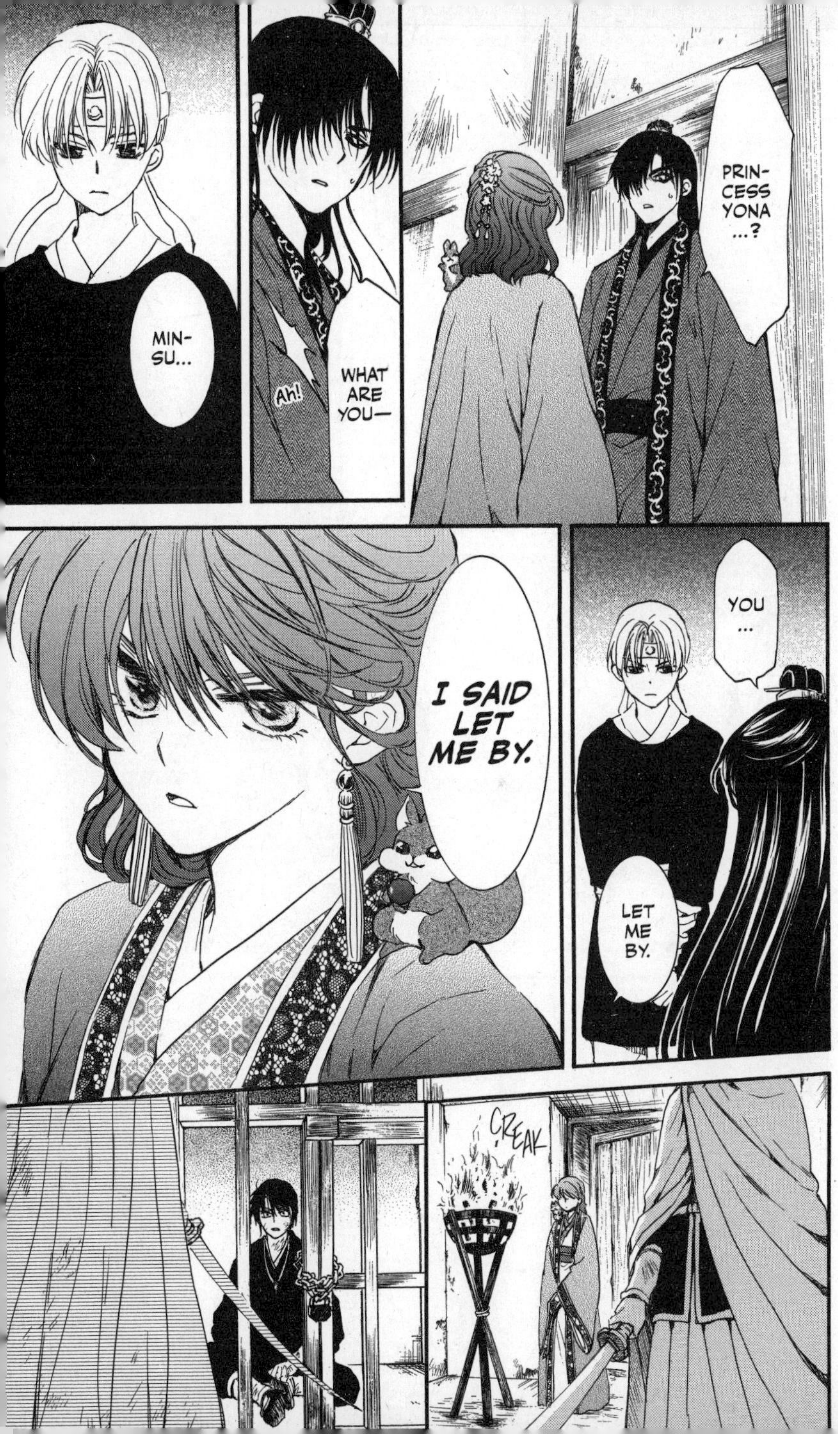
PRIN-CESS YONA ...?
Ah!
WHAT ARE YOU—
MIN-SU...
YOU ...
LET ME BY.
I SAID LET ME BY.
CREAK

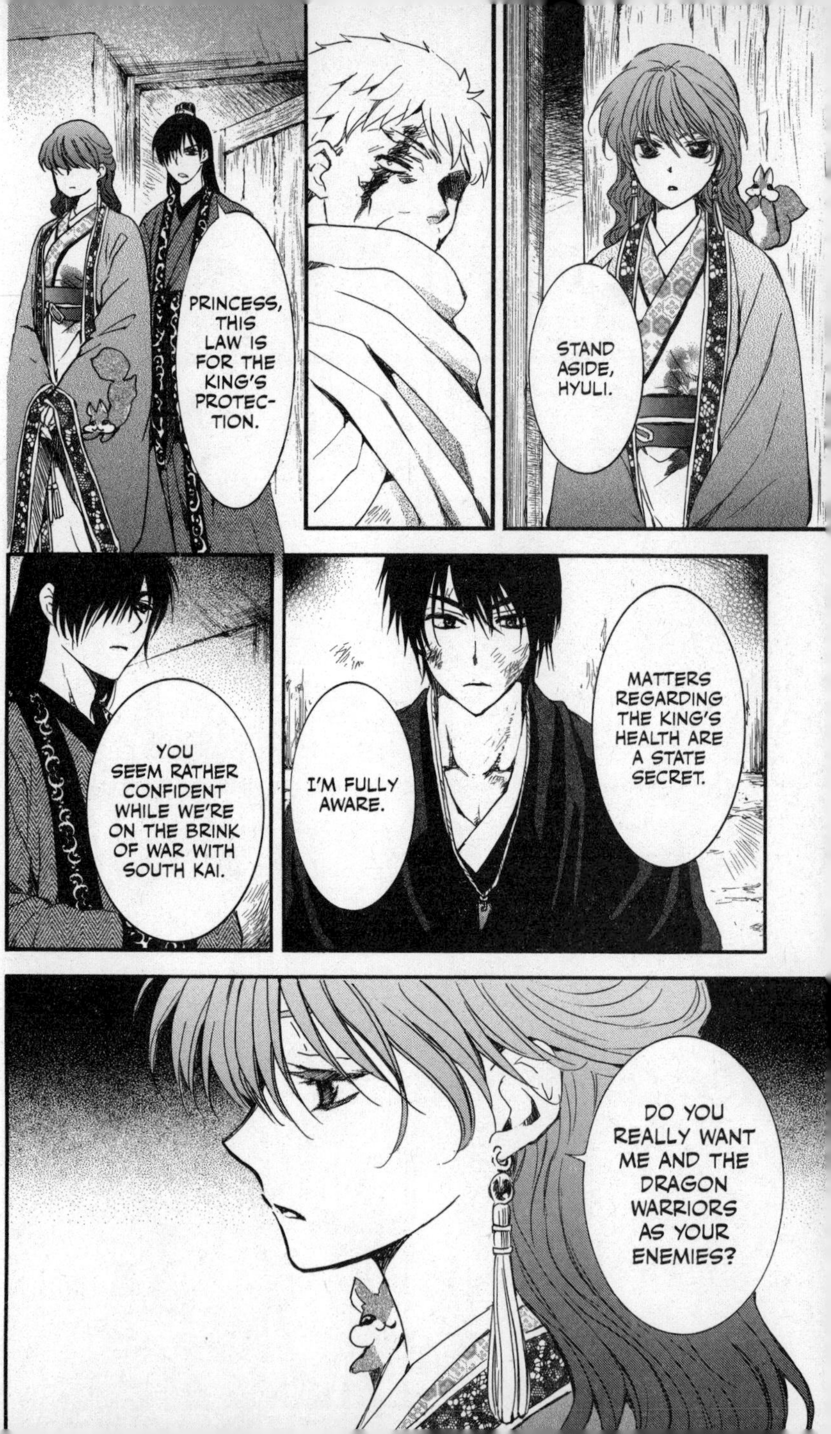
STAND ASIDE, HYULI.
PRINCESS, THIS LAW IS FOR THE KING'S PROTECTION.
MATTERS REGARDING THE KING'S HEALTH ARE A STATE SECRET.
I'M FULLY AWARE.
YOU SEEM RATHER CONFIDENT WHILE WE'RE ON THE BRINK OF WAR WITH SOUTH KAI.
DO YOU REALLY WANT ME AND THE DRAGON WARRIORS AS YOUR ENEMIES?

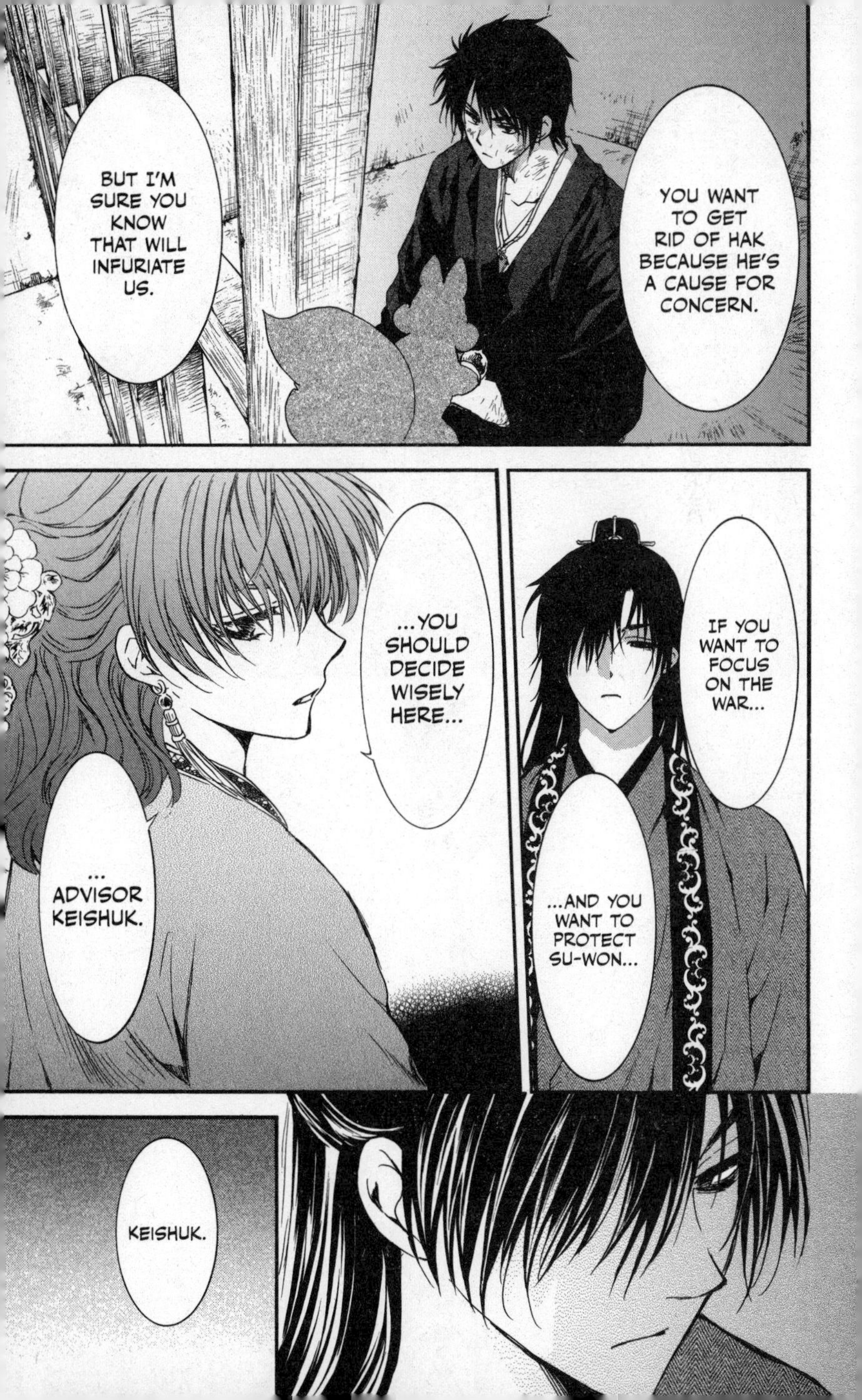
YOU WANT TO GET RID OF HAK BECAUSE HE'S A CAUSE FOR CONCERN.
BUT I'M SURE YOU KNOW THAT WILL INFURIATE US.
IF YOU WANT TO FOCUS ON THE WAR...
...AND YOU WANT TO PROTECT SU-WON...
...YOU SHOULD DECIDE WISELY HERE...
... ADVISOR KEISHUK.
KEISHUK.

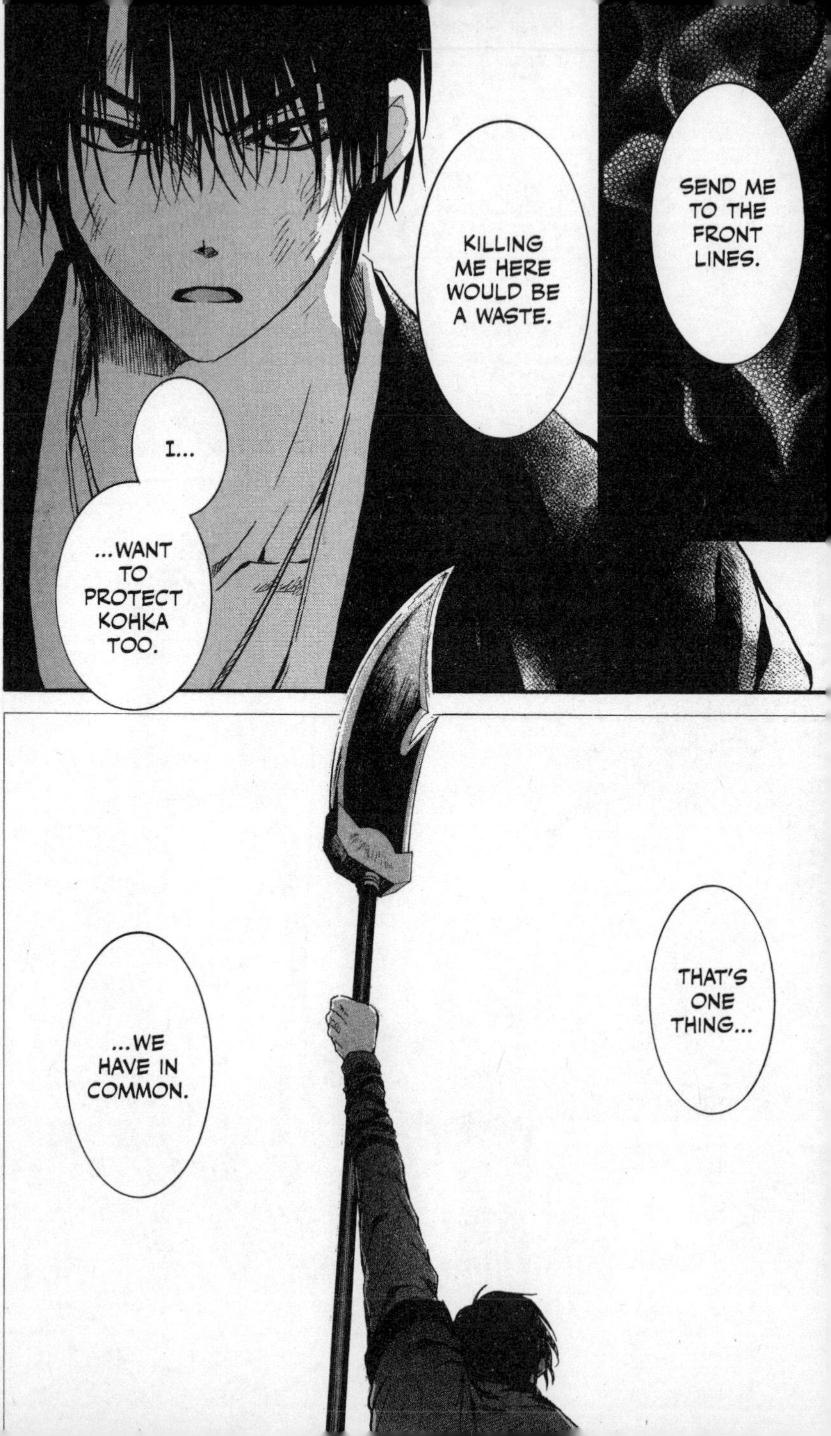
SEND ME TO THE FRONT LINES.
KILLING ME HERE WOULD BE A WASTE.
I...
...WANT TO PROTECT KOHKA TOO.
THAT'S ONE THING...
...WE HAVE IN COMMON.

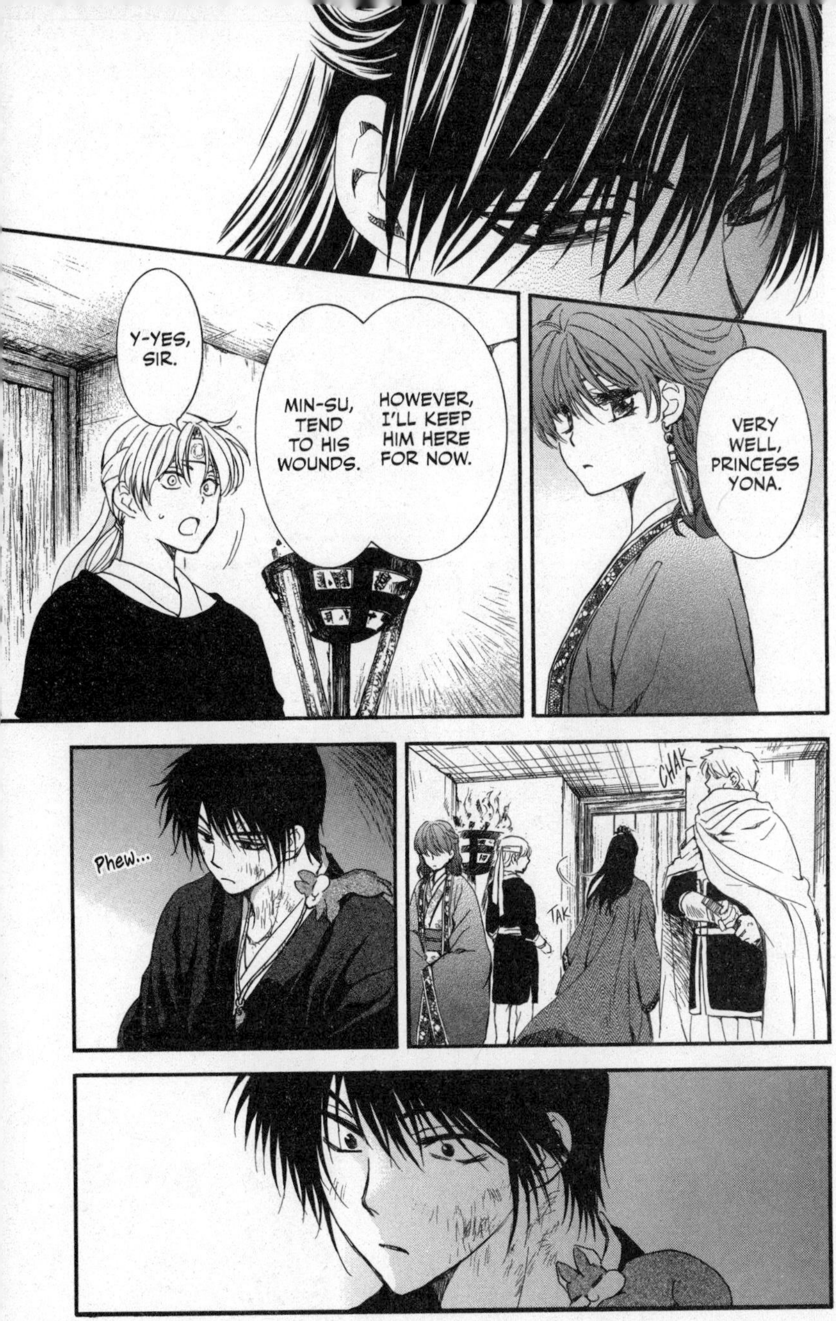
VERY WELL, PRINCESS YONA.
HOWEVER, I'LL KEEP HIM HERE FOR NOW.
MIN-SU, TEND TO HIS WOUNDS.
Y-YES, SIR.
CHAK
TAK
Phew...

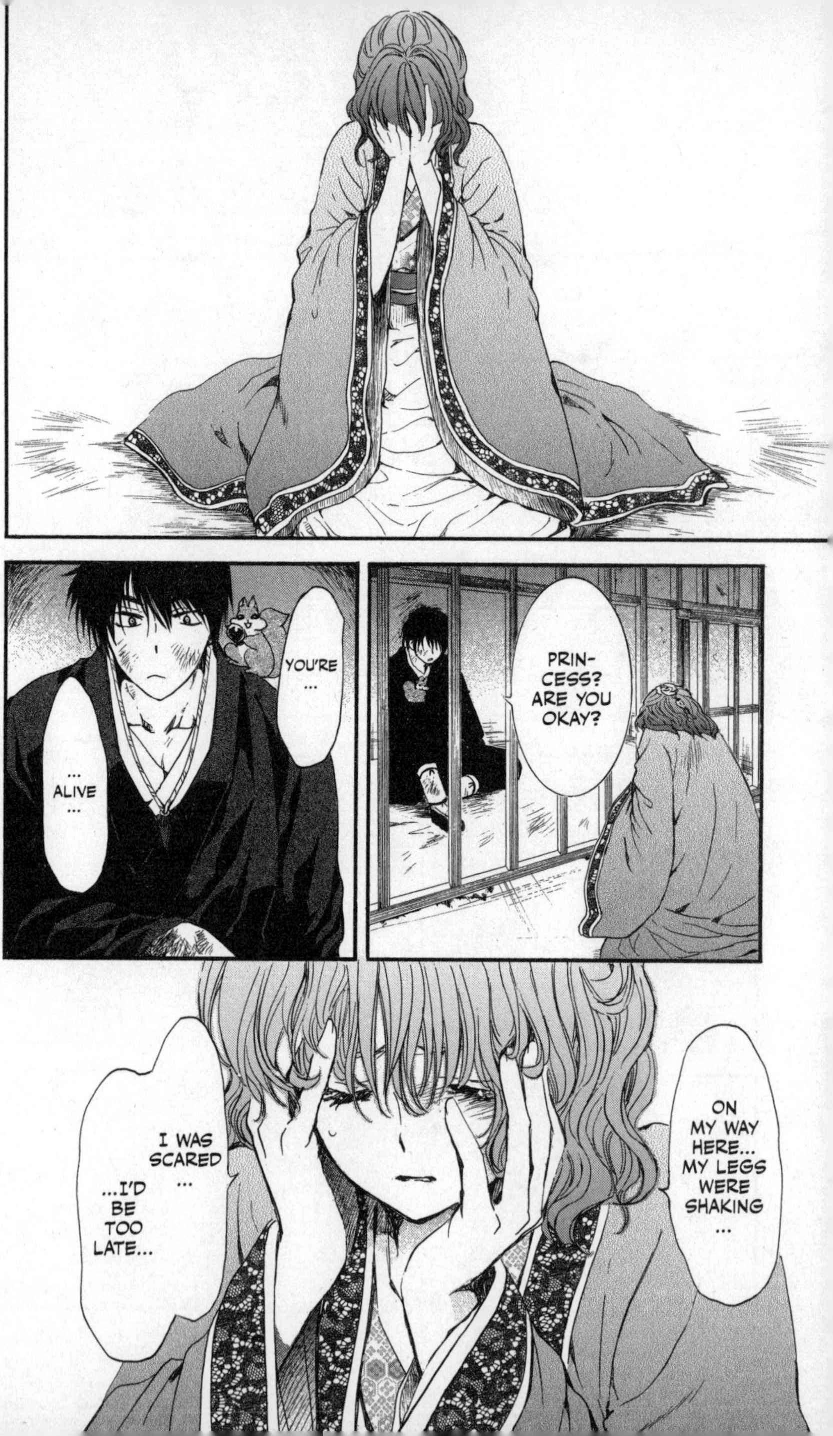
PRIN-CESS? ARE YOU OKAY?
YOU'RE ...
... ALIVE ...
ON MY WAY HERE... MY LEGS WERE SHAKING ...
I WAS SCARED ...
...I'D BE TOO LATE...

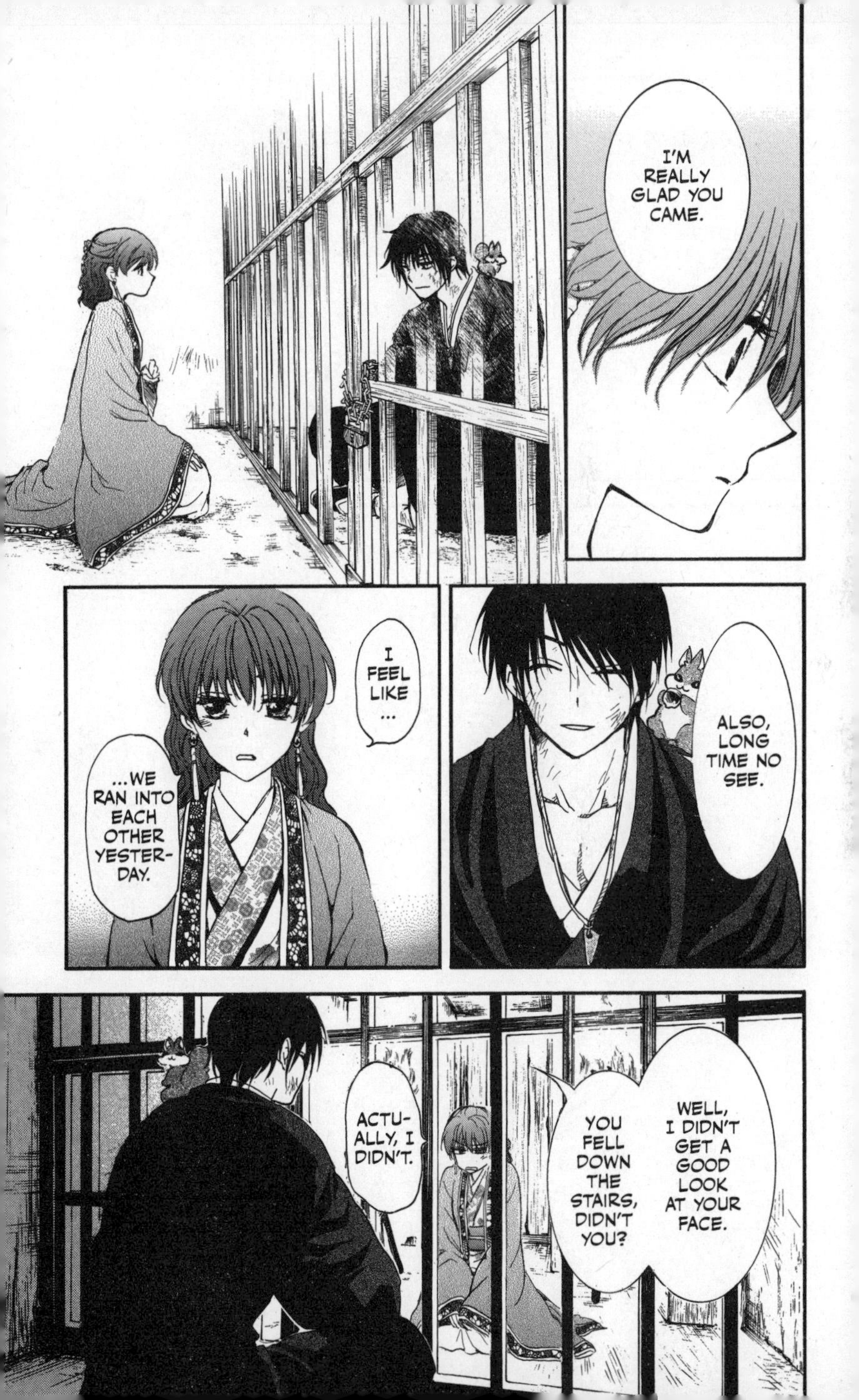
I'M REALLY GLAD YOU CAME.
ALSO, LONG TIME NO SEE.
I FEEL LIKE ...
...WE RAN INTO EACH OTHER YESTER-DAY.
WELL, I DIDN'T GET A GOOD LOOK AT YOUR FACE.
YOU FELL DOWN THE STAIRS, DIDN'T YOU?
ACTU-ALLY, I DIDN'T.

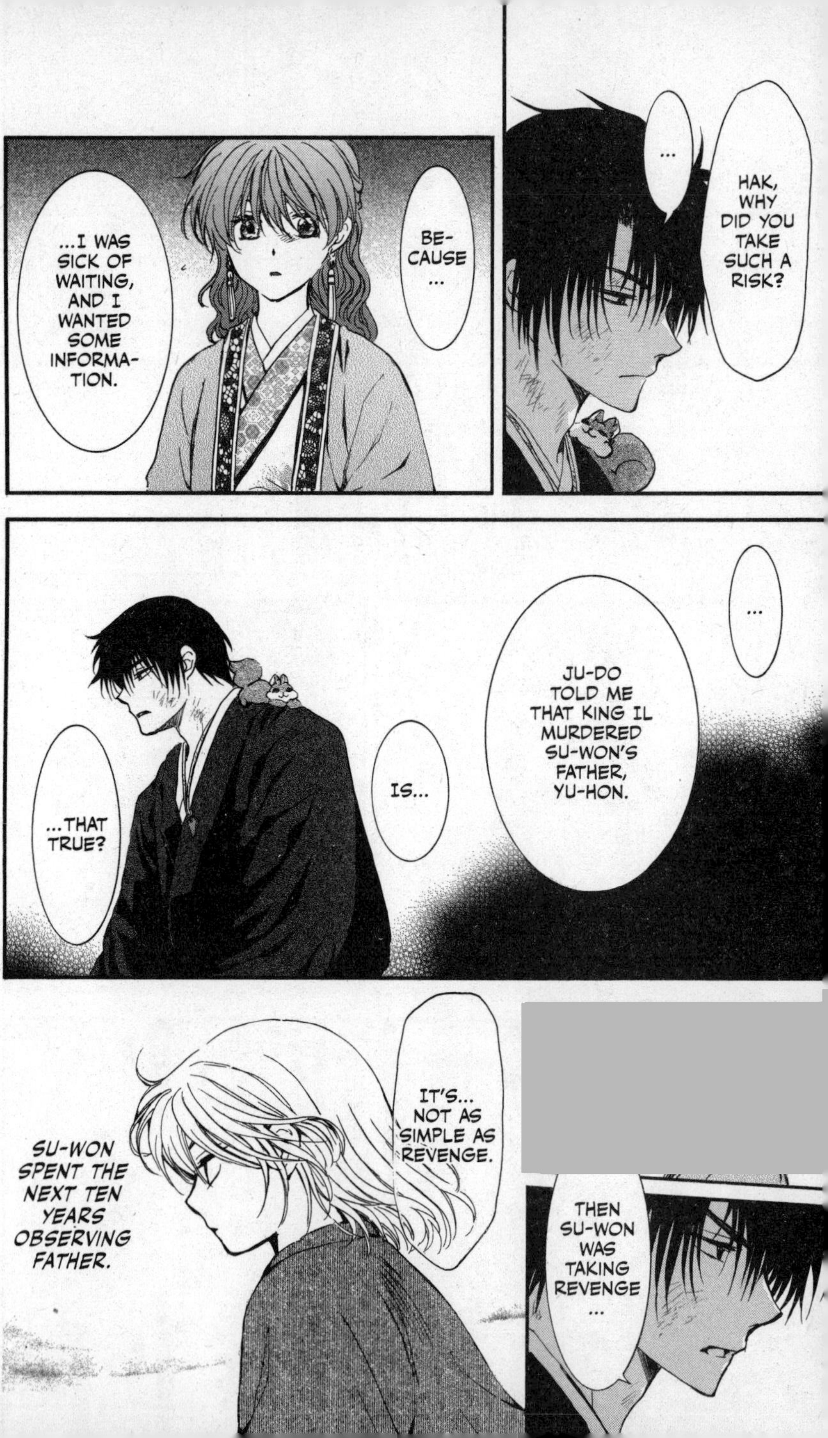
HAK, WHY DID YOU TAKE SUCH A RISK?
...
BE-CAUSE...
...I WAS SICK OF WAITING, AND I WANTED SOME INFORMA-TION.
...
JU-DO TOLD ME THAT KING IL MURDERED SU-WON'S FATHER, YU-HON.
IS...
...THAT TRUE?
THEN SU-WON WAS TAKING REVENGE...
IT'S... NOT AS SIMPLE AS REVENGE.
SU-WON SPENT THE NEXT TEN YEARS OBSERVING FATHER.

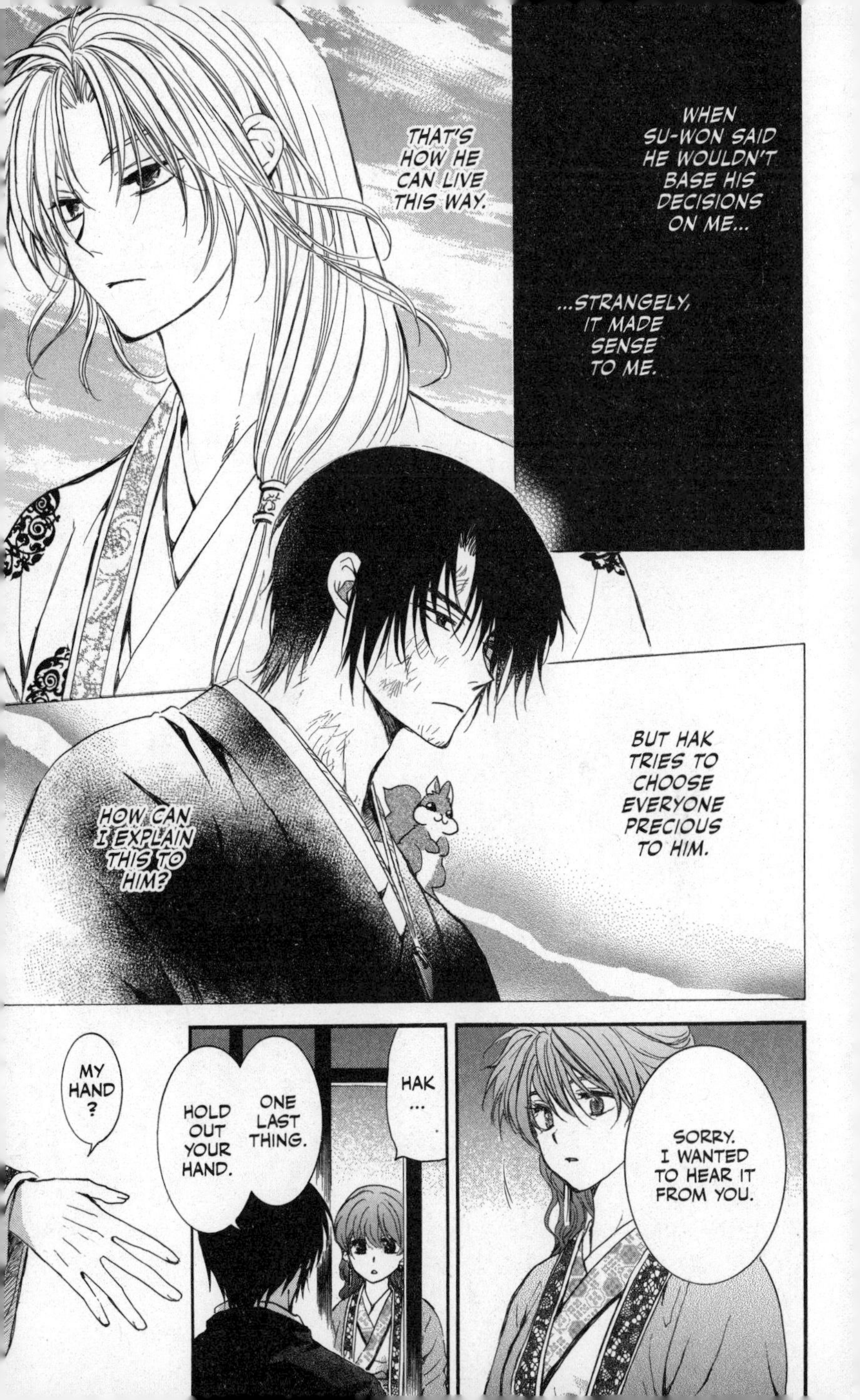
WHEN SU-WON SAID HE WOULDN'T BASE HIS DECISIONS ON ME...
...STRANGELY, IT MADE SENSE TO ME.
THAT'S HOW HE CAN LIVE THIS WAY.
BUT HAK TRIES TO CHOOSE EVERYONE PRECIOUS TO HIM.
HOW CAN I EXPLAIN THIS TO HIM?
SORRY. I WANTED TO HEAR IT FROM YOU.
HAK...
ONE LAST THING.
HOLD OUT YOUR HAND.
MY HAND?

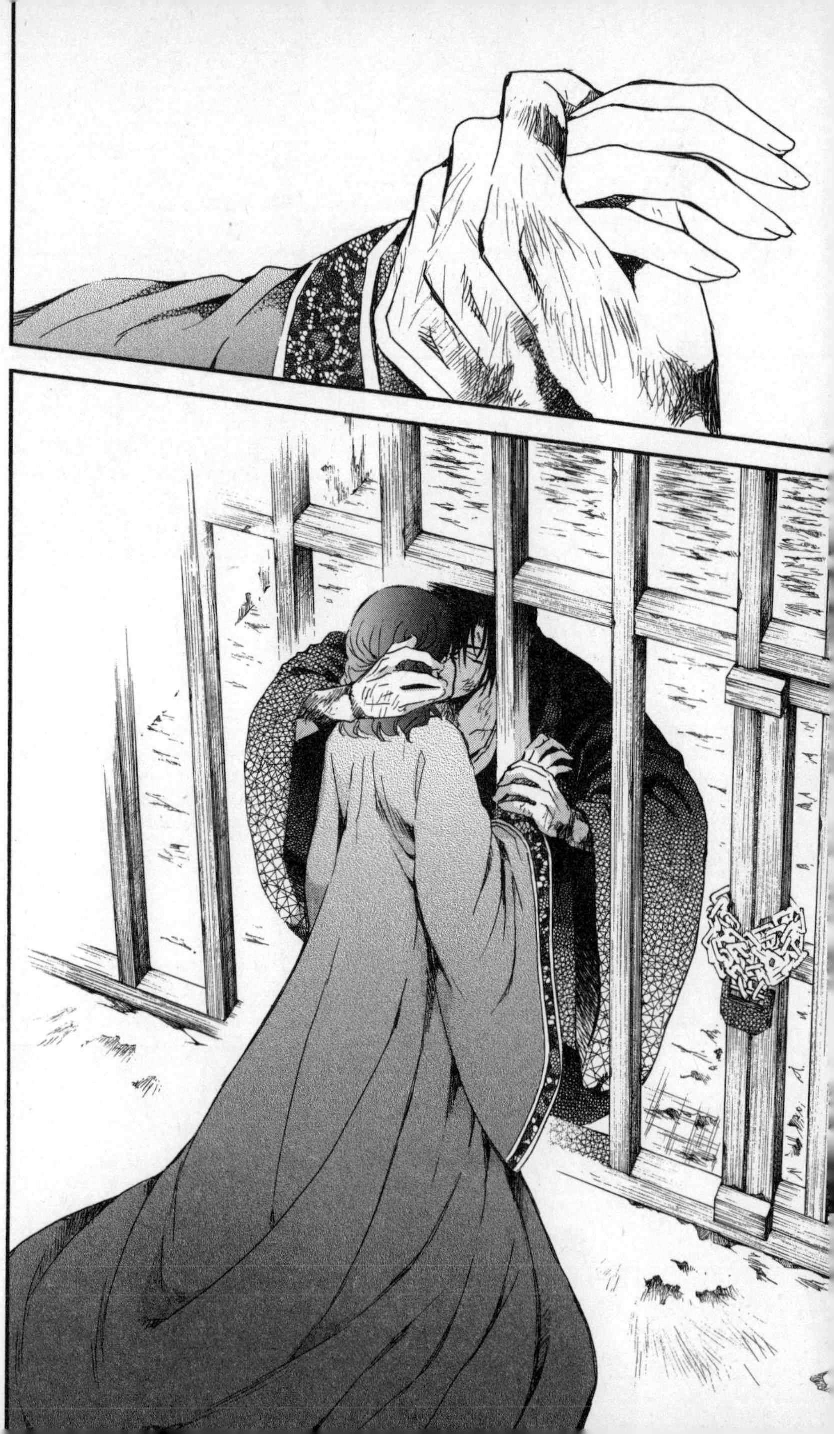

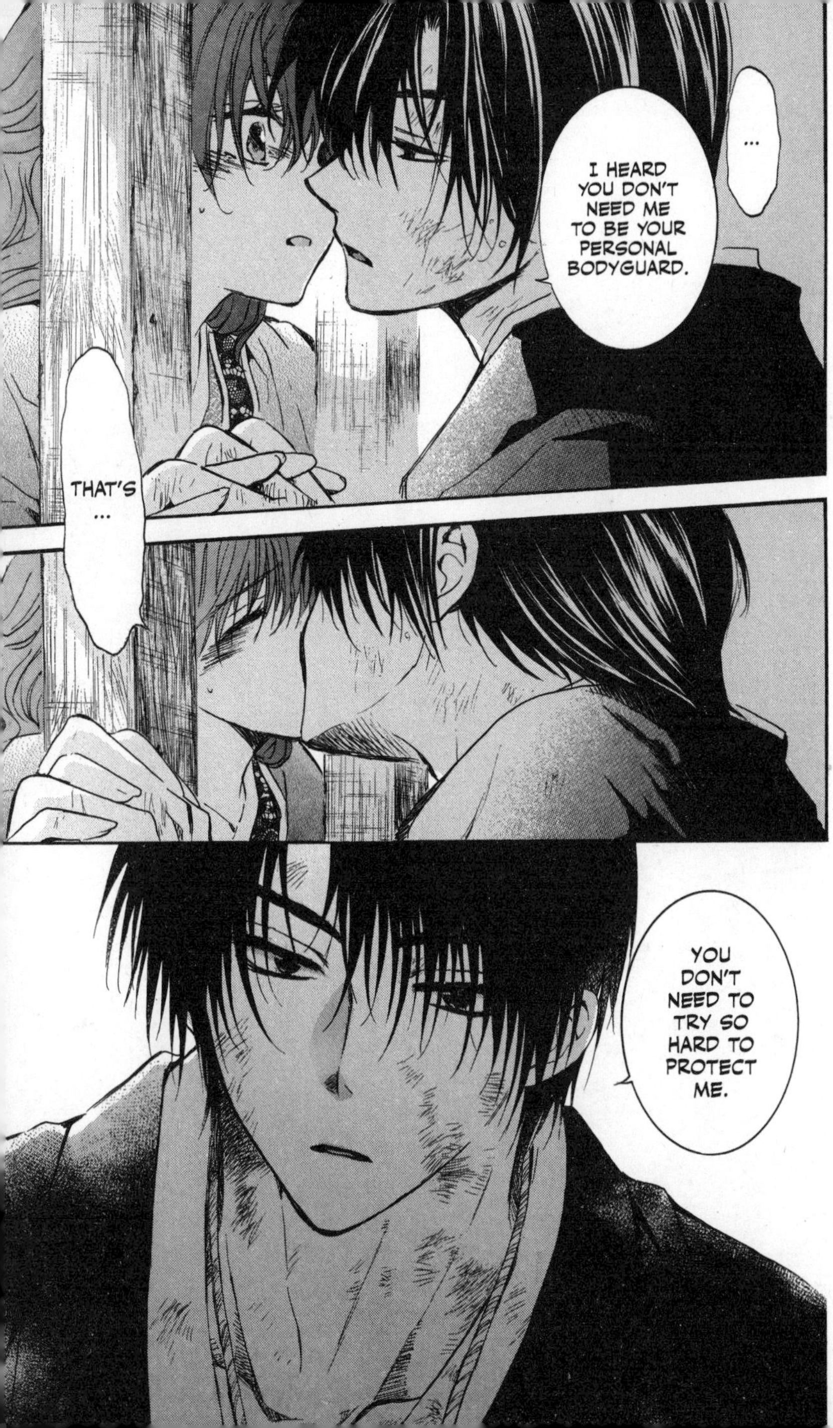
...
I HEARD YOU DON'T NEED ME TO BE YOUR PERSONAL BODYGUARD.
THAT'S ...
YOU DON'T NEED TO TRY SO HARD TO PROTECT ME.

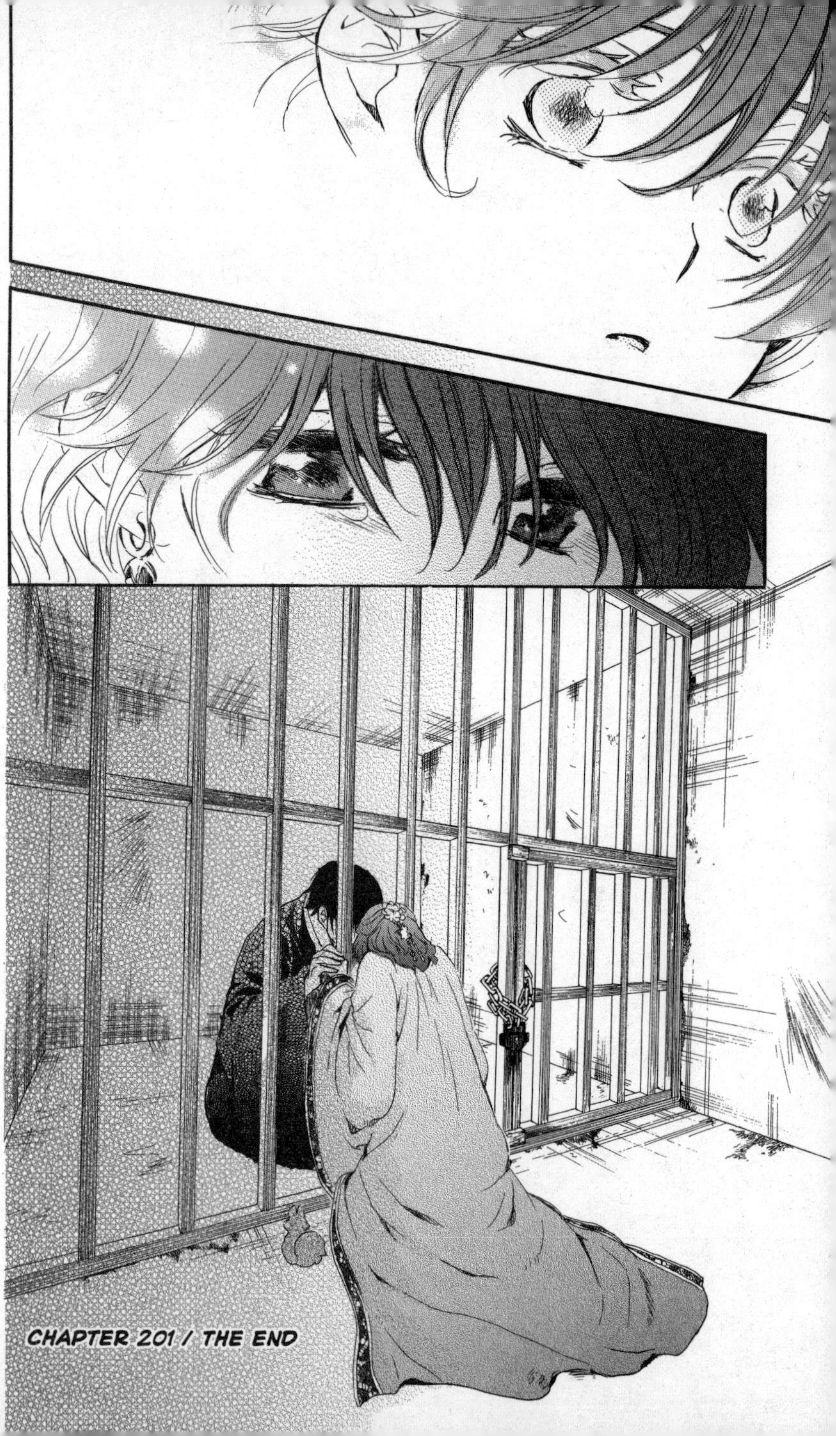
CHAPTER 201 / THE END

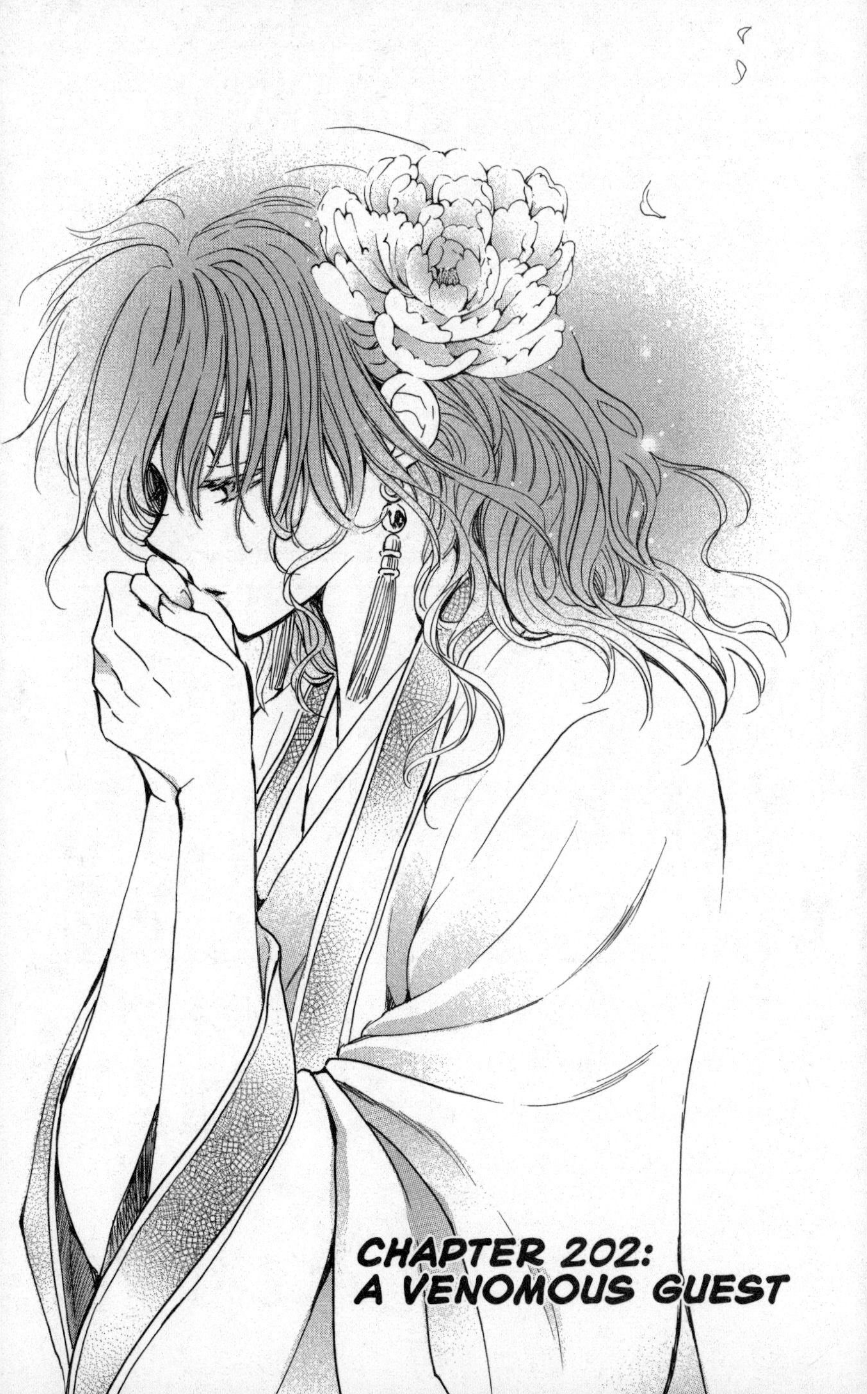
CHAPTER 202:
A VENOMOUS GUEST

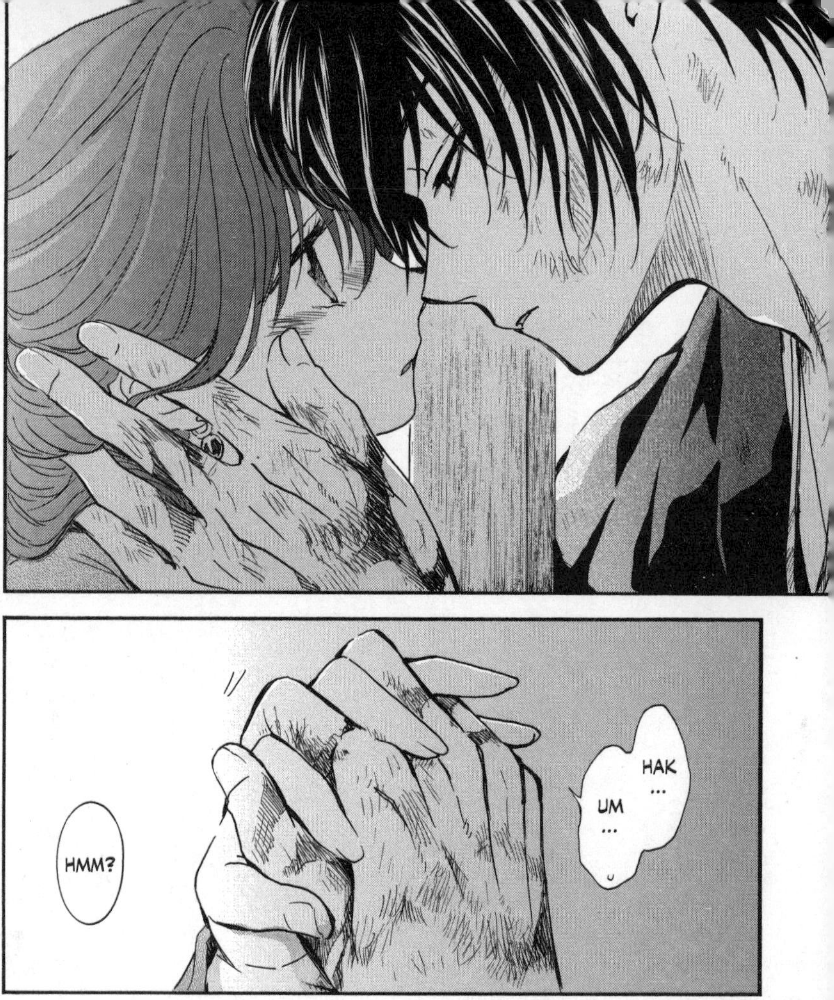
HAK... UM...
HMM?

Yona of the Dawn

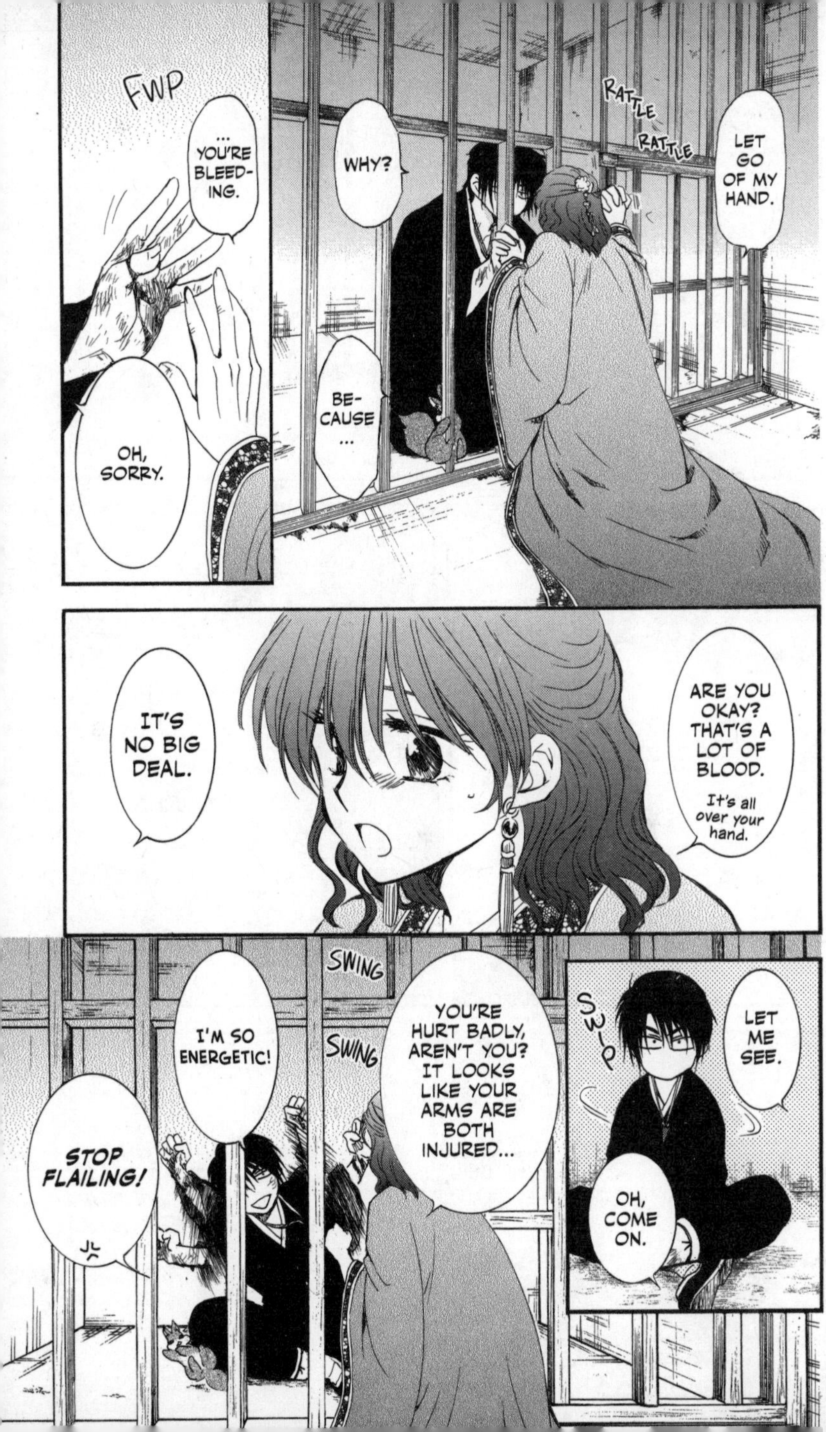
RATTLE RATTLE
LET GO OF MY HAND.
WHY?
BE-CAUSE...
FWP
...YOU'RE BLEED-ING.
OH, SORRY.
ARE YOU OKAY? THAT'S A LOT OF BLOOD.
It's all over your hand.
IT'S NO BIG DEAL.
SWP
LET ME SEE.
OH, COME ON.
SWING
SWING
YOU'RE HURT BADLY, AREN'T YOU? IT LOOKS LIKE YOUR ARMS ARE BOTH INJURED...
I'M SO ENERGETIC!
STOP FLAILING!

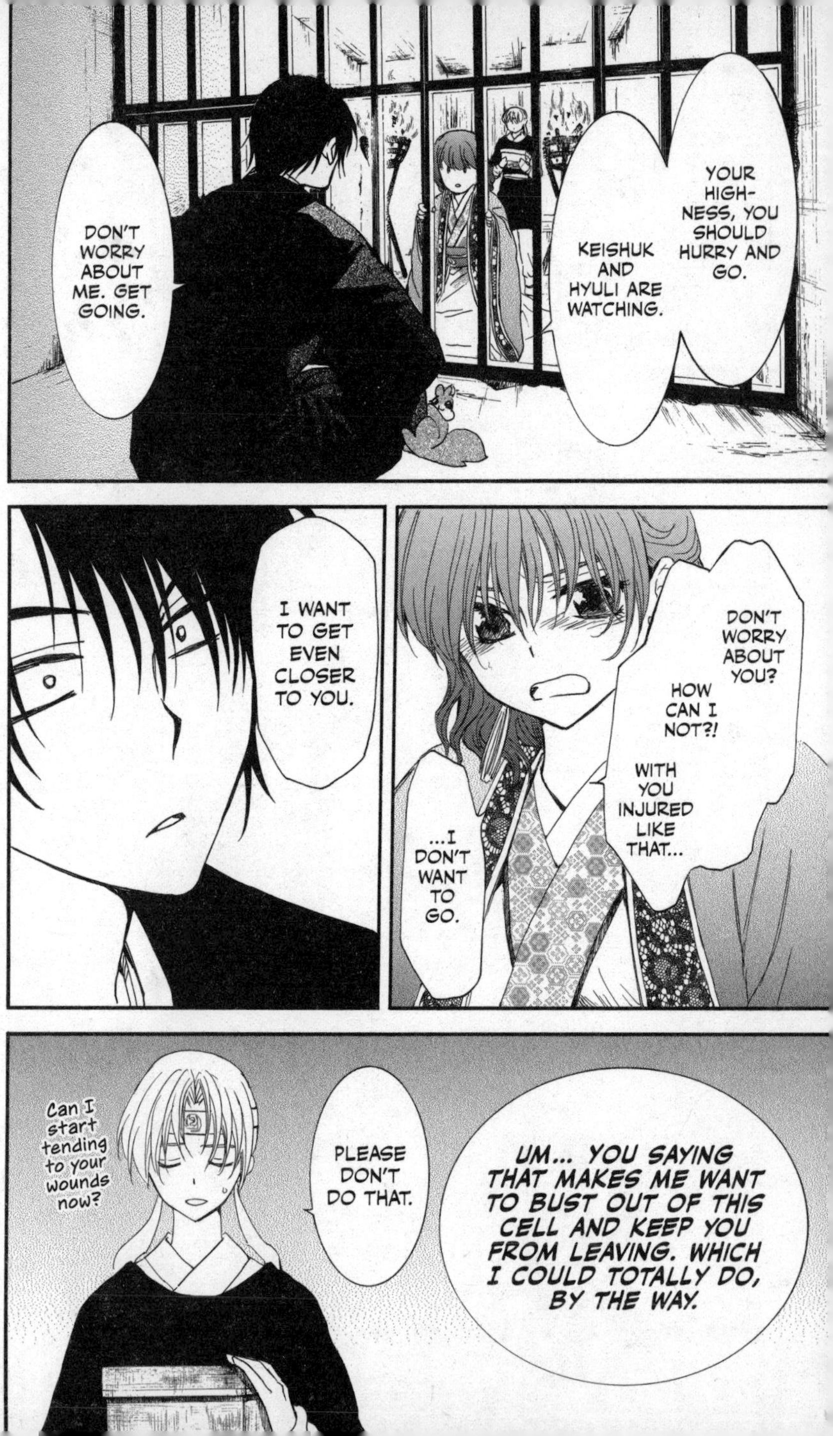
YOUR HIGHNESS, YOU SHOULD HURRY AND GO.
KEISHUK AND HYULI ARE WATCHING.
DON'T WORRY ABOUT ME. GET GOING.
DON'T WORRY ABOUT YOU?
HOW CAN I NOT?!
WITH YOU INJURED LIKE THAT...
...I DON'T WANT TO GO.
I WANT TO GET EVEN CLOSER TO YOU.
UM... YOU SAYING THAT MAKES ME WANT TO BUST OUT OF THIS CELL AND KEEP YOU FROM LEAVING. WHICH I COULD TOTALLY DO, BY THE WAY.
PLEASE DON'T DO THAT.
Can I start tending to your wounds now?

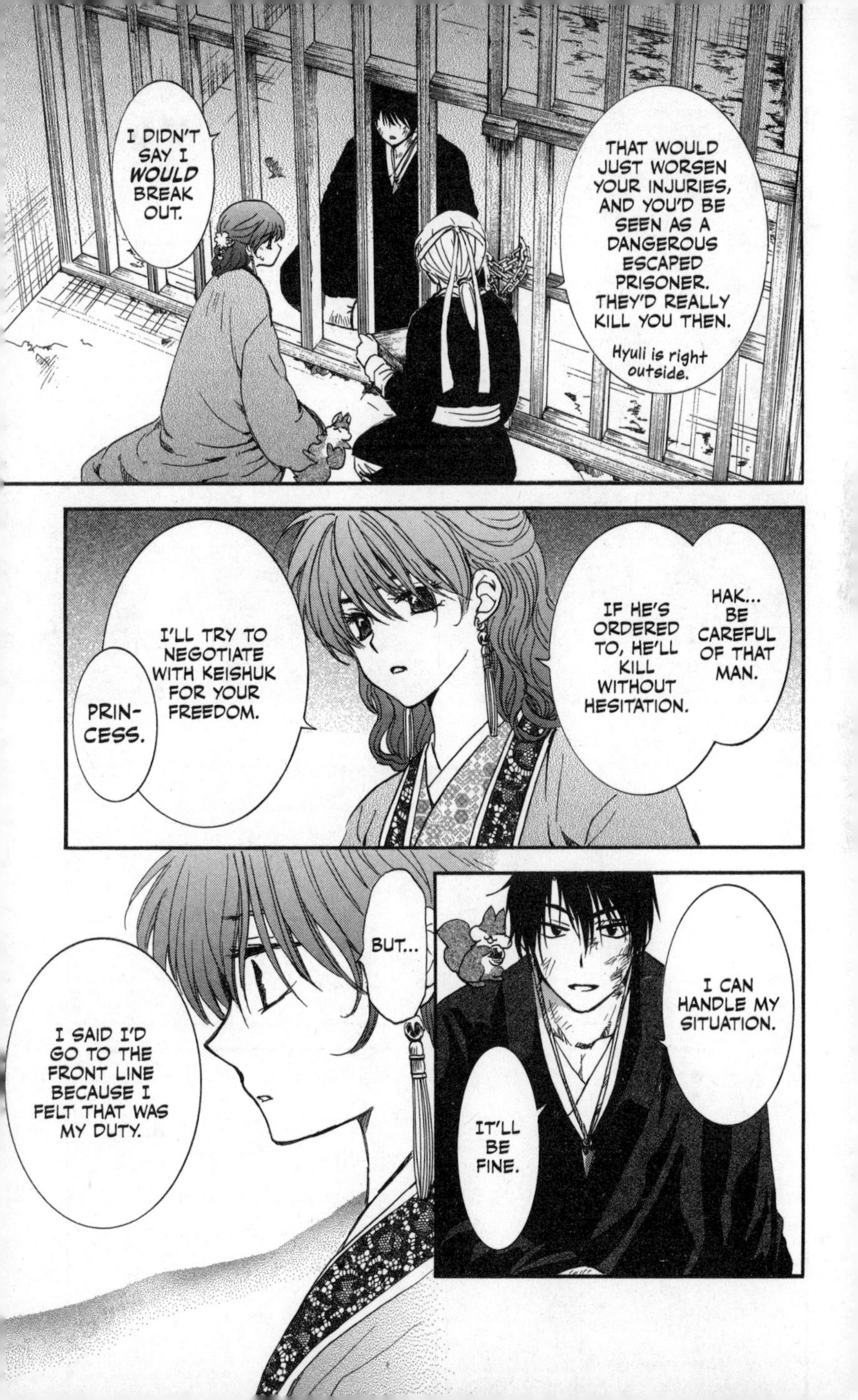
THAT WOULD JUST WORSEN YOUR INJURIES, AND YOU'D BE SEEN AS A DANGEROUS ESCAPED PRISONER. THEY'D REALLY KILL YOU THEN.
Hyuli is right outside.
I DIDN'T SAY I WOULD BREAK OUT.
HAK... BE CAREFUL OF THAT MAN.
IF HE'S ORDERED TO, HE'LL KILL WITHOUT HESITATION.
I'LL TRY TO NEGOTIATE WITH KEISHUK FOR YOUR FREEDOM.
PRIN-CESS.
I CAN HANDLE MY SITUATION.
IT'LL BE FINE.
BUT...
I SAID I'D GO TO THE FRONT LINE BECAUSE I FELT THAT WAS MY DUTY.

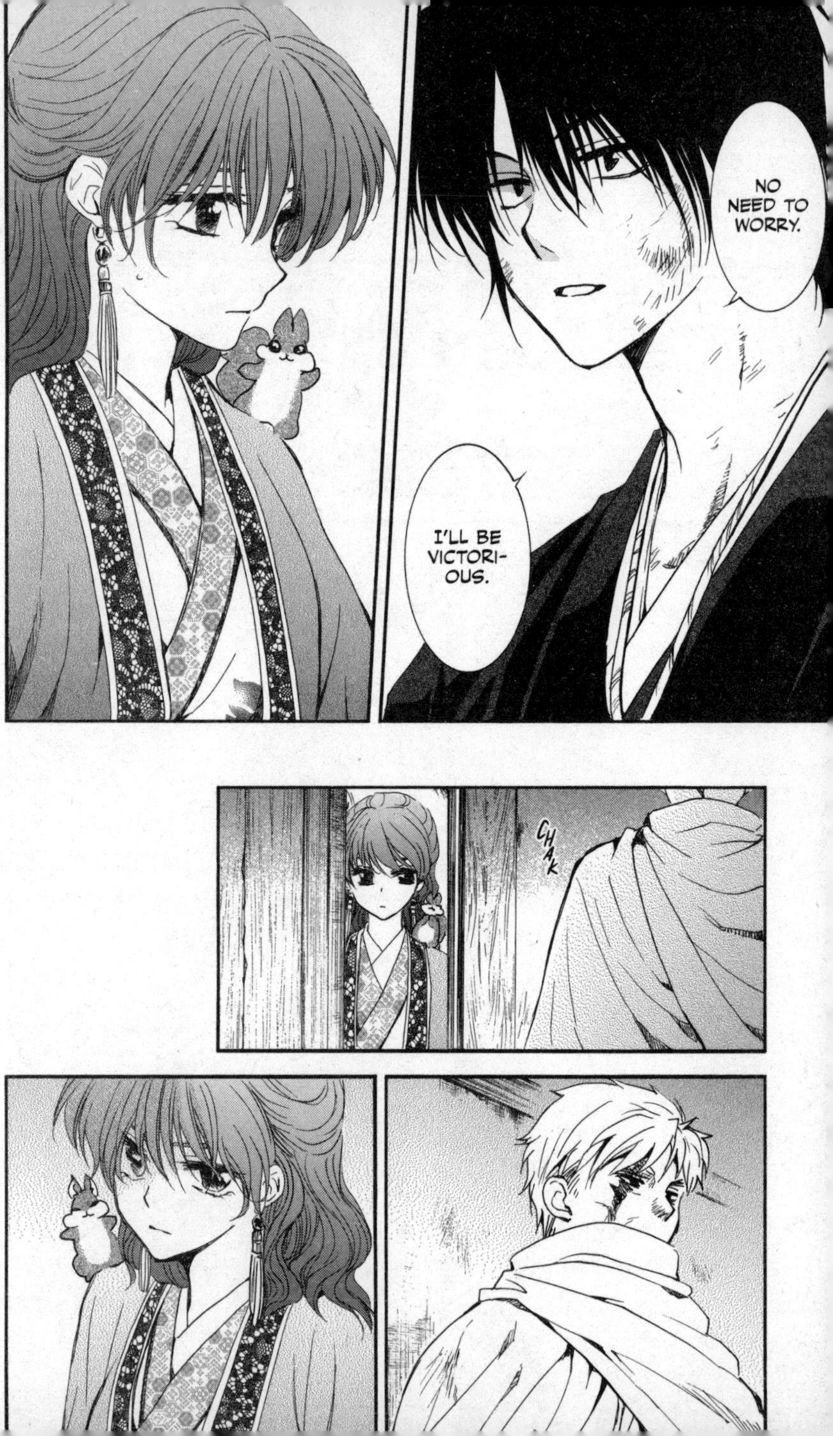
NO NEED TO WORRY.
I'LL BE VICTORI-OUS.
CHAK

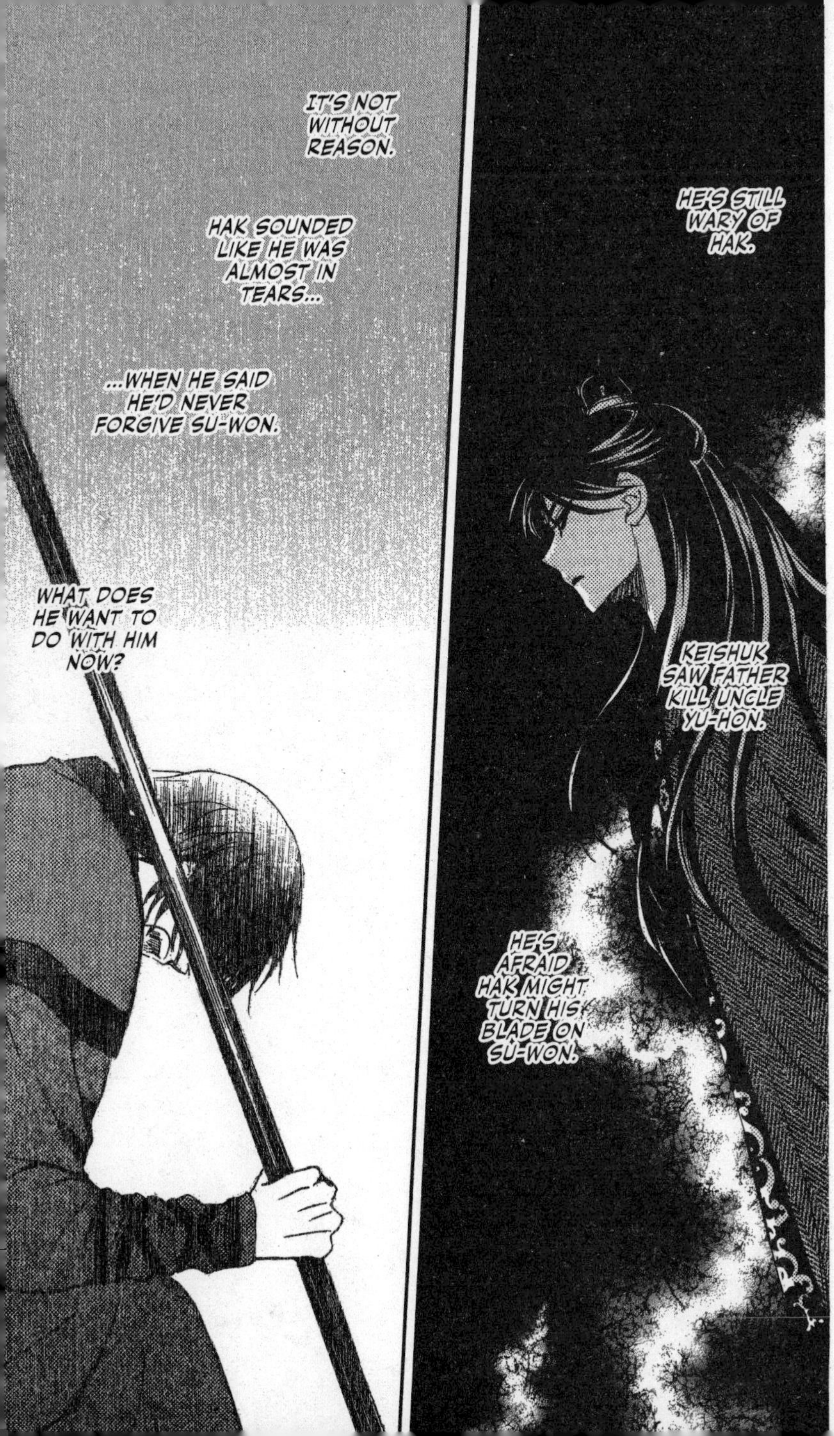
HE'S STILL WARY OF HAK.
KEISHUK SAW FATHER KILL UNCLE YU-HON.
HE'S AFRAID HAK MIGHT TURN HIS BLADE ON SU-WON.
IT'S NOT WITHOUT REASON.
HAK SOUNDED LIKE HE WAS ALMOST IN TEARS...
...WHEN HE SAID HE'D NEVER FORGIVE SU-WON.
WHAT DOES HE WANT TO DO WITH HIM NOW?

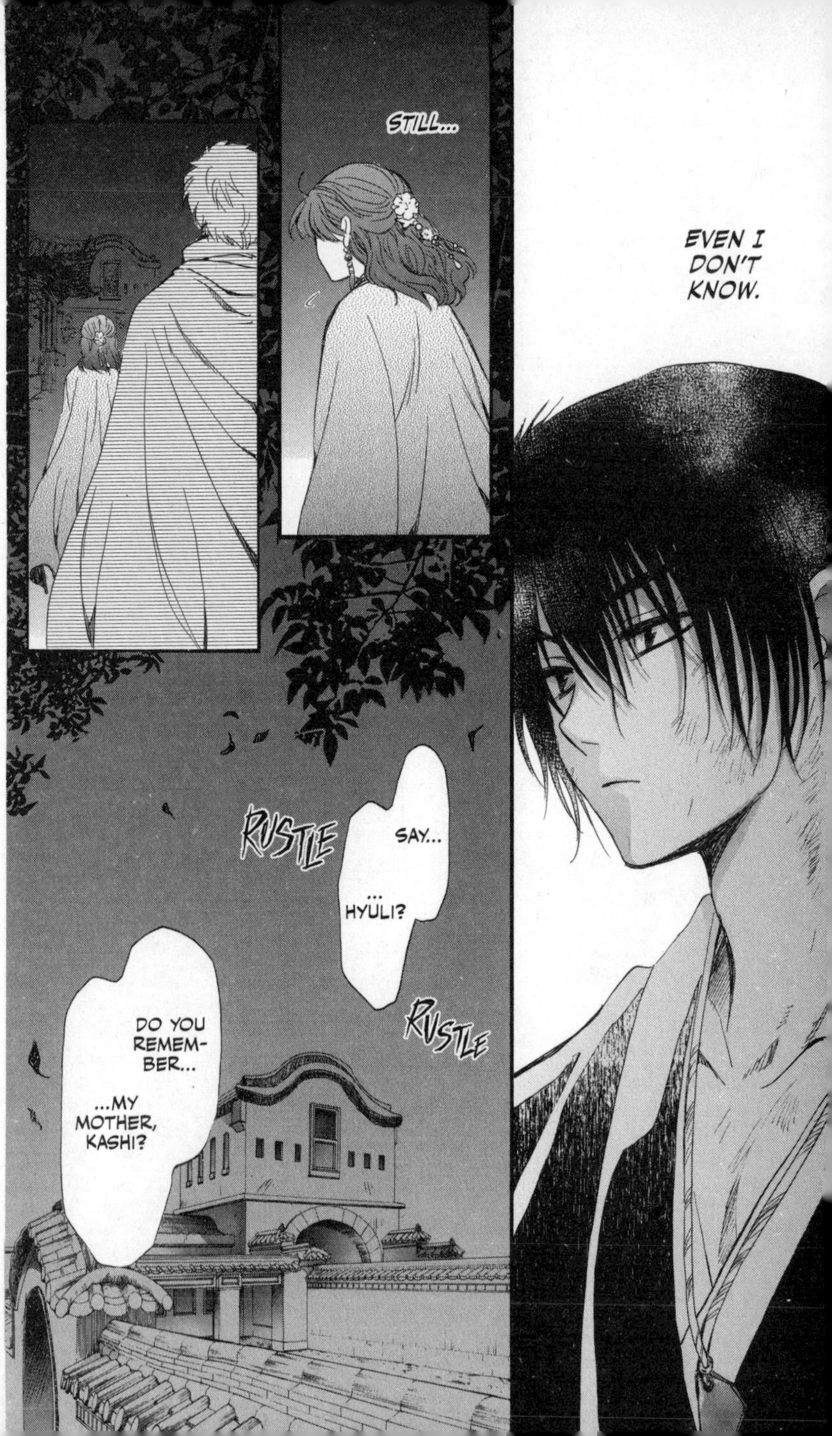
EVEN I DON'T KNOW.
STILL...
RUSTLE
SAY...
...HYULI?
RUSTLE
DO YOU REMEMBER...
...MY MOTHER, KASHI?

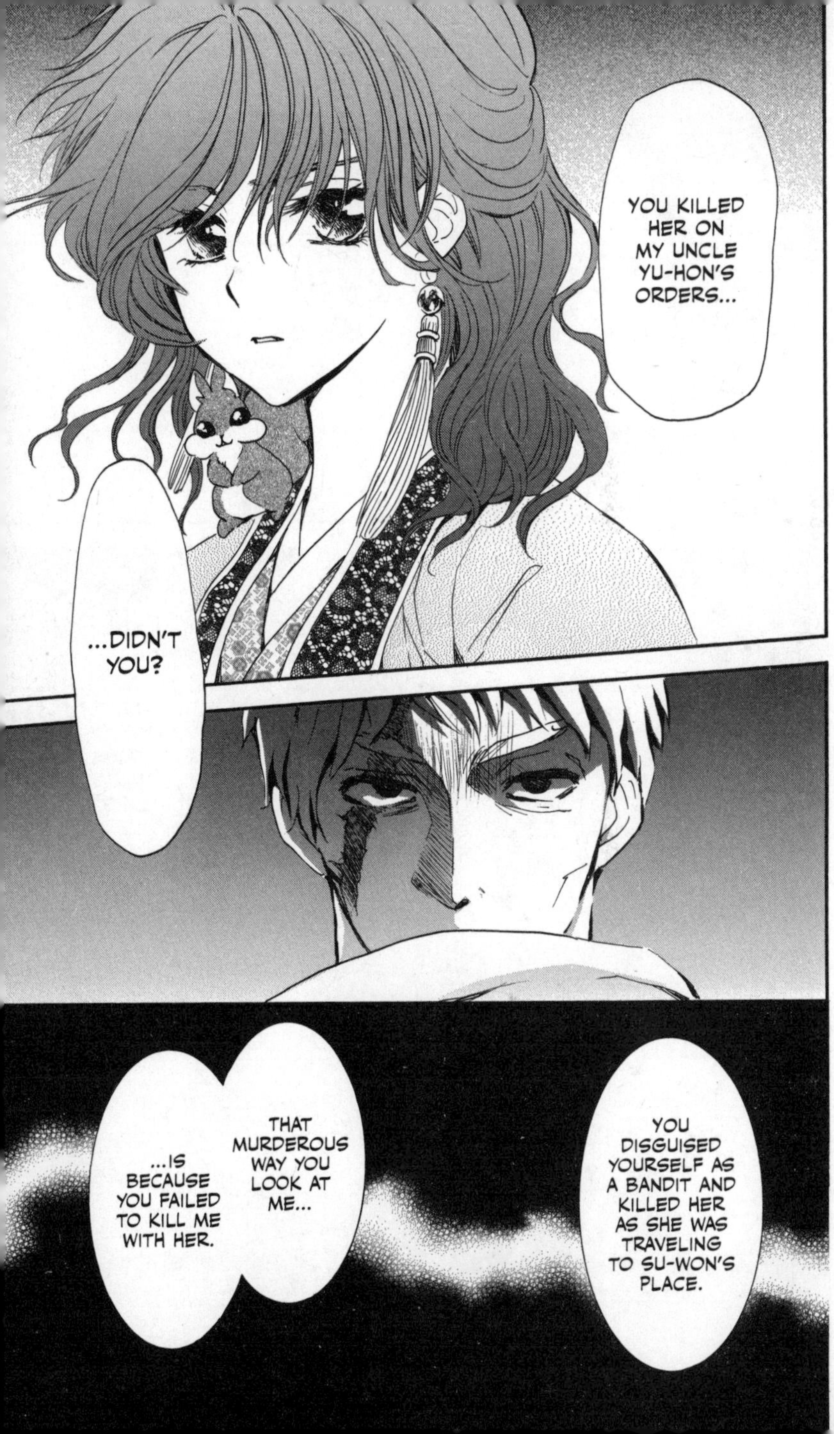
YOU KILLED HER ON MY UNCLE YU-HON'S ORDERS...
...DIDN'T YOU?
YOU DISGUISED YOURSELF AS A BANDIT AND KILLED HER AS SHE WAS TRAVELING TO SU-WON'S PLACE.
THAT MURDEROUS WAY YOU LOOK AT ME...
...IS BECAUSE YOU FAILED TO KILL ME WITH HER.

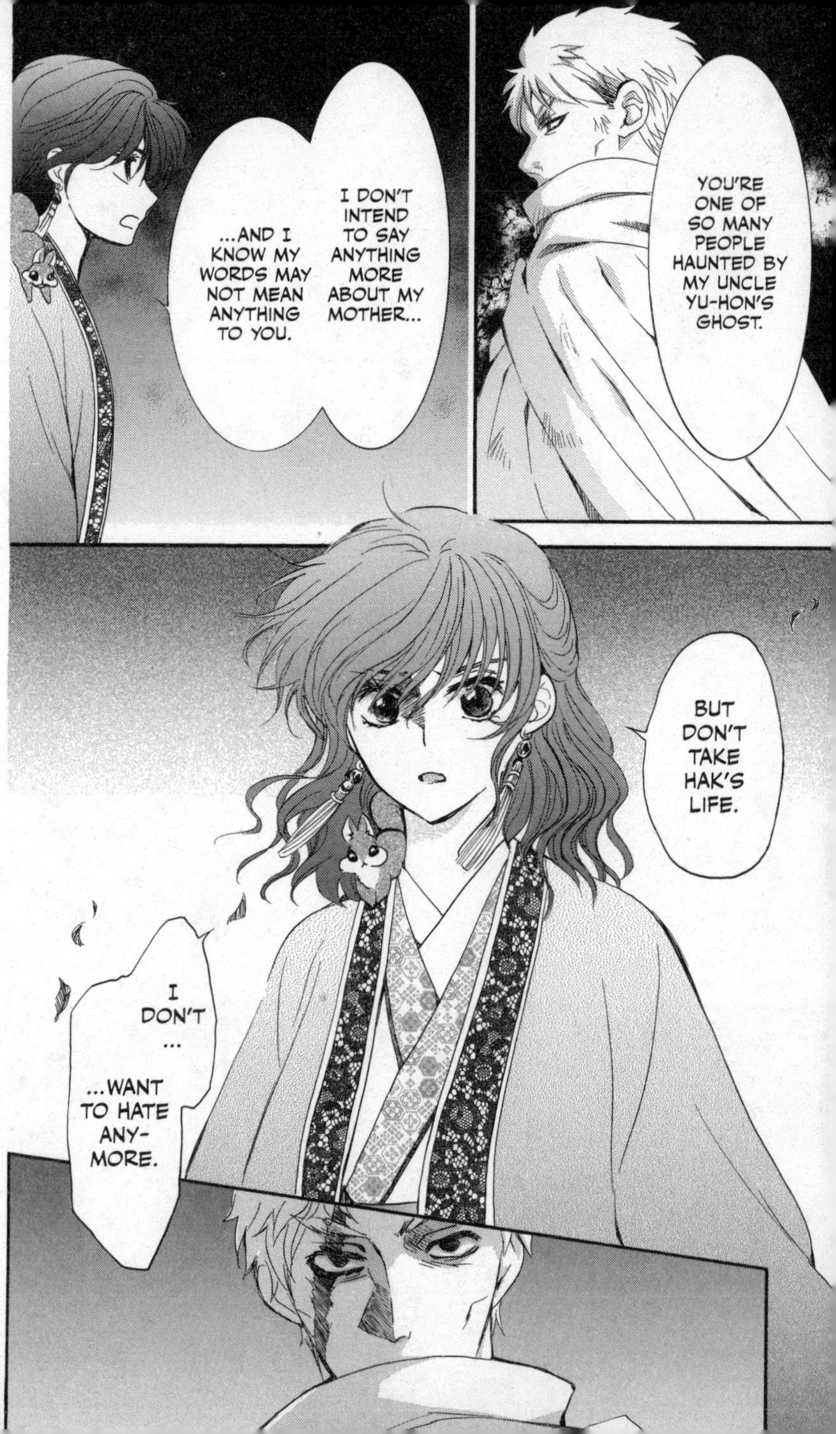
YOU'RE ONE OF SO MANY PEOPLE HAUNTED BY MY UNCLE YU-HON'S GHOST.
I DON'T INTEND TO SAY ANYTHING MORE ABOUT MY MOTHER...
...AND I KNOW MY WORDS MAY NOT MEAN ANYTHING TO YOU.
BUT DON'T TAKE HAK'S LIFE.
I DON'T ...
...WANT TO HATE ANY-MORE.

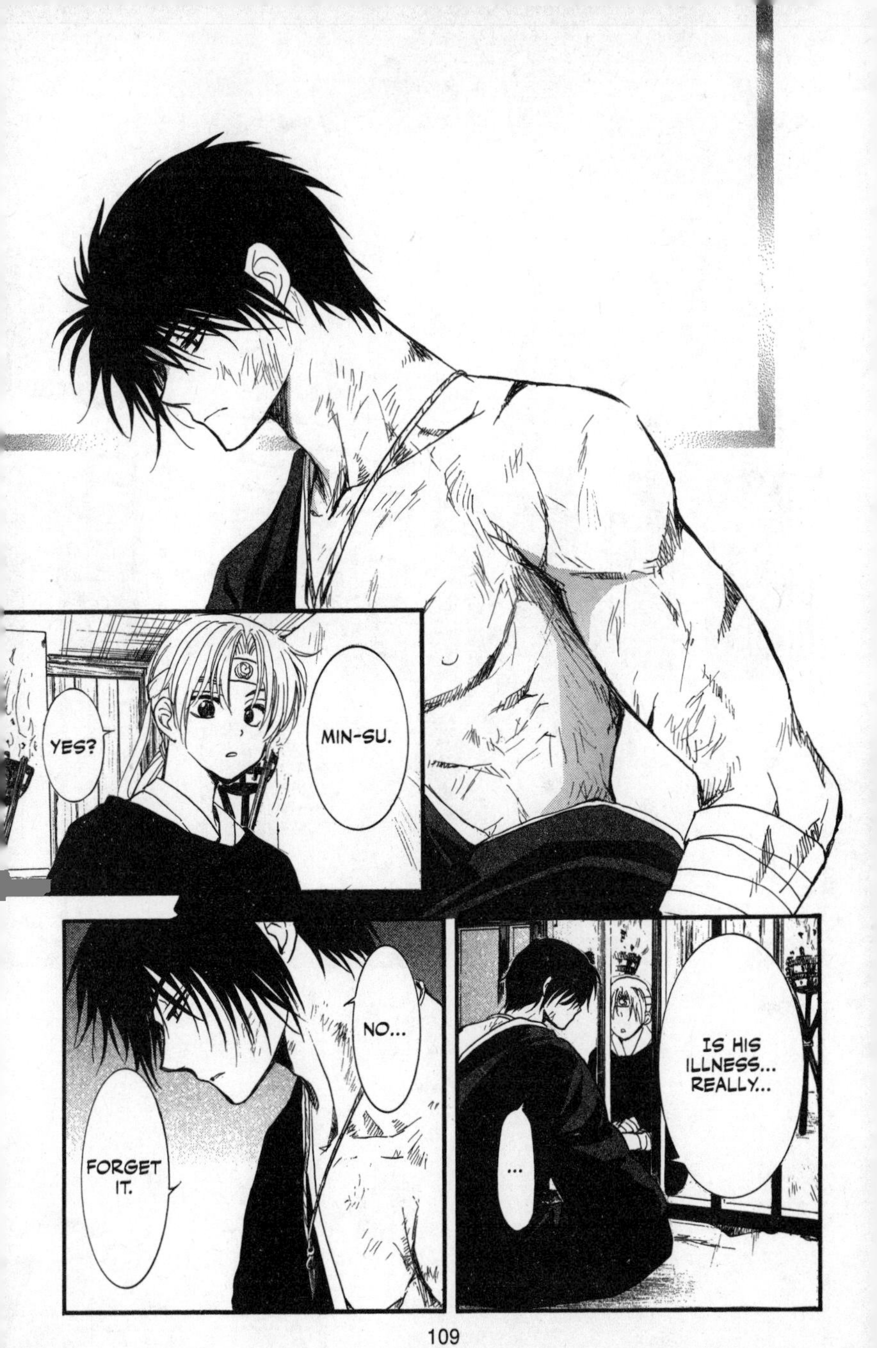
MIN-SU.
YES?
IS HIS ILLNESS... REALLY...
...
NO...
FORGET IT.

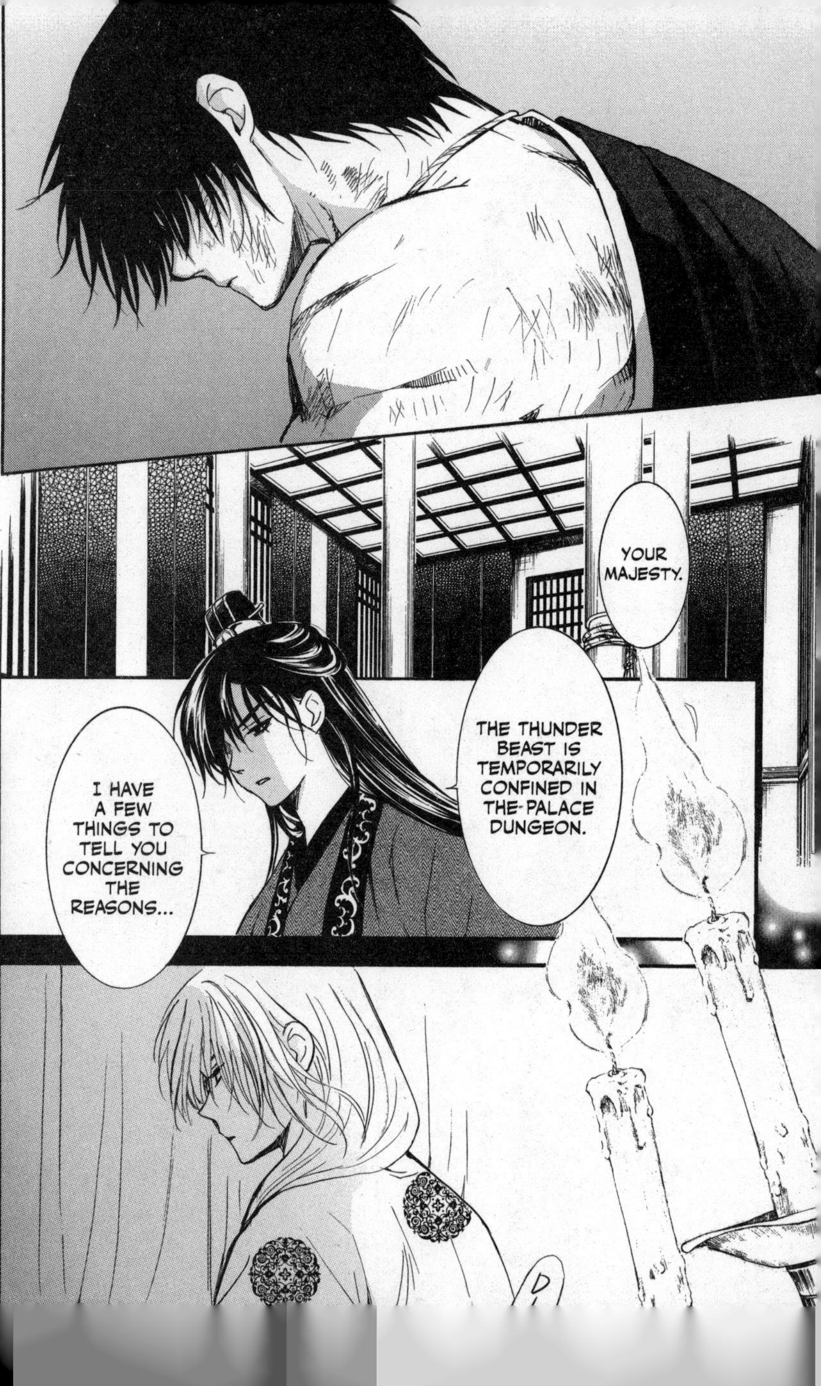
YOUR MAJESTY.
THE THUNDER BEAST IS TEMPORARILY CONFINED IN THE-PALACE DUNGEON.
I HAVE A FEW THINGS TO TELL YOU CONCERNING THE REASONS...

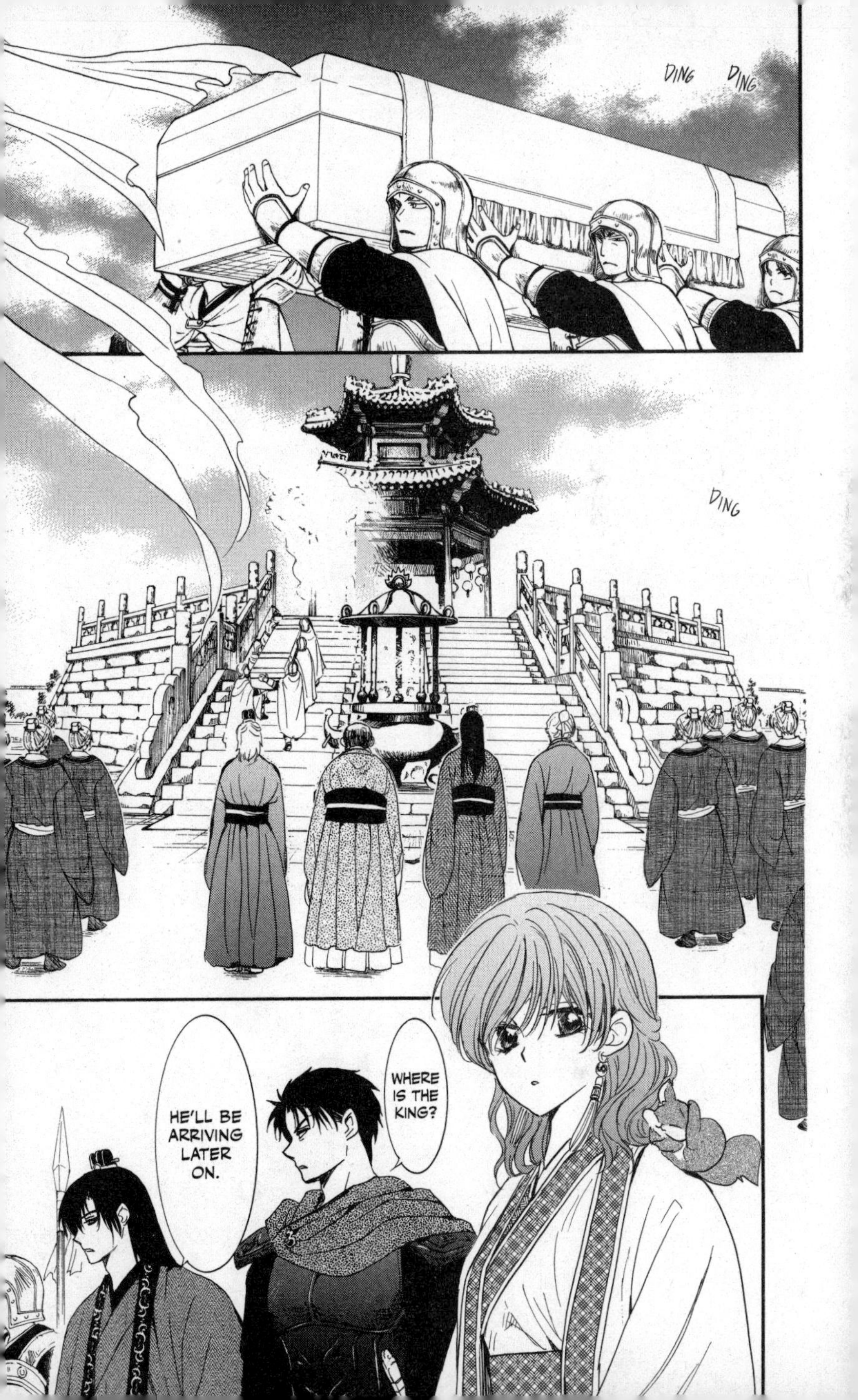
DING DING
DING
WHERE IS THE KING?
HE'LL BE ARRIVING LATER ON.

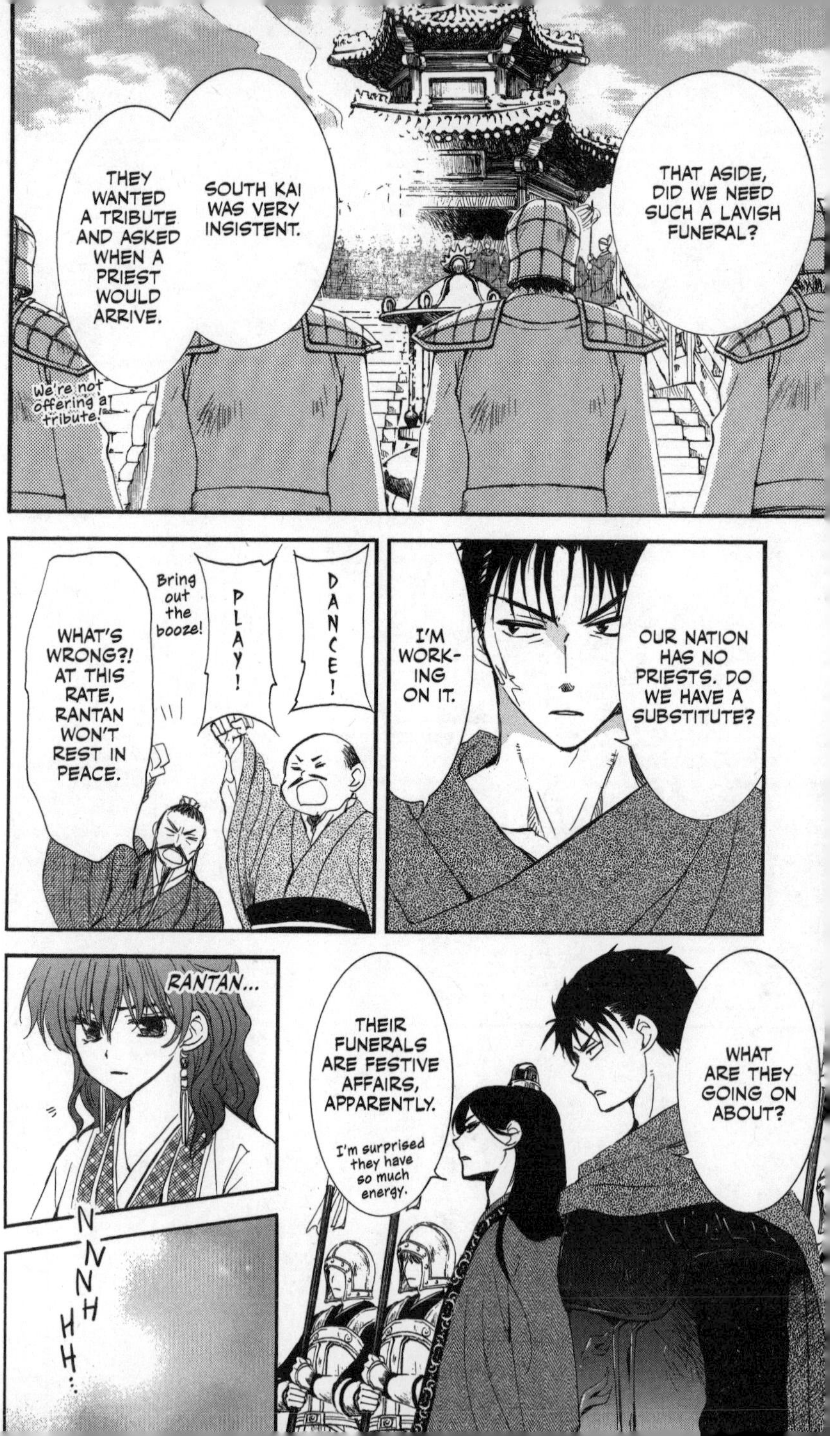
THAT ASIDE, DID WE NEED SUCH A LAVISH FUNERAL?
SOUTH KAI WAS VERY INSISTENT.
THEY WANTED A TRIBUTE AND ASKED WHEN A PRIEST WOULD ARRIVE.
We're not offering a tribute!
OUR NATION HAS NO PRIESTS. DO WE HAVE A SUBSTITUTE?
I'M WORKING-ING ON IT.
DANCE!
PLAY!
Bring out the booze!
WHAT'S WRONG?! AT THIS RATE, RANTAN WON'T REST IN PEACE.
WHAT ARE THEY GOING ON ABOUT?
THEIR FUNERALS ARE FESTIVE AFFAIRS, APPARENTLY.
I'm surprised they have so much energy.
RANTAN...
NNNHHH...

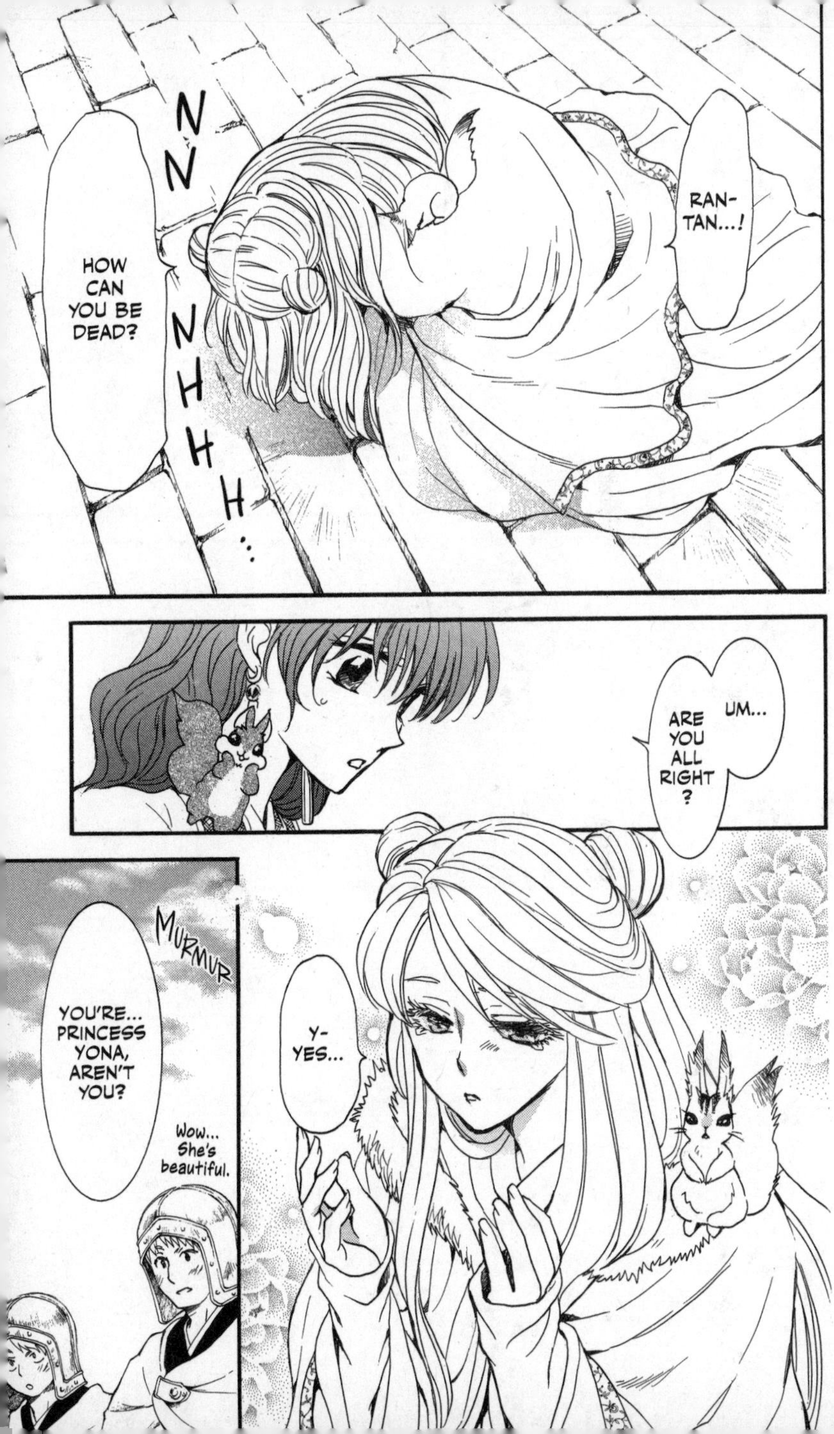
RAN-TAN...!
NNNHHH...
HOW CAN YOU BE DEAD?
UM... ARE YOU ALL RIGHT?
Y-YES...
MURMUR
YOU'RE... PRINCESS YONA, AREN'T YOU?
Wow... She's beautiful.

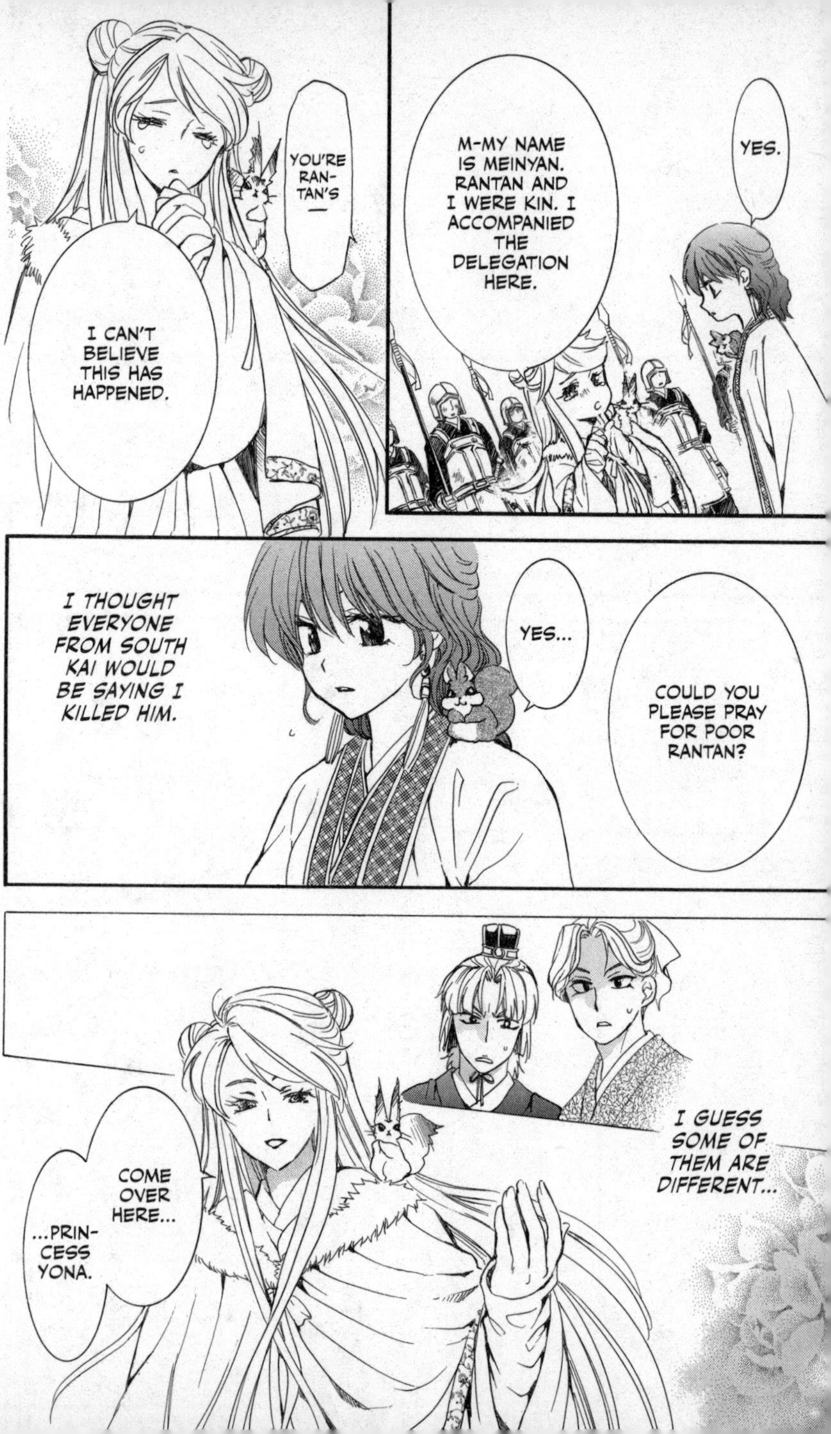
YES.
M-MY NAME IS MEINYAN. RANTAN AND I WERE KIN. I ACCOMPANIED THE DELEGATION HERE.
YOU'RE RAN-TAN'S —
I CAN'T BELIEVE THIS HAS HAPPENED.
COULD YOU PLEASE PRAY FOR POOR RANTAN?
YES...
I THOUGHT EVERYONE FROM SOUTH KAI WOULD BE SAYING I KILLED HIM.
I GUESS SOME OF THEM ARE DIFFERENT...
COME OVER HERE...
...PRIN-CESS YONA.

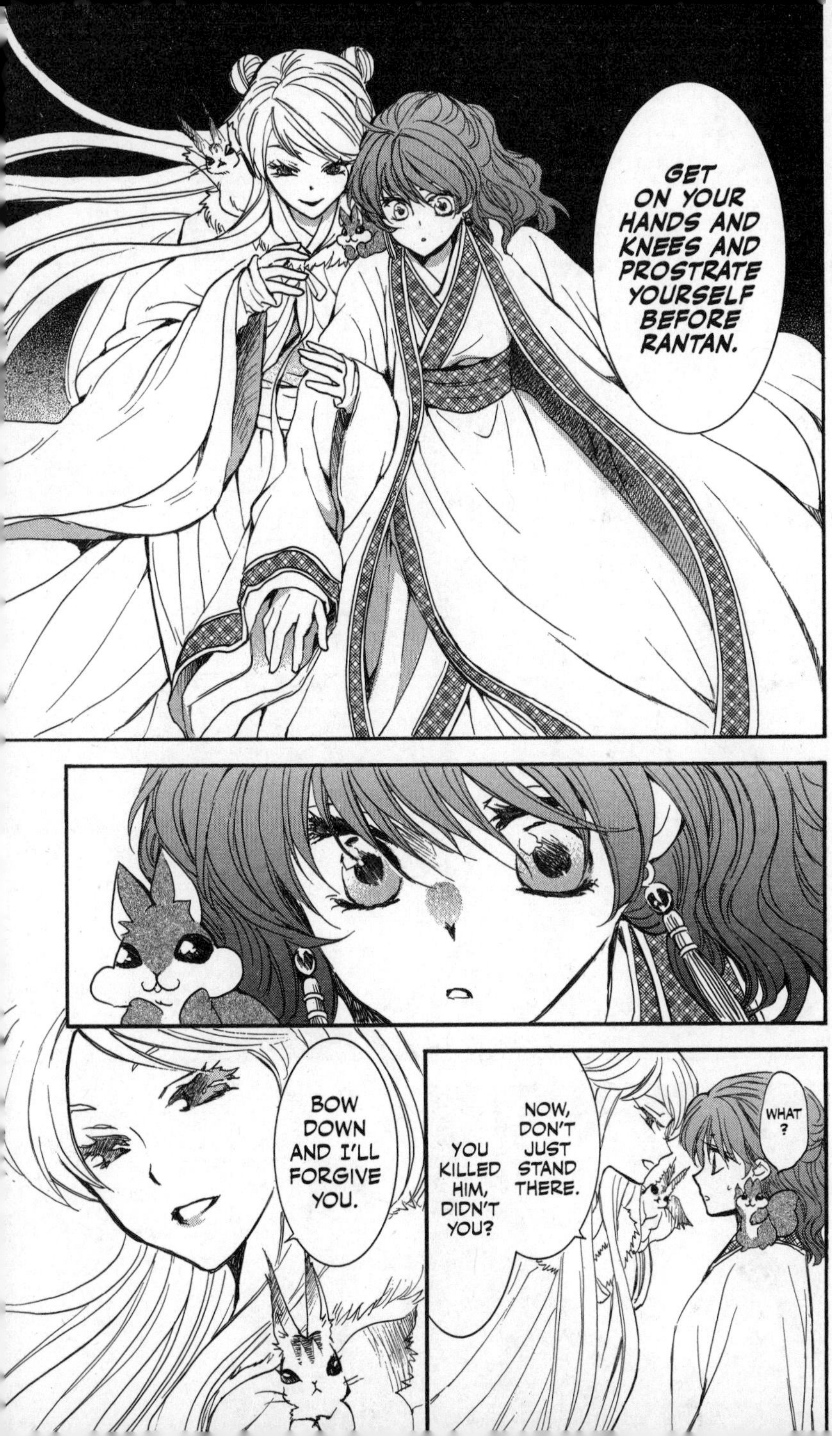
GET ON YOUR HANDS AND KNEES AND PROSTRATE YOURSELF BEFORE RANTAN.
WHAT?
NOW, DON'T JUST STAND THERE.
YOU KILLED HIM, DIDN'T YOU?
BOW DOWN AND I'LL FORGIVE YOU.

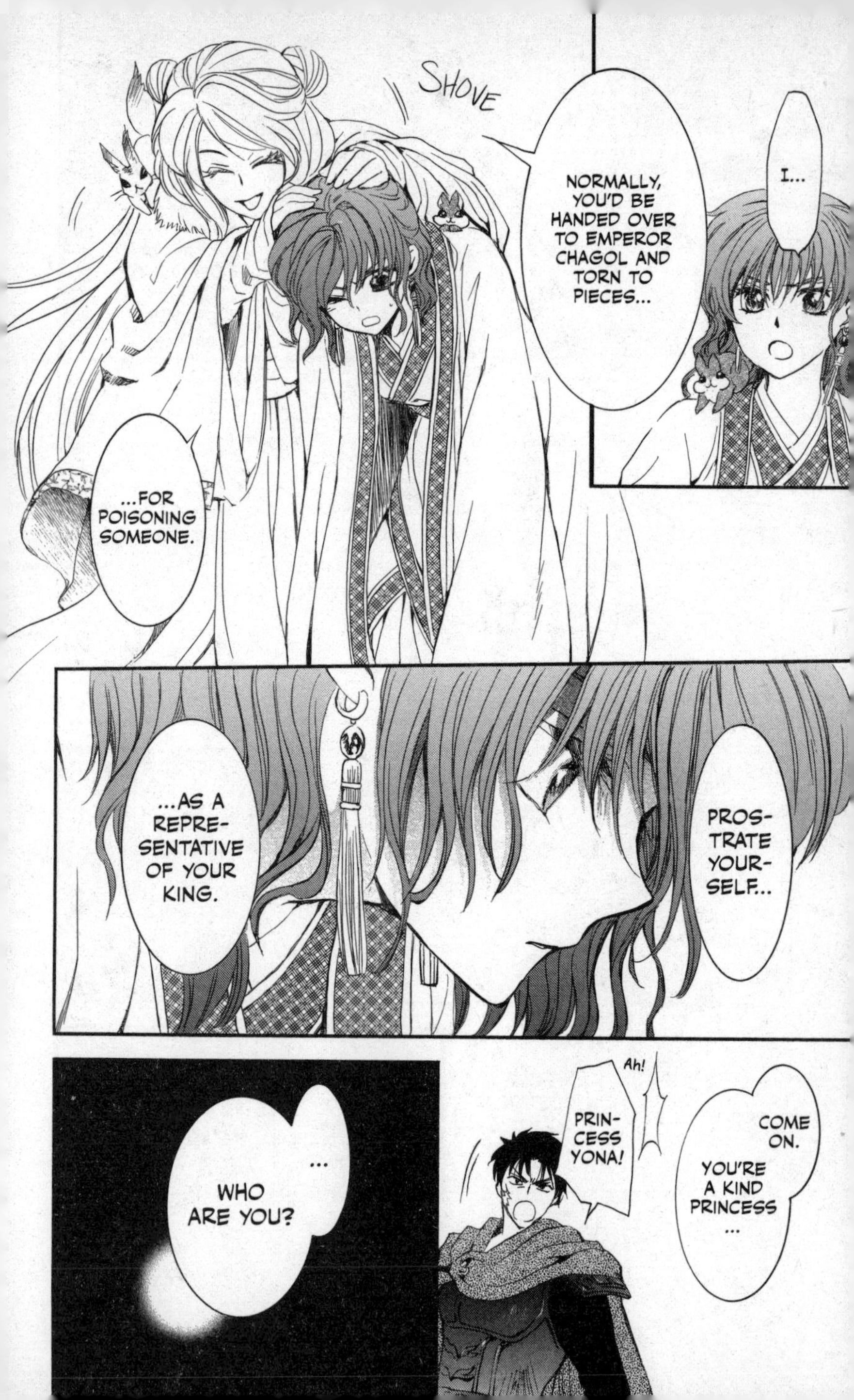
I...
SHOVE
NORMALLY, YOU'D BE HANDED OVER TO EMPEROR CHAGOL AND TORN TO PIECES...
...FOR POISONING SOMEONE.
PROS-TRATE YOUR-SELF...
...AS A REPRE-SENTATIVE OF YOUR KING.
COME ON. YOU'RE A KIND PRINCESS ...
Ah!
PRIN-CESS YONA!
... WHO ARE YOU?

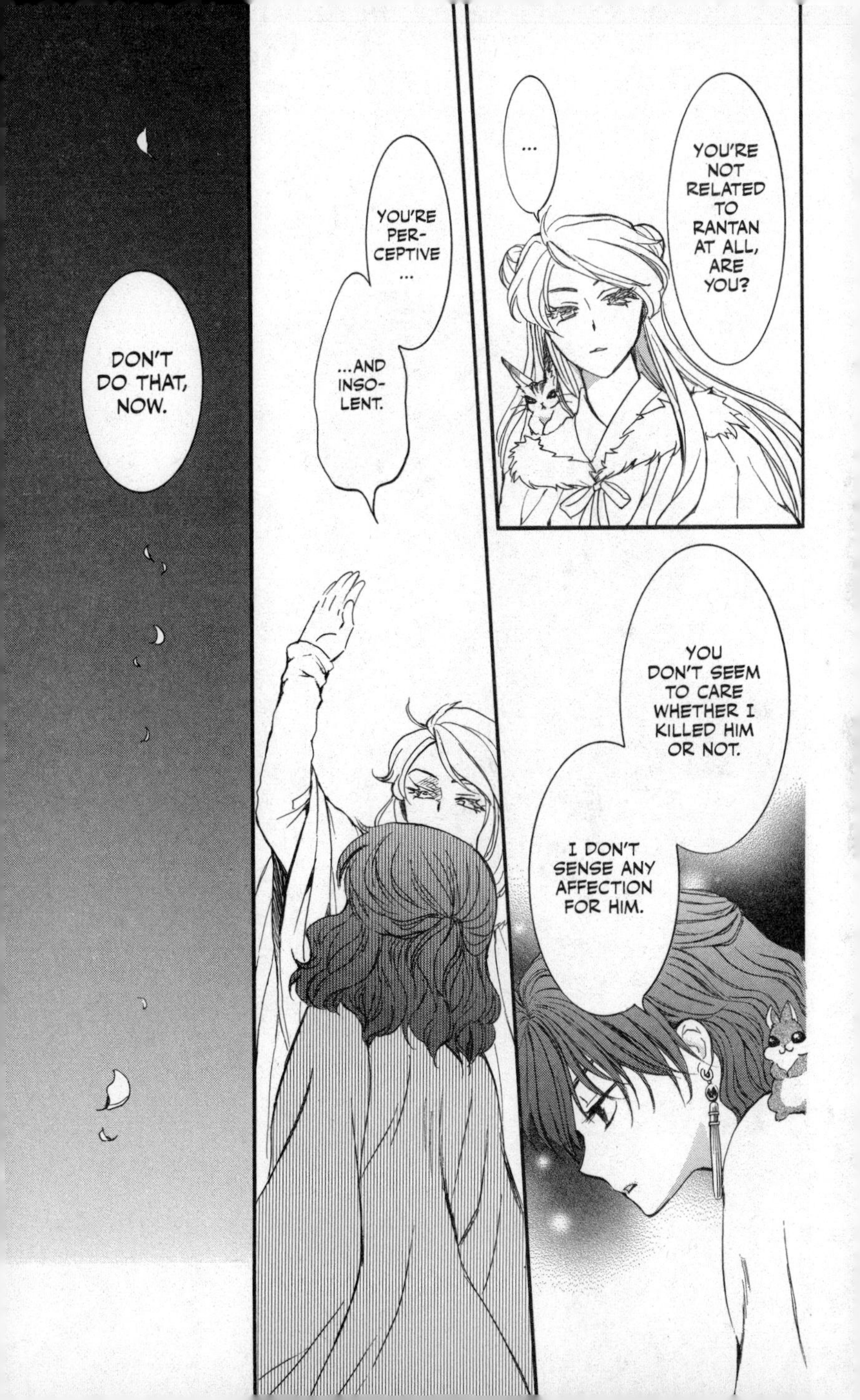
YOU'RE NOT RELATED TO RANTAN AT ALL, ARE YOU?
...
YOU DON'T SEEM TO CARE WHETHER I KILLED HIM OR NOT.
I DON'T SENSE ANY AFFECTION FOR HIM.
YOU'RE PER-CEPTIVE ...
...AND INSO-LENT.
DON'T DO THAT, NOW.

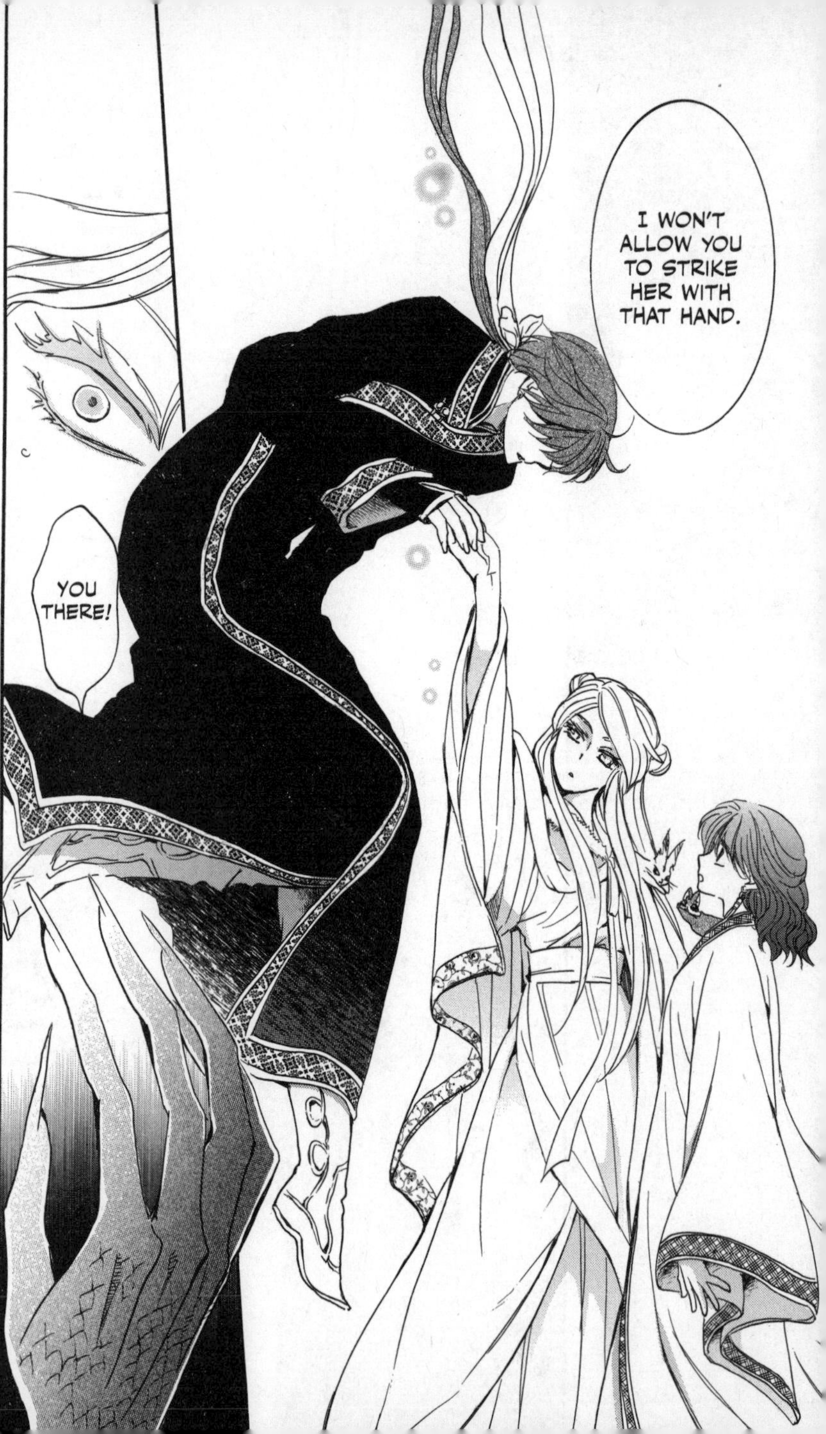
I WON'T ALLOW YOU TO STRIKE HER WITH THAT HAND.
YOU THERE!

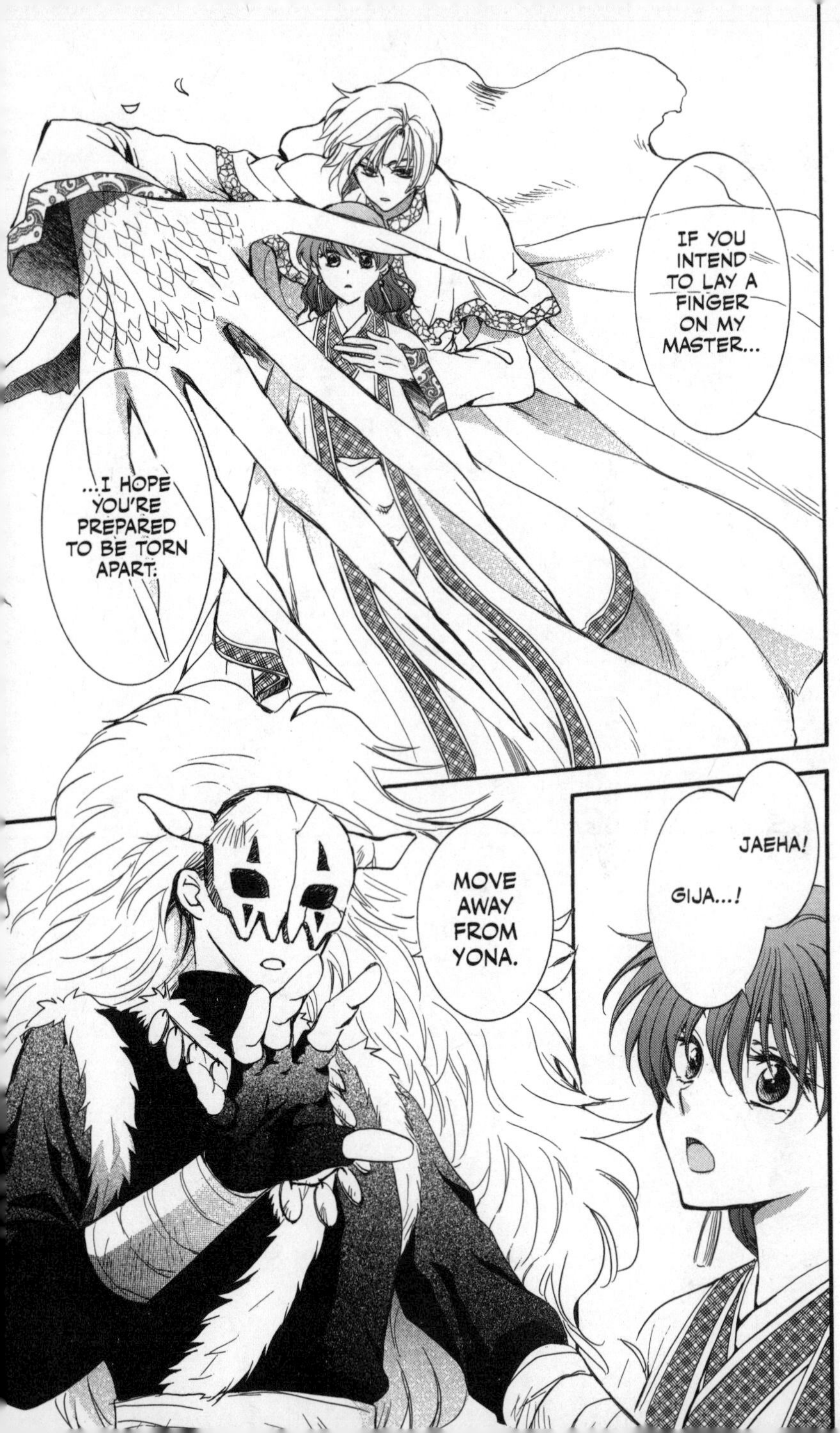
IF YOU INTEND TO LAY A FINGER ON MY MASTER...
...I HOPE YOU'RE PREPARED TO BE TORN APART.
JAEHA!
GIJA...!
MOVE AWAY FROM YONA.

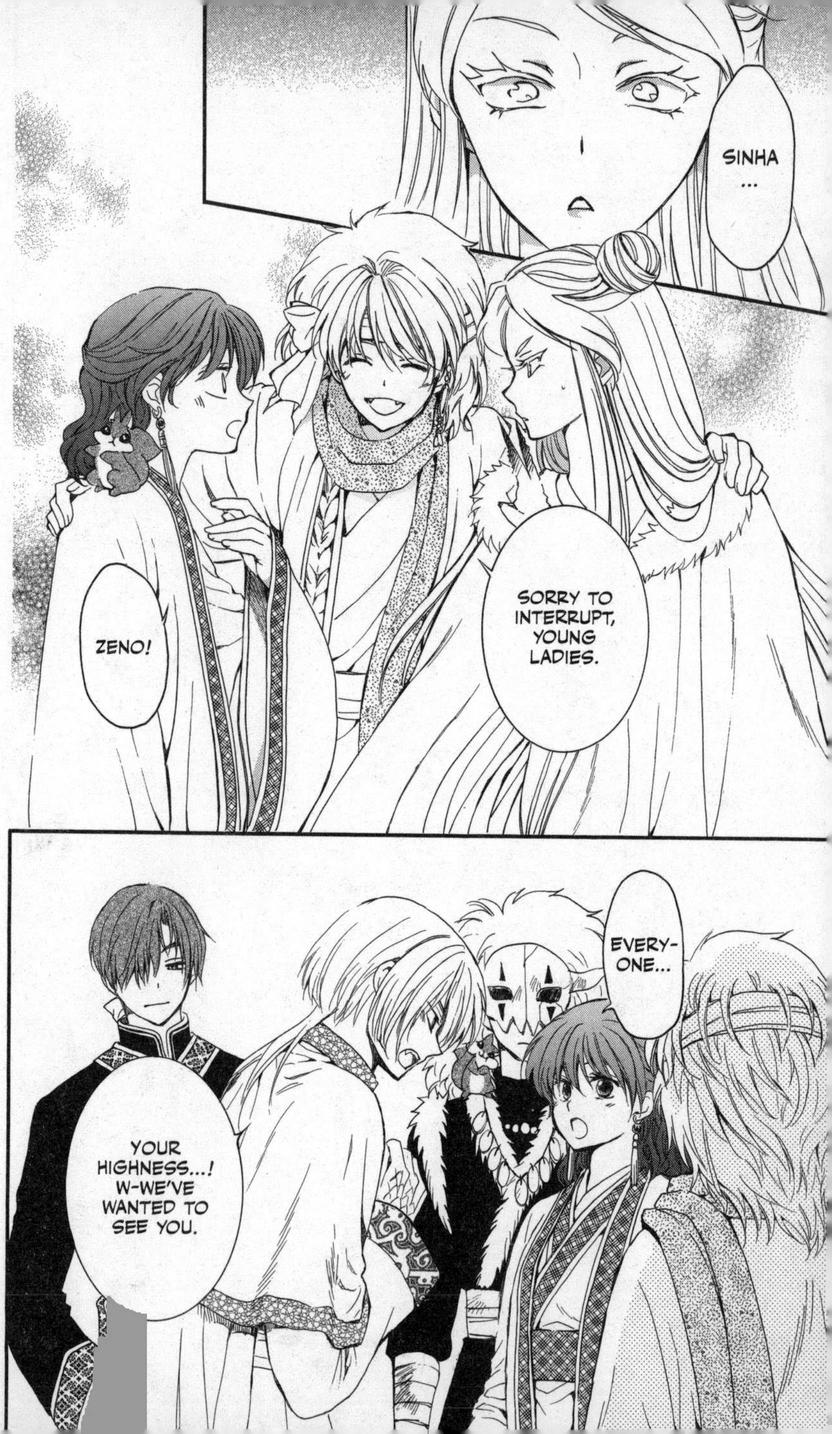
SINHA ...
SORRY TO INTERRUPT, YOUNG LADIES.
ZENO!
EVERY-ONE...
YOUR HIGHNESS...! W-WE'VE WANTED TO SEE YOU.

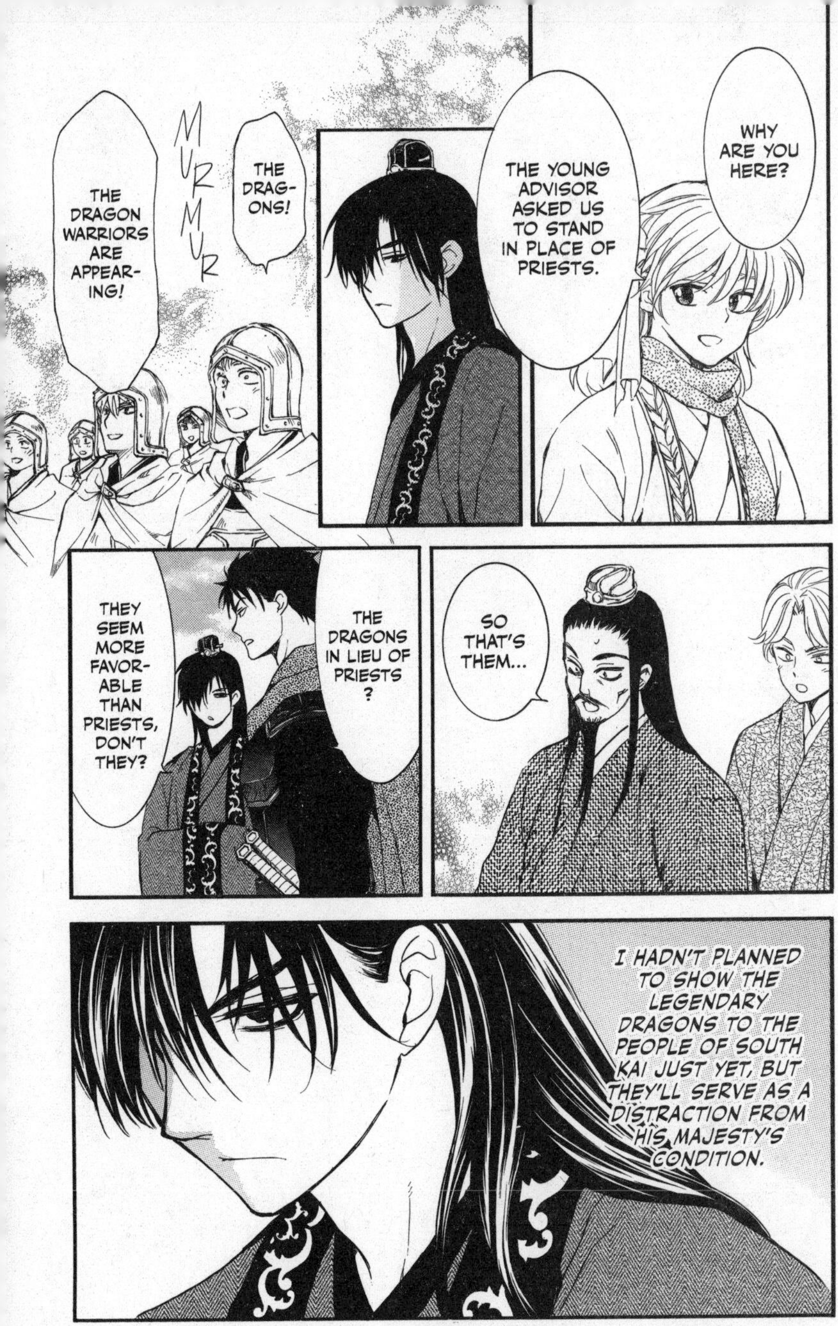
WHY ARE YOU HERE?
THE YOUNG ADVISOR ASKED US TO STAND IN PLACE OF PRIESTS.
THE DRAGONS!
MURMUR
THE DRAGON WARRIORS ARE APPEARING!
SO THAT'S THEM...
THE DRAGONS IN LIEU OF PRIESTS?
THEY SEEM MORE FAVORABLE THAN PRIESTS, DON'T THEY?
I HADN'T PLANNED TO SHOW THE LEGENDARY DRAGONS TO THE PEOPLE OF SOUTH KAI JUST YET, BUT THEY'LL SERVE AS A DISTRACTION FROM HIS MAJESTY'S CONDITION.

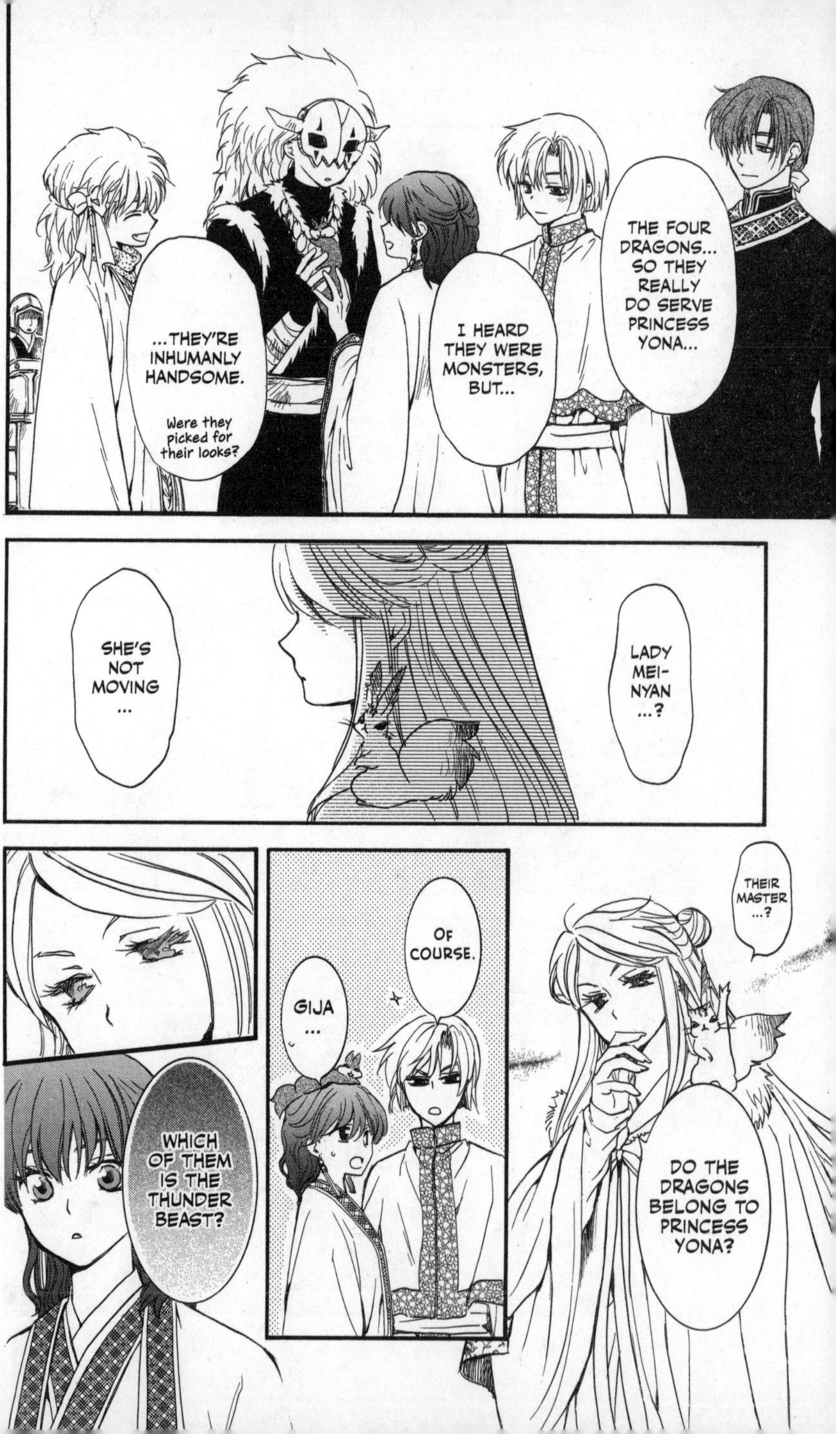
THE FOUR DRAGONS... SO THEY REALLY DO SERVE PRINCESS YONA...
I HEARD THEY WERE MONSTERS, BUT...
...THEY'RE INHUMANLY HANDSOME.
Were they picked for their looks?
LADY MEI-NYAN ...?
SHE'S NOT MOVING ...
THEIR MASTER ...?
DO THE DRAGONS BELONG TO PRINCESS YONA?
OF COURSE.
GIJA ...
WHICH OF THEM IS THE THUNDER BEAST?

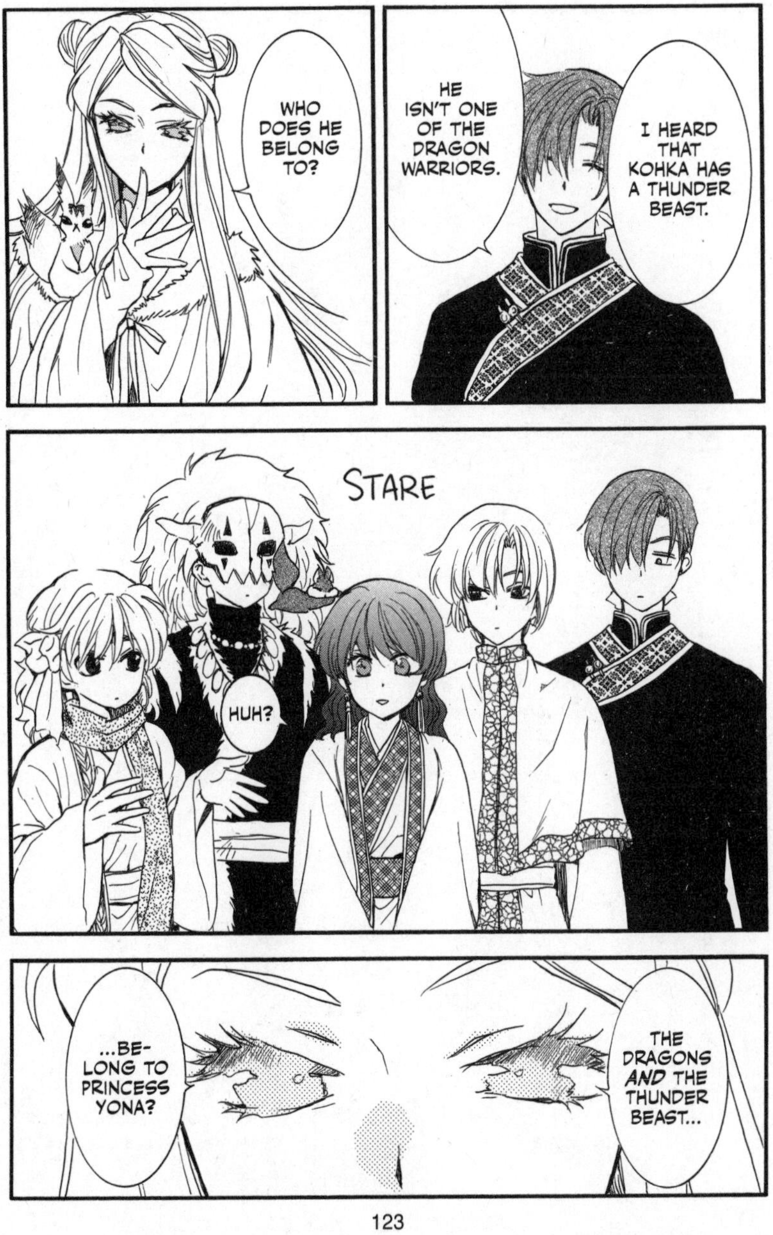
I HEARD THAT KOHKA HAS A THUNDER BEAST.
HE ISN'T ONE OF THE DRAGON WARRIORS.
WHO DOES HE BELONG TO?
STARE
HUH?
THE DRAGONS *AND* THE THUNDER BEAST...
...BE-LONG TO PRINCESS YONA?

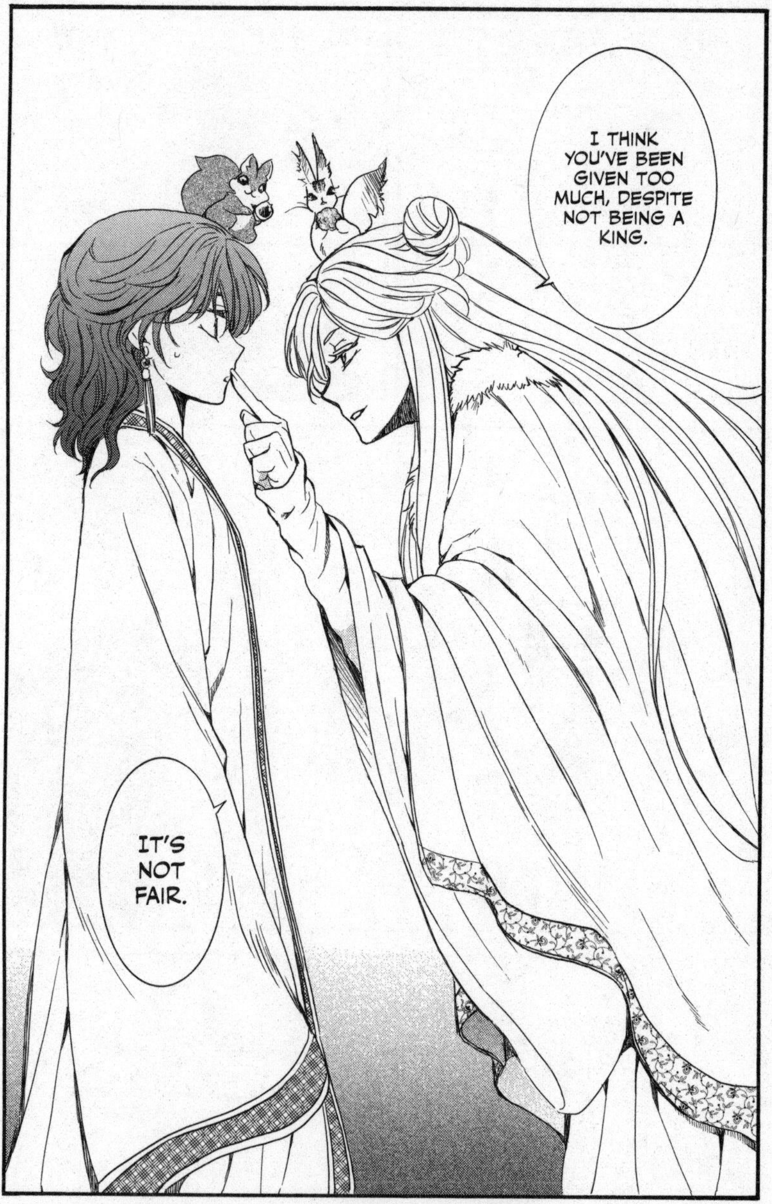
I THINK YOU'VE BEEN GIVEN TOO MUCH, DESPITE NOT BEING A KING.
IT'S NOT FAIR.

CHAPTER 202 / THE END

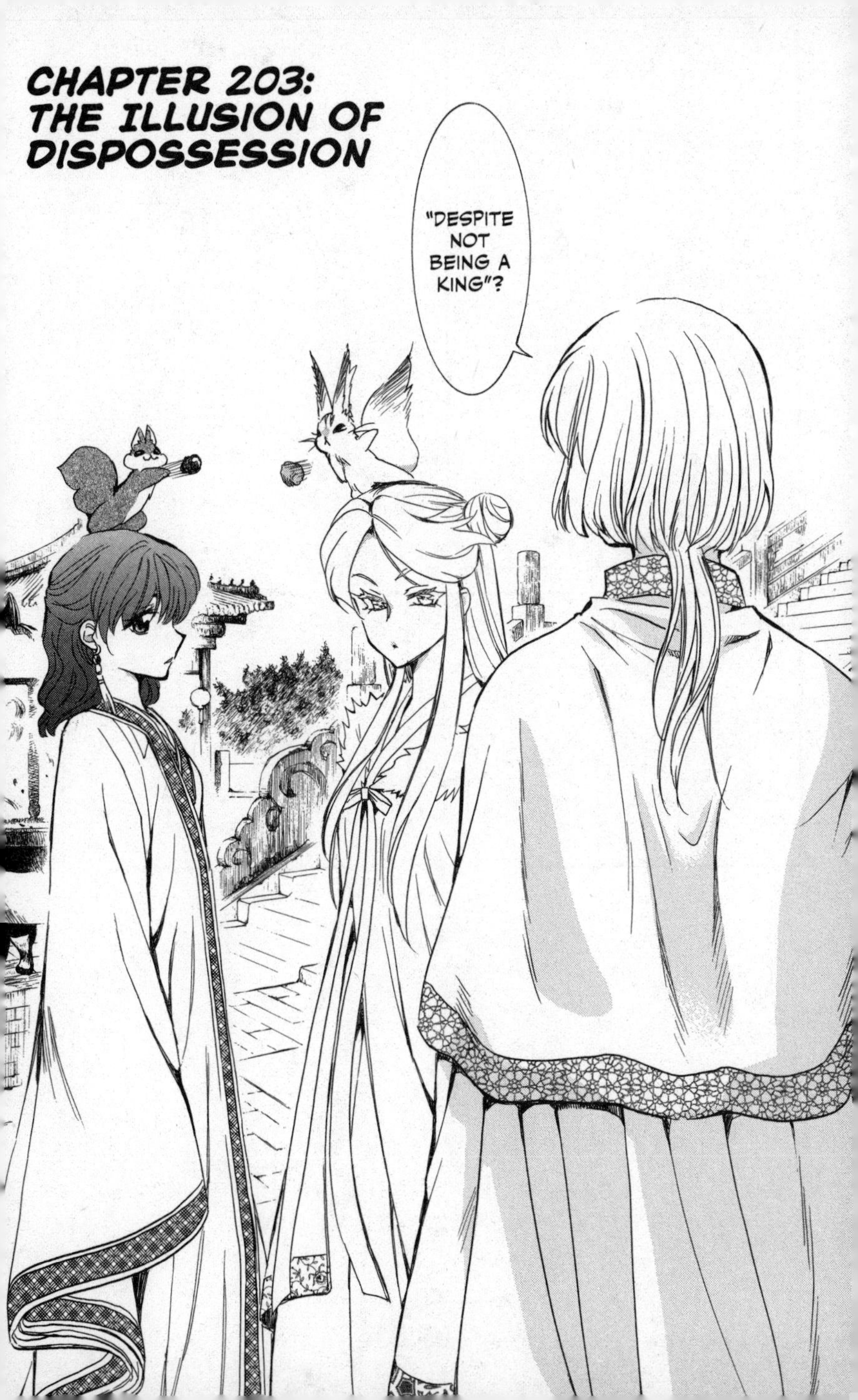
CHAPTER 203:
THE ILLUSION OF
DISPOSSESSION
"DESPITE NOT BEING A KING"?

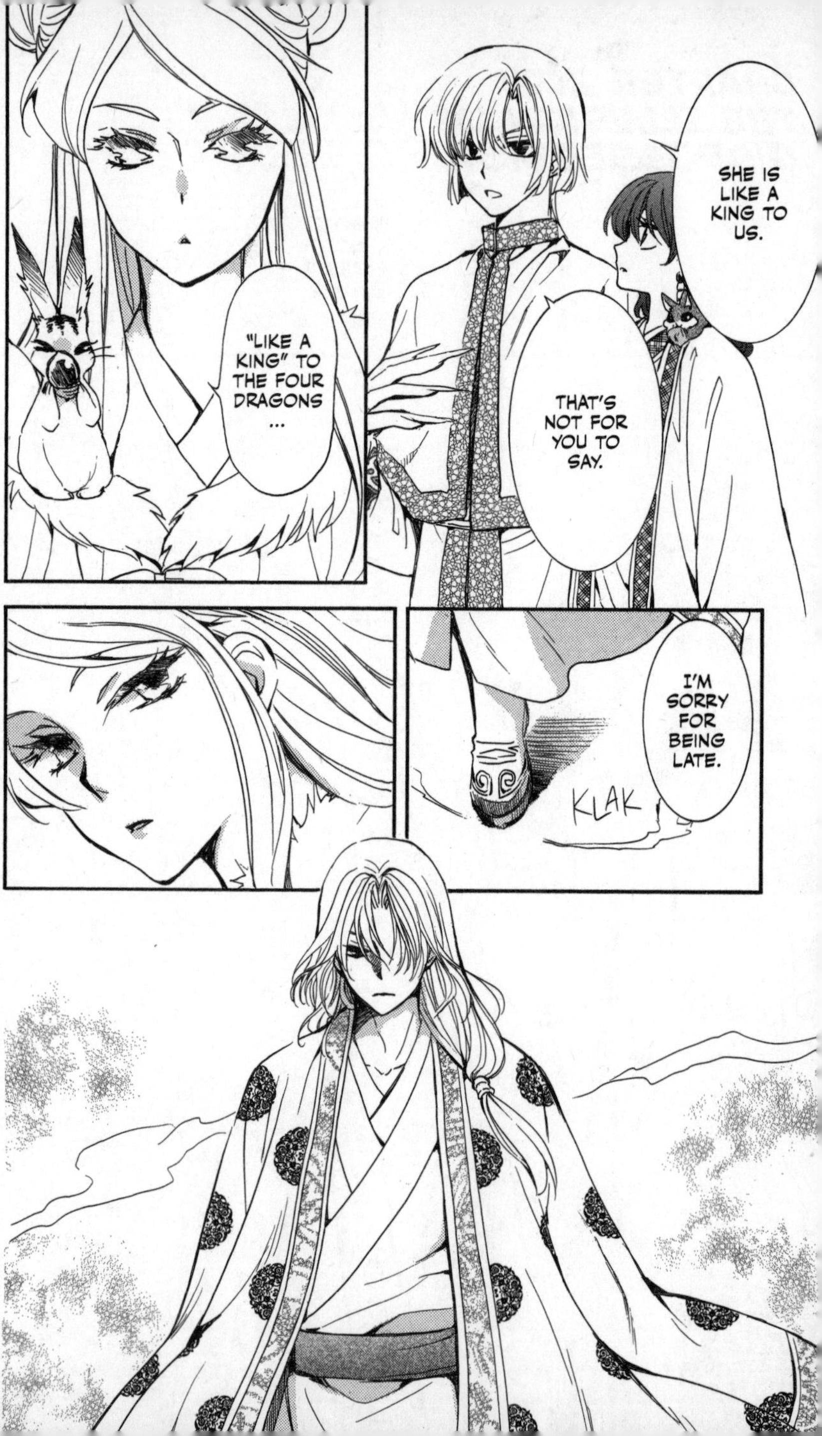
SHE IS LIKE A KING TO US.
THAT'S NOT FOR YOU TO SAY.
"LIKE A KING" TO THE FOUR DRAGONS ...
I'M SORRY FOR BEING LATE.
KLAK

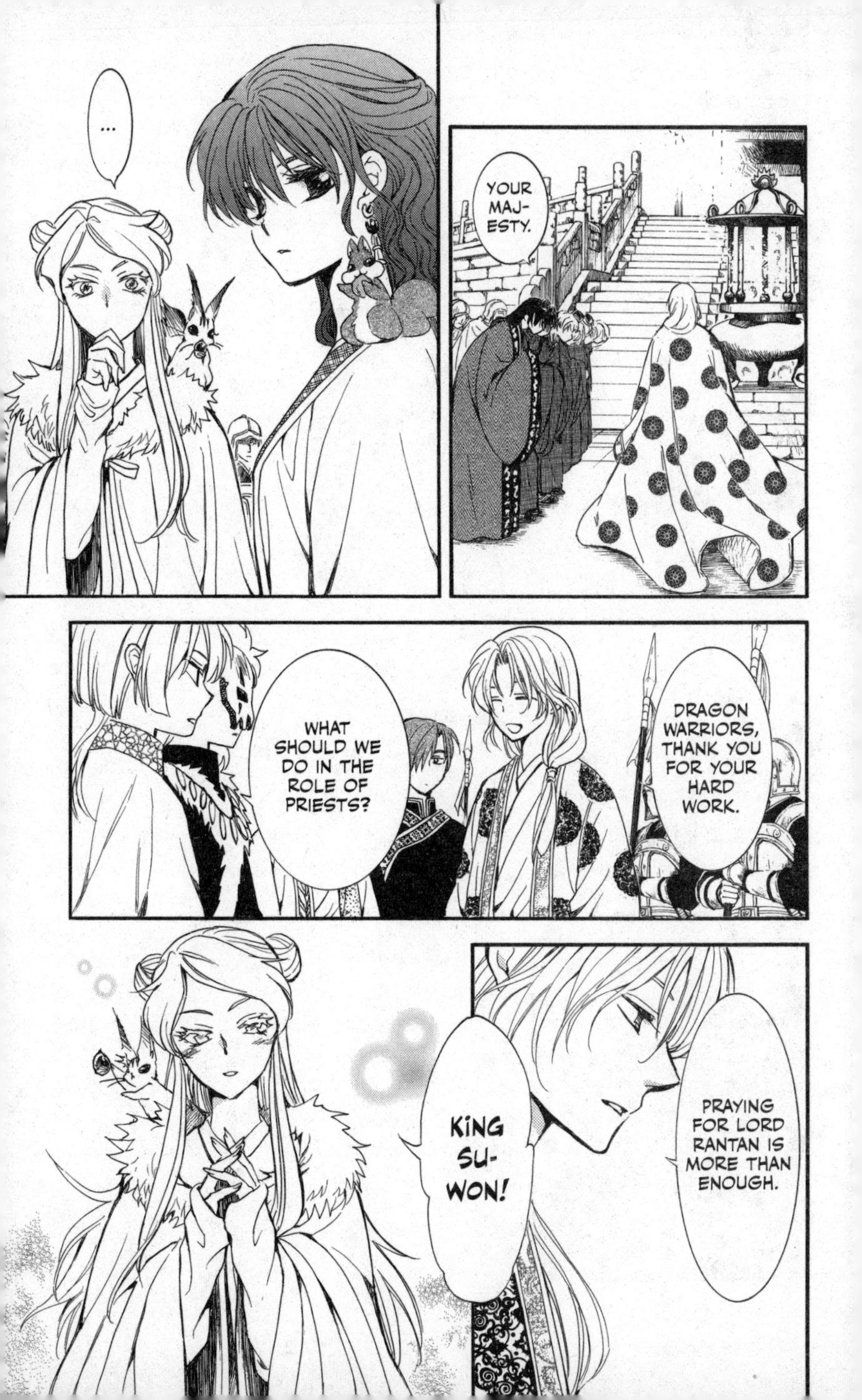
YOUR MAJESTY.
...
DRAGON WARRIORS, THANK YOU FOR YOUR HARD WORK.
WHAT SHOULD WE DO IN THE ROLE OF PRIESTS?
PRAYING FOR LORD RANTAN IS MORE THAN ENOUGH.
KING SU-WON!

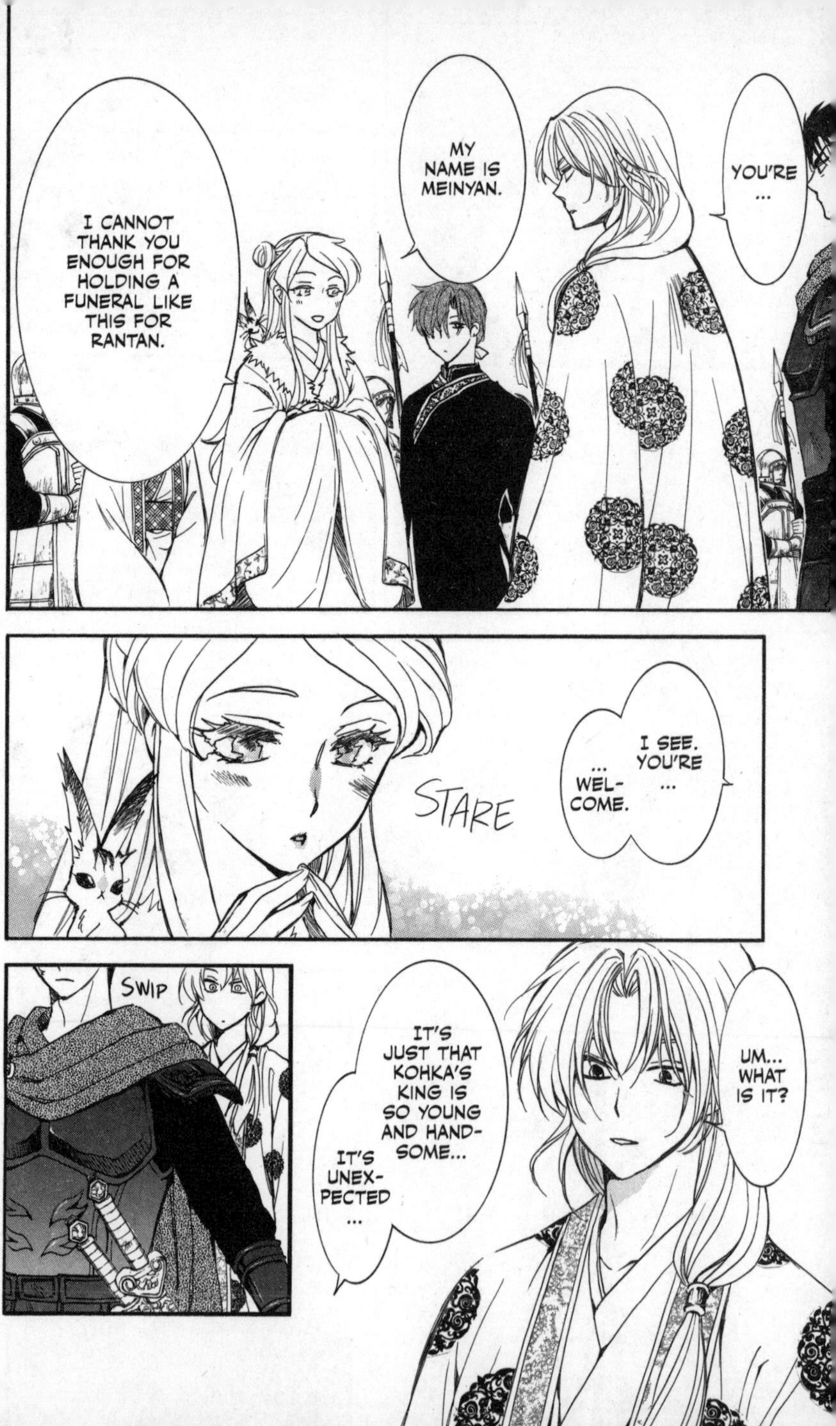
YOU'RE ...
MY NAME IS MEINYAN.
I CANNOT THANK YOU ENOUGH FOR HOLDING A FUNERAL LIKE THIS FOR RANTAN.
I SEE. YOU'RE ... ... WEL-COME.
STARE
UM... WHAT IS IT?
IT'S JUST THAT KOHKA'S KING IS SO YOUNG AND HAND-SOME...
IT'S UNEX-PECTED ...
SWIP

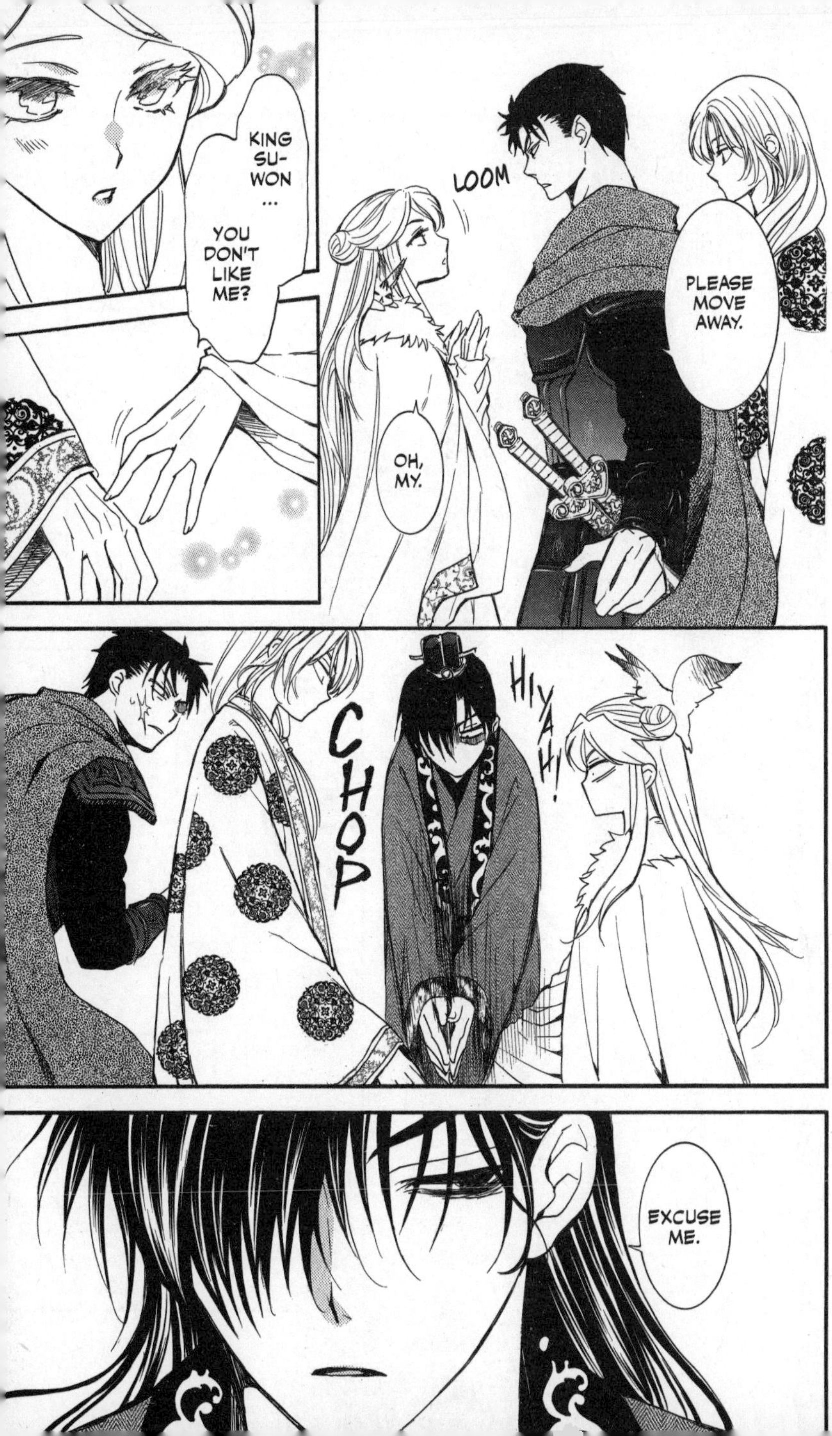
LOOM
PLEASE MOVE AWAY.
OH, MY.
KING SU-WON...
YOU DON'T LIKE ME?
HIYAH!
CHOP
EXCUSE ME.

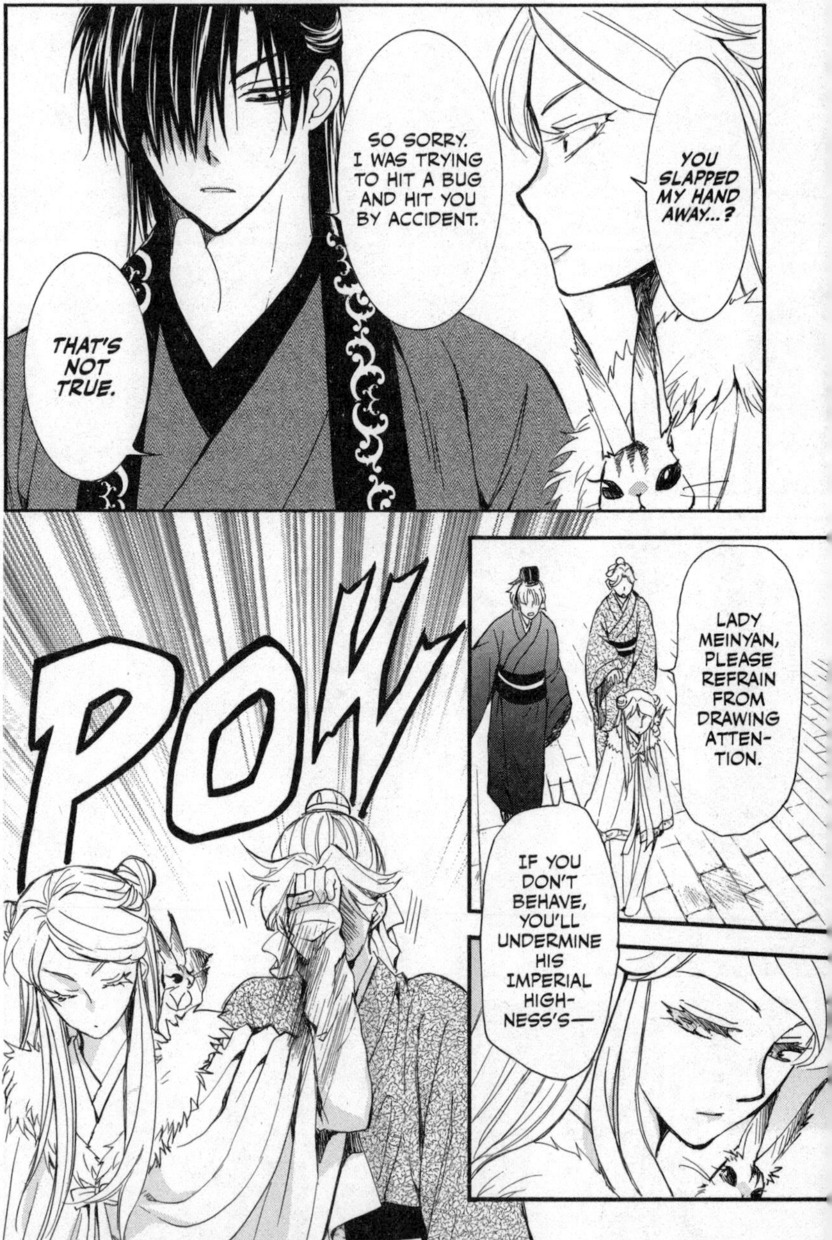
YOU SLAPPED MY HAND AWAY...?
SO SORRY. I WAS TRYING TO HIT A BUG AND HIT YOU BY ACCIDENT.
THAT'S NOT TRUE.
LADY MEINYAN, PLEASE REFRAIN FROM DRAWING ATTEN-TION.
IF YOU DON'T BEHAVE, YOU'LL UNDERMINE HIS IMPERIAL HIGH-NESS'S—
POW

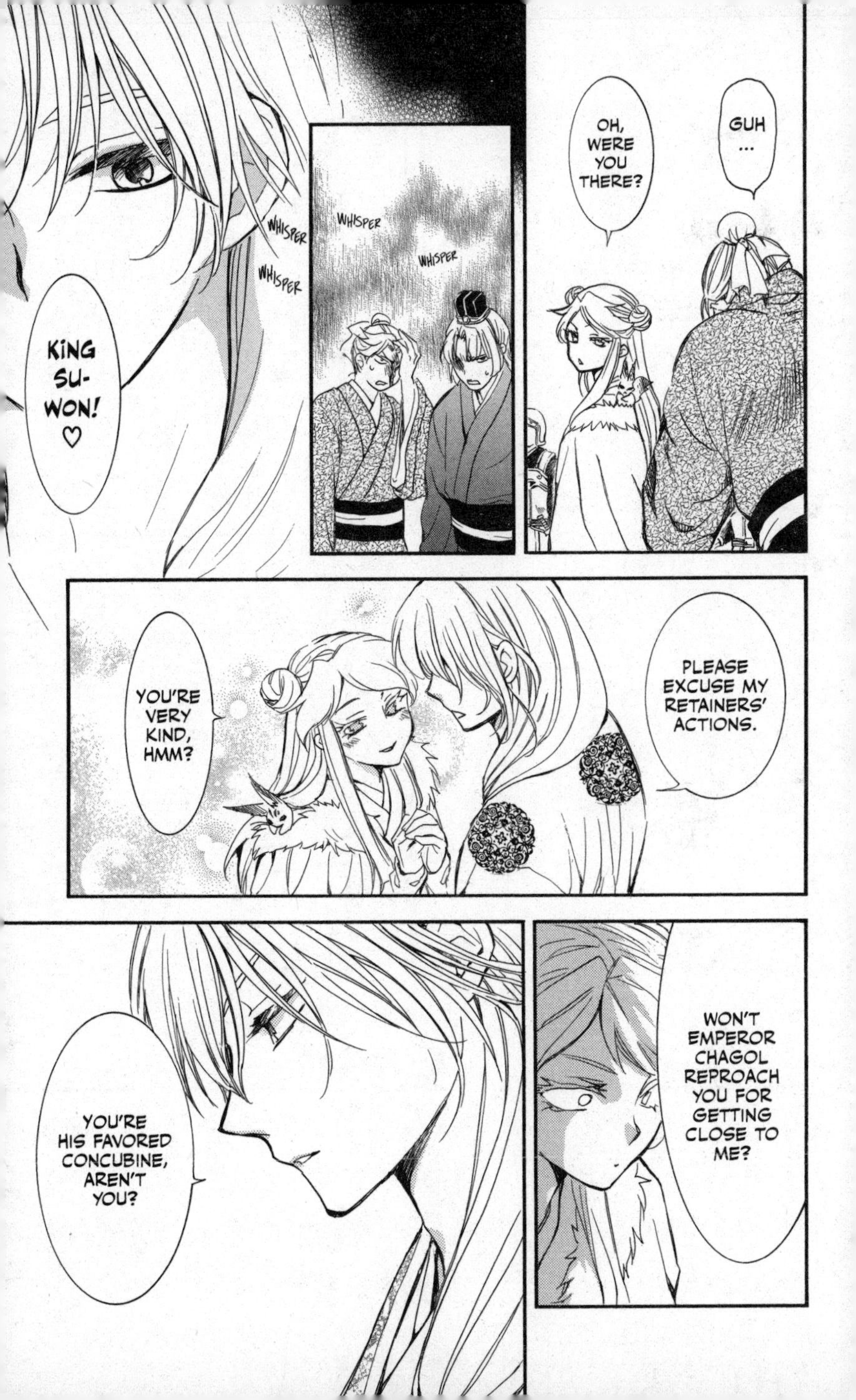
GUH ...
OH, WERE YOU THERE?
WHISPER
WHISPER
WHISPER
WHISPER
KING SU-WON! ♡
PLEASE EXCUSE MY RETAINERS' ACTIONS.
YOU'RE VERY KIND, HMM?
WON'T EMPEROR CHAGOL REPROACH YOU FOR GETTING CLOSE TO ME?
YOU'RE HIS FAVORED CONCUBINE, AREN'T YOU?

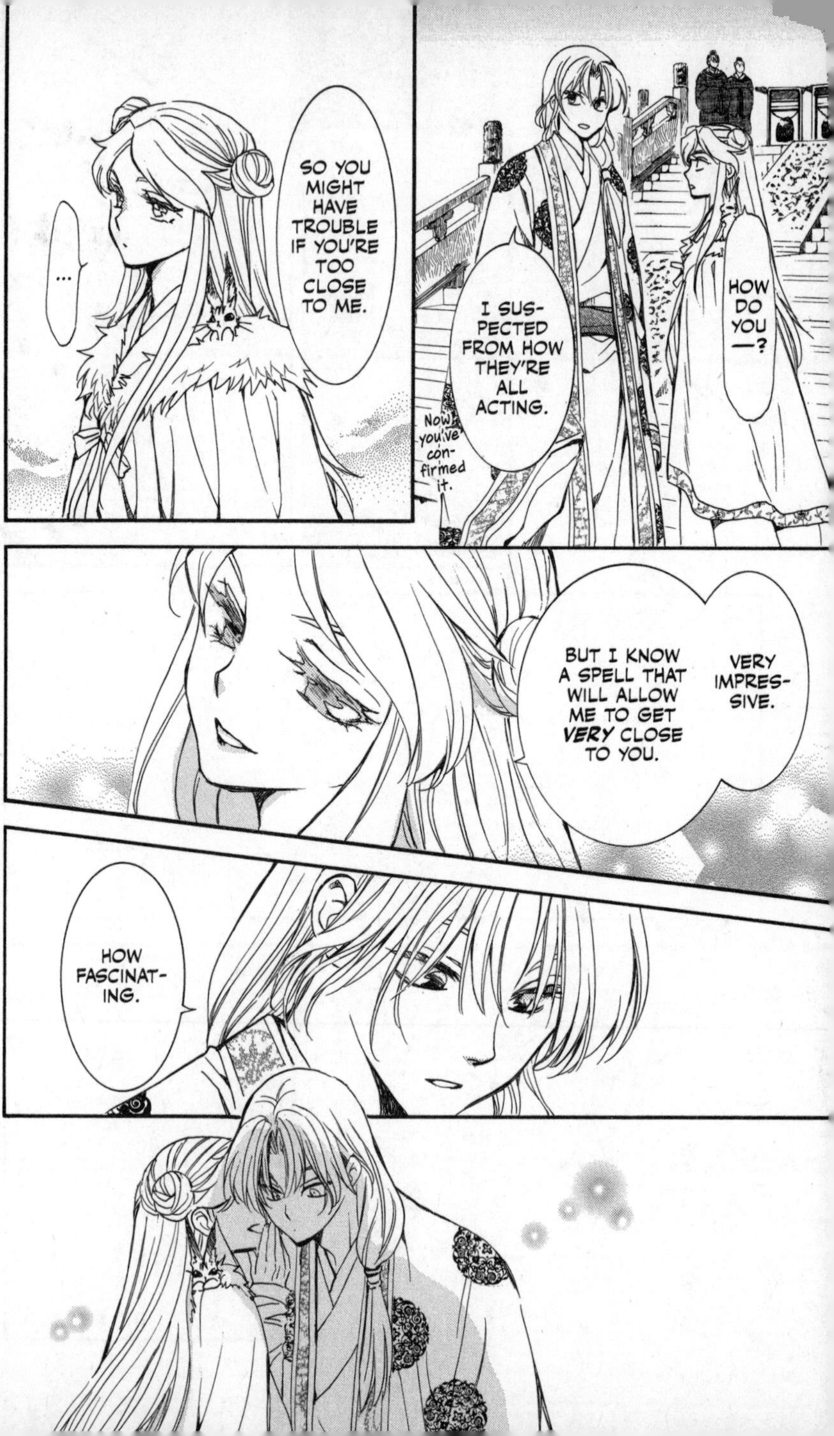
HOW DO YOU—?
I SUS-PECTED FROM HOW THEY'RE ALL ACTING.
Now you've con-firmed it.
SO YOU MIGHT HAVE TROUBLE IF YOU'RE TOO CLOSE TO ME.
...
VERY IMPRES-SIVE.
BUT I KNOW A SPELL THAT WILL ALLOW ME TO GET *VERY* CLOSE TO YOU.
HOW FASCINAT-ING.

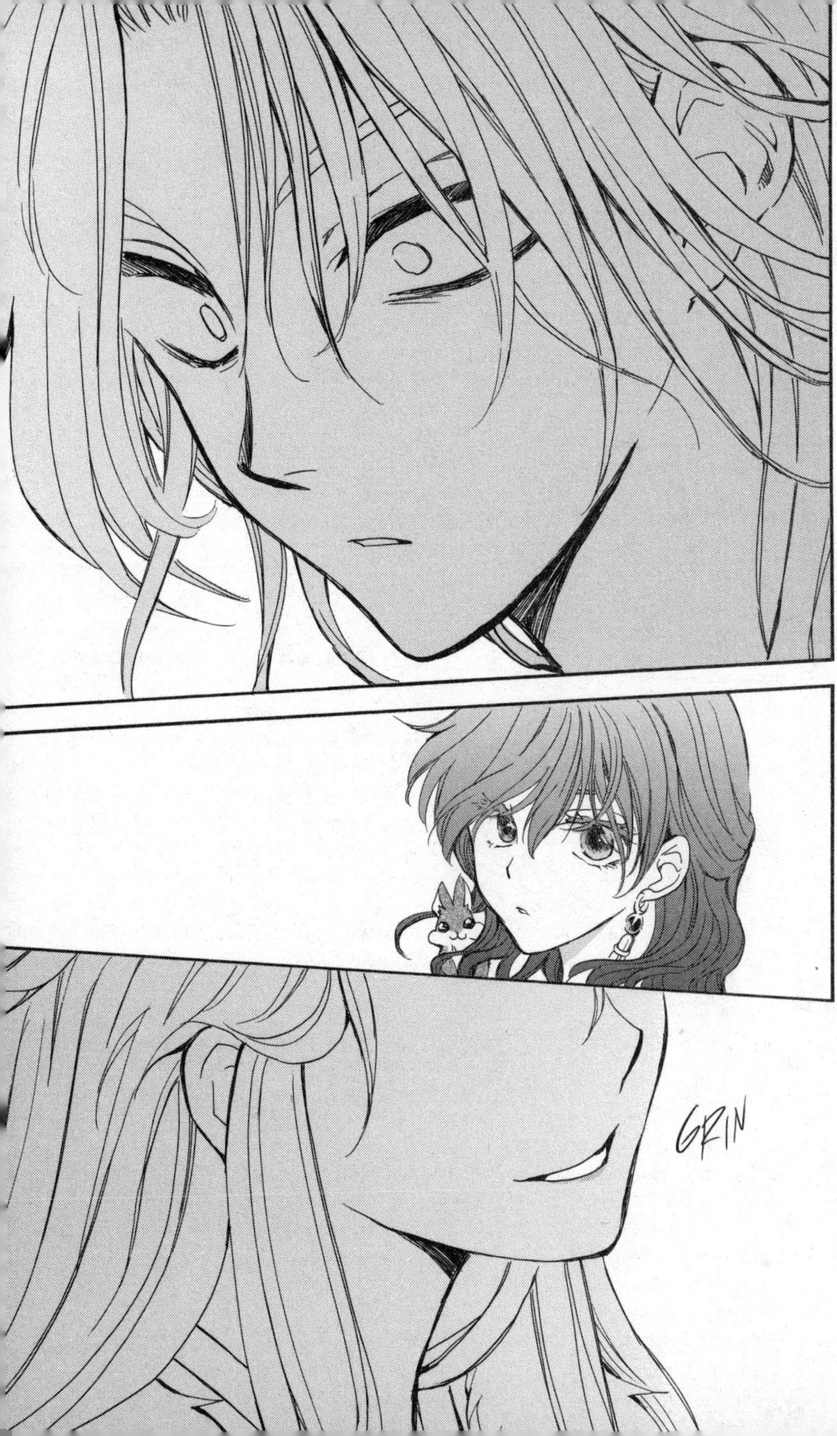
GRIN

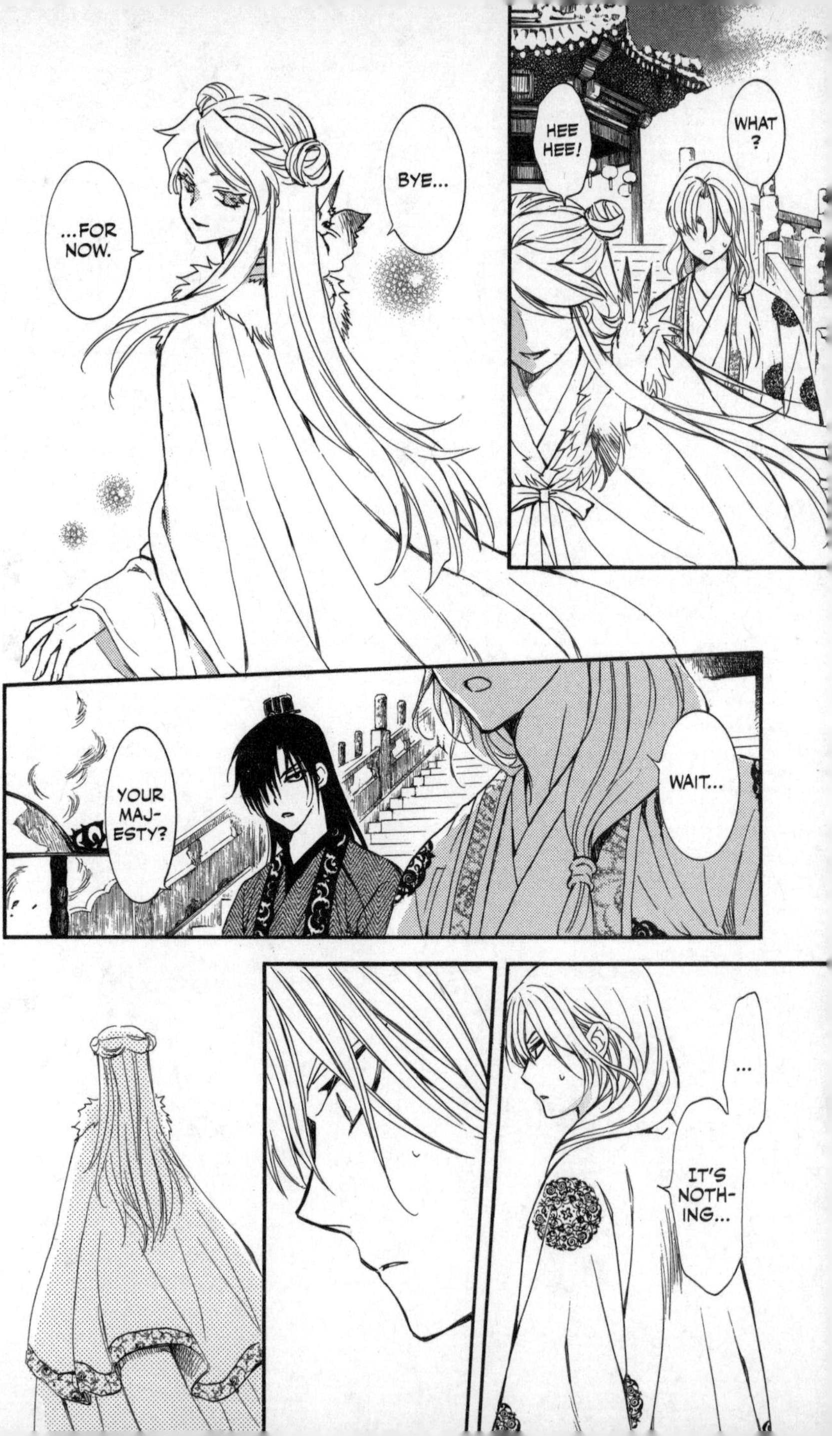
BYE...
...FOR NOW.
HEE HEE!
WHAT?
WAIT...
YOUR MAJESTY?
...
IT'S NOTHING...

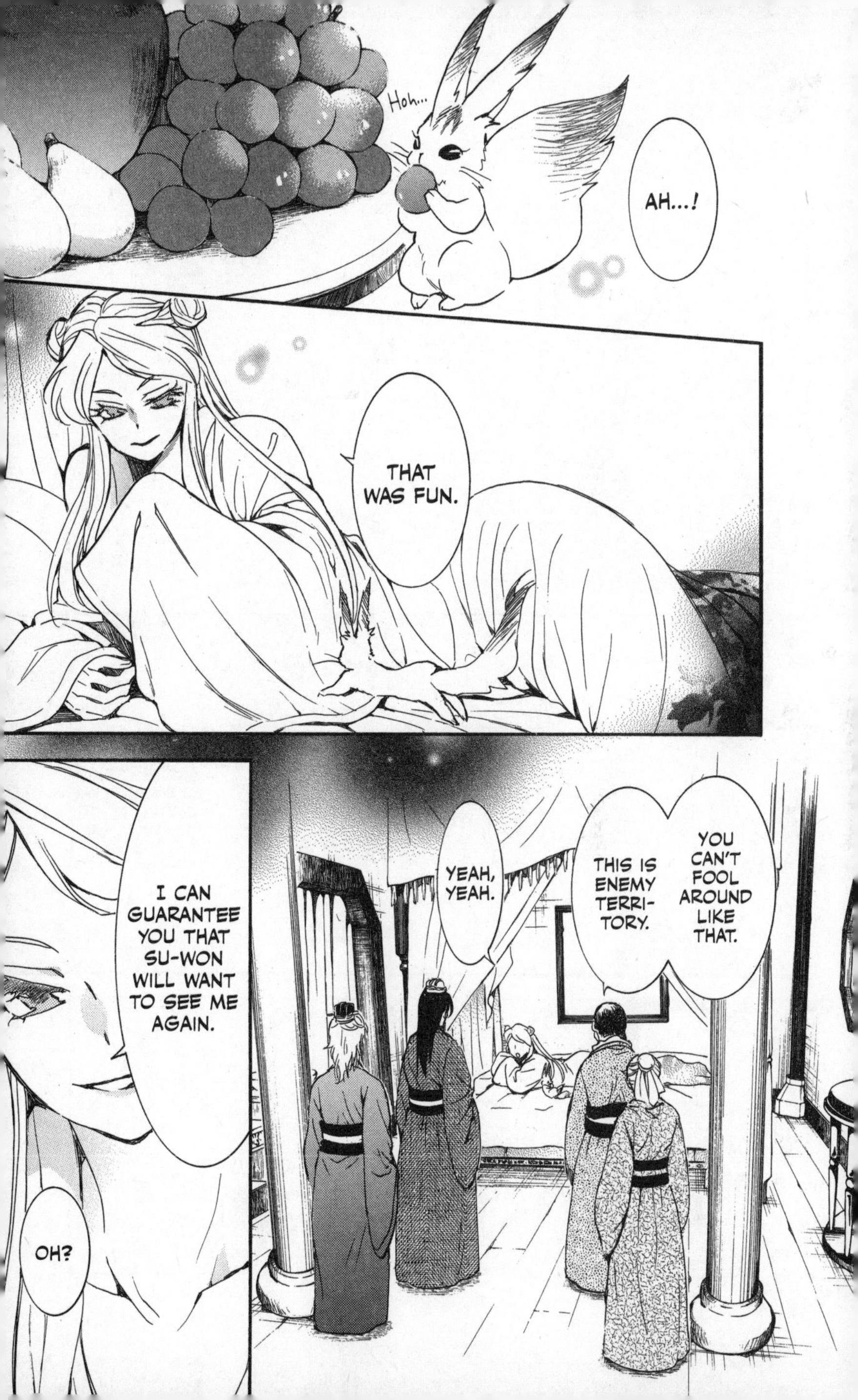
Hoh...
AH...!
THAT WAS FUN.
YOU CAN'T FOOL AROUND LIKE THAT.
THIS IS ENEMY TERRITORY.
YEAH, YEAH.
I CAN GUARANTEE YOU THAT SU-WON WILL WANT TO SEE ME AGAIN.
OH?

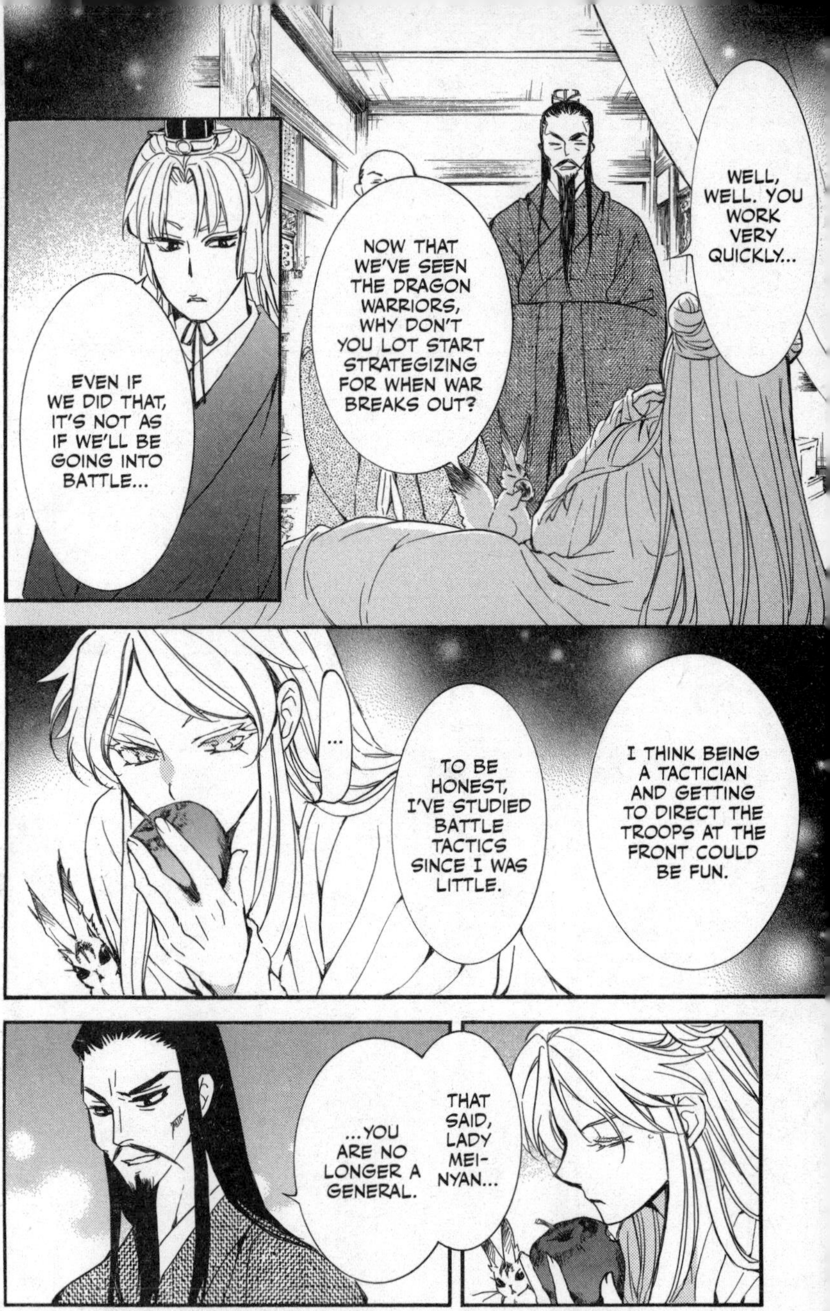
WELL, WELL. YOU WORK VERY QUICKLY...
NOW THAT WE'VE SEEN THE DRAGON WARRIORS, WHY DON'T YOU LOT START STRATEGIZING FOR WHEN WAR BREAKS OUT?
EVEN IF WE DID THAT, IT'S NOT AS IF WE'LL BE GOING INTO BATTLE...
I THINK BEING A TACTICIAN AND GETTING TO DIRECT THE TROOPS AT THE FRONT COULD BE FUN.
TO BE HONEST, I'VE STUDIED BATTLE TACTICS SINCE I WAS LITTLE.
...
THAT SAID, LADY MEI-NYAN...
...YOU ARE NO LONGER A GENERAL.

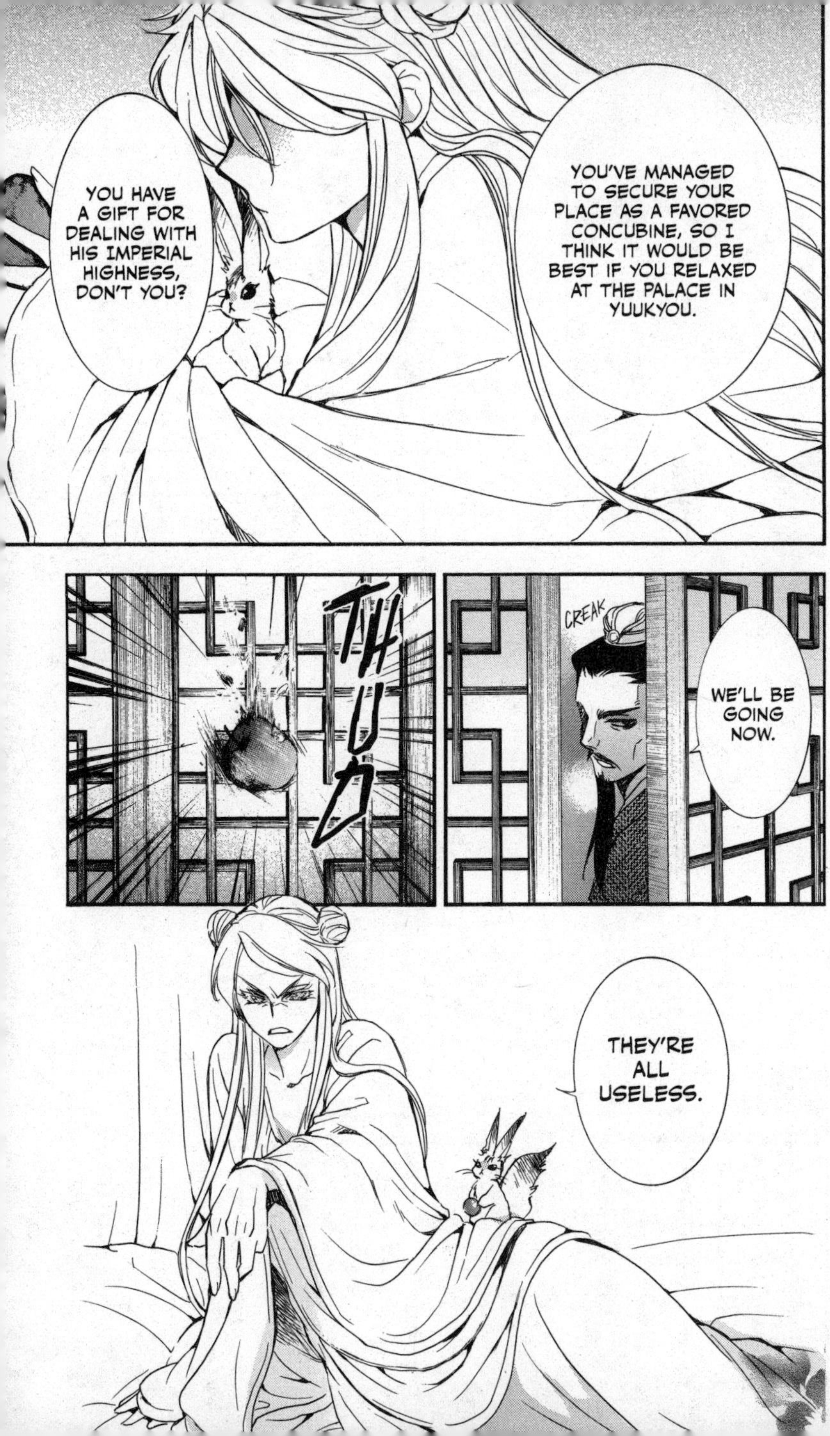
YOU'VE MANAGED TO SECURE YOUR PLACE AS A FAVORED CONCUBINE, SO I THINK IT WOULD BE BEST IF YOU RELAXED AT THE PALACE IN YUUKYOU.
YOU HAVE A GIFT FOR DEALING WITH HIS IMPERIAL HIGHNESS, DON'T YOU?
CREAK
WE'LL BE GOING NOW.
THUD
THEY'RE ALL USELESS.

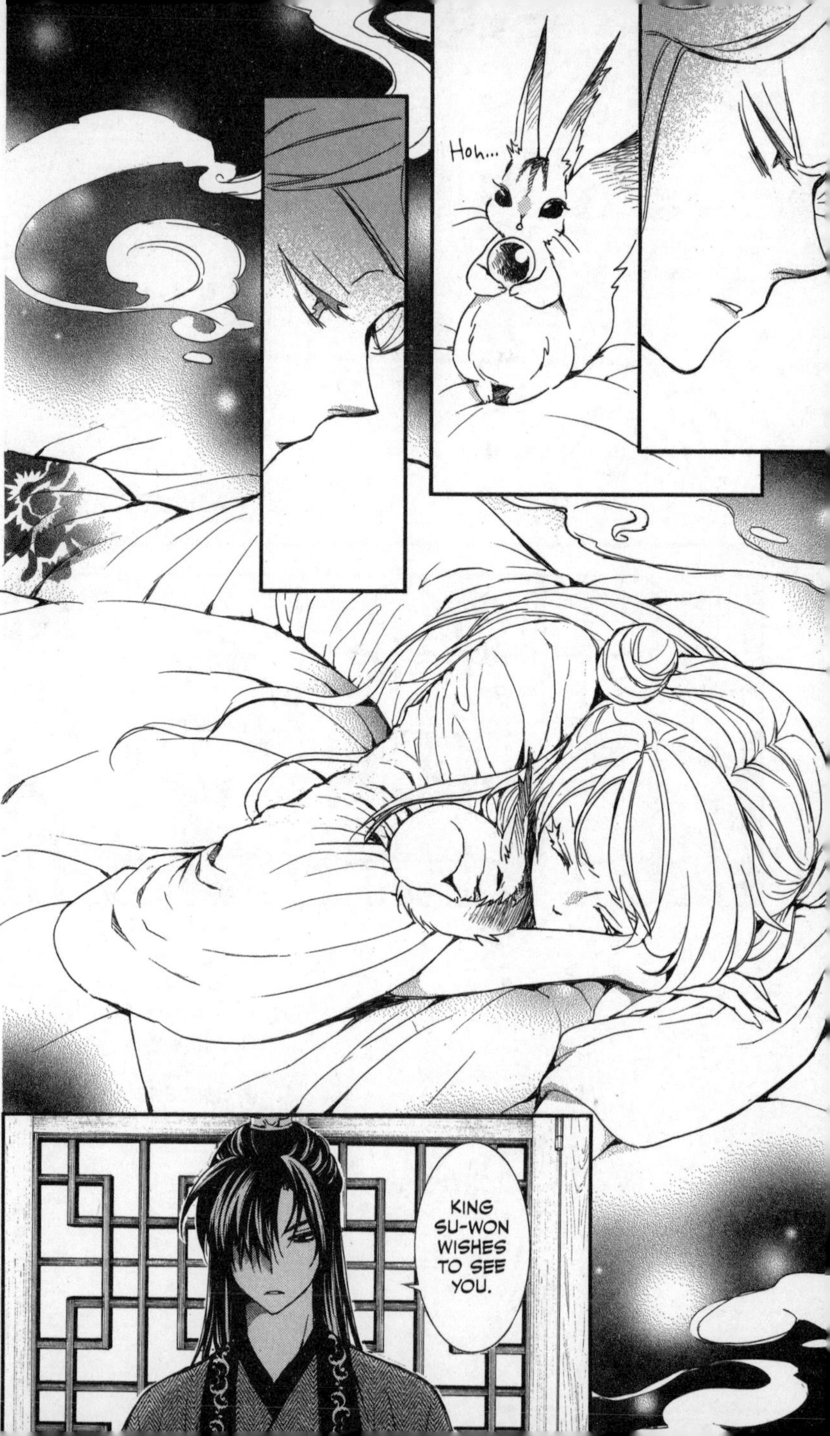
Hoh...
KING SU-WON WISHES TO SEE YOU.

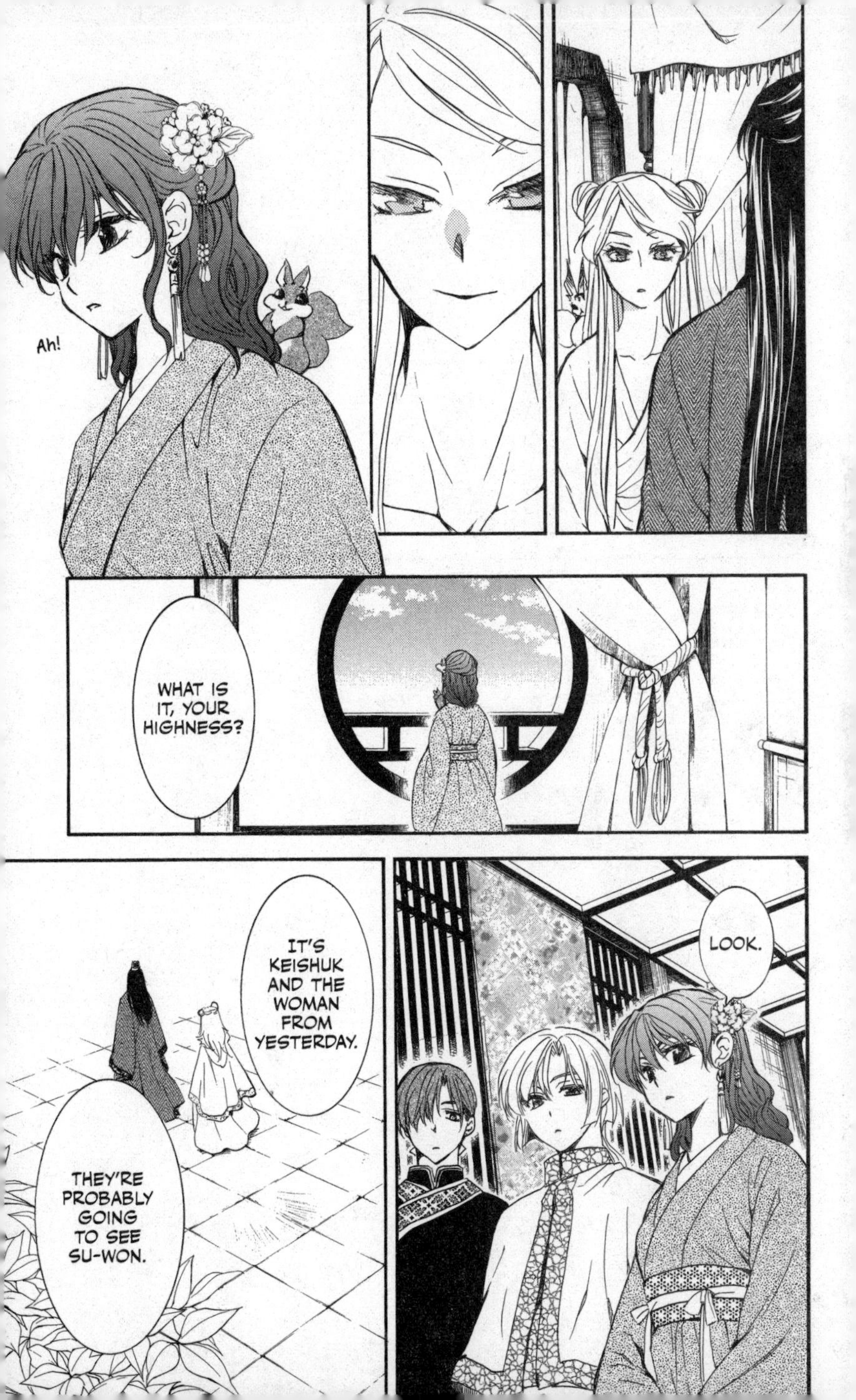
Ah!
WHAT IS IT, YOUR HIGHNESS?
LOOK.
IT'S KEISHUK AND THE WOMAN FROM YESTERDAY.
THEY'RE PROBABLY GOING TO SEE SU-WON.

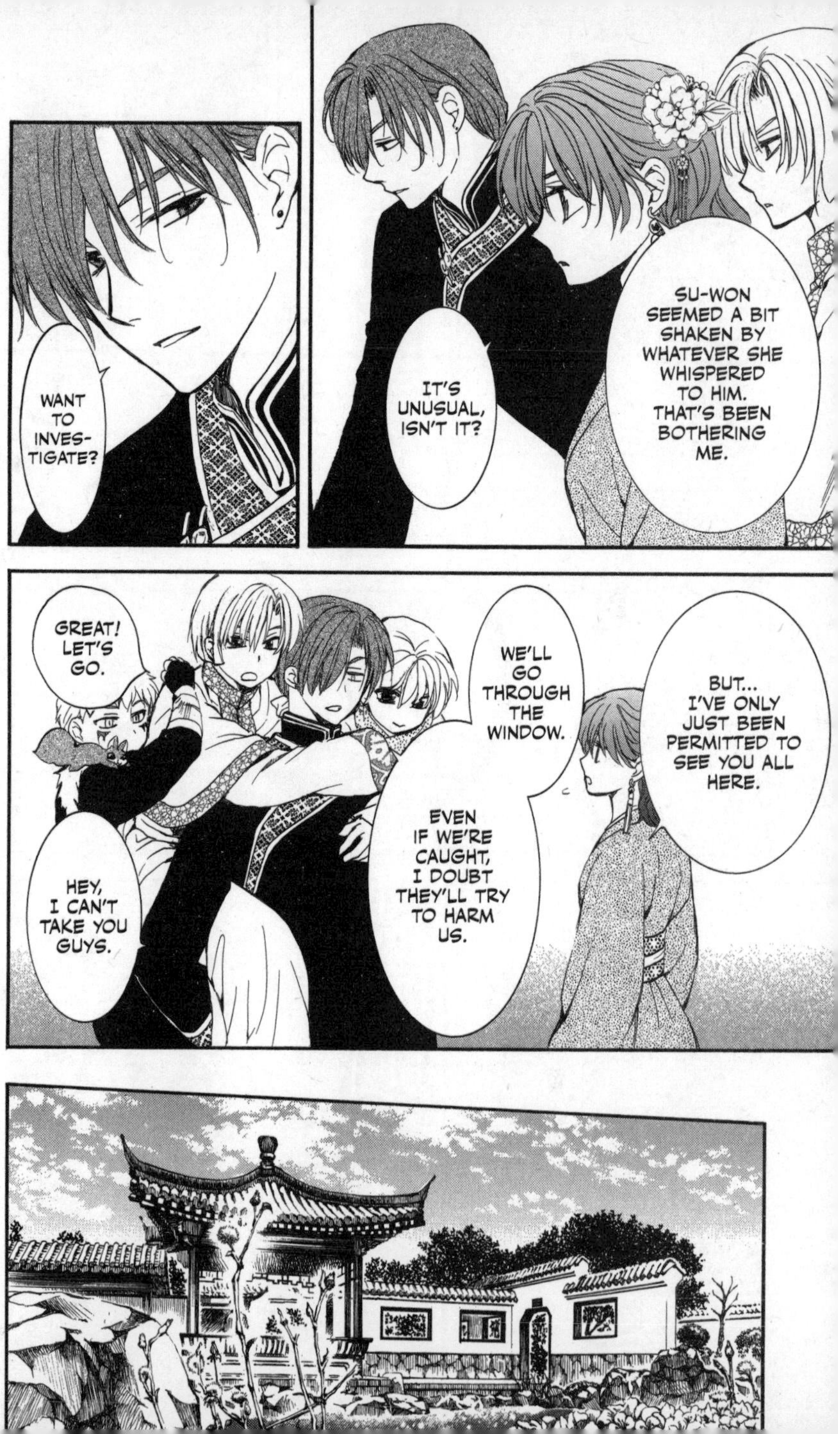
SU-WON SEEMED A BIT SHAKEN BY WHATEVER SHE WHISPERED TO HIM. THAT'S BEEN BOTHERING ME.
IT'S UNUSUAL, ISN'T IT?
WANT TO INVES-TIGATE?
BUT... I'VE ONLY JUST BEEN PERMITTED TO SEE YOU ALL HERE.
WE'LL GO THROUGH THE WINDOW.
EVEN IF WE'RE CAUGHT, I DOUBT THEY'LL TRY TO HARM US.
GREAT! LET'S GO.
HEY, I CAN'T TAKE YOU GUYS.

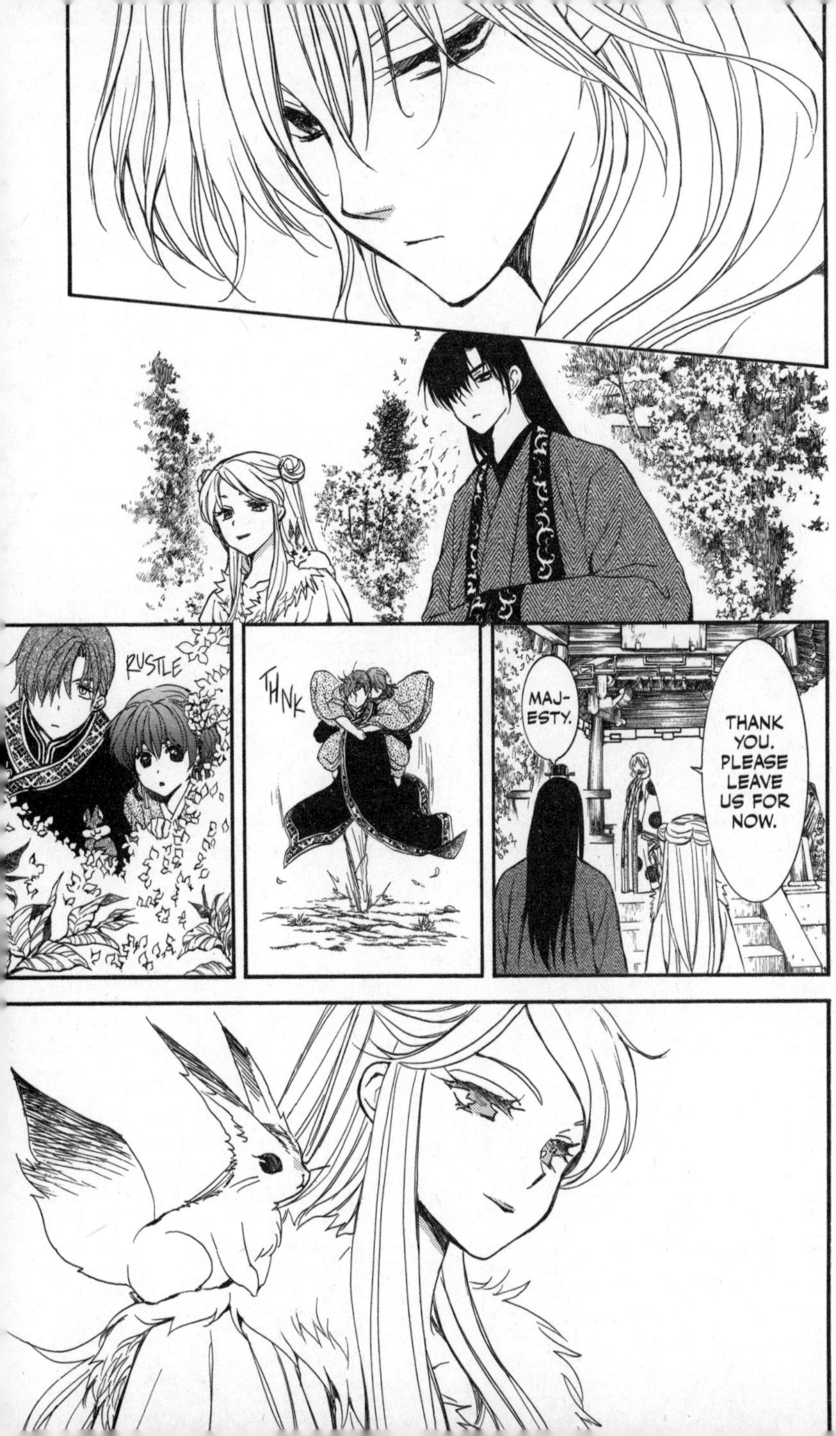
THANK YOU. PLEASE LEAVE US FOR NOW.
MAJ-ESTY.
THNK
RUSTLE

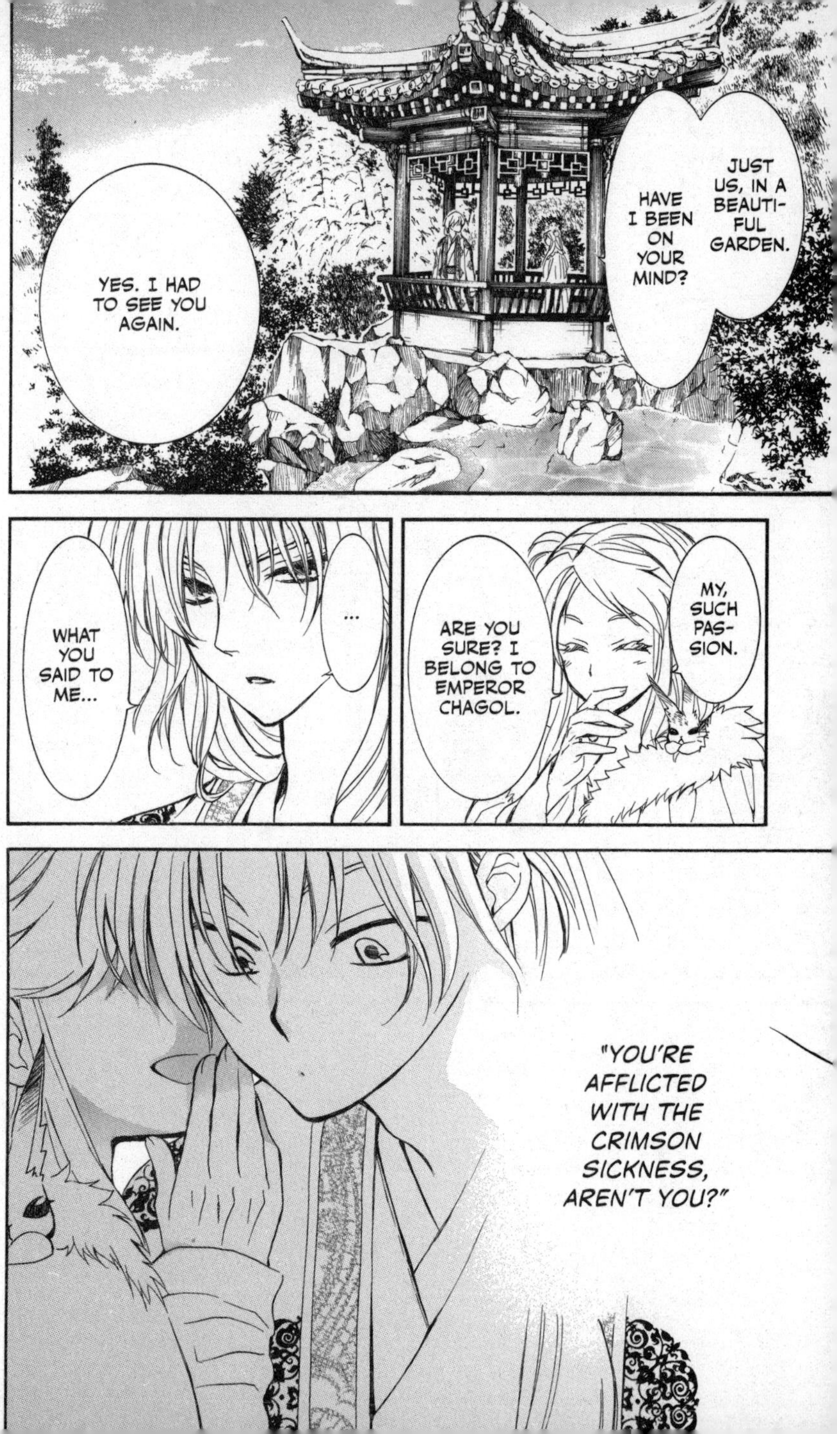
JUST US, IN A BEAUTIFUL GARDEN.
HAVE I BEEN ON YOUR MIND?
YES. I HAD TO SEE YOU AGAIN.
MY, SUCH PASSION.
ARE YOU SURE? I BELONG TO EMPEROR CHAGOL.
...
WHAT YOU SAID TO ME...
"YOU'RE AFFLICTED WITH THE CRIMSON SICKNESS, AREN'T YOU?"

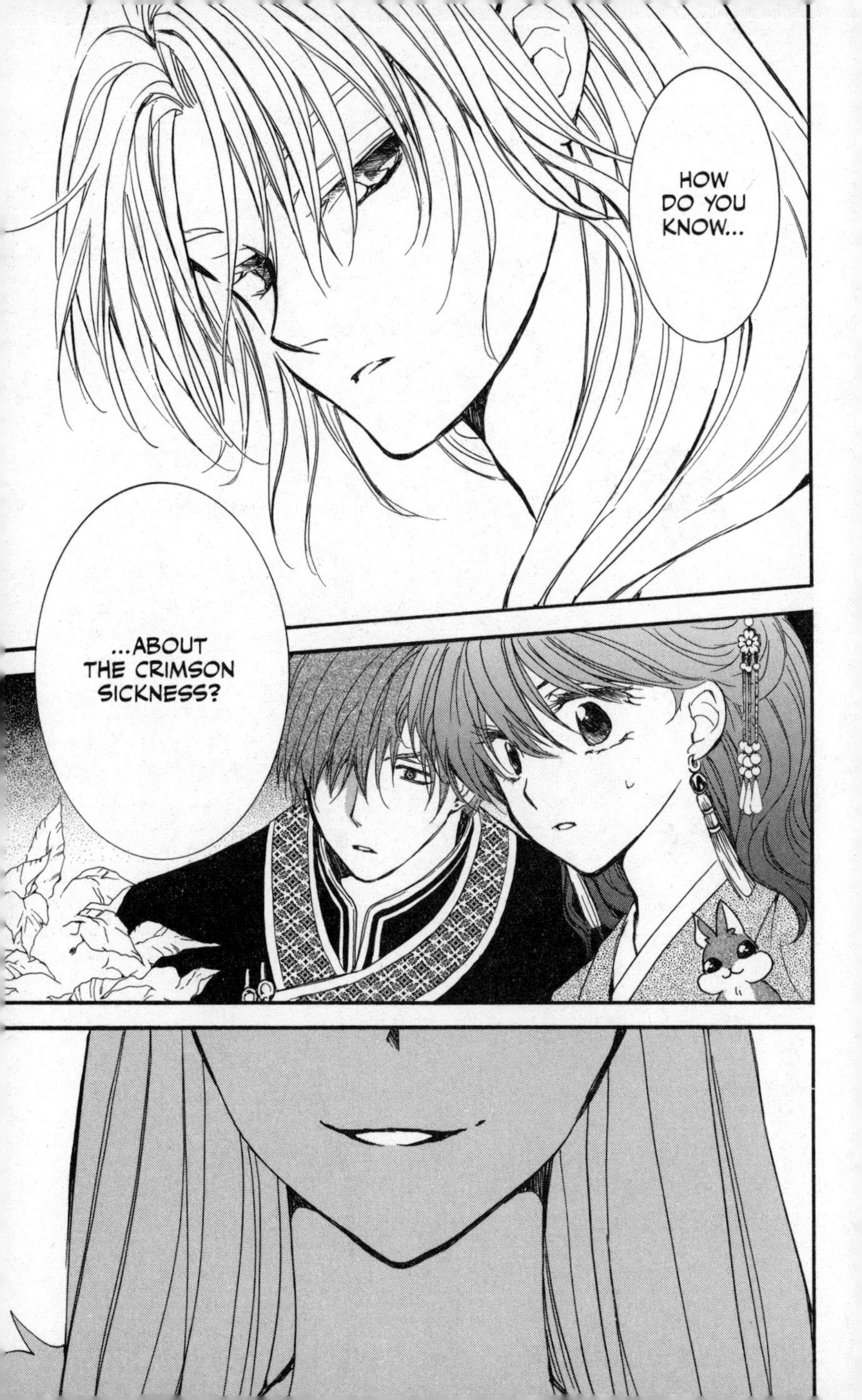
HOW DO YOU KNOW...
...ABOUT THE CRIMSON SICKNESS?

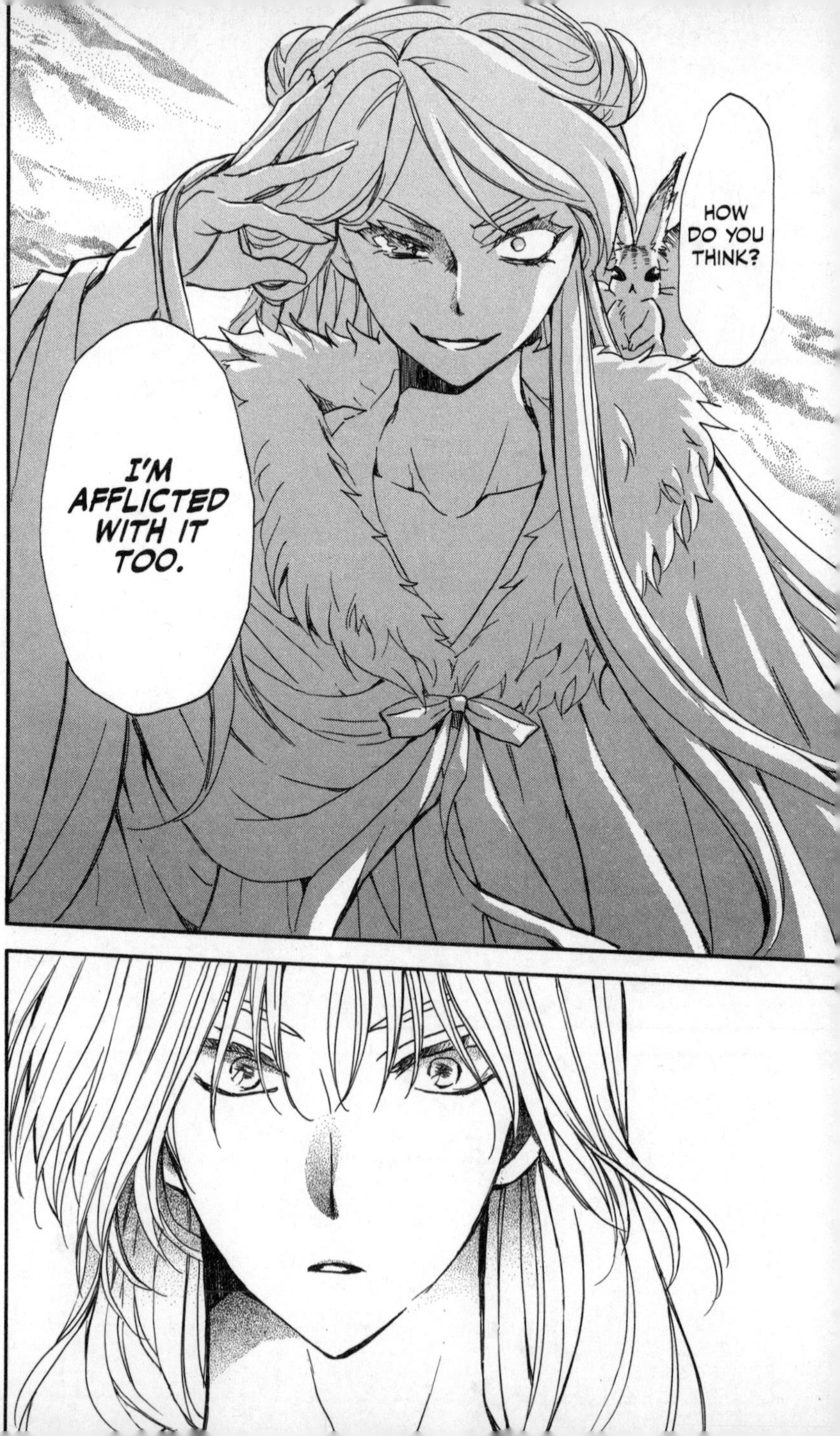
HOW DO YOU THINK?
I'M AFFLICTED WITH IT TOO.

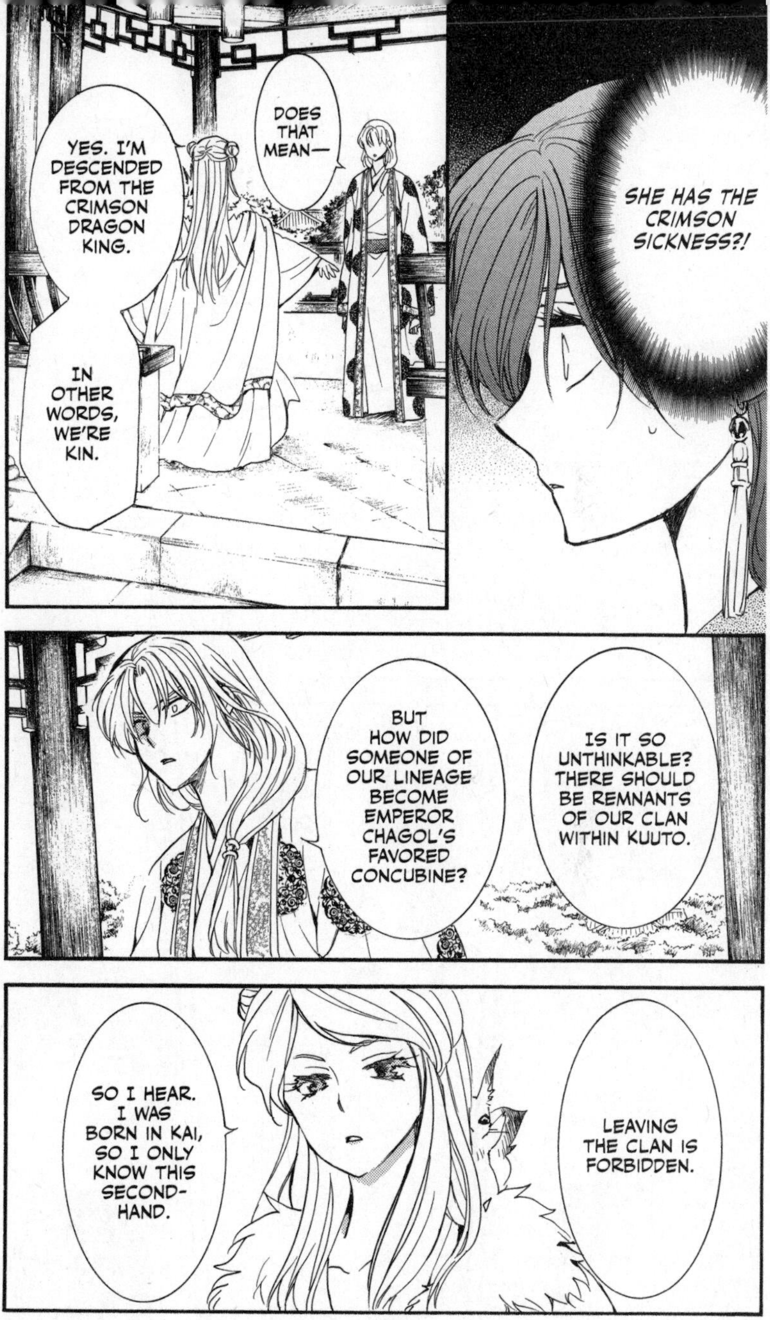
SHE HAS THE CRIMSON SICKNESS?!
DOES THAT MEAN—
YES. I'M DESCENDED FROM THE CRIMSON DRAGON KING.
IN OTHER WORDS, WE'RE KIN.
IS IT SO UNTHINKABLE? THERE SHOULD BE REMNANTS OF OUR CLAN WITHIN KUUTO.
BUT HOW DID SOMEONE OF OUR LINEAGE BECOME EMPEROR CHAGOL'S FAVORED CONCUBINE?
LEAVING THE CLAN IS FORBIDDEN.
SO I HEAR. I WAS BORN IN KAI, SO I ONLY KNOW THIS SECOND-HAND.

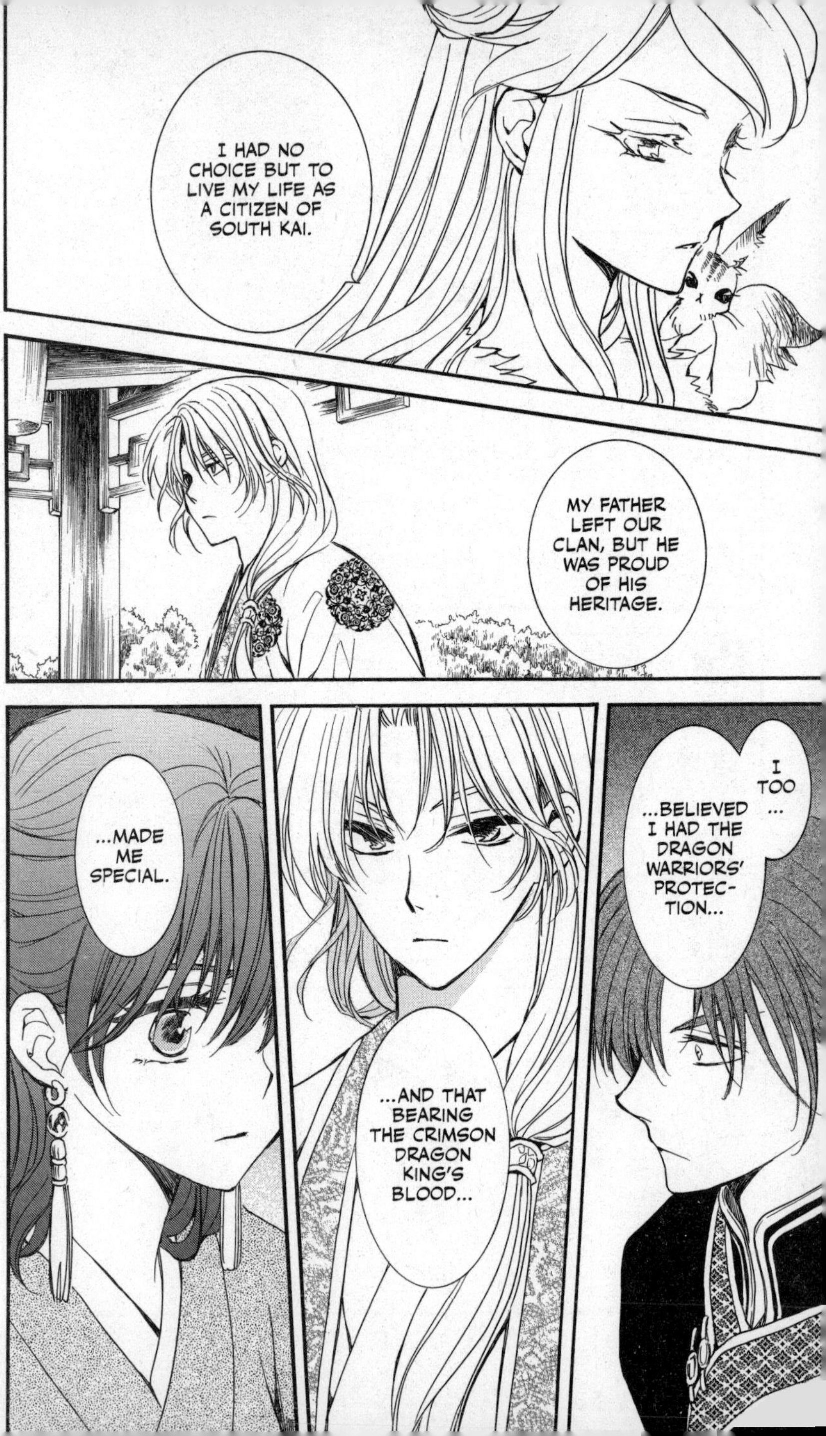
I HAD NO CHOICE BUT TO LIVE MY LIFE AS A CITIZEN OF SOUTH KAI.
MY FATHER LEFT OUR CLAN, BUT HE WAS PROUD OF HIS HERITAGE.
I TOO ...
...BELIEVED I HAD THE DRAGON WARRIORS' PROTECTION...
...AND THAT BEARING THE CRIMSON DRAGON KING'S BLOOD...
...MADE ME SPECIAL.

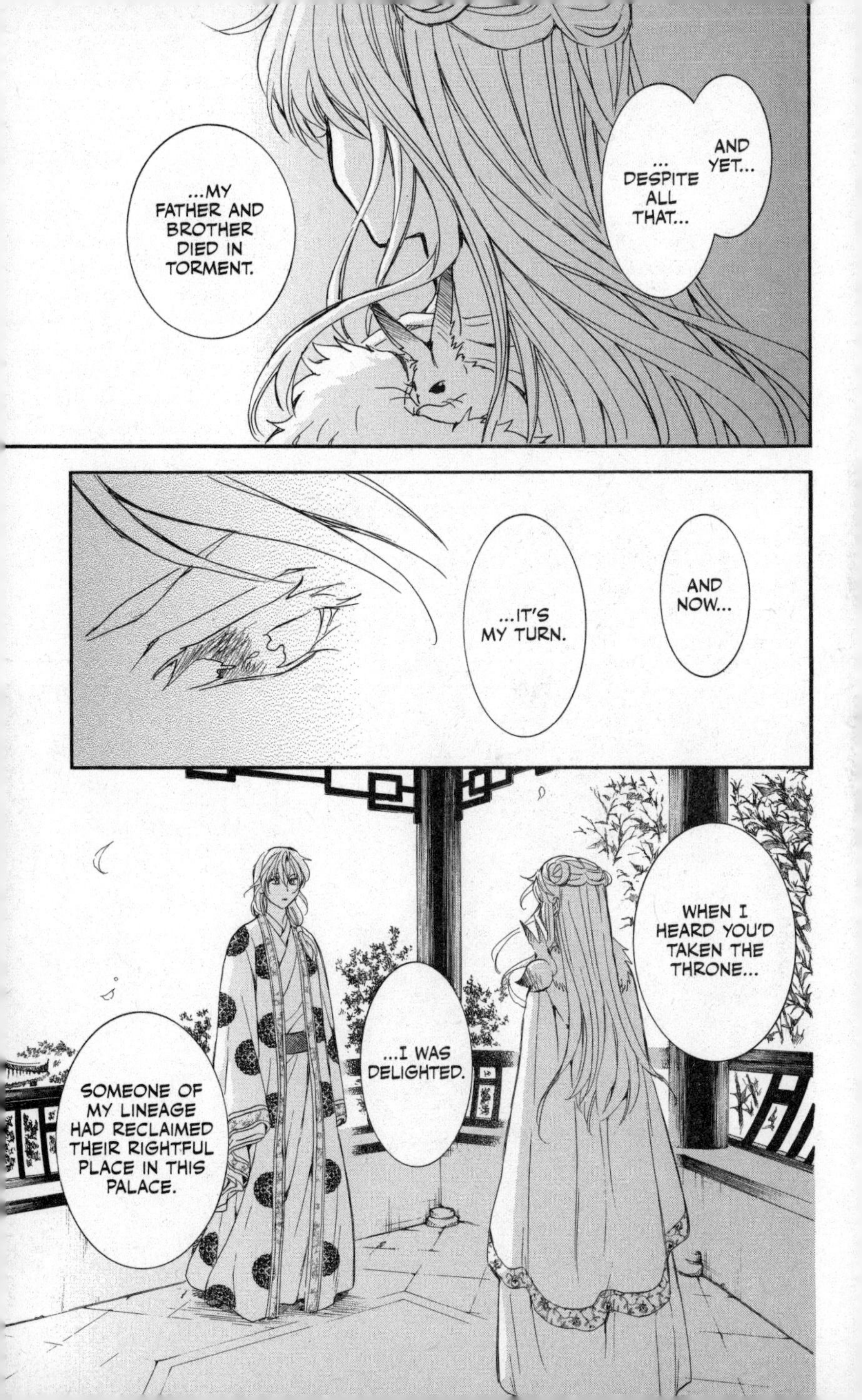
AND YET...
...DESPITE ALL THAT...
...MY FATHER AND BROTHER DIED IN TORMENT.
AND NOW...
...IT'S MY TURN.
WHEN I HEARD YOU'D TAKEN THE THRONE...
...I WAS DELIGHTED.
SOMEONE OF MY LINEAGE HAD RECLAIMED THEIR RIGHTFUL PLACE IN THIS PALACE.

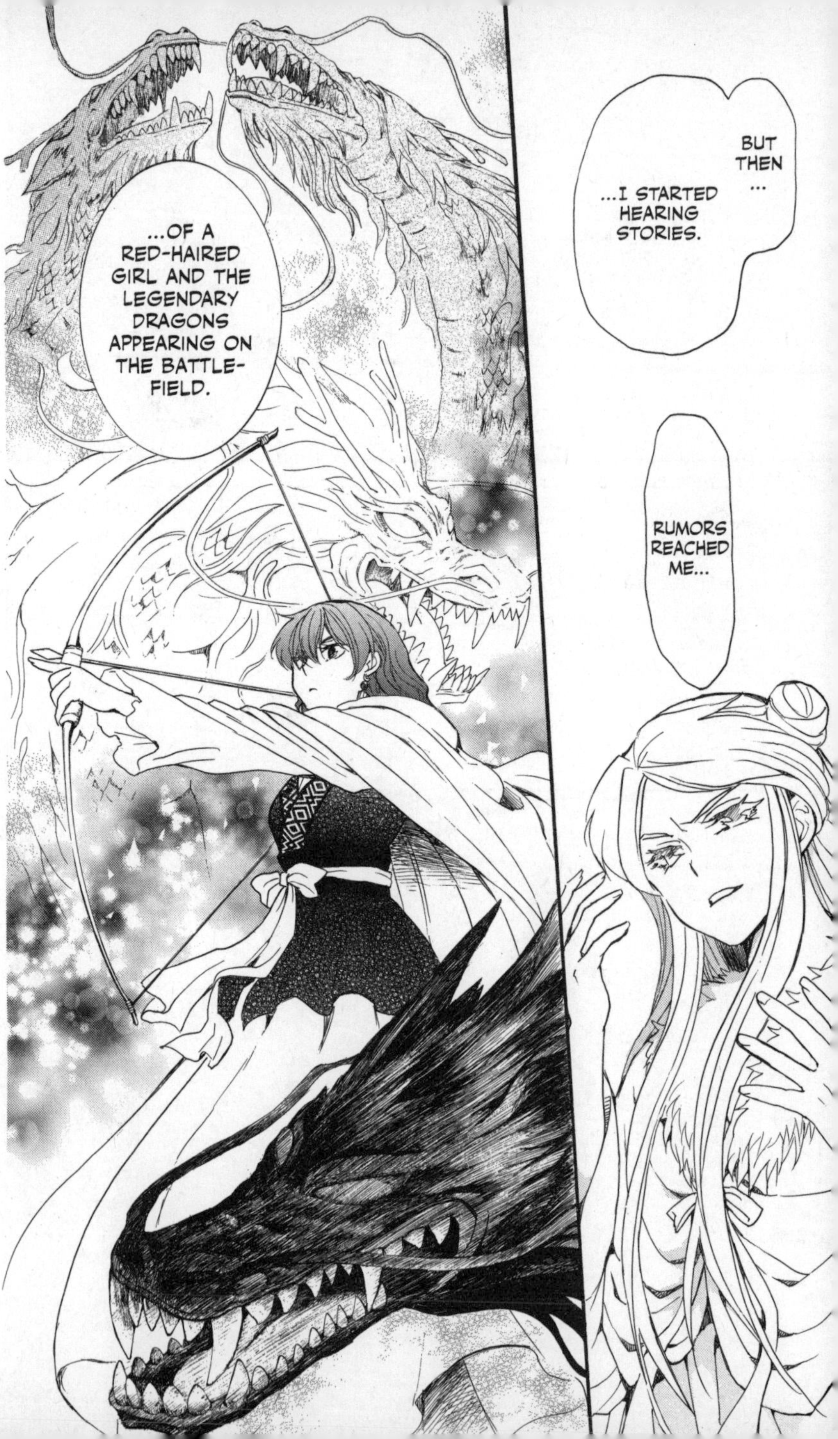
BUT THEN ...
...I STARTED HEARING STORIES.
RUMORS REACHED ME...
...OF A RED-HAIRED GIRL AND THE LEGENDARY DRAGONS APPEARING ON THE BATTLE-FIELD.

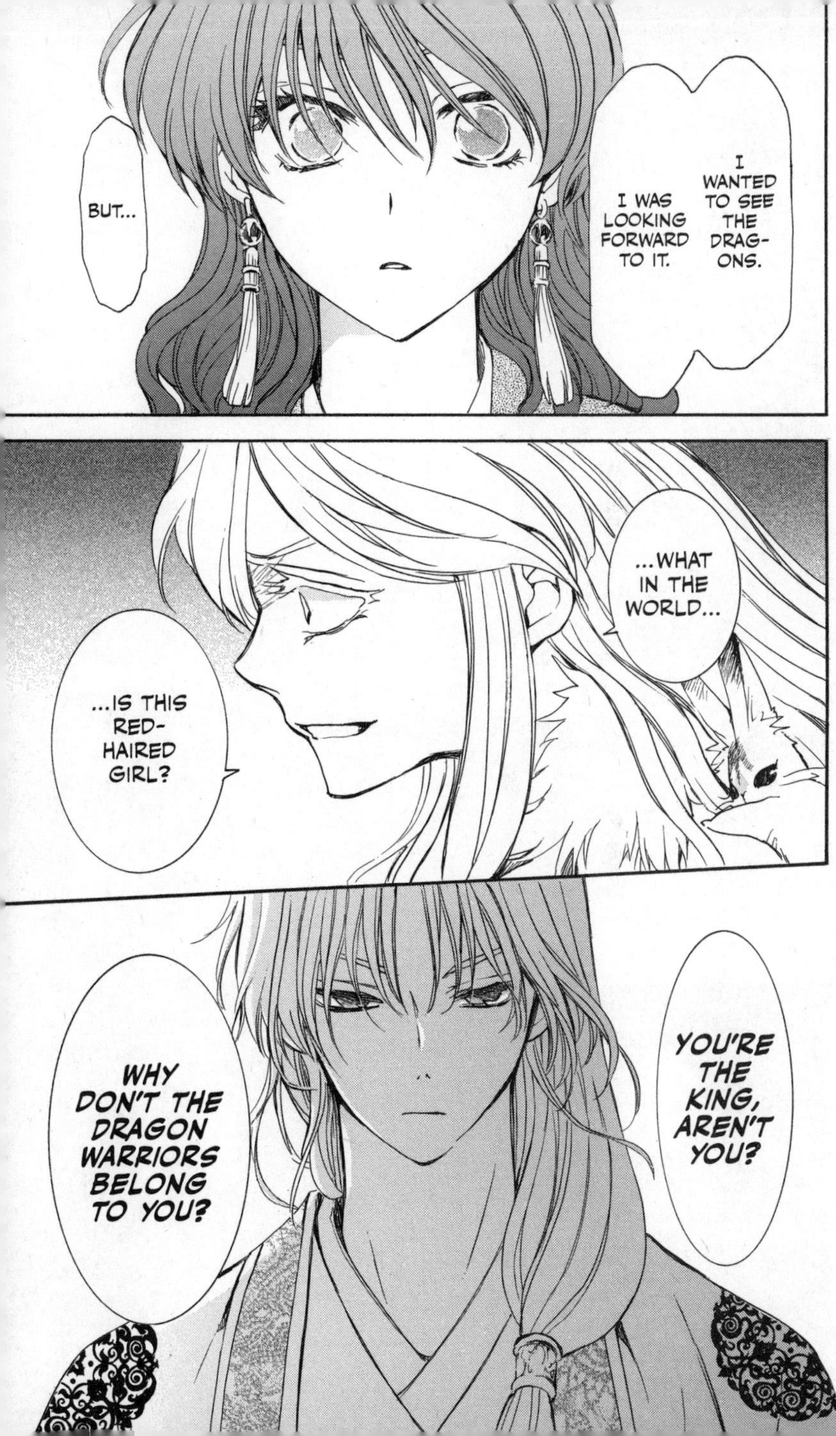
I WANTED TO SEE THE DRAG-ONS.
I WAS LOOKING FORWARD TO IT.
BUT...
...WHAT IN THE WORLD...
...IS THIS RED-HAIRED GIRL?
YOU'RE THE KING, AREN'T YOU?
WHY DON'T THE DRAGON WARRIORS BELONG TO YOU?

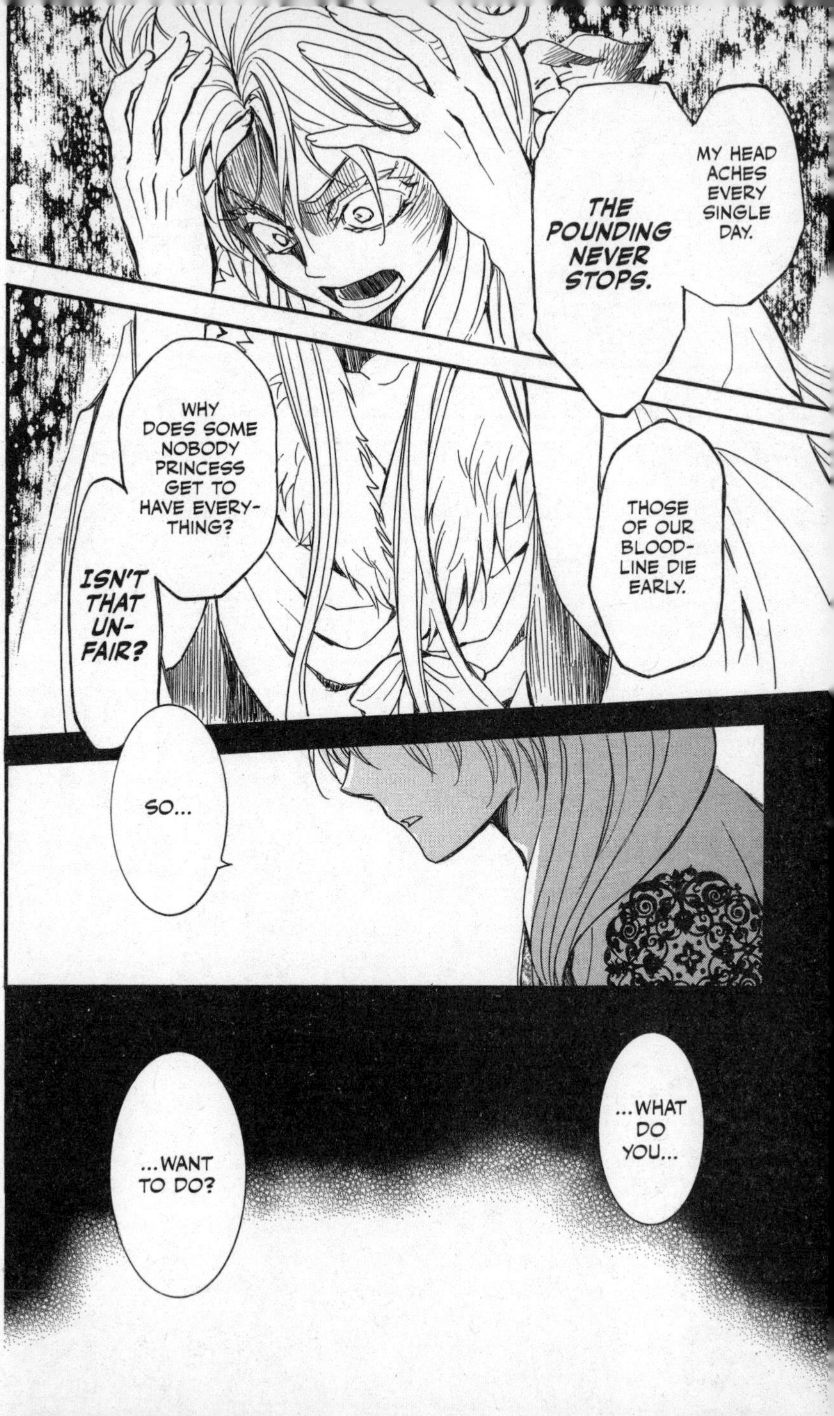
MY HEAD ACHES EVERY SINGLE DAY.
THE POUNDING NEVER STOPS.
THOSE OF OUR BLOOD-LINE DIE EARLY.
WHY DOES SOME NOBODY PRINCESS GET TO HAVE EVERY-THING?
ISN'T THAT UN-FAIR?
SO...
...WHAT DO YOU...
...WANT TO DO?

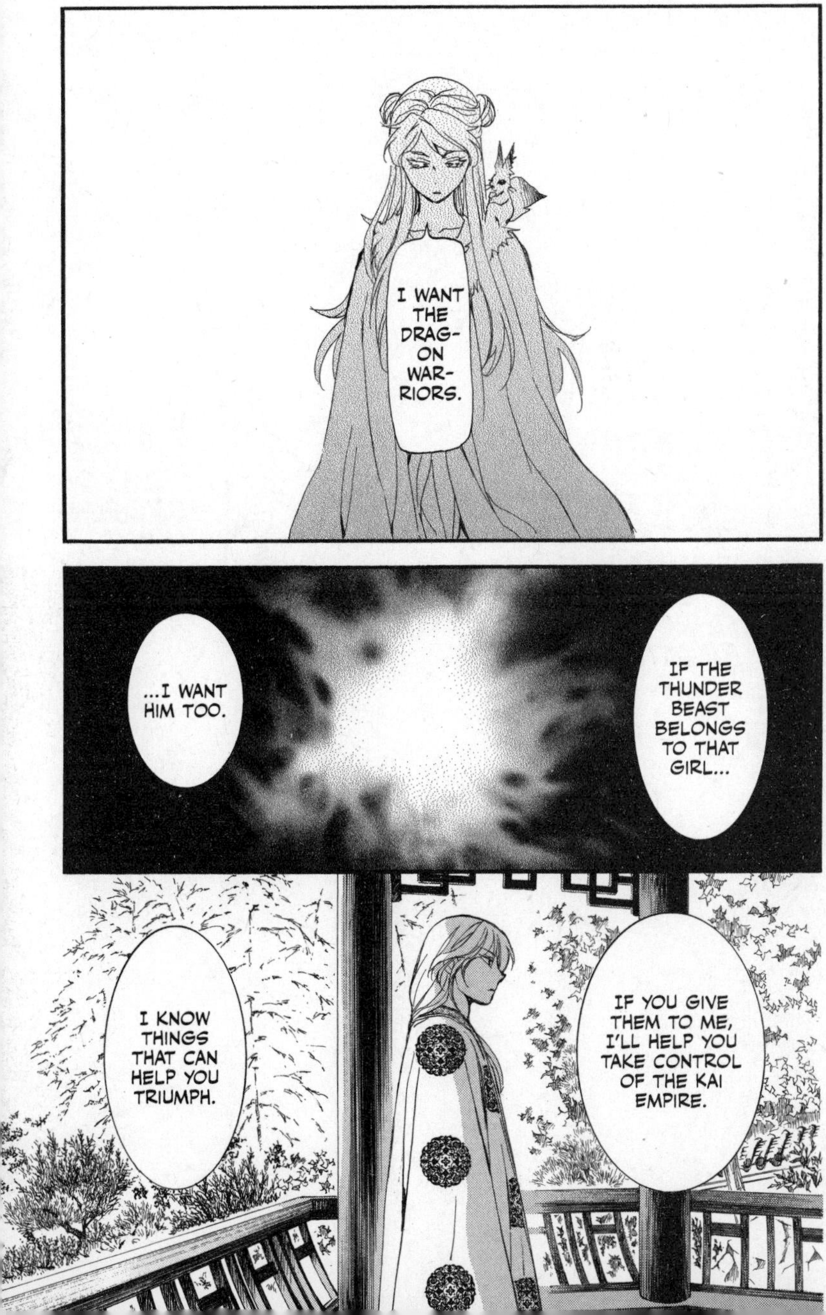
I WANT THE DRAG-ON WAR-RIORS.
IF THE THUNDER BEAST BELONGS TO THAT GIRL...
...I WANT HIM TOO.
IF YOU GIVE THEM TO ME, I'LL HELP YOU TAKE CONTROL OF THE KAI EMPIRE.
I KNOW THINGS THAT CAN HELP YOU TRIUMPH.

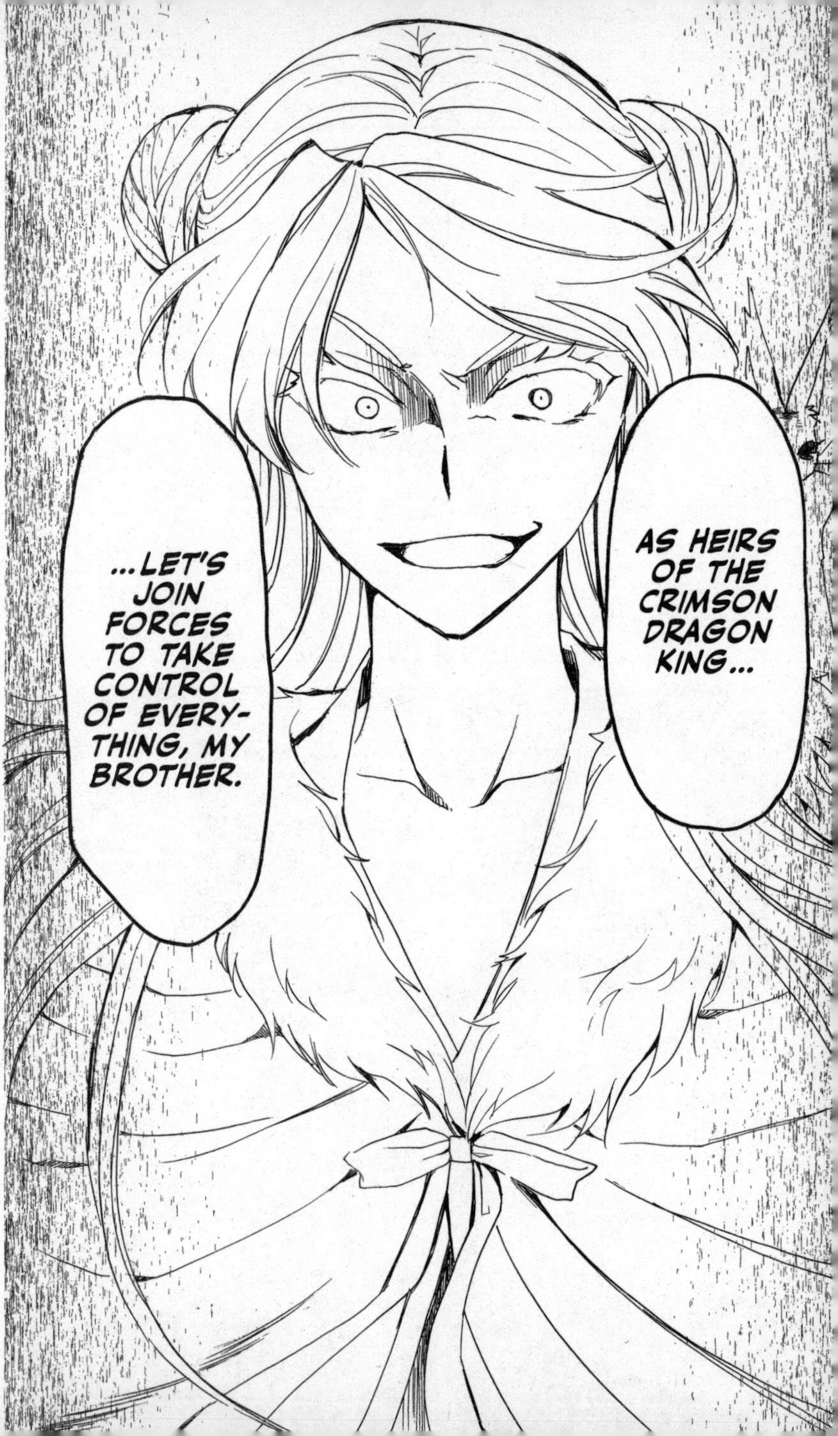
AS HEIRS OF THE CRIMSON DRAGON KING...
...LET'S JOIN FORCES TO TAKE CONTROL OF EVERY-THING, MY BROTHER.

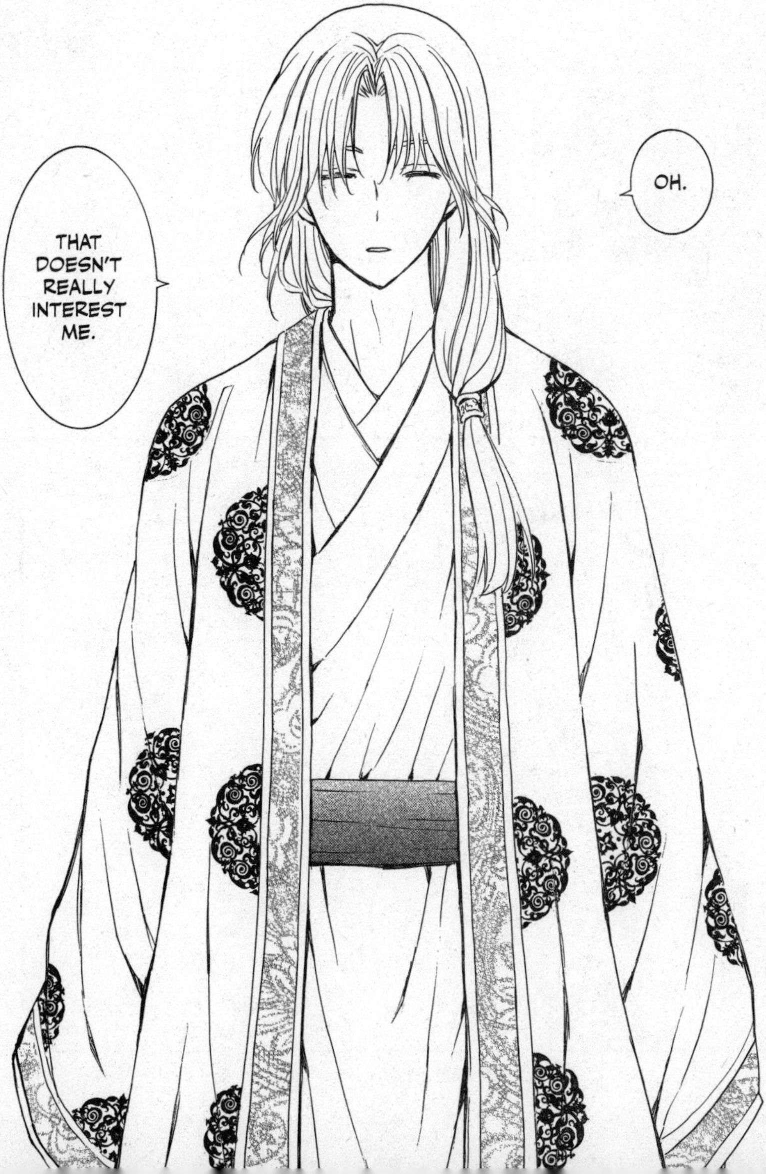
OH.
THAT DOESN'T REALLY INTEREST ME.

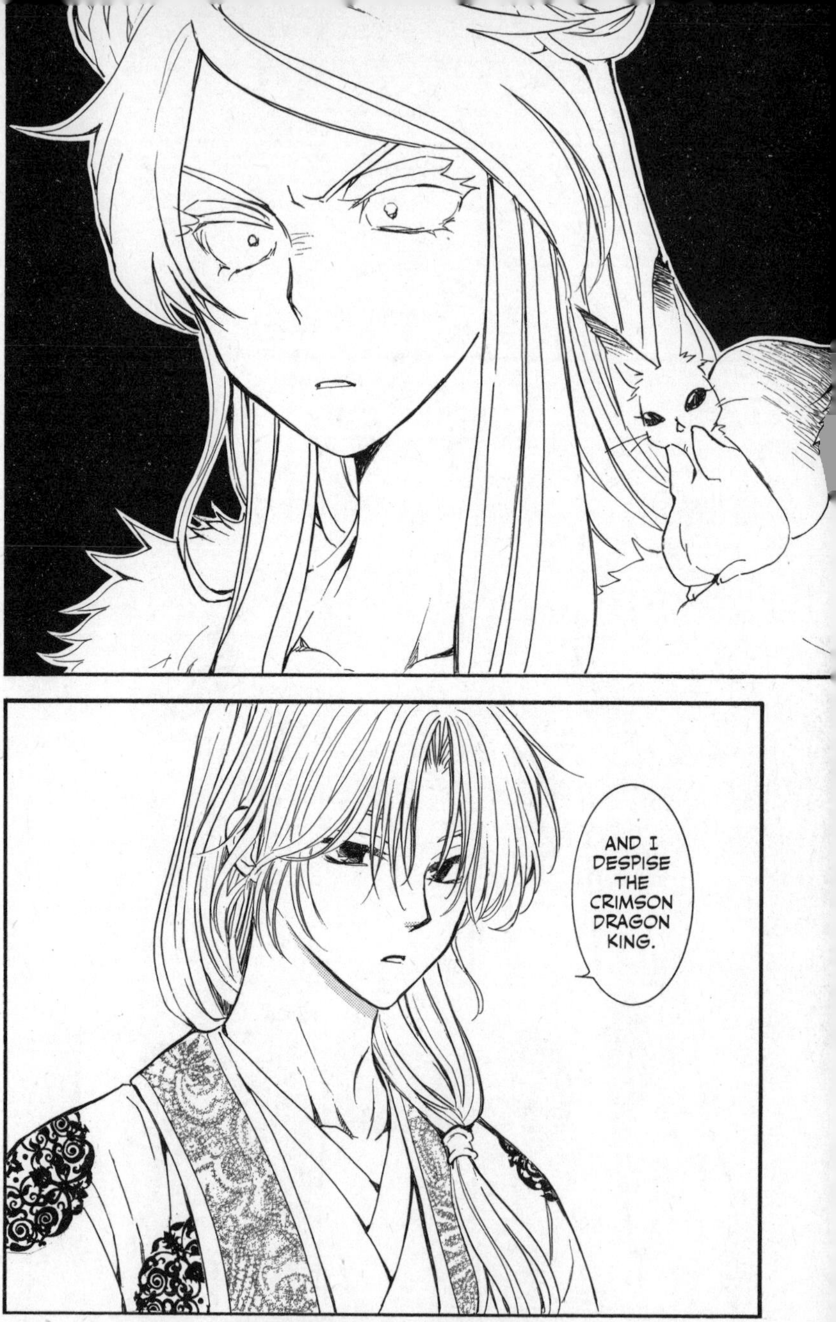
AND I DESPISE THE CRIMSON DRAGON KING.

CHAPTER 203 / THE END

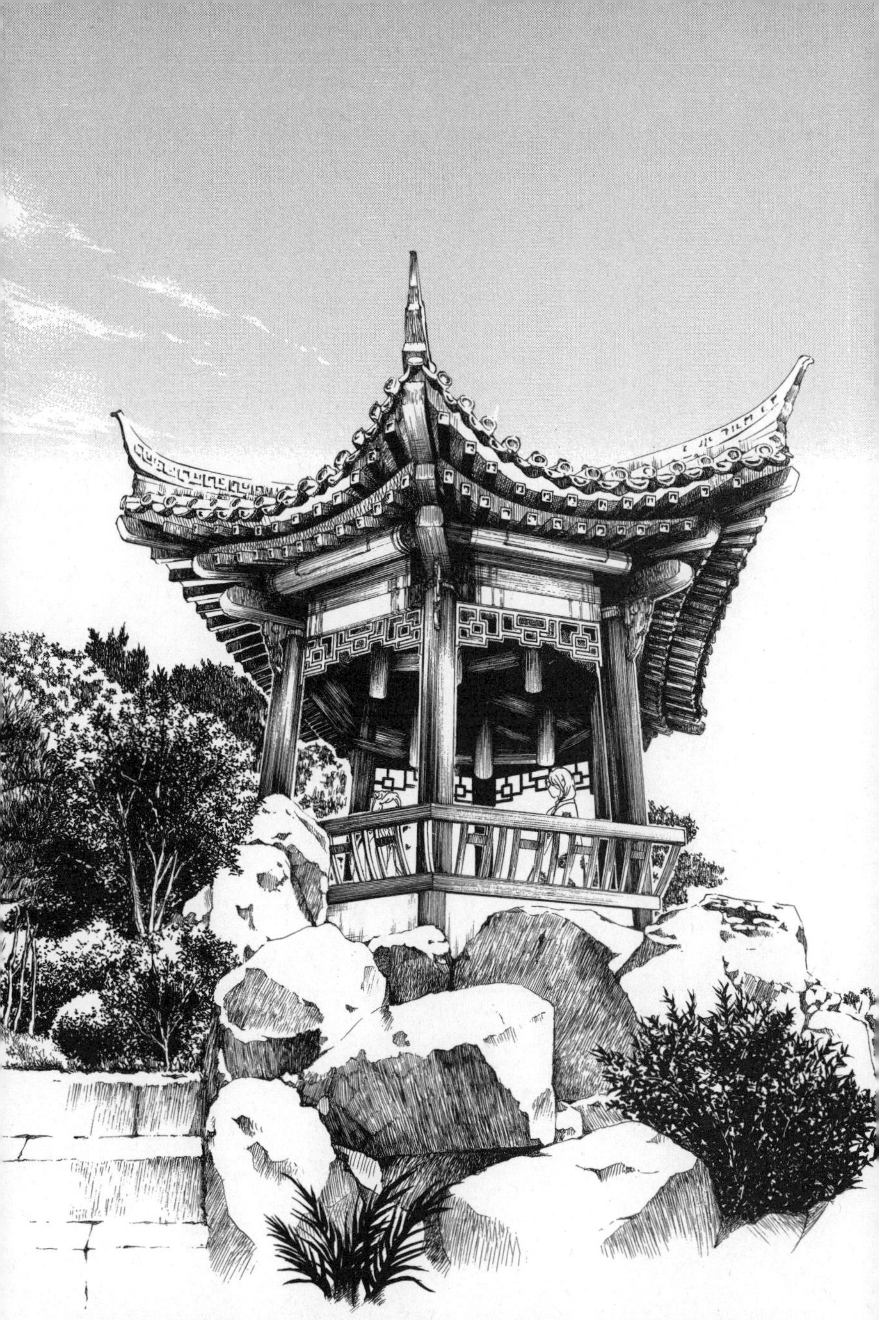

CHAPTER 204: ONE-SIDED AFFECTION

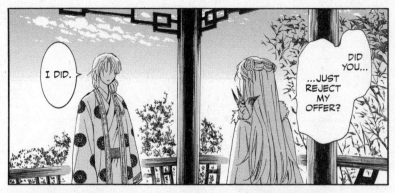

DID YOU... ...JUST REJECT MY OFFER?
I DID.
YOU DESPISE THE CRIMSON DRAGON KING? DO YOU DENY YOUR OWN HERITAGE?
I DON'T DENY BEING HIS DESCENDANT...
...BUT I DON'T SEE WHAT'S SO SPECIAL ABOUT IT.
YOU'RE NOT INTERESTED?
IMPOSSIBLE!

Yona of the Dawn

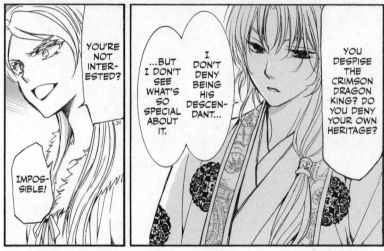

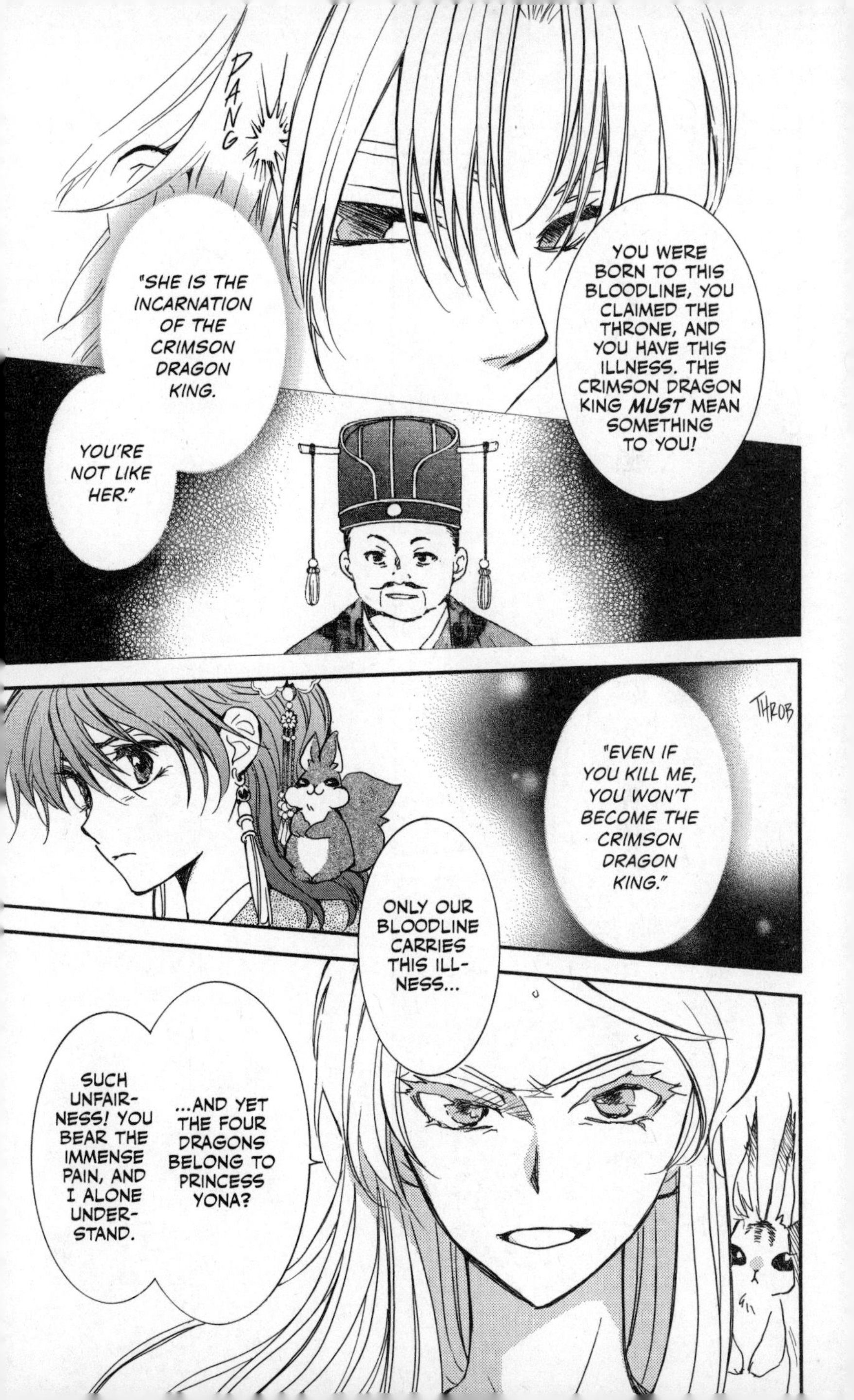
PANG
YOU WERE BORN TO THIS BLOODLINE, YOU CLAIMED THE THRONE, AND YOU HAVE THIS ILLNESS. THE CRIMSON DRAGON KING *MUST* MEAN SOMETHING TO YOU!
"SHE IS THE INCARNATION OF THE CRIMSON DRAGON KING.
YOU'RE NOT LIKE HER."
THROB
"EVEN IF YOU KILL ME, YOU WON'T BECOME THE CRIMSON DRAGON KING."
ONLY OUR BLOODLINE CARRIES THIS ILL-NESS...
...AND YET THE FOUR DRAGONS BELONG TO PRINCESS YONA?
SUCH UNFAIR-NESS! YOU BEAR THE IMMENSE PAIN, AND I ALONE UNDER-STAND.

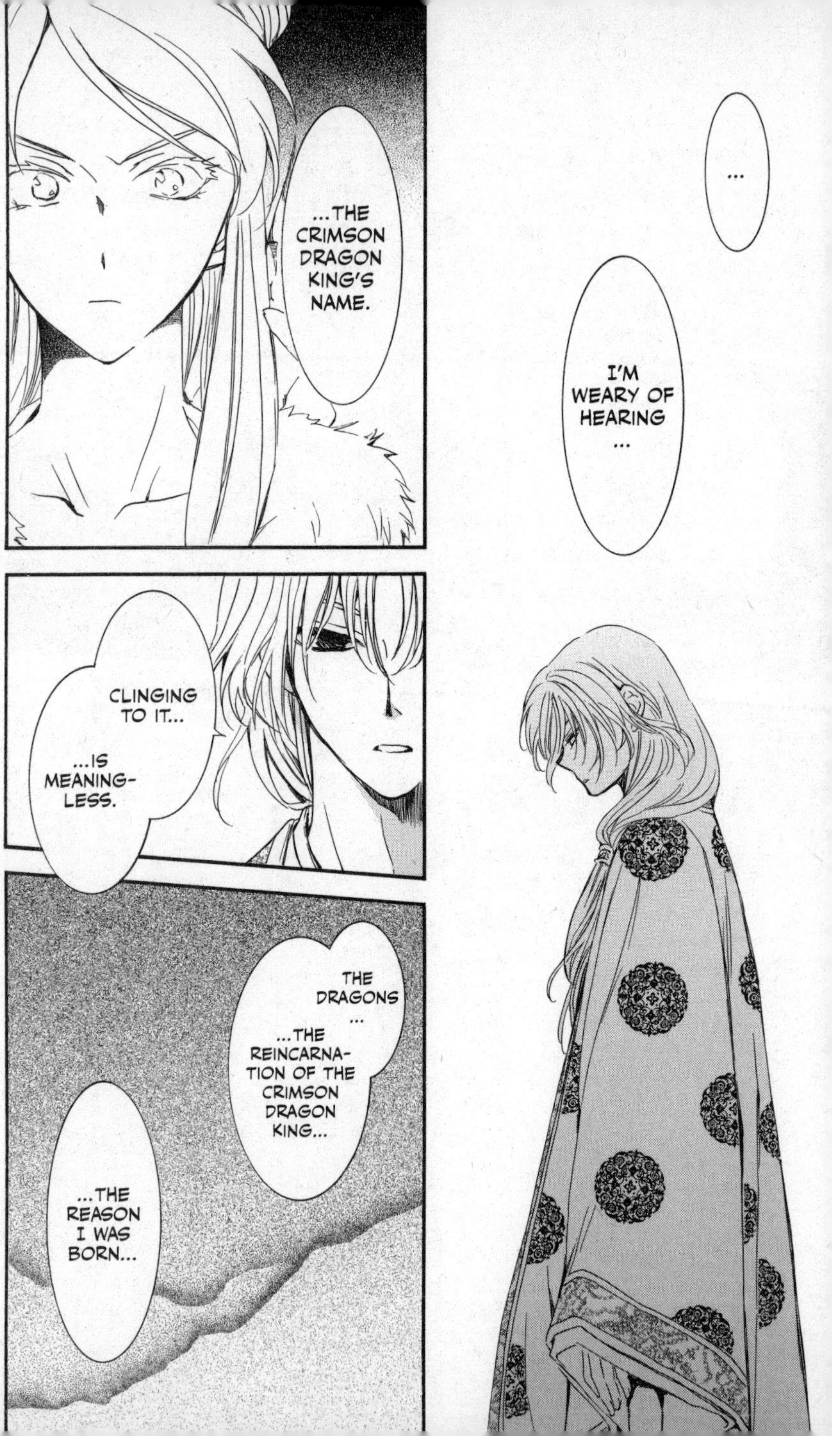
...
I'M WEARY OF HEARING ...
...THE CRIMSON DRAGON KING'S NAME.
CLINGING TO IT...
...IS MEANING-LESS.
THE DRAGONS ... ...THE REINCARNA-TION OF THE CRIMSON DRAGON KING...
...THE REASON I WAS BORN...

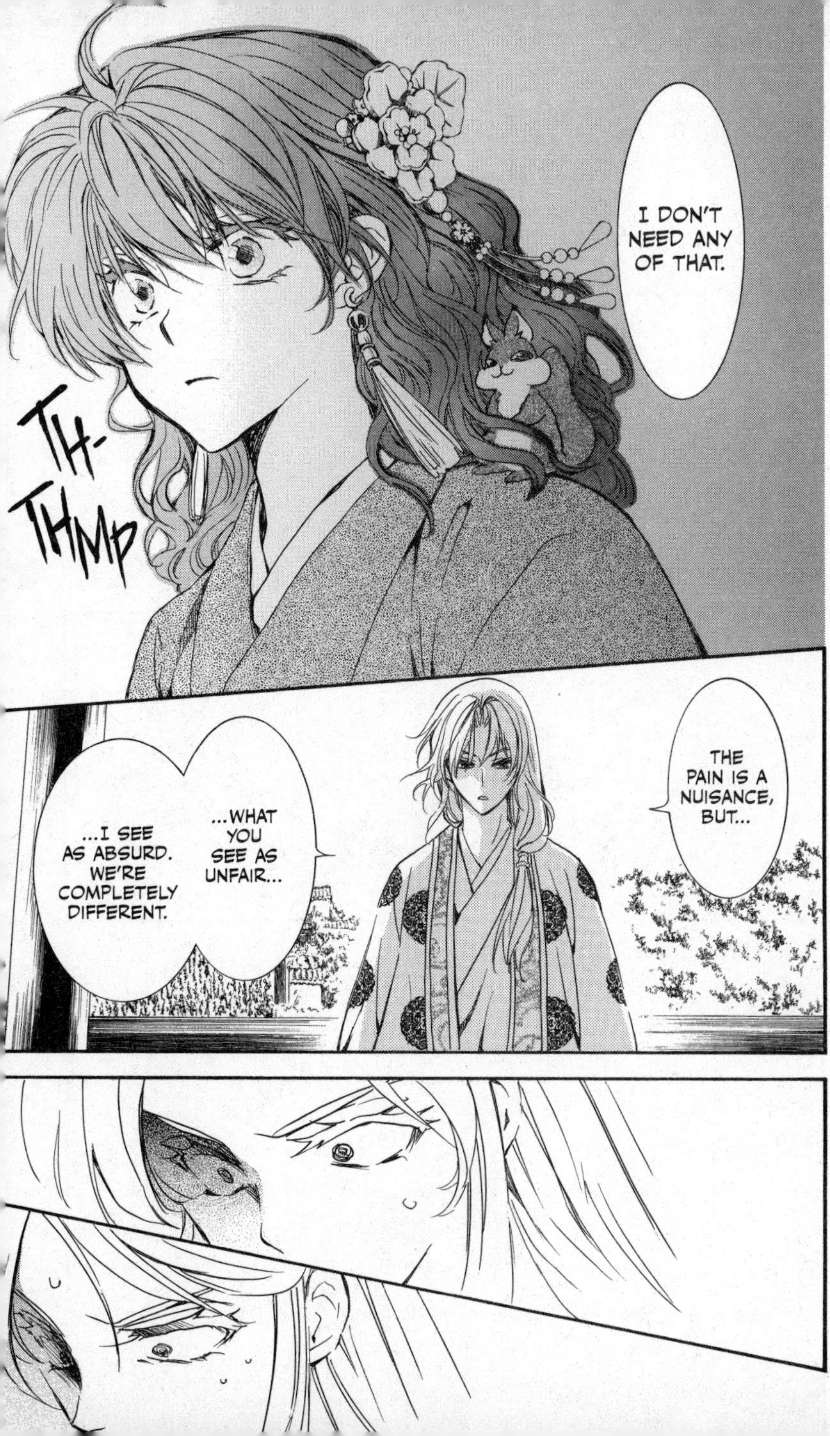
I DON'T NEED ANY OF THAT.
TH-THMP
THE PAIN IS A NUISANCE, BUT...
...WHAT YOU SEE AS UNFAIR...
...I SEE AS ABSURD. WE'RE COMPLETELY DIFFERENT.

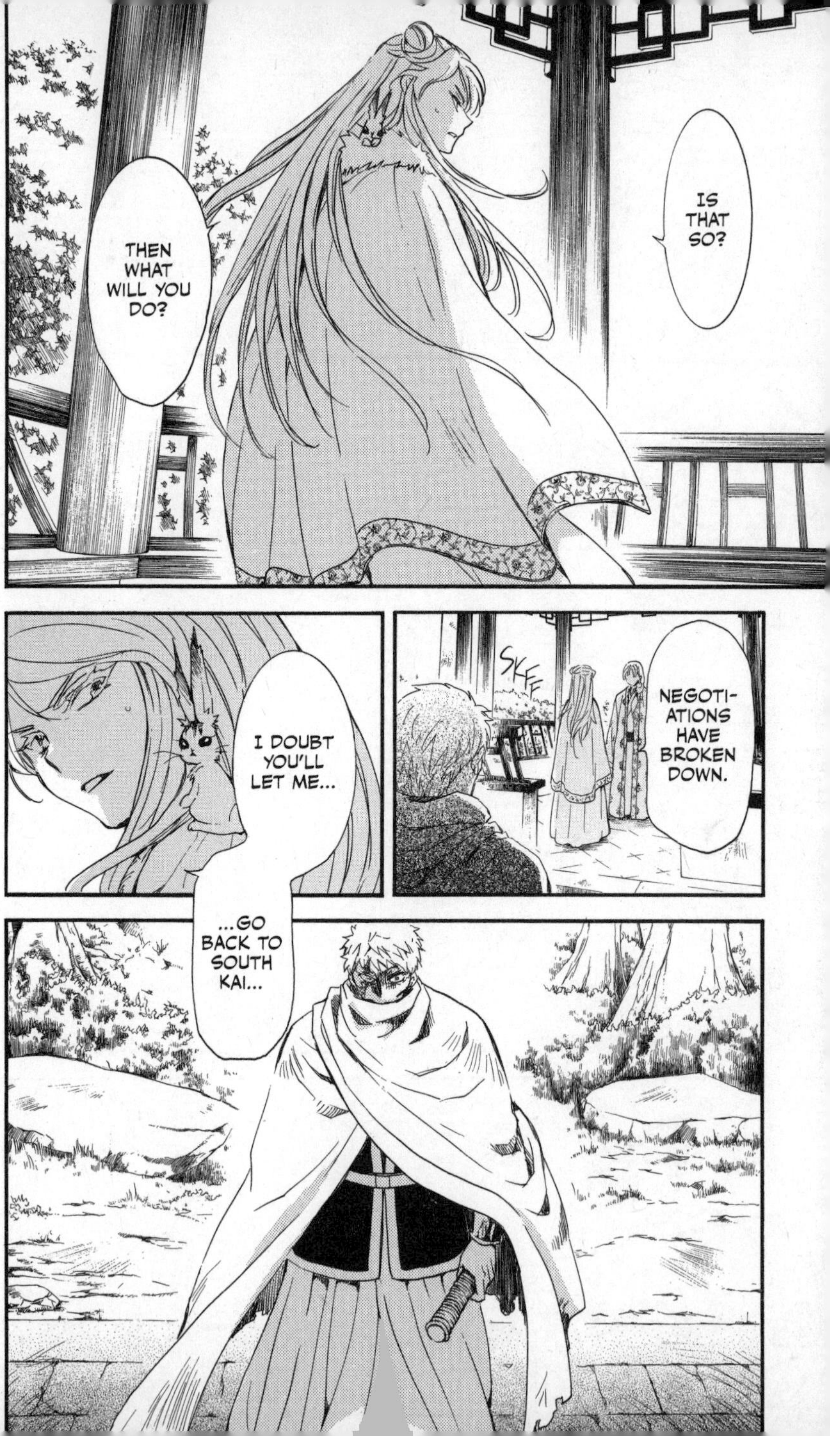
IS THAT SO?
THEN WHAT WILL YOU DO?
SKFF
NEGOTIATIONS HAVE BROKEN DOWN.
I DOUBT YOU'LL LET ME...
...GO BACK TO SOUTH KAI...

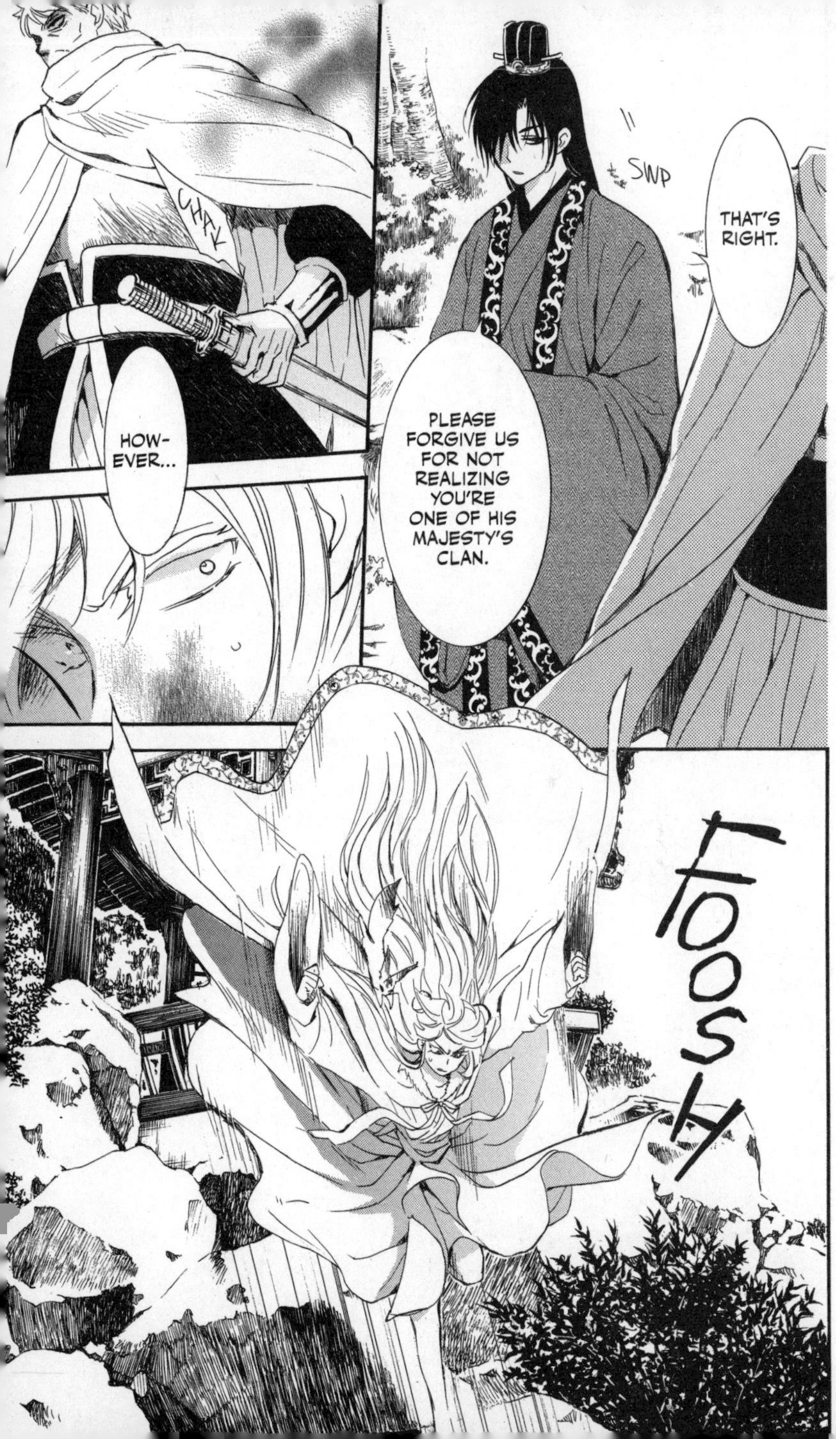
SWP
THAT'S RIGHT.
PLEASE FORGIVE US FOR NOT REALIZING YOU'RE ONE OF HIS MAJESTY'S CLAN.
CHAK
HOW-EVER...
FOOSH

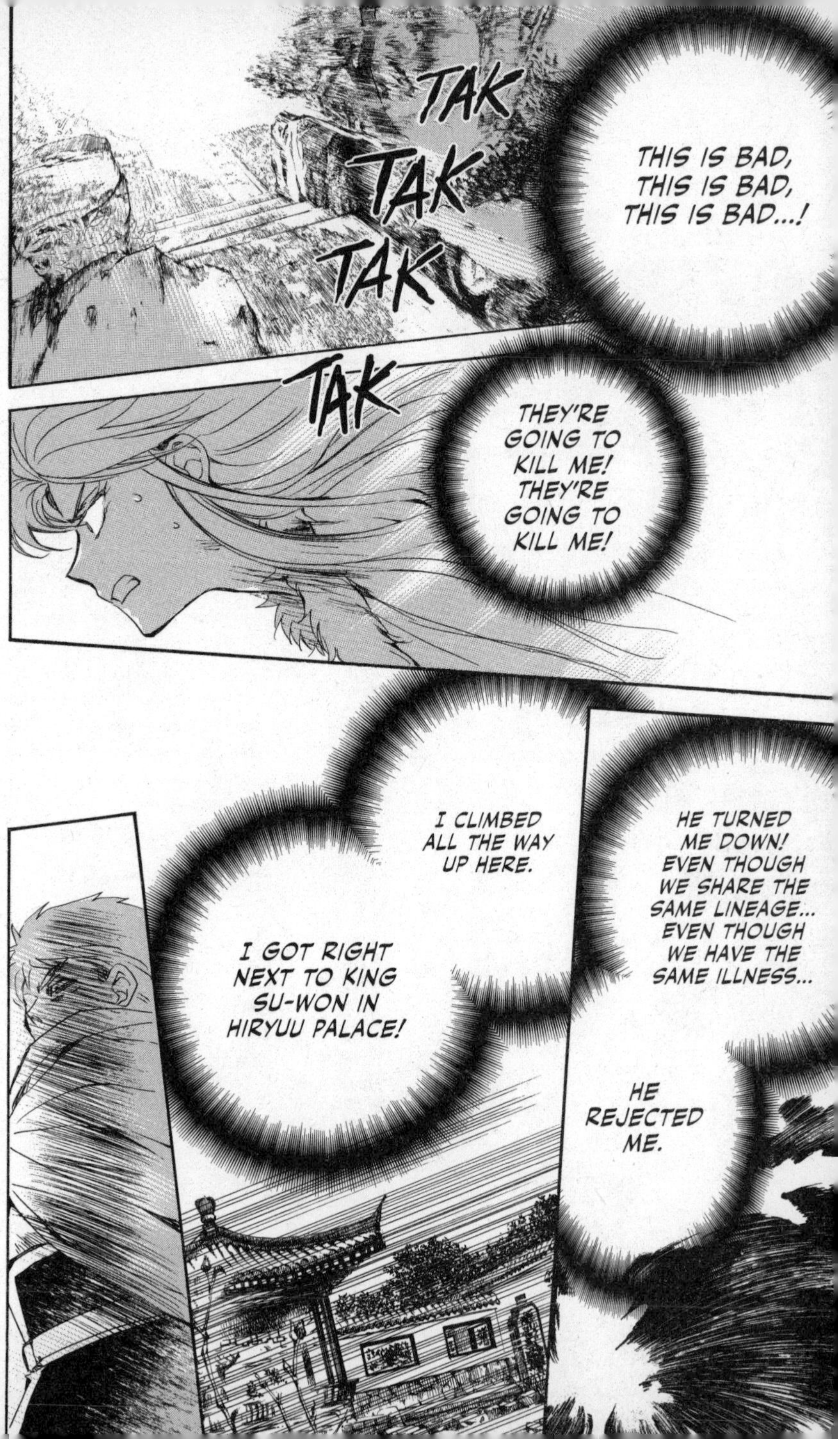
THIS IS BAD, THIS IS BAD, THIS IS BAD...!
TAK
TAK
TAK
TAK
THEY'RE GOING TO KILL ME! THEY'RE GOING TO KILL ME!
I CLIMBED ALL THE WAY UP HERE.
I GOT RIGHT NEXT TO KING SU-WON IN HIRYUU PALACE!
HE TURNED ME DOWN! EVEN THOUGH WE SHARE THE SAME LINEAGE... EVEN THOUGH WE HAVE THE SAME ILLNESS...
HE REJECTED ME.

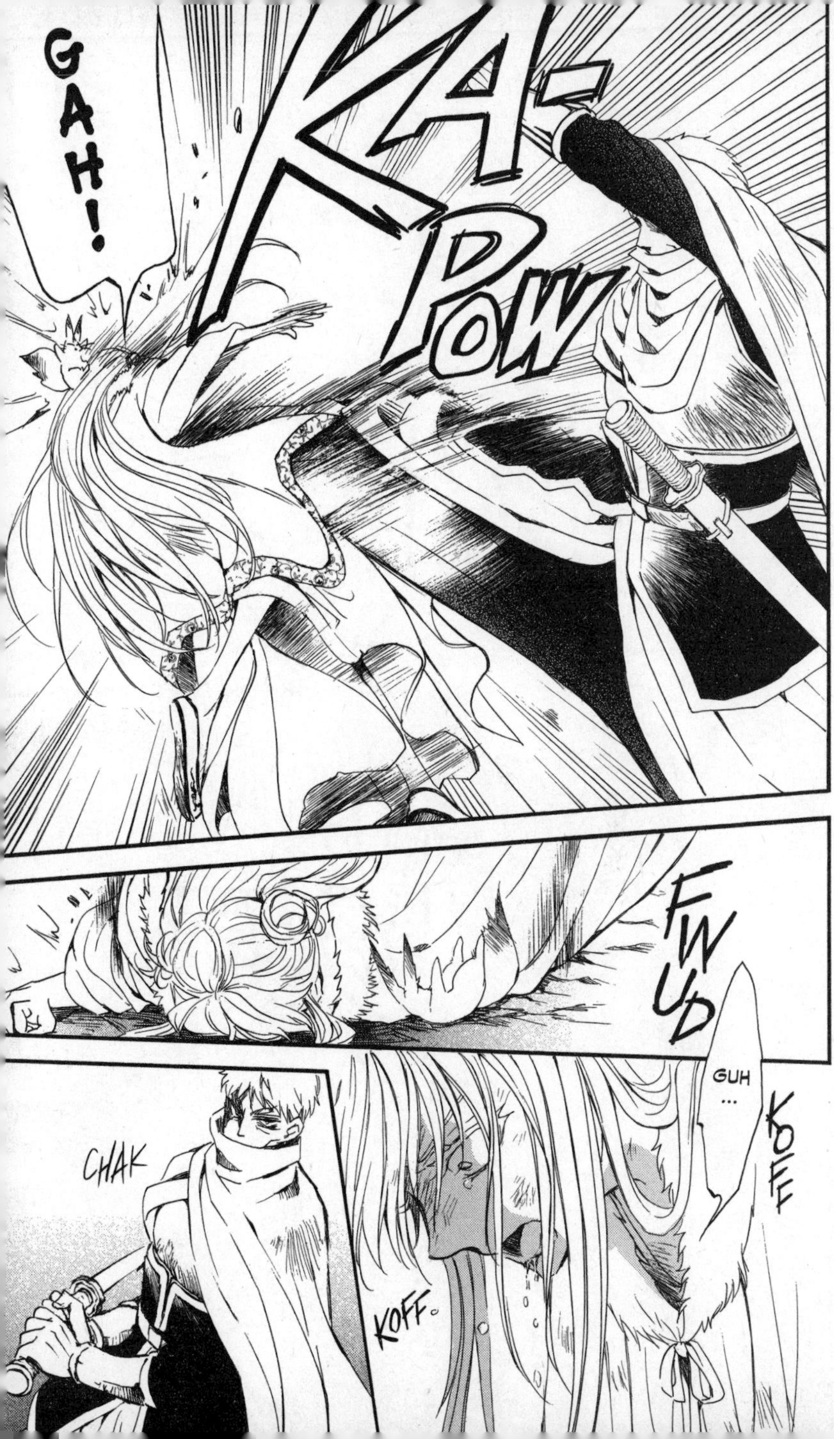
KA-POW
GAH!
FWUD
GUH ...
KOFF
CHAK
KOFF

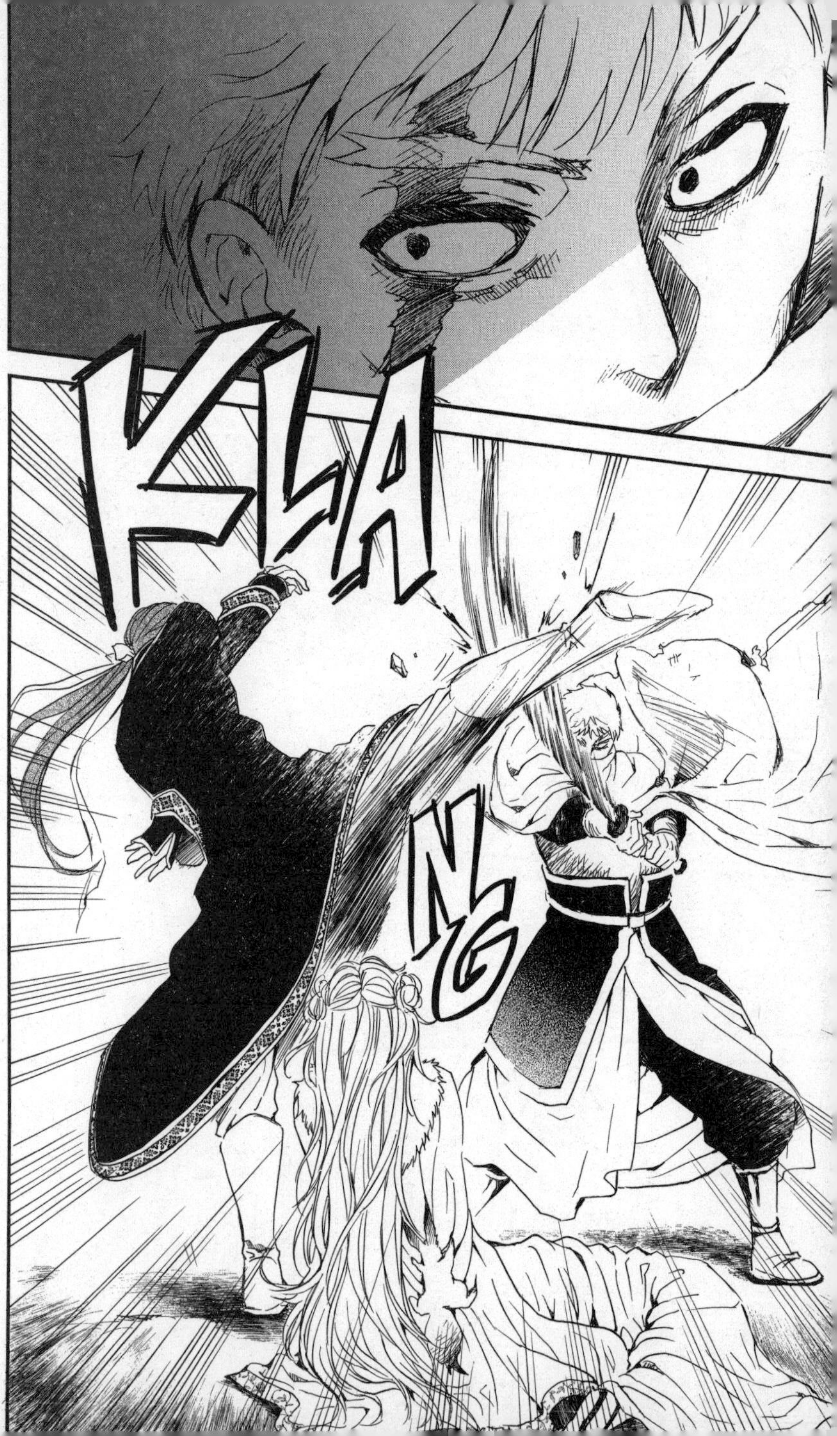
KLA
NG

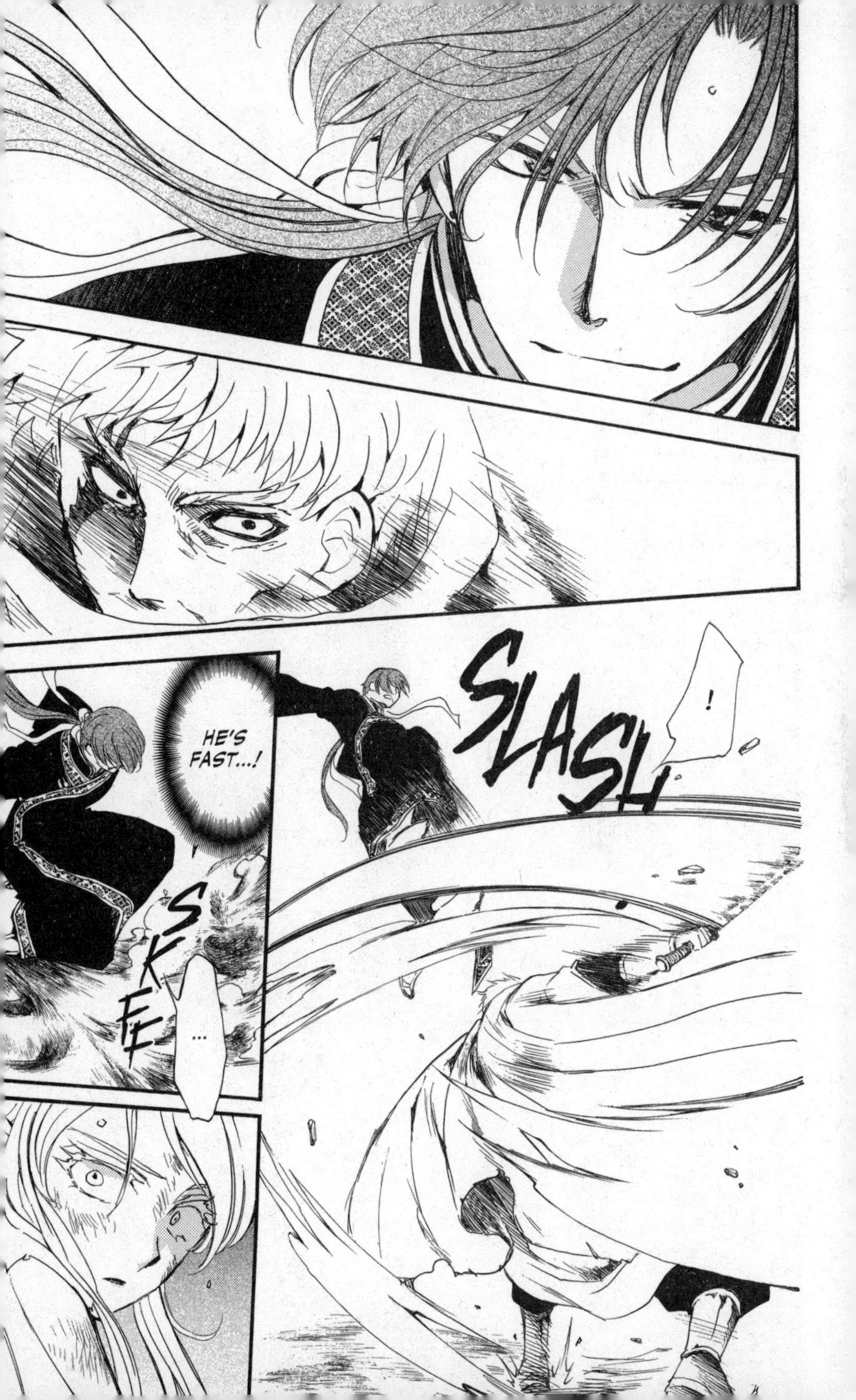
SLASH
!
HE'S FAST...!
SKEE
...

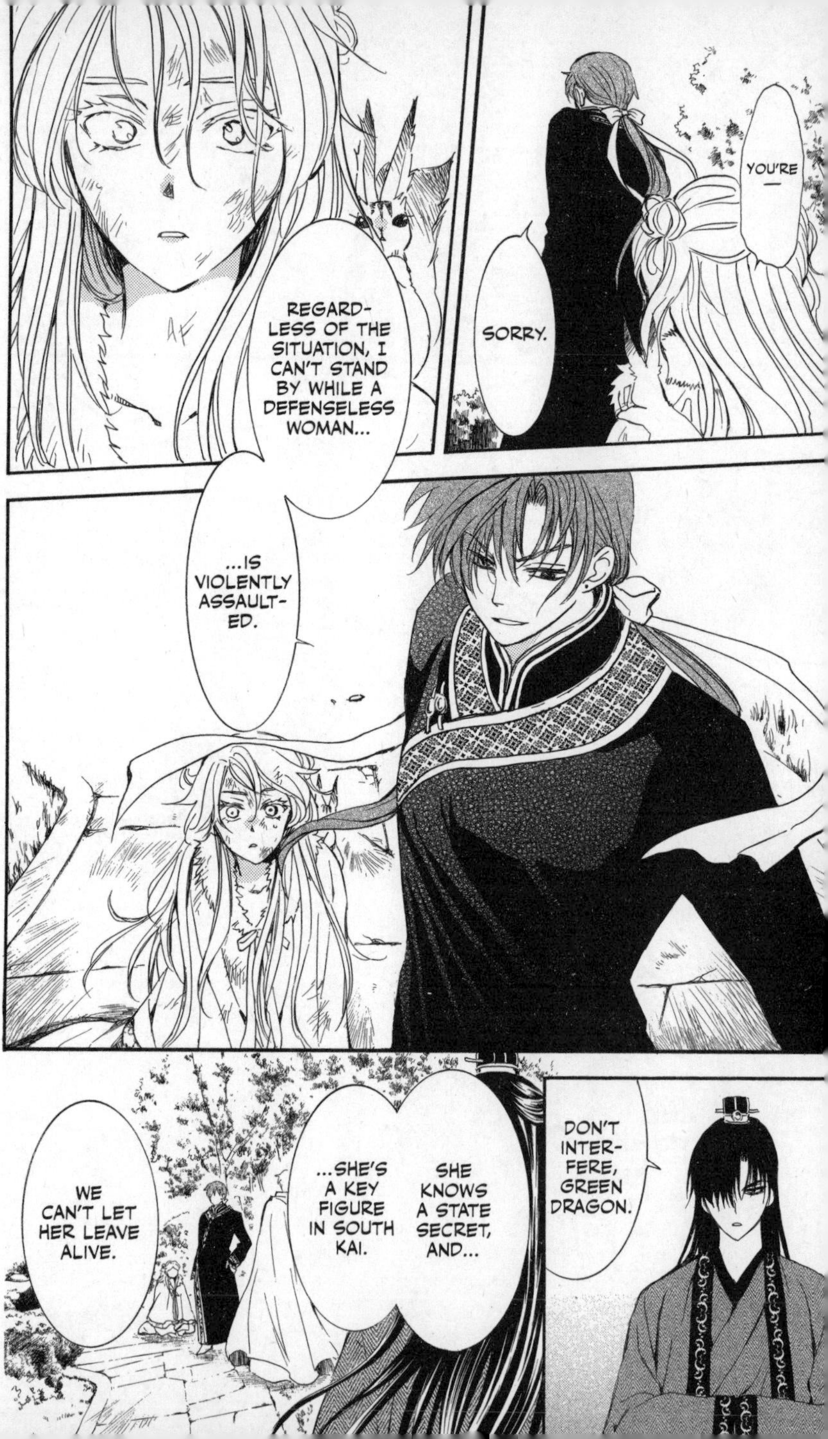
YOU'RE —
SORRY.
REGARDLESS OF THE SITUATION, I CAN'T STAND BY WHILE A DEFENSELESS WOMAN...
...IS VIOLENTLY ASSAULTED.
DON'T INTERFERE, GREEN DRAGON.
SHE KNOWS A STATE SECRET, AND...
...SHE'S A KEY FIGURE IN SOUTH KAI.
WE CAN'T LET HER LEAVE ALIVE.

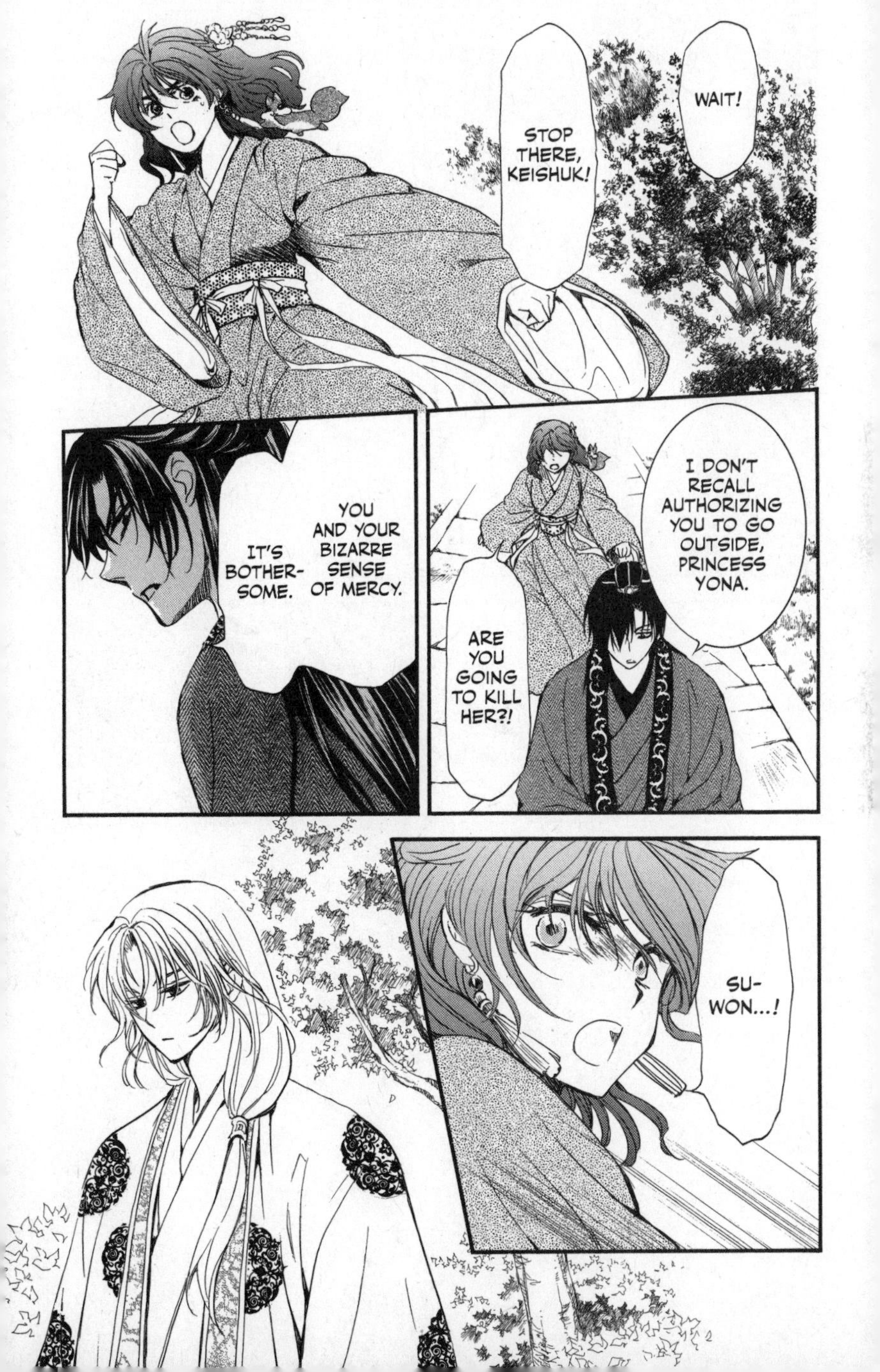
WAIT!
STOP THERE, KEISHUK!
I DON'T RECALL AUTHORIZING YOU TO GO OUTSIDE, PRINCESS YONA.
ARE YOU GOING TO KILL HER?!
YOU AND YOUR BIZARRE SENSE OF MERCY.
IT'S BOTHER-SOME.
SU-WON...!

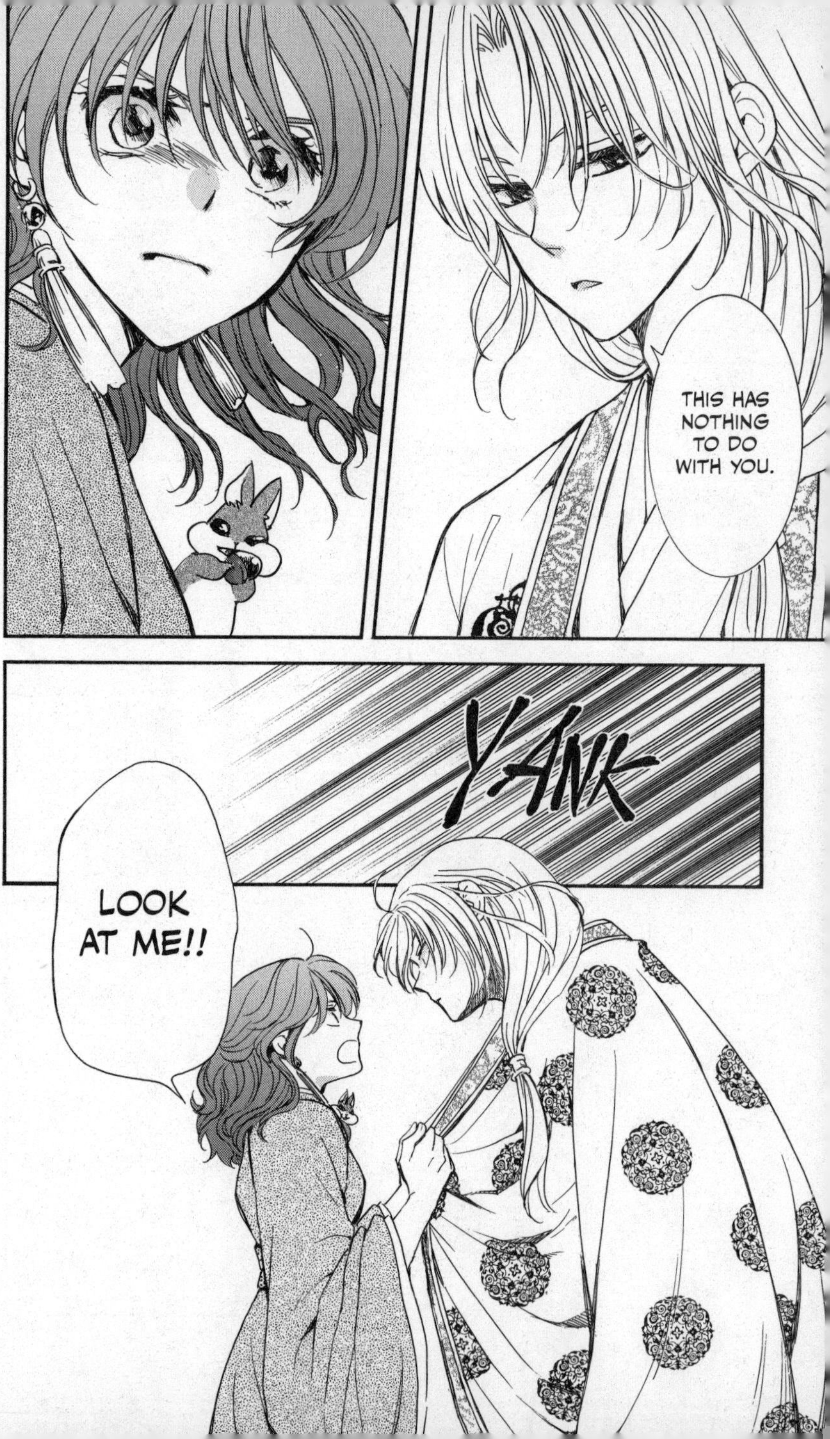
THIS HAS NOTHING TO DO WITH YOU.
YANK
LOOK AT ME!!

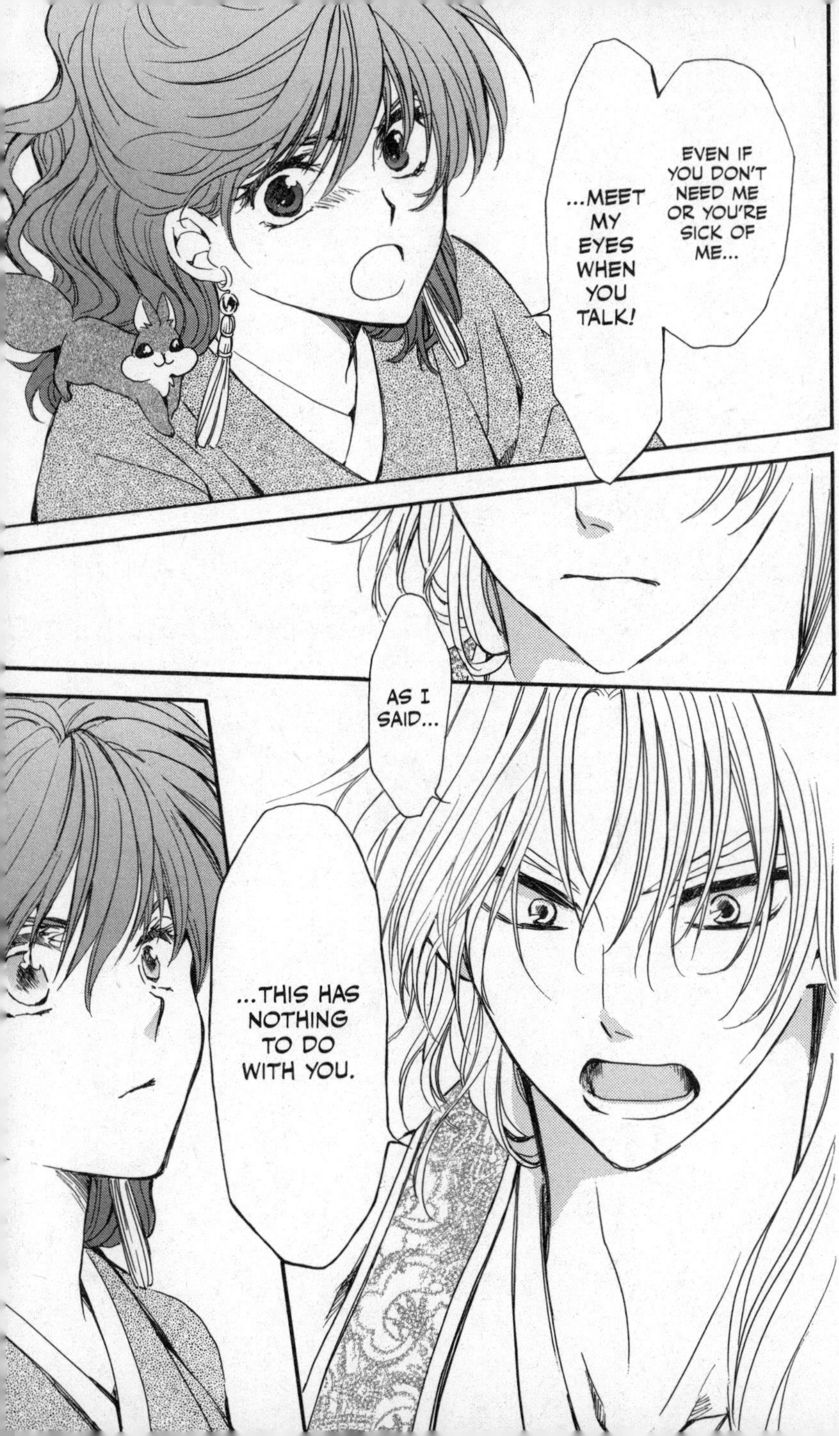
EVEN IF YOU DON'T NEED ME OR YOU'RE SICK OF ME...
...MEET MY EYES WHEN YOU TALK!
AS I SAID...
...THIS HAS NOTHING TO DO WITH YOU.

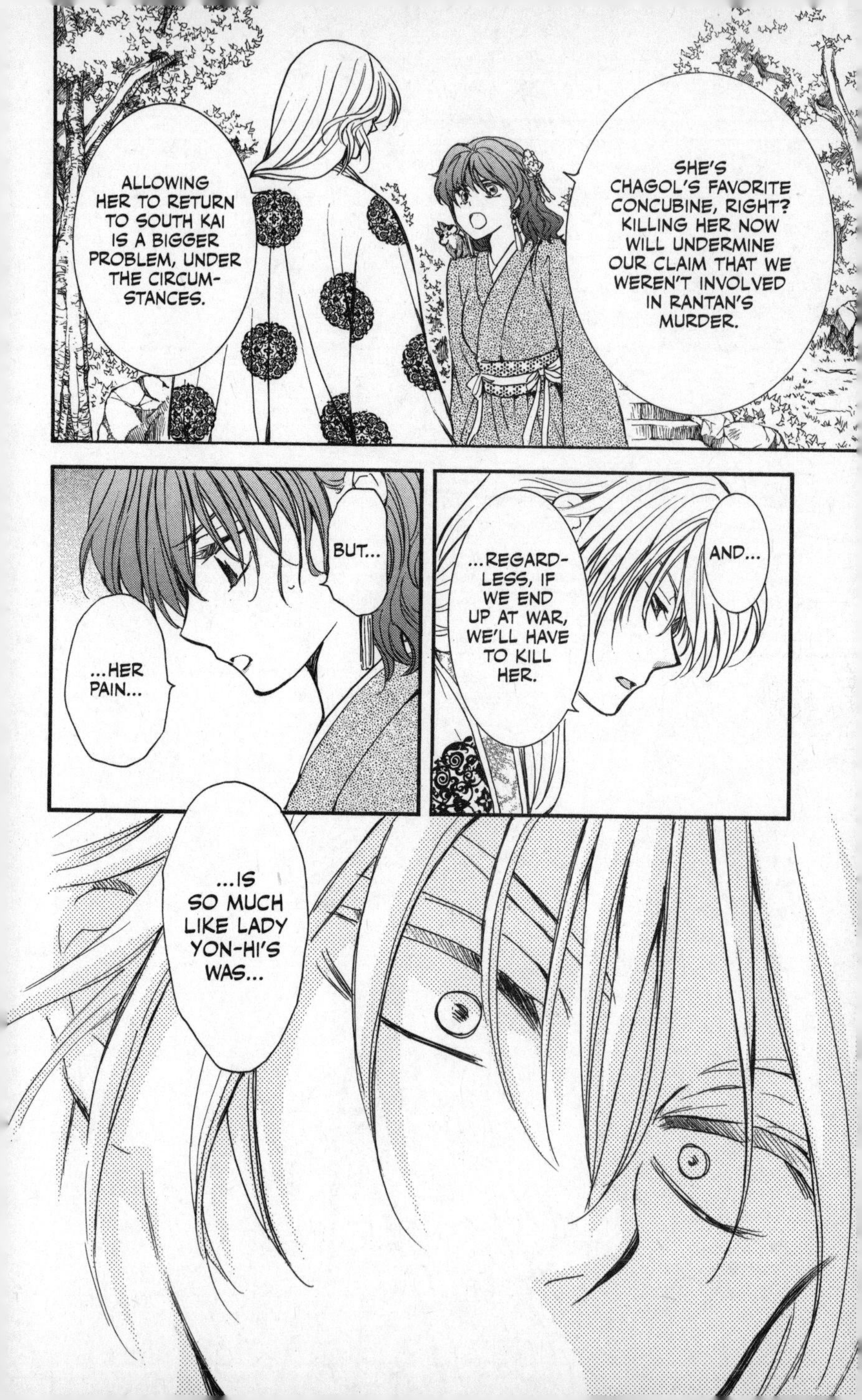
SHE'S CHAGOL'S FAVORITE CONCUBINE, RIGHT? KILLING HER NOW WILL UNDERMINE OUR CLAIM THAT WE WEREN'T INVOLVED IN RANTAN'S MURDER.
ALLOWING HER TO RETURN TO SOUTH KAI IS A BIGGER PROBLEM, UNDER THE CIRCUM-STANCES.
AND...
...REGARD-LESS, IF WE END UP AT WAR, WE'LL HAVE TO KILL HER.
BUT...
...HER PAIN...
...IS SO MUCH LIKE LADY YON-HI'S WAS...

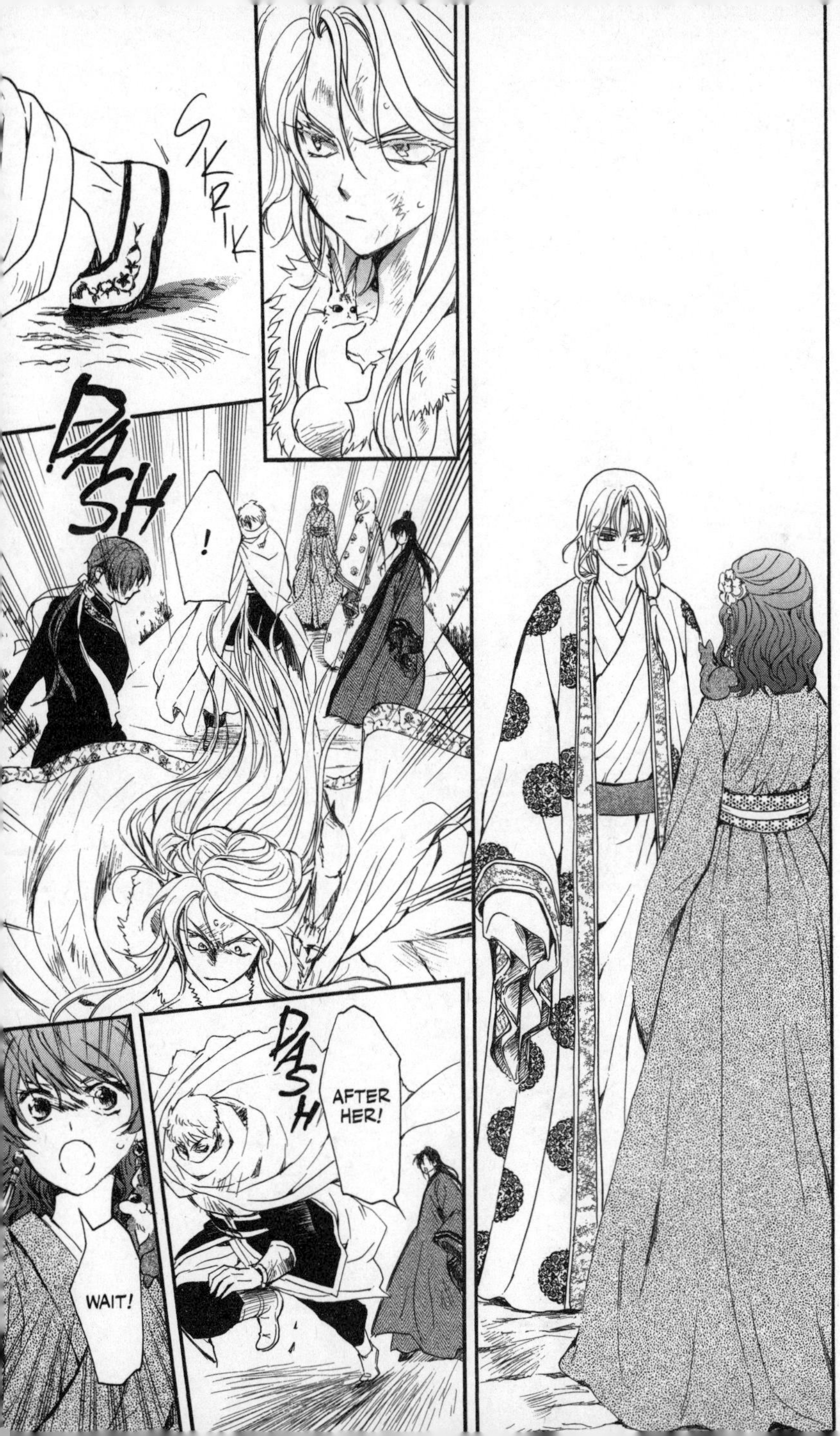
SKRIK
DASH
!
AFTER HER!
DASH
WAIT!

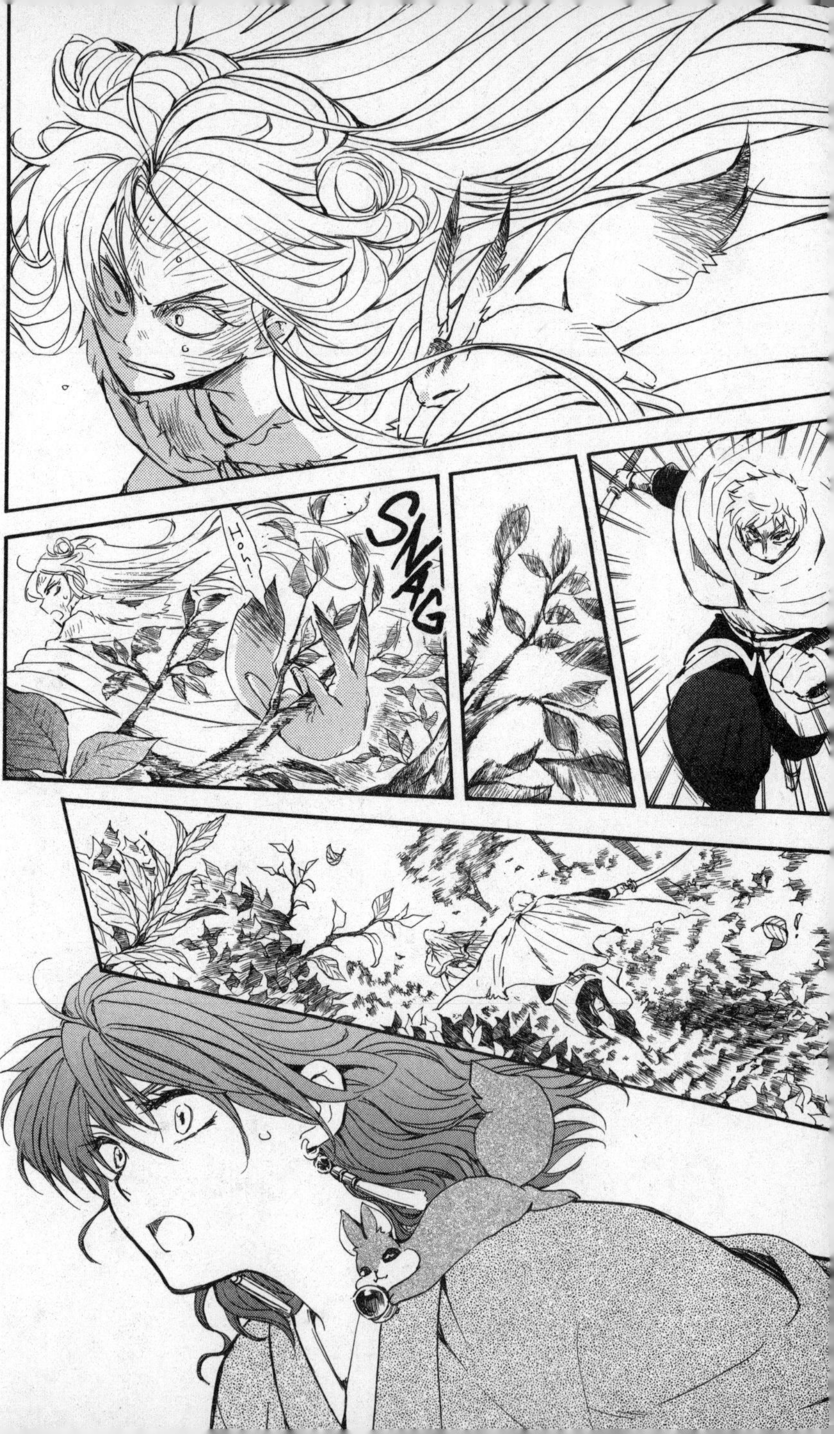
SNAG
Hoh!

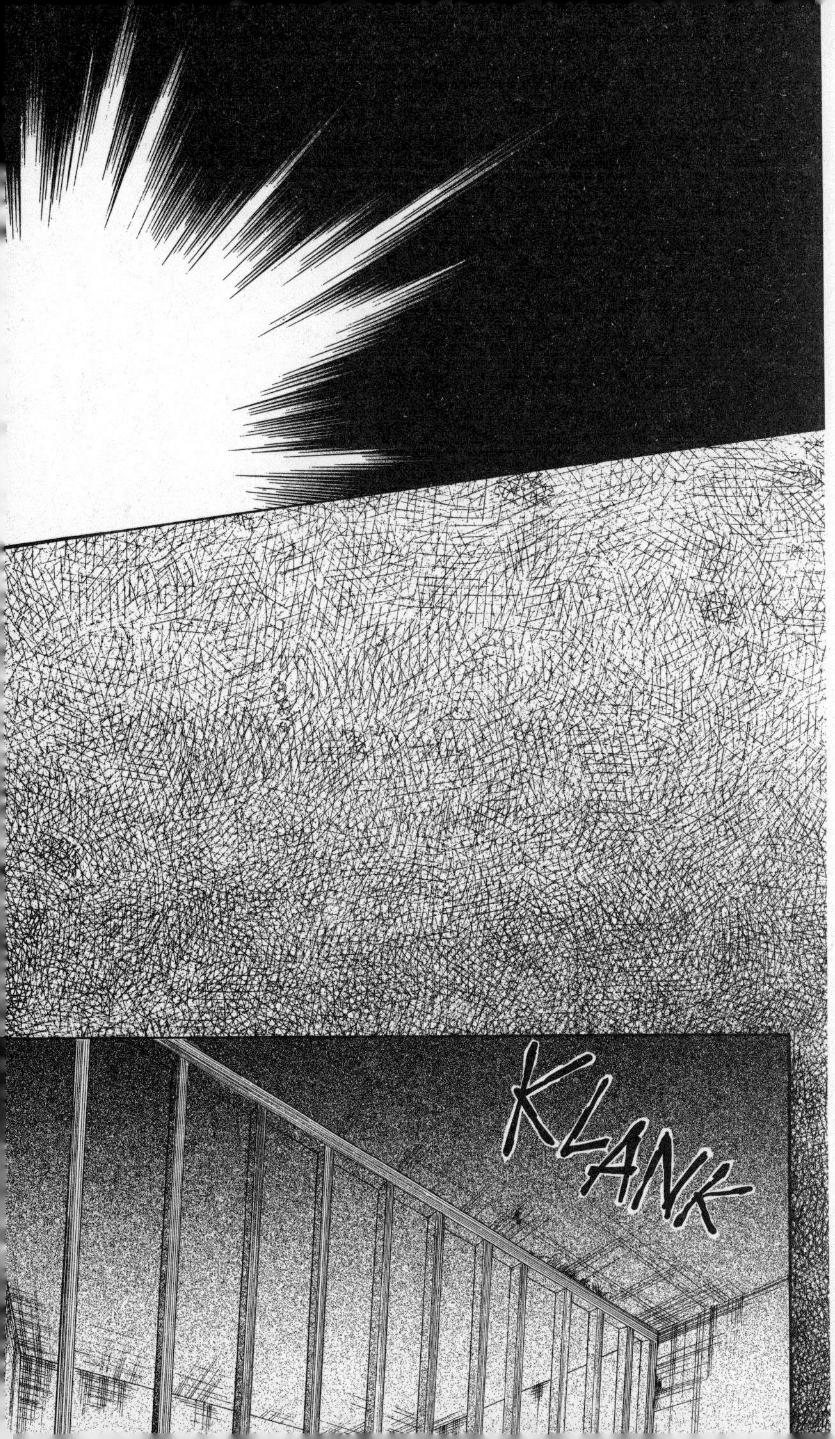
KLANK

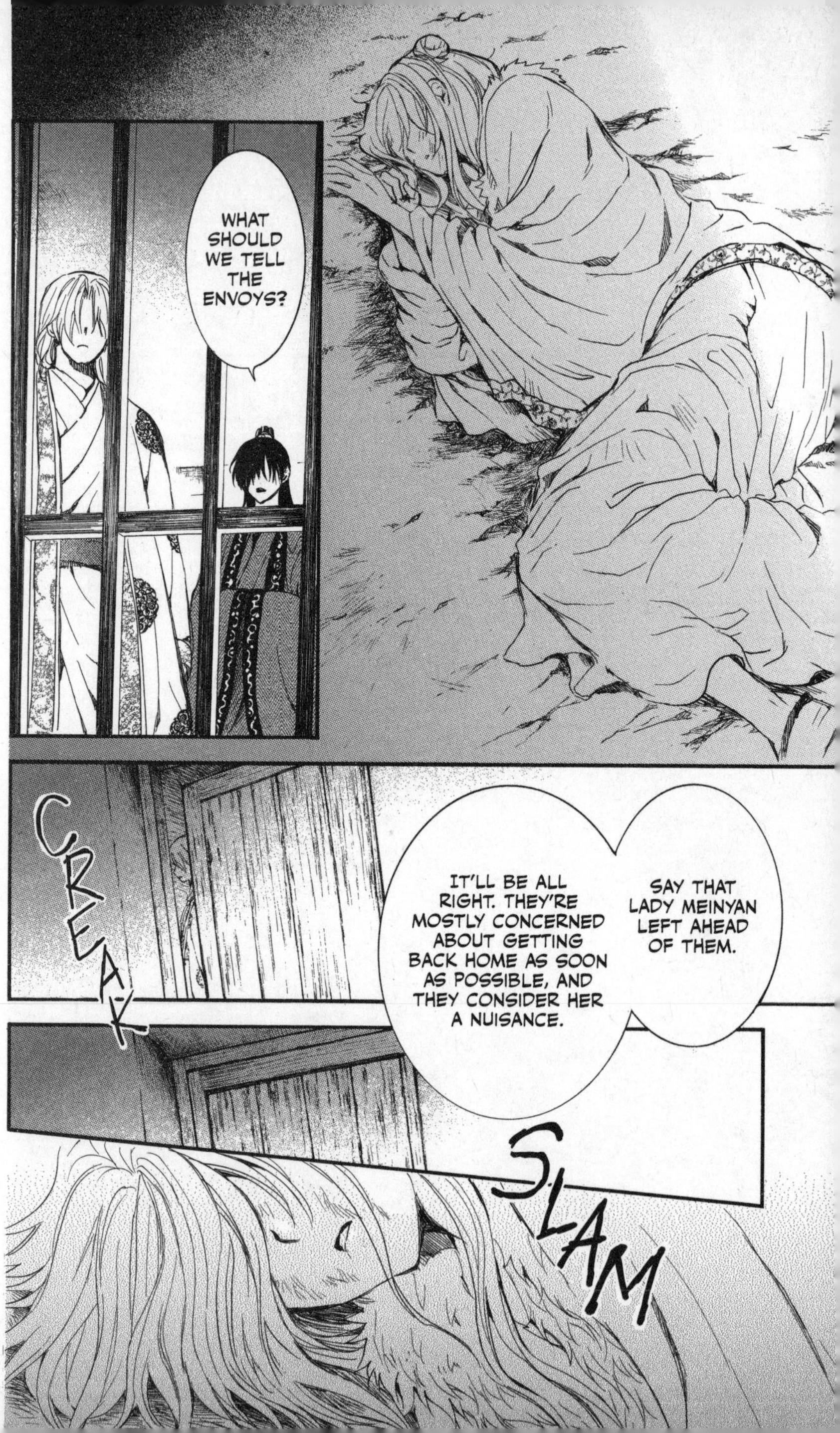
WHAT SHOULD WE TELL THE ENVOYS?
SAY THAT LADY MEINYAN LEFT AHEAD OF THEM.
IT'LL BE ALL RIGHT. THEY'RE MOSTLY CONCERNED ABOUT GETTING BACK HOME AS SOON AS POSSIBLE, AND THEY CONSIDER HER A NUISANCE.
CREAK
SLAM

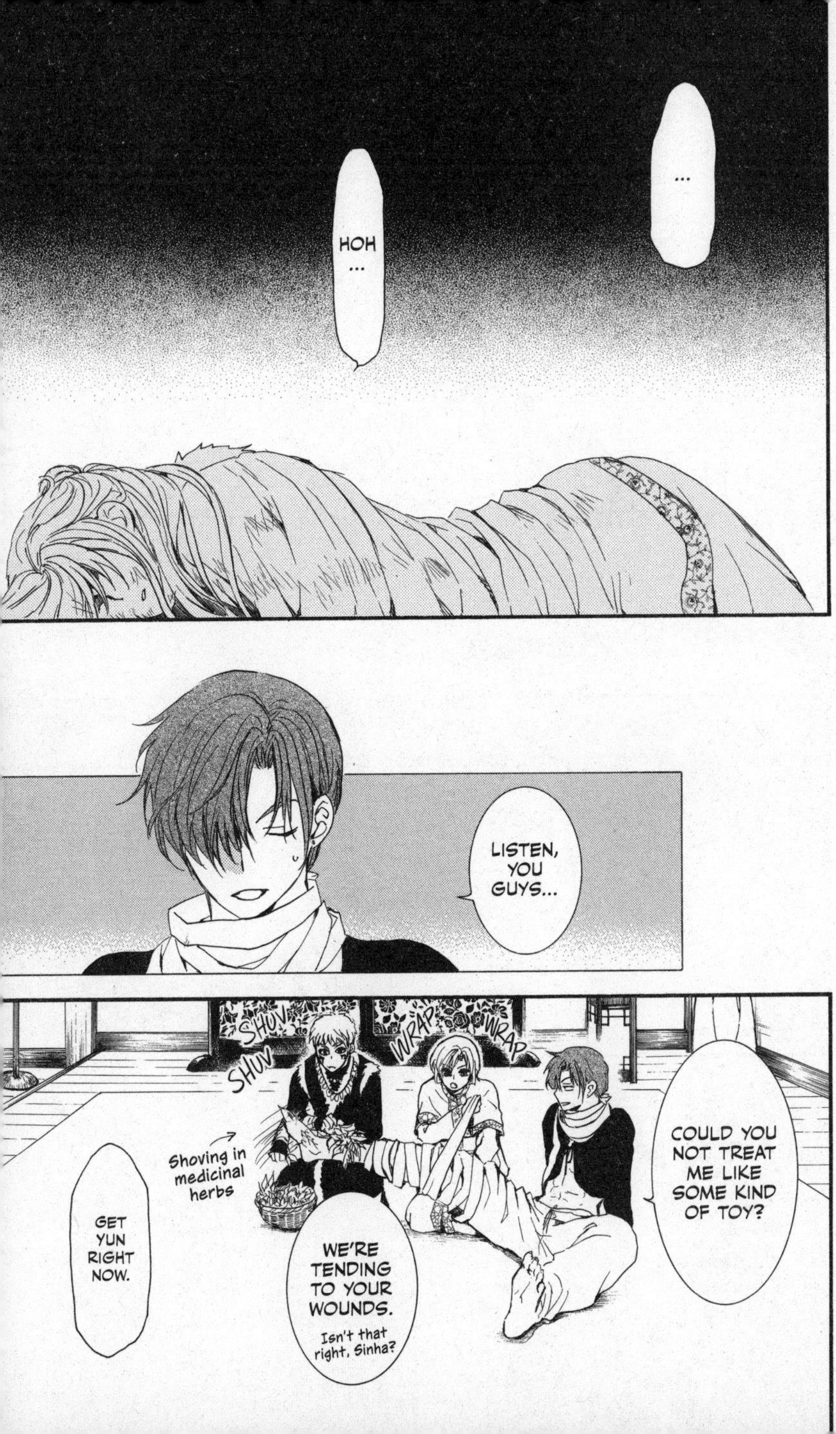
...
HOH ...
LISTEN, YOU GUYS...
COULD YOU NOT TREAT ME LIKE SOME KIND OF TOY?
WRAP WRAP
SHUV SHUV
WE'RE TENDING TO YOUR WOUNDS.
Isn't that right, Sinha?
Shoving in medicinal herbs
GET YUN RIGHT NOW.

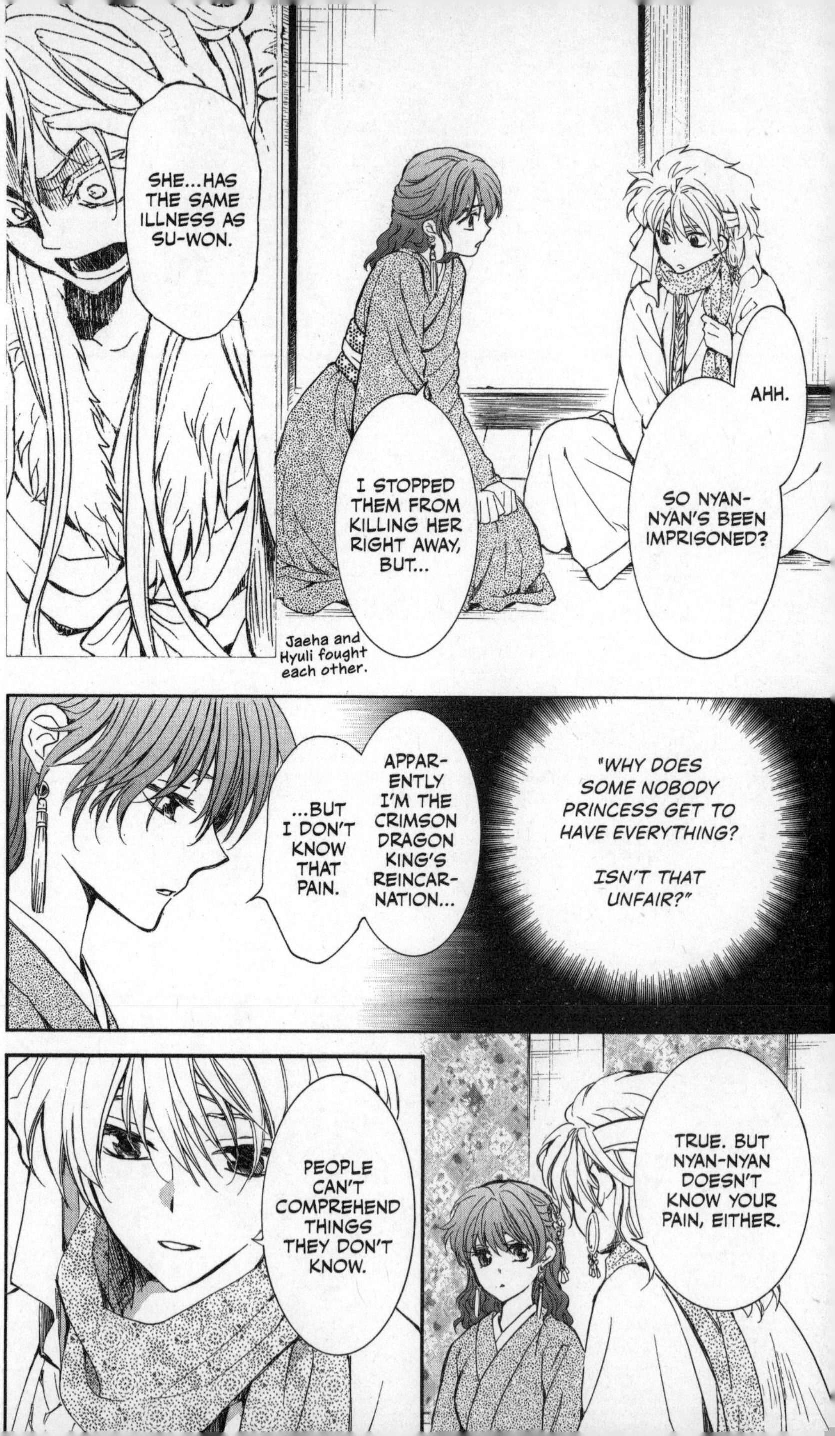
AHH.
SO NYAN-NYAN'S BEEN IMPRISONED?
I STOPPED THEM FROM KILLING HER RIGHT AWAY, BUT...
Jaeha and Hyuli fought each other.
SHE...HAS THE SAME ILLNESS AS SU-WON.
"WHY DOES SOME NOBODY PRINCESS GET TO HAVE EVERYTHING?
ISN'T THAT UNFAIR?"
APPARENTLY I'M THE CRIMSON DRAGON KING'S REINCARNATION...
...BUT I DON'T KNOW THAT PAIN.
TRUE. BUT NYAN-NYAN DOESN'T KNOW YOUR PAIN, EITHER.
PEOPLE CAN'T COMPREHEND THINGS THEY DON'T KNOW.

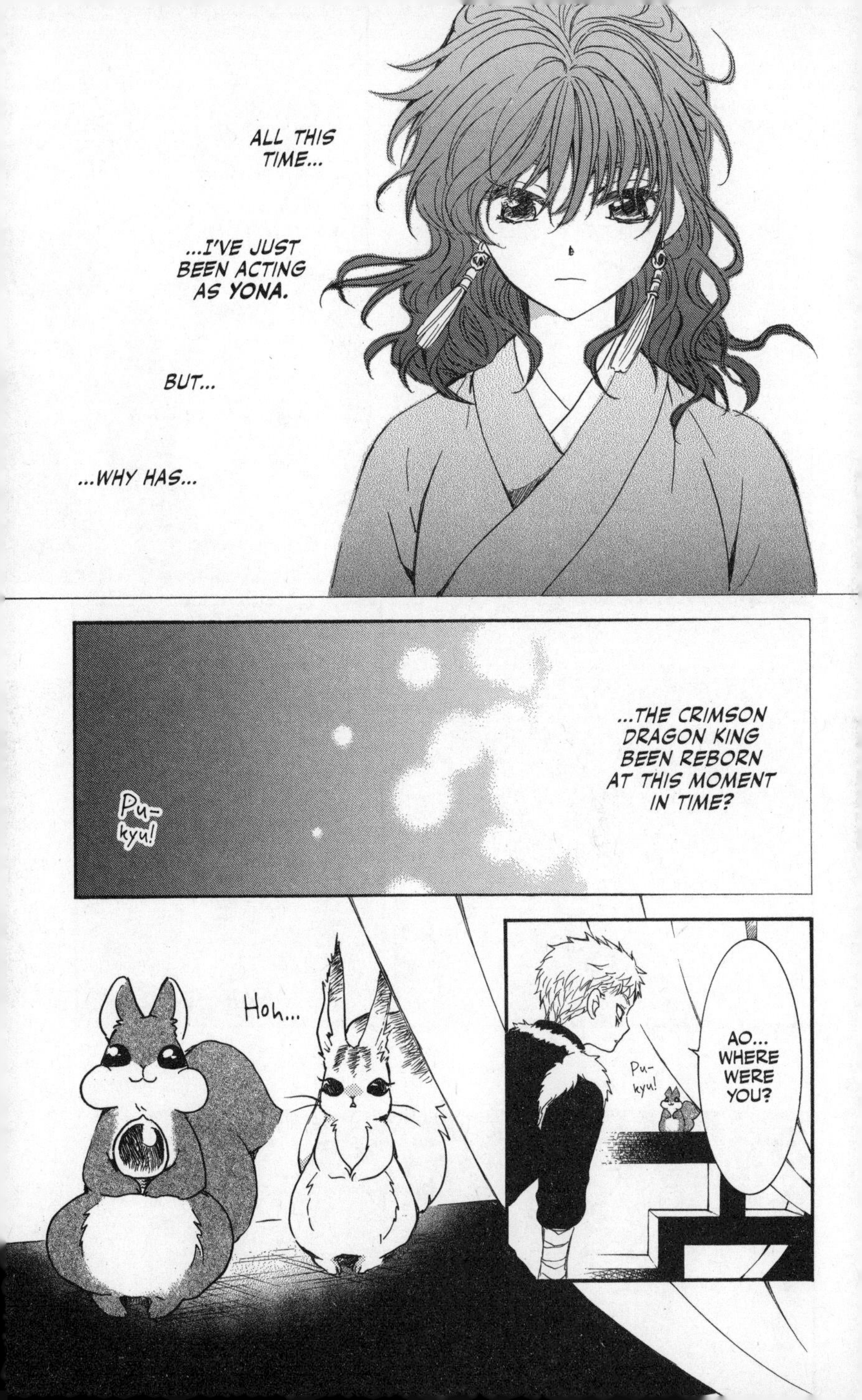
ALL THIS TIME...
...I'VE JUST BEEN ACTING AS YONA.
BUT...
...WHY HAS...
...THE CRIMSON DRAGON KING BEEN REBORN AT THIS MOMENT IN TIME?
Pu-kyu!
AO... WHERE WERE YOU?
Pu-kyu!
Hoh...

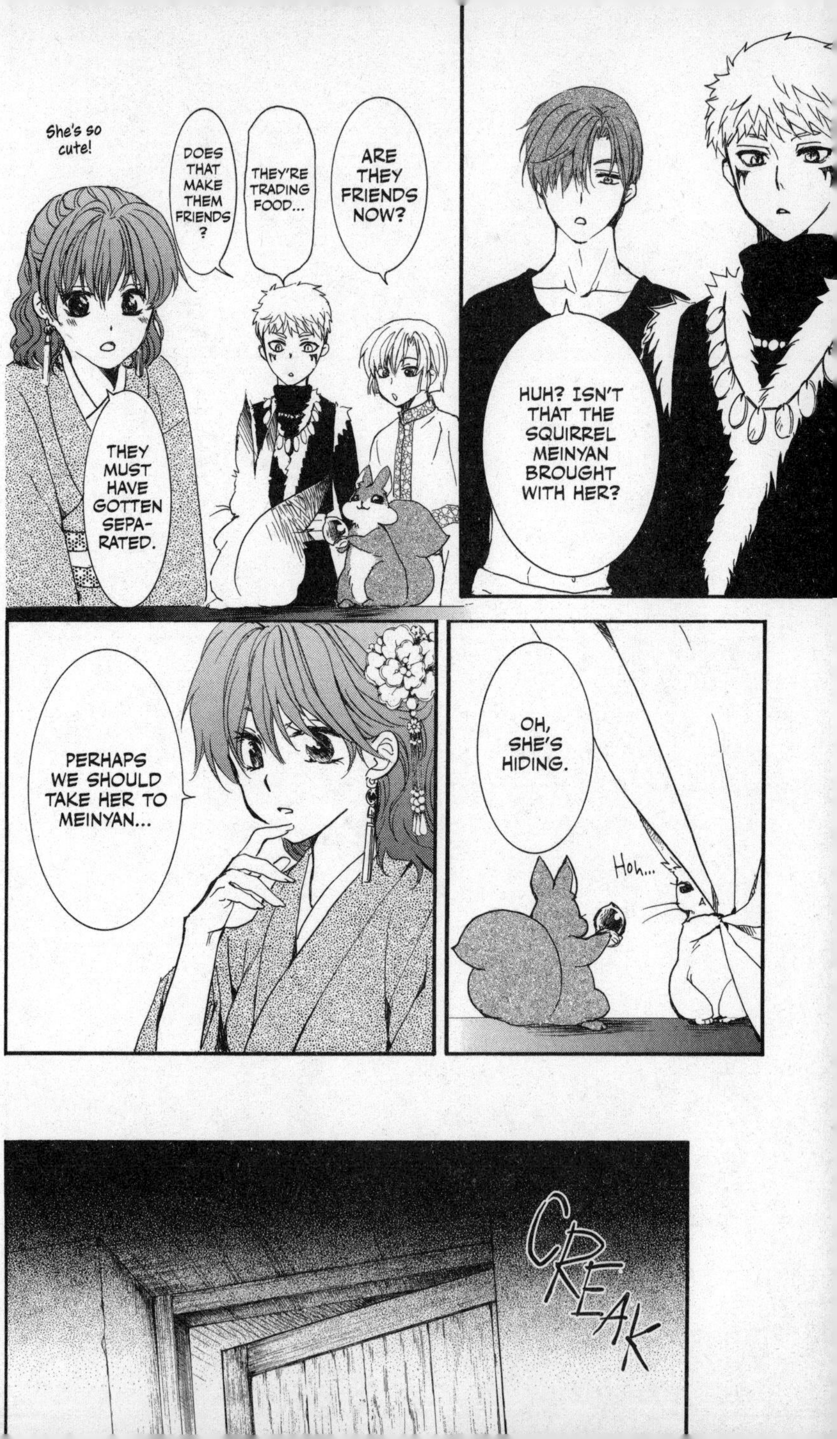
HUH? ISN'T THAT THE SQUIRREL MEINYAN BROUGHT WITH HER?
ARE THEY FRIENDS NOW?
THEY'RE TRADING FOOD...
DOES THAT MAKE THEM FRIENDS?
She's so cute!
THEY MUST HAVE GOTTEN SEPA-RATED.
OH, SHE'S HIDING.
Hoh...
PERHAPS WE SHOULD TAKE HER TO MEINYAN...
CREAK

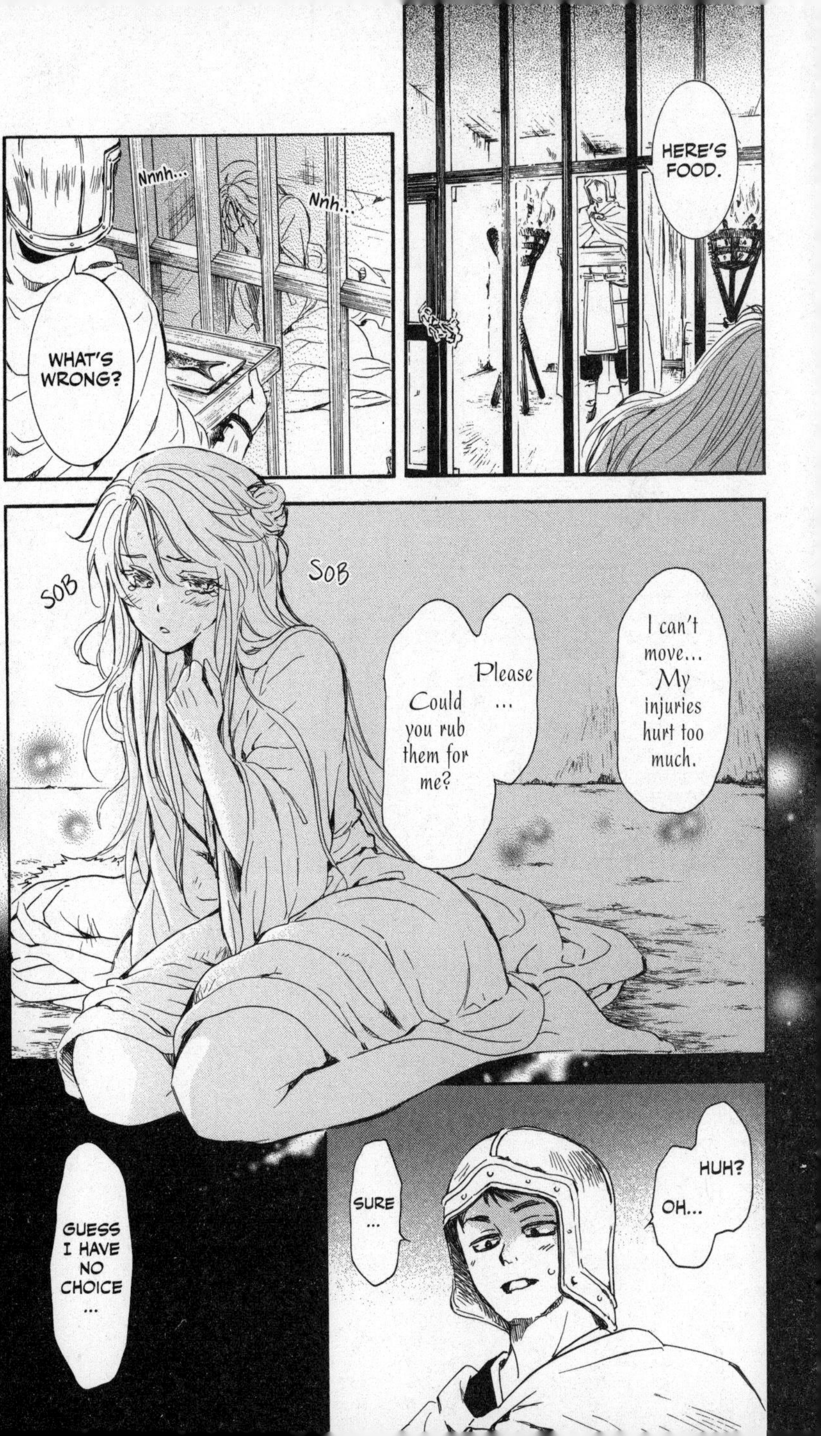
HERE'S FOOD.
Nnh...
Nnnh...
WHAT'S WRONG?
SOB
SOB
I can't move... My injuries hurt too much.
Please... Could you rub them for me?
HUH? OH...
SURE ...
GUESS I HAVE NO CHOICE ...

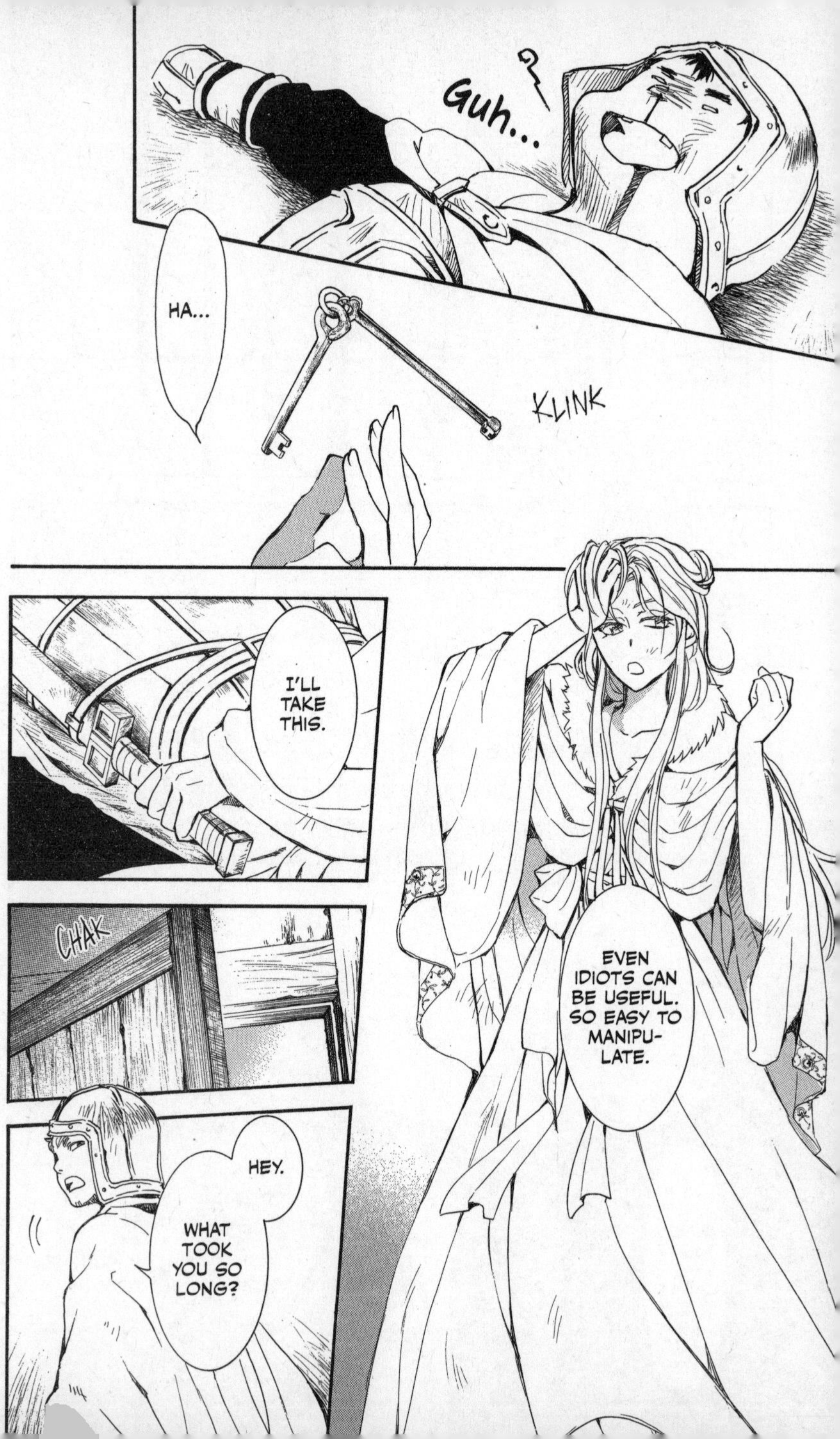

?
Guh...
KLINK
HA...
EVEN IDIOTS CAN BE USEFUL. SO EASY TO MANIPU-LATE.
I'LL TAKE THIS.
CHAK
HEY.
WHAT TOOK YOU SO LONG?

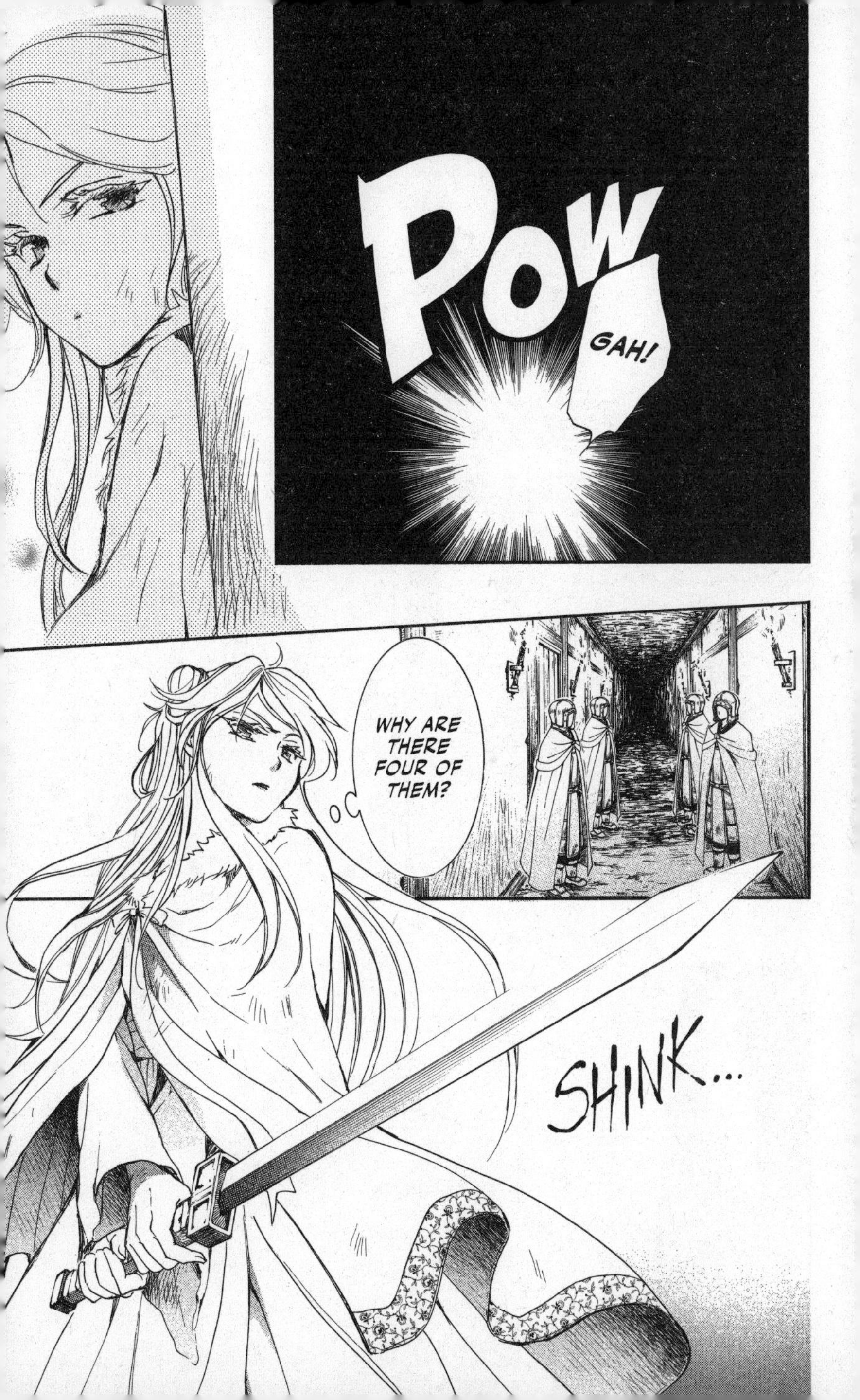
POW
GAH!
WHY ARE THERE FOUR OF THEM?
SHINK...

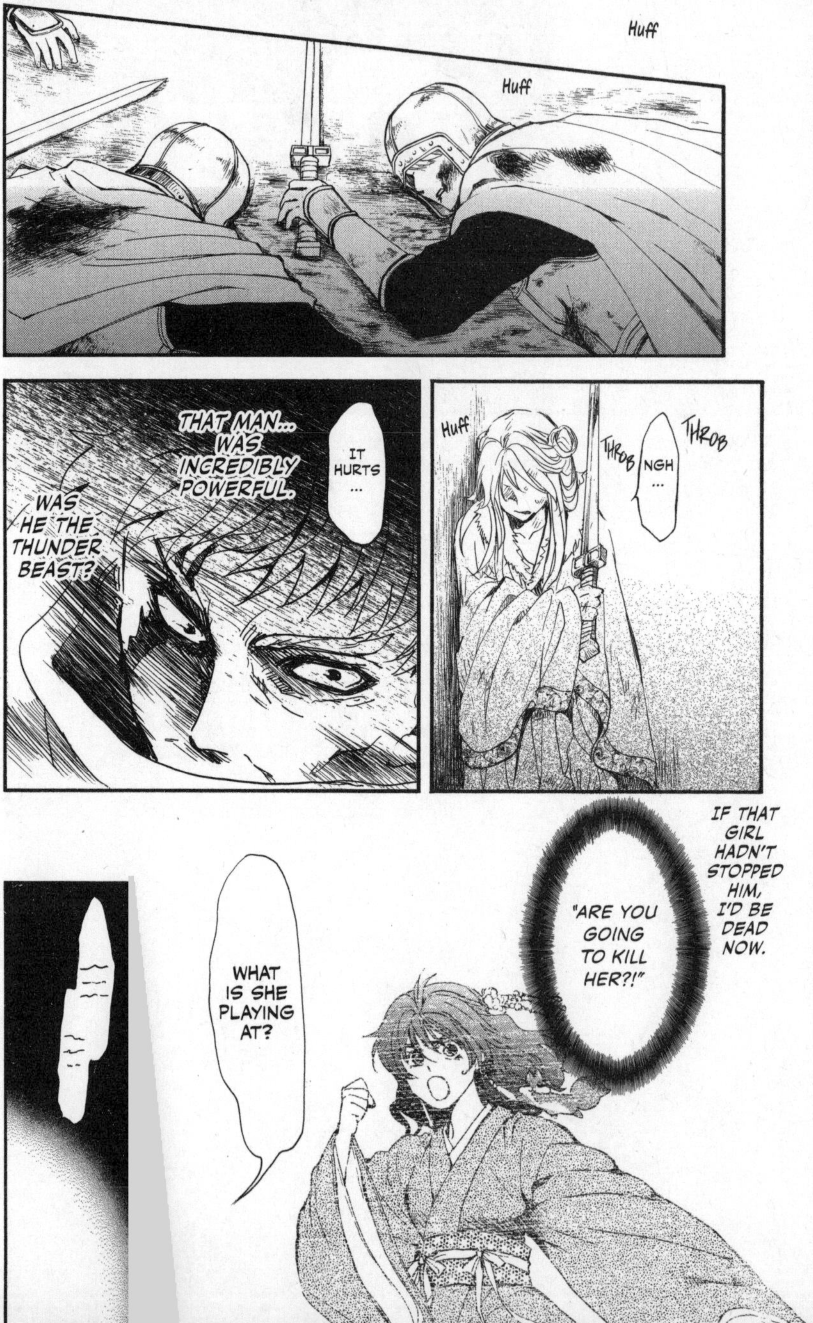
Huff
Huff
Huff
THROB
NGH...
THROB
IT HURTS...
THAT MAN... WAS INCREDIBLY POWERFUL.
WAS HE THE THUNDER BEAST?
IF THAT GIRL HADN'T STOPPED HIM, I'D BE DEAD NOW.
"ARE YOU GOING TO KILL HER?!"
WHAT IS SHE PLAYING AT?

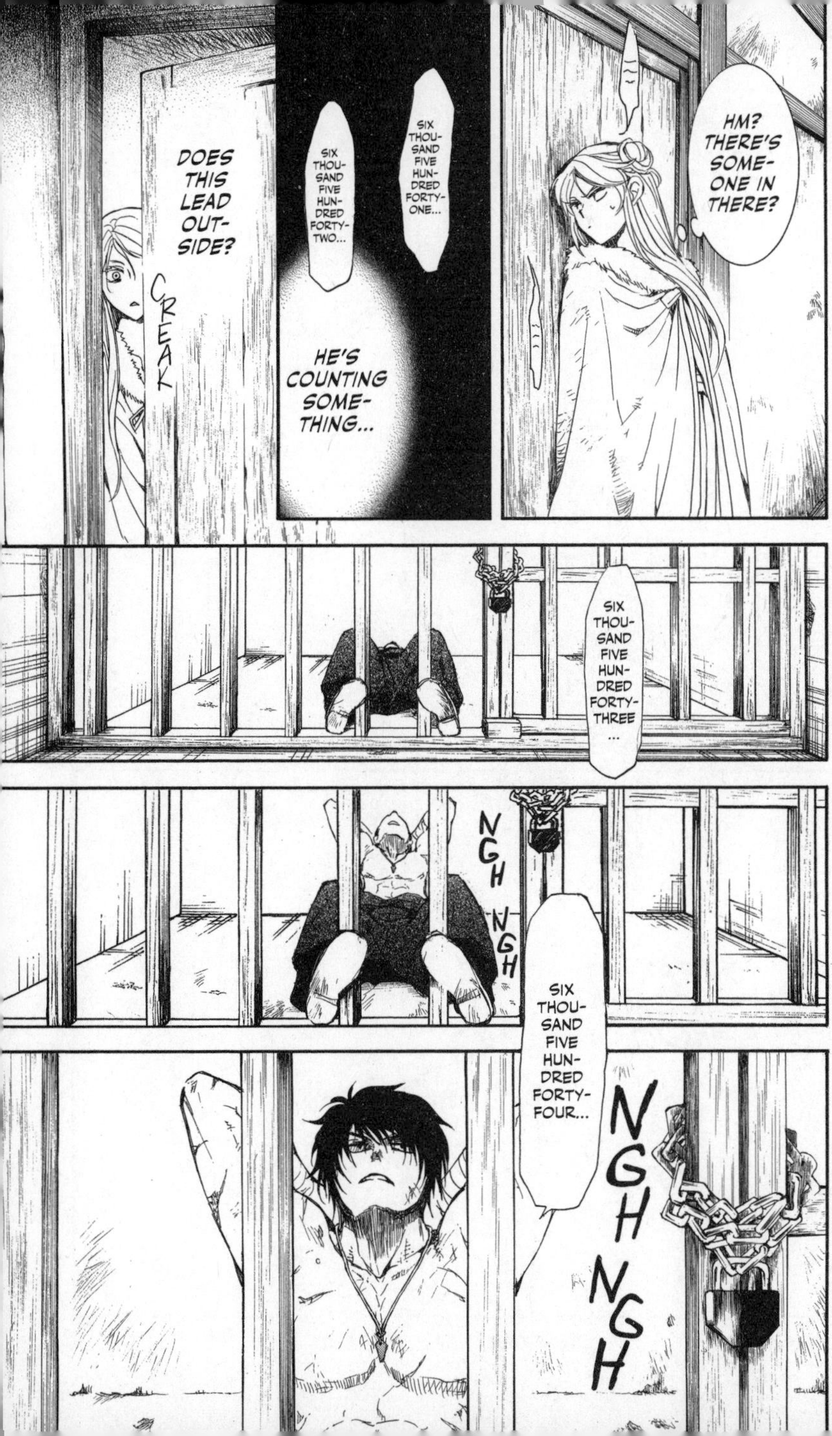
HM? THERE'S SOMEONE IN THERE?
SIX THOUSAND FIVE HUNDRED FORTY-ONE...
SIX THOUSAND FIVE HUNDRED FORTY-TWO...
HE'S COUNTING SOMETHING...
DOES THIS LEAD OUTSIDE?
CREAK
SIX THOUSAND FIVE HUNDRED FORTY-THREE...
NGH NGH
SIX THOUSAND FIVE HUNDRED FORTY-FOUR...
NGH NGH

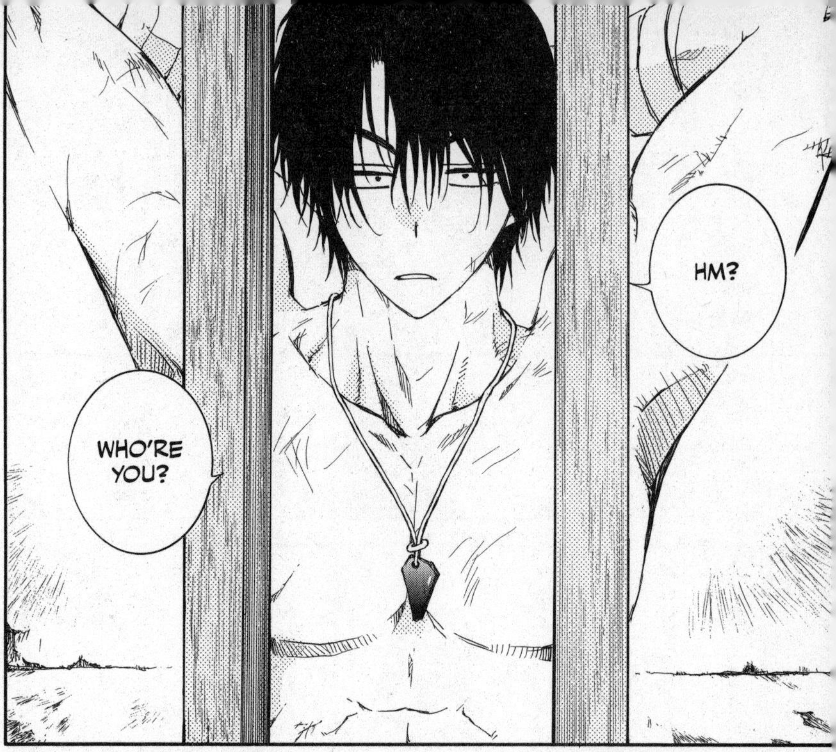
HM?
WHO'RE YOU?

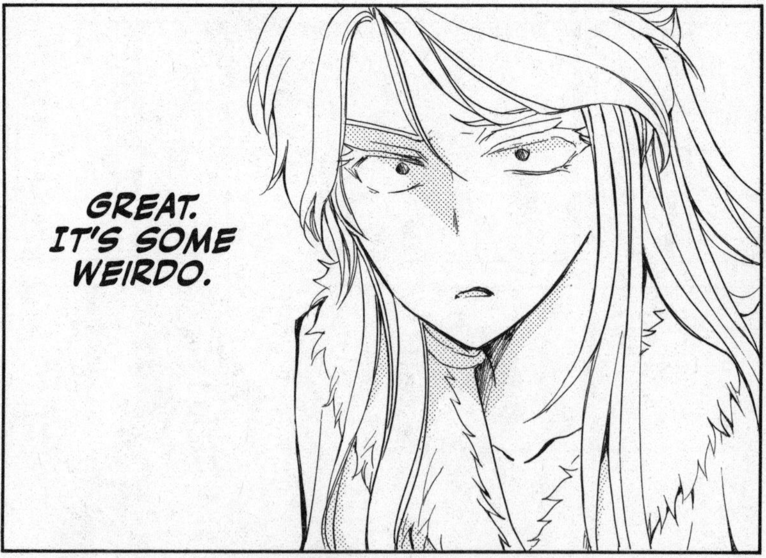
GREAT. IT'S SOME WEIRDO.

CHAPTER 204 / THE END

A special thanks to these people who always help me out!

My assistants who have worked with me → Mikorun, C.F., Ryo Sakura,
Ryo, and my little sister

My editors → Hasegawa (Sho), my previous editors, and the *Hana to
Yume* editorial office

Everyone who is involved with the sale of *Yona*...

My family and friends who always encourage and support me...

My cats, who make me feel better...

My longtime readers and those who have only recently started reading!

Thanks to all of you, I'm able to draw manga.

I can't make a series by myself. Thank you very much.

I'm going to stay focused and do my best!

Afterword

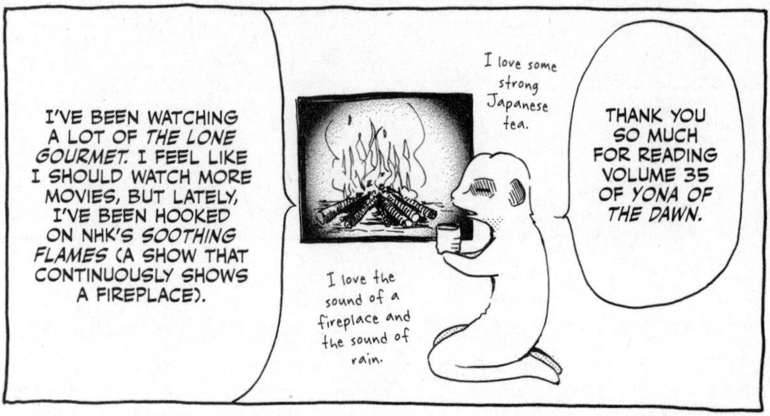
THANK YOU SO MUCH FOR READING VOLUME 35 OF *YONA OF THE DAWN.*
I love some strong Japanese tea.
I'VE BEEN WATCHING A LOT OF *THE LONE GOURMET.* I FEEL LIKE I SHOULD WATCH MORE MOVIES, BUT LATELY, I'VE BEEN HOOKED ON NHK'S *SOOTHING FLAMES* (A SHOW THAT CONTINUOUSLY SHOWS A FIREPLACE).
I love the sound of a fireplace and the sound of rain.

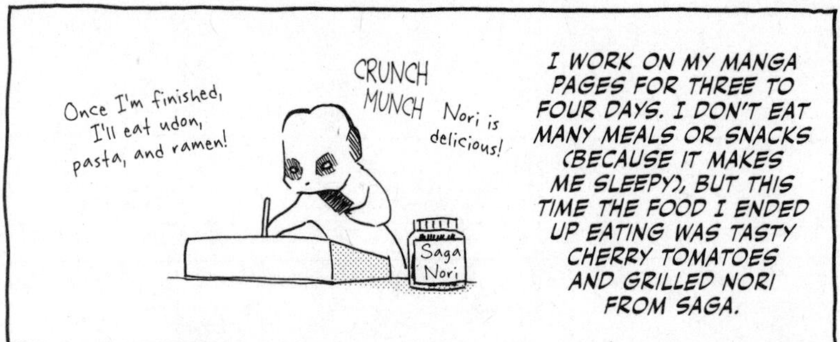
I WORK ON MY MANGA PAGES FOR THREE TO FOUR DAYS. I DON'T EAT MANY MEALS OR SNACKS (BECAUSE IT MAKES ME SLEEPY), BUT THIS TIME THE FOOD I ENDED UP EATING WAS TASTY CHERRY TOMATOES AND GRILLED NORI FROM SAGA.
CRUNCH
MUNCH
Nori is delicious!
Once I'm finished, I'll eat udon, pasta, and ramen!
Saga Nori

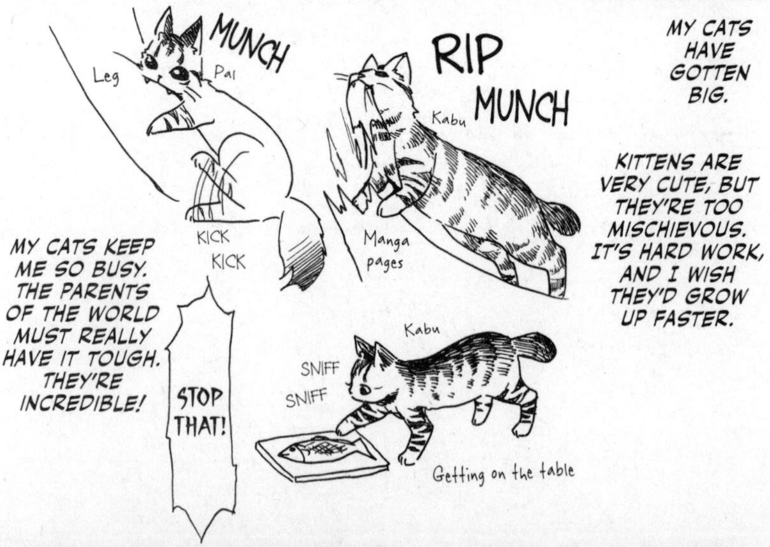
MY CATS HAVE GOTTEN BIG.
KITTENS ARE VERY CUTE, BUT THEY'RE TOO MISCHIEVOUS. IT'S HARD WORK, AND I WISH THEY'D GROW UP FASTER.
RIP
MUNCH
Kabu
Manga pages
MUNCH
Leg
Pal
KICK
KICK
Kabu
SNIFF
SNIFF
Getting on the table
STOP THAT!
MY CATS KEEP ME SO BUSY. THE PARENTS OF THE WORLD MUST REALLY HAVE IT TOUGH. THEY'RE INCREDIBLE!

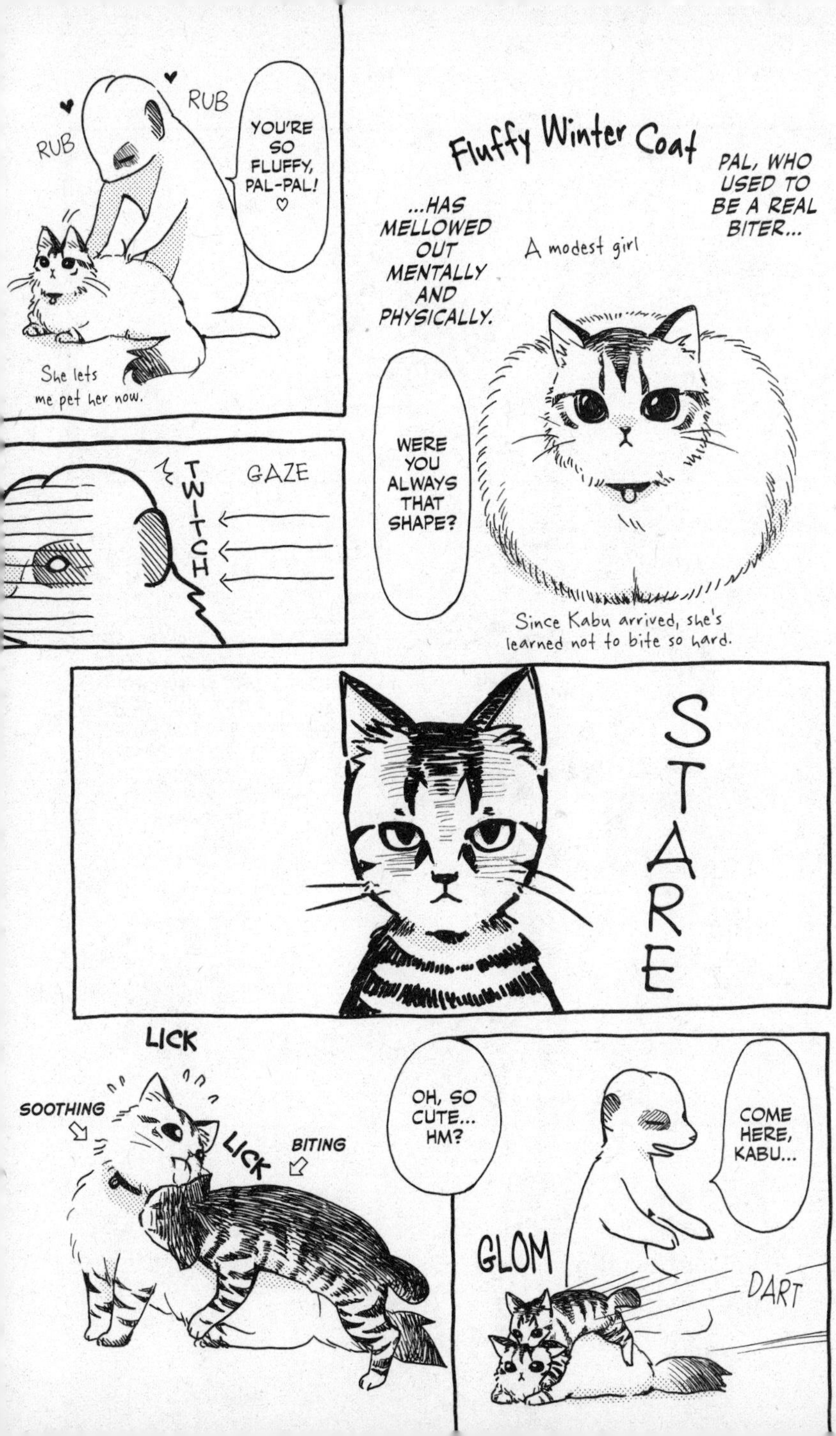
Fluffy Winter Coat
PAL, WHO USED TO BE A REAL BITER...
...HAS MELLOWED OUT MENTALLY AND PHYSICALLY.
A modest girl
WERE YOU ALWAYS THAT SHAPE?
Since Kabu arrived, she's learned not to bite so hard.
RUB
RUB
YOU'RE SO FLUFFY, PAL-PAL! ♡
She lets me pet her now.
GAZE
TWITCH
STARE
COME HERE, KABU...
OH, SO CUTE... HM?
GLOM
DART
LICK
LICK
SOOTHING
BITING

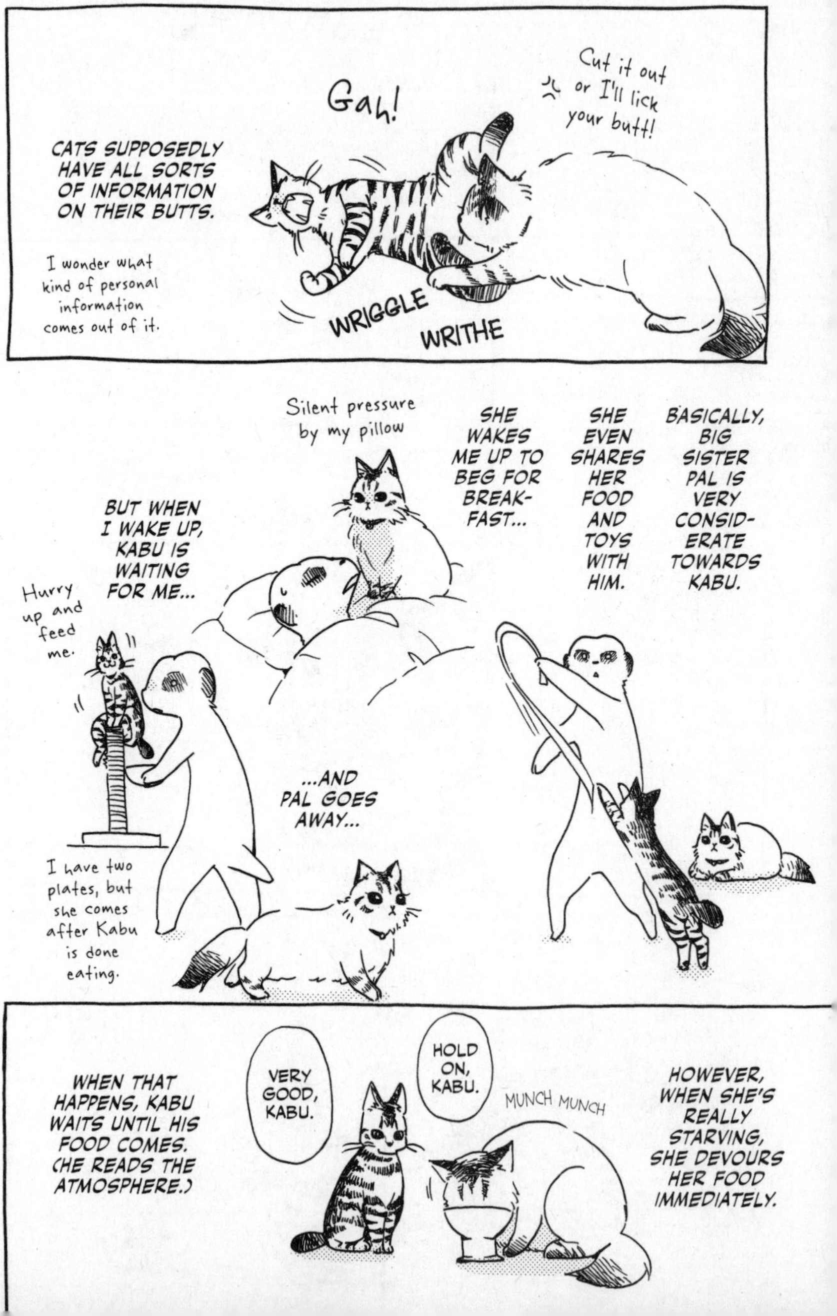
Cut it out or I'll lick your butt!
Gah!
CATS SUPPOSEDLY HAVE ALL SORTS OF INFORMATION ON THEIR BUTTS.
I wonder what kind of personal information comes out of it.
WRIGGLE
WRITHE
BASICALLY, BIG SISTER PAL IS VERY CONSID-ERATE TOWARDS KABU.
SHE EVEN SHARES HER FOOD AND TOYS WITH HIM.
SHE WAKES ME UP TO BEG FOR BREAK-FAST...
Silent pressure by my pillow
BUT WHEN I WAKE UP, KABU IS WAITING FOR ME...
Hurry up and feed me.
...AND PAL GOES AWAY...
I have two plates, but she comes after Kabu is done eating.
HOWEVER, WHEN SHE'S REALLY STARVING, SHE DEVOURS HER FOOD IMMEDIATELY.
HOLD ON, KABU.
MUNCH MUNCH
VERY GOOD, KABU.
WHEN THAT HAPPENS, KABU WAITS UNTIL HIS FOOD COMES. (HE READS THE ATMOSPHERE.)

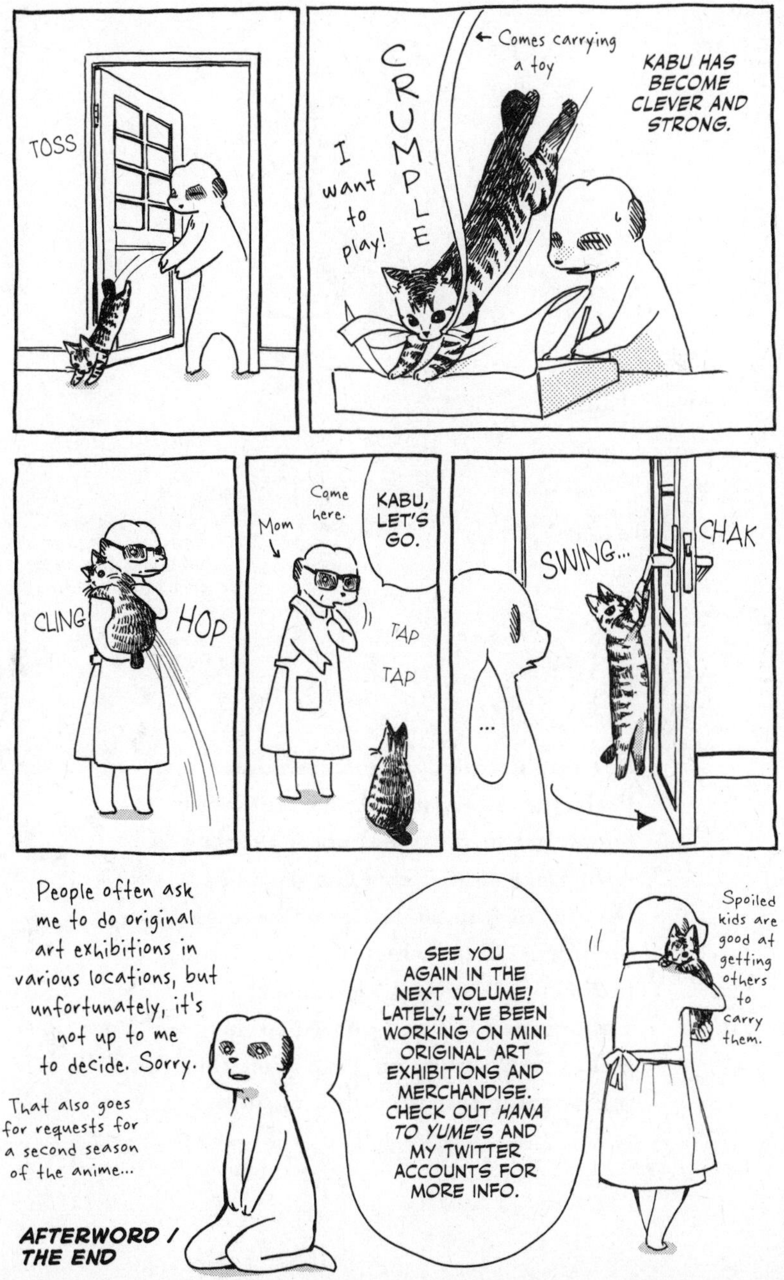
KABU HAS BECOME CLEVER AND STRONG.
← Comes carrying a toy
CRUMPLE
I want to play!
TOSS
CHAK
SWING...
...
KABU, LET'S GO.
Come here.
Mom
TAP
TAP
HOP
CLING
Spoiled kids are good at getting others to carry them.
SEE YOU AGAIN IN THE NEXT VOLUME! LATELY, I'VE BEEN WORKING ON MINI ORIGINAL ART EXHIBITIONS AND MERCHANDISE. CHECK OUT *HANA TO YUME'S* AND MY TWITTER ACCOUNTS FOR MORE INFO.
People often ask me to do original art exhibitions in various locations, but unfortunately, it's not up to me to decide. Sorry.
That also goes for requests for a second season of the anime...
AFTERWORD / THE END

Thank you so much for buying volume 35!

—Mizuho Kusanagi

Born on February 3 in Kumamoto Prefecture in Japan, Mizuho Kusanagi began her professional manga career with *Yoiko no Kokoroe* (The Rules of a Good Child) in 2003. Her other works include *NG Life*, which was serialized in *Hana to Yume* and *The Hana to Yume* magazines and published by Hakusensha in Japan. *Yona of the Dawn* was adapted into an anime in 2014.

YONA OF THE DAWN
VOL.35
Shojo Beat Edition

STORY AND ART BY
MIZUHO KUSANAGI

English Adaptation/Ysabet Reinhardt MacFarlane
Translation/JN Productions
Touch-Up Art & Lettering/Lys Blakeslee
Design/Philana Chen
Editor/Amy Yu

Akatsuki no Yona by Mizuho Kusanagi
© Mizuho Kusanagi 2021
All rights reserved.
First published in Japan in 2021 by HAKUSENSHA, Inc., Tokyo.
English language translation rights arranged with
HAKUSENSHA, Inc., Tokyo.

Printed in the U.S.A.

Published by VIZ Media, LLC
P.O. Box 77010
San Francisco, CA 94107

10 9 8 7 6 5 4 3 2 1
First printing, April 2022

viz.com   shojobeat.com

This is the last page.

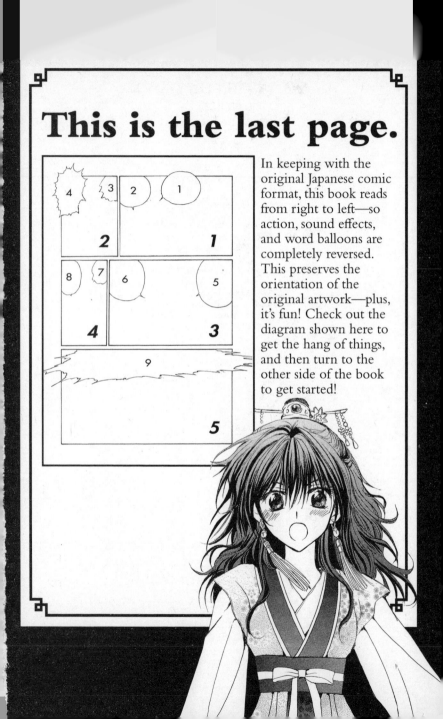

In keeping with the original Japanese comic format, this book reads from right to left—so action, sound effects, and word balloons are completely reversed. This preserves the orientation of the original artwork—plus, it's fun! Check out the diagram shown here to get the hang of things, and then turn to the other side of the book to get started!